FOREIGNERS IN THEIR NATIVE LAND

Foreigners in Their Native Land

Historical Roots of the Mexican Americans

edited by
David J. Weber

30th Anniversary Edition

New Foreword by
Arnoldo De León

New Afterword by
David J. Weber

University of New Mexico Press
Albuquerque

© 1973 by the University of New Mexico Press
© 2003 Foreword and Afterword by the University of New Mexico Press
All rights reserved.
Manufactured in the United States of America
Original ISBN 0-8263-0278-5 (cloth) • ISBN 0-8263-0279-3 (paper)

30th Anniversary Edition

13 12 11 10 09   16 17 18 19 20

ISBN-13: 978-0-8263-3510-4

Library of Congress Cataloging-in-Publication Data

Weber, David J.
    Foreigners in their native land : historical roots of the Mexican
Americans / David J. Weber.—30th anniversary pbk. ed.
        p.   cm.
Includes index.
    ISBN 0-8263-3510-1 (pbk. : alk paper)
    1. Mexican Americans—History. I. Title.
    E184.M5W42 2003
    973.0468072—dc22
                                        2003020529

For my wife
CAROL BRYANT WEBER

A victim to the wickedness of a few men, whose imposture was favored by their origin, and recent domination over the country; *a foreigner in my native land;* could I be expected stoically to endure their outrages and insults?

Juan Nepomuceno Seguín

Texas, 1858

It is the conquered who are humbled before the conqueror asking for his protection, while enjoying what little their misfortune has left them. It is those who have been sold like sheep—it is those who were abandoned by Mexico. They do not understand the prevalent language of their native soil. They are *foreigners in their own land.* I have seen seventy and sixty year olds cry like children because they had been uprooted from the lands of their fathers. They have been humiliated and insulted. They have been refused the privilege of taking water from their own wells. They have been denied the privilege of cutting their own firewood.

Pablo de la Guerra
Speech to the California Senate, 1856

It is very natural that the history written by the victim does not altogether chime with the story of the victor.

José Fernández
California, 1874

Foreword to the Thirtieth Anniversary Edition

Foreigners in Their Native Land has enjoyed a remarkable life over the last thirty years. In its twelfth paperbound printing as of last count, *Foreigners* continues as a favorite classroom adoption despite the odds. It is older, for instance, than most students who read it! In 1973 the study of Mexican American history was in its infancy and facing an uncertain future. In 2003, anyone interested in Mexican American history would find extraordinary advances: several survey textbooks, specialized overviews of state histories, and comprehensive bibliographical and historiographical essays assessing three decades of scholarship.[1] But amid this new literature, *Foreigners in Their Native Land* has retained its value and appeal.

Professional historians who have studied Mexican American history would not find it difficult to determine the reasons for the book's durability. Disadvantaged though he was by a paucity of literature, David J. Weber touched on issues, approaches, topics, premises, and interpretations that remain the subject of debate, elucidation, and inquiry today. He took on, for instance, the irksome question of periodization. Which event/episode represented a juncture in Mexican American history, he wondered. Was it the Treaty of Guadalupe Hidalgo of 1848 (or in the case of Texas, the War for Independence of 1836)? While these two episodes transformed Mexican citizens into Mexican Americans, he thought the delineation too confining, explaining that the study of Mexicans in the U.S. should embrace their background in the Far North when the region still belonged to New Spain or independent Mexico. Almost half of the book, therefore, treated the pre-1848 era.

The larger body of the monographic literature, however, has not abided by Weber's thinking, and instead has focused on post-1848 events as a general understanding has emerged by those who study the U.S. Southwest (or Mexico's Far North) that the era preceding the Treaty of Guadalupe Hidalgo should be the domain of Borderlands scholars. Recently, in fact, published studies have even questioned the validity of 1848 as a starting point for Mexican American history. According to scholars Gilbert G. González and Raúl Fernández, a better point of focus for Chicano history is the twentieth century. As this school of thought has it, the pre-1900

Mexicano experience revolved around a pre-capitalist pastoral society (Mexicans) coming in contact with the capitalist system introduced by Anglos. The large waves of immigration that began in the 1890s and early 1900s introduced new and different players into Mexican American history, and at a time when few questioned capitalism. Conflict between Mexicans and Anglos now centered on working-class needs instead of lynching or land dispossession, as exploited laborers sought economic improvement from agribusiness enterprises and corporate giants.[2]

Advocates of cultural studies would similarly question the wisdom of 1848 as a date of new beginnings. Studying literary works (short stories, poetry, novels, and the like), these newer practitioners of Chicano Studies find writers of fiction to have only passing use for turning points in history such as 1848. Emotion, characters, and plots in fiction often do not coincide with the historical reality that historians associate with an event of monumental significance.[3]

Despite such objections, some scholars who consider themselves students of what is still referred to as "Chicano history" would nonetheless accept Weber's demarcation. Most prominent would be Ramón A. Gutiérrez, author of the award-winning *When Jesus Came, the Corn Mothers Went Away: Marriage, Sexuality, and Power in New Mexico, 1500–1846* (Stanford: Stanford University Press, 1991). As Gutiérrez sees things, the marriage relations involving Spanish/Mexican settlers and Native Americans in colonial New Mexico shaped class differentiation and social life and were key to structuring the New Mexico community during the first half of the nineteenth century. Other proponents of the pre-1848 date also find the Spanish-Mexican era to be an integral part of Chicano history. They find a connection in aspects of community that revolve around civil government, the *presidios,* the missions, and other colonial institutions, as well as in everyday experiences.[4]

Foreigners in Their Native Land remains relevant in 2003 not solely because of the issues it addressed, but because its approach remains as sound today (when contemporary scholars experiment with novel and sometimes faddish techniques) as when first published. Trained as a Borderlands scholar, Weber subscribed to traditional Borderlands standards (rigorous research, scrupulous evaluation of the documents, and clear writing). He wisely eschewed the colonial model (which likened the domination of Mexican Americans in the U.S. to colonial structures between imperial powers and third world countries) then in vogue among some Chicano historians. Long defunct, the colonial model—had Weber used it—would have rendered *Foreigners* anachronistic by now. On the other hand, his scholarly insights stirred him into joining the ongoing dispute of the 1970s that asked what forces lay behind Mexican American societal disadvantages. He rejected the social science explanation that a Mexican American non-competitive and unambitious culture lurked behind the group's low socioeconomic achievements. Instead, he attributed (as did early revisionists) the causes for Mexican American lag to the odious bane of white supremacy, racism, disenfranchisement, and other disabling forces. Moreover, he argued that Mexican Americans had historically pursued self-improvement and that they had sought a measure of accommodation into the larger society as a means of self-preservation.

Modern scholarship has corroborated Weber's positions. His argument that external forces deterred Mexican Americans from attaining the American promise remains valid today. The new social history of the last few decades that finds ordinary people have an impact on history equal to that of elites has completely negated the 1960s popular stereotype of the "passive Mexican." Instead, it has detected a drive for individual and group amelioration in every aspect of the Chicano community: in its diverse ideologies, its folklore, artistic displays, literary expressions, social clubs, entertainment forms, religious observances, labor unionism, and in numerous other manifestations of culture. The New Western History has drawn a similar picture: as Mexicans entered western America (either as a conquered people or as immigrants), they struggled to get ahead as competitively as Anglos, Africans, or Chinese. Few took a defeatist or fatalistic attitude toward their new circumstance.[5]

So, too, have historians validated Weber's understanding that accommodation has been a survival technique for Mexicans over the decades. Armed with approaches from gender, ethnography, and cultural sociology, however, scholars today have expanded on the meaning of accommodation. To them, such a negotiation was more complex than Weber saw it. Historical sociologist David Montejano, for example, advances a more sophisticated explanation of what transpired among oligarchs, referring to a "peace structure." An understanding ensued, he argues, between Anglo and Mexican elites wherein Anglos would rule a conquered area and the latter would not resist their domination. In exchange, Mexicans of the upper strata would have the flexibility to participate in the Anglo economic and political structure (this peace structure left little space for the rank-and-file within Mexican American society to improve themselves).[6] Then, too, scholars who study gender in Chicano history see women as active agents in the process of accommodation. Women planned (or had their fathers do so) for their own well-being and that of their offspring by courting white males, seeing Anglos as better able to offer them material security than could their own countrymen. Accommodation of this kind did not necessarily mean repudiation of old customs; often, Mexican American women made sure that their children retained the Spanish language and Catholicism.[7]

Further contributing to *Foreigners'* reputation as a classic is its discussion of topics that are as relevant today as they were in 1973. Weber, for example, alluded to the significance of *mutualistas,* to the function of newspapers within Mexican American communities, to efforts by communities to educate the young, and to the presence of political bossism as a nineteenth-century reality. He singled out particular episodes and group movements unique to Mexican American history. Among these would have been the El Paso Salt War of 1877, the campaigns of Las Gorras Blancas in New Mexico, the story of the "forty blond babies," social banditry, leadership figures, and the efforts undertaken by the Mexican government to found colonies for Mexican Americans in northern Mexico in 1848.[8] He referenced the issue of Mexican American "culture" and the difficulty social scientists were having in defining it precisely. All these topics have become the subject of more sophisticated scholarly attention since 1973.

Where Weber noted, for instance, that "Thus far, Chicano sociologists have found it easier to say what Mexican American culture is *not,* than to suggest a model for what Mexican American culture *is,*" modern day social scientists would have no great difficulty doing so. Inter-disciplinary studies have advanced to such a degree that every discipline appears to have its own refined definition of Mexican American "culture." For those who study Chicano history through a "gendered context," at least a segment of the Mexican American female population engaged in actions that would modify traditional definitions of culture. For them, women often acted historically in ways that ignored the limitations that men placed on them. Role reversals occurred when women ran businesses or managed the family farm or ranch during their husbands' absences. Sexual democracy on the frontier therefore derived from the actions of women themselves. Some women questioned patriarchy by ignoring a man's wish that they not work outside the household, that they not join religious clubs, or get politically involved. When women re-defined male/female roles in this way, they influenced culture. Considering the advances made in cultural studies, social scientists today would not find it problematic to say what Mexican American culture *is.*[9]

Nor would students of literature who discern identity in the creative works of writers (generally elites) and the folklore of common folks find it difficult. Weber scarcely touched on the subject, but modern-day scholars from literary studies (another of history's companion disciplines) have found many modes of cultural self-expression among nineteenth-century Mexican Americans in vehicles as common as newspapers. As a matter of policy, newspapers issued editorials, took political stands on the questions of the day, and published short stories, novels in serialized forms, or poetry; such creative literature often revealed the cultural identity of a community that saw itself as constrained by racial inequality. Other writers found alternative outlets for their creative impulses and the number of literary forms (novels, poetry, plays, chronicles, missionary texts, folklore, *dichos,* and the like) currently being "recovered" by academic sleuths is impressive.[10] Mexican Americans also left autobiographies, some of them in the form of "*testimonios,*" or "elicited dictations" (as one scholar has labeled them). Solicited by Hubert Howe Bancroft for his histories of the West from Californios during the 1870s, these testimonios reveal much about how the Anglo American conquest shaped culture. The testimonios show bitterness toward the political system (which in part held responsibility for the Californios' land loss), toward the discriminatory nature of the new capitalism, and toward Anglo distortions of historical events in the West.[11]

Premises and interpretations that have been substantiated by modern scholarship or that have been updated by new evidence further explain the longevity of *Foreigners in Their Native Land.* The broader outlines that Weber (and other contemporaries of the early 1970s) recognized as constituting nineteenth-century Chicano history have generally been corroborated. The reasoning that Mexican Americans as an ethnic group have historically been victimized by racism and by deliberate designs to subordinate them, for instance, is as much a tenet of modern-day Chicano history as it was in 1973. Numerous studies by historians and researchers from allied fields continue to pour forth buttressing this judgment.[12] Weber's view that Mexican Americans have historically resisted Anglo rule has similarly been proven correct by modern-day studies. Resistance—seen mainly during the early 1970s in the activities of the aforementioned "social bandits"—is now also argued to be evident in newly discovered episodes involving community organizing, political involvement, labor struggles, and ethnic riots, as well as in the literary and folkloric mocking of Anglo Americans.[13]

Weber's statement that "85 percent" of Mexican Americans "live in the four Southwestern states adjacent to the United States-Mexican border" is also essentially correct, but needs amending. The Mexican American community of 1970 has of course expanded and grown. A flood of immigration and natural increase has changed the demographic picture, so that the 2000 census placed the total Mexican-descent population in these four states at 14,923,516, a figure almost thrice as large as the one Weber gave for 1970. As of 2000, however, 72 percent of the total Mexican American population still lived in the U.S. Southwest. The remainder was dispersed throughout other parts of the country, including the Midwest where almost 10 percent of the population is Mexican-origin (Chicago alone had a Mexican population of more than one-half million).[14]

Several of Weber's other seminal observations have likewise been revised. It is true that Mexican Americans lost much of their land to governmental indifference, political chicanery, and selfish land-grabbers. But today some scholars place blame on Mexican Americans for their own land loss, citing their refusal to modernize their ranches or their habit of dividing lands to heirs, thus ensuring the dissolution of their original grants.[15] Racism toward Mexican Americans, as Weber pointed out, was severe, but according to the current debate, not as vile as previously thought. At least in nineteenth-century Texas, racism came in different degrees, certainly violent but at other times subtle and measured.[16] And it was also true that many elites partnered with Anglo Americans to either protect their property or to enhance their standing in post-1848 society. At the same time, these "race traitors" did not entirely reject their own past nor embrace everything in the dominant system. According to what the aforementioned students who have studied the Californio testimonios and Mexican American autobiographies reveal, many of these old elites resented Anglo Americans their crude manner, controlling nature, and wanton disregard for truth in history. It was this latter concern that led José Antonio Navarro and Juan N. Seguín, both of San Antonio, to pen their memoirs. Each hoped to correct the ways in which Anglos depicted both them and fellow Spaniards/Mexicans in Texas history.[17] Moreover, elites in places such as frontier Arizona retained close ties to their communities, participating in activities that helped improve conditions for fellow Hispanics. They addressed education, supported the work of the Catholic Church, kept the welfare of laborers in mind, and in other ways strove for the "collective good."[18]

A last thing that makes *Foreigners* a landmark publication is its judicious selection of primary sources. All the documents Weber chose remain as pertinent to Mexican American history today as when first compiled. Some lay hidden in dusty archives or on microfilm until Weber discovered them. He traveled to several depositories across the U.S. Southwest to locate them. Many remained in the original Spanish, but Weber translated them. More significantly, he placed them in historical context, thus providing credibility to new approaches, premises, and interpretations then under debate.[19] He balanced the documents by telling different stories with them. In Chapter 4, for instance, the weight of the documents points to the victimization of Mexican Americans in the nineteenth century, but the primary sources in Chapter 5 counterweigh that theme by giving agency to their subjects. Balance is also evident in the care Weber took to give voice to Mexican Americans. In Chapters 2 and 3, outsiders are the observers and commentators, but in several of the documents found in Chapters 4 and 5, Mexican Americans are speaking for themselves. All these qualities continue to attract both students and professors to *Foreigners in Their Native Land.*

Historians and students of the humanities today would not have to do the yeoman work that Weber did, and a newer anthology of documents would thus emphasize a different side of the Mexican American experience. Researchers have found sources for writing Mexican American history to be plentiful; the once accepted axiom that it was impossible to write Mexican American history because of a scarcity of documents is no longer tenable. The proliferation of writings for the colonial epoch and the nineteenth century attest to that, and give modern-day editors more choices to reflect today's concerns. In portraying Mexican-origin communities, contemporary historians can probably find more writings that reveal social life, gender, and nationalist identity. Documents for the chapter titled "Yankee Infiltration and the Hardening of Stereotypes," which explain how Yankees mistreated Mexicans, could focus on the techniques that Mexicans utilized to ward off Yankee domination. The same emphasis could probably be given to Chapter 3 ("Cultures Collide"), which examines the Texas War for Independence and the War with Mexico, two topics that may no longer hold the same fascination they once did. The book's last chapter on "Accommodation, Assimilation, and Resistance" could today be complemented by documents about the theater, popular religiosity, migrant work or tenant farming, group entertainment, material culture, community building, and involvement with the Knights of Labor or with the *Partido Liberal Mexicano.* Were Weber to have written *Foreigners* in 2003, however, he would have done just that and ensured the book's life span well into the twenty-first century.

Over time, *Foreigners in Their Native Land* has weathered new directions in scholarship and remains an authoritative volume in Mexican American history. With practically no literature behind him nor the spate of works to be issued by what would come to be called "Chicano historians," Weber nonetheless capably navigated the history of Mexican Americans. In so doing, he set standards, established guidepost, advanced challenging interpretations, proposed imaginative arguments, and launched a career that would make him the premier historian of the Spanish/Mexican Borderlands. With a historian's instinct, he predicted a venerable future for Chicano history. Time has not proved him wrong.

Arnoldo De León
C. J. "Red" Davidson Professor of History
Angelo State University
San Angelo, Texas
Spring 2003

Notes

1. Examples of current surveys would be Rodolfo Acuña, *Occupied America: A History of Chicanosi*, 4th ed. (New York: Langman 2000); Matt S. Meier and Feliciano Ribera, *Mexican Americans, American Mexicans: From Conquistadores to Chicanos*, 2nd ed. (New York: Hill and Wang, 1993); Richard Griswold del Castillo and Arnoldo De León, *North to Aztlán: A History of Mexican Americans in the United States* (New York: Twayne Publishers, 1996); Manuel G. Gonzales, *Mexicanos: A History of Mexicans in the United States* (Bloomington and Indianapolis: Indiana University Press, 1999); Julian Samora and Patricia Vandel Simon, *A History of the Mexican-American People*, 2nd ed. (Notre Dame: University of Notre Dame Press, 1993); and F. Arturo Rosales, *Chicano! The History of the Mexican American Civil Rights Movement* (Houston: Arte Público Press, 1996). Select books that focus on Mexican Americans in specific states would be Arnoldo De León, *Mexican Americans in Texas: A Brief History*, 2nd ed. (Arlington Heights, Ill.: Harlan Davidson, 1999); Albert Camarillo, *Chicanos in California History: A History of Mexican Americans in California* (San Francisco: Boyd & Fraser Publishing Co, 1984); and Erlinda Gonzales-Berry and David R. Maciel (eds.), *The Contested Homeland: A Chicano History of New Mexico* (Albuquerque: University of New Mexico Press, 2000). Recent bibliographical and historiographical essays assessing the state of the scholarship would include Alex Zaragosa, "The Significance of Recent Chicano-Related Historical Writings: An Appraisal," *Ethnic Affairs* 1 (1987); Richard Griswold del Castillo, "Chicano Historical Discourse: An Overview and Evaluation of the 1980s," *Perspectives in Mexican American Studies* vol. 4 (Tucson: Mexican American Studies Research Center, University of Arizona, 1993); Richard Griswold del Castillo, "History from the Margins: Chicana/o History in the 1990s." *JSRI Occasional Paper No. 28* (Lansing: University of Michigan, 1998); Arnoldo De León, "Whither Tejano History: Origins, Development, and Status," *Southwestern Historical Quarterly* 106 (January 2003); and Refugio I. Rochín and Dennis N. Valdes, *Voices of a New Chicana/o History* (East Lansing: Michigan State University Press, 2000).

2. Gilbert G. González and Raúl Fernández, "Chicano History: Transcending Cultural Models," *Pacific Historical Review* LXIII (November 1994), 485–90.

3. Louis Gerard Mendoza, *Historia: the Literary Making of Chicana & Chicano History* (College Station: Texas A & M University Press, 2001), 16–23, chapter 1, and Conclusion.

4. These might be Antonia I. Castañeda, *"Presidarias y Pobladoras*: Spanish Mexican Women in Frontier Monterey, Alta California, 1770–1821" (Ph.D. dissertation, Stanford University 1990); Deena J. González, *Refusing the Favor: The Spanish-Mexican Women of Santa Fe, 1820–1880* (New York: Oxford University Press, 1999); and Douglas Monroy, *Thrown Among Strangers: The Making of Mexican Culture in Frontier California* (Berkeley: University of California Press, 1990).

5. One example is my own *Racial Frontiers: Africans, Chinese, and Mexicans in Western America, 1848–1890* (Albuquerque: University of New Mexico Press, 2002).

6. David Montejano, *Anglos and Mexicans in the Making of Texas, 1836–1986* (Austin: University of Texas Press, 1987), 8, 34, 310.

7. Darlis A. Miller, "Cross-Cultural Marriages in the Southwest: The New Mexico Experience, 1846–1900," in Joan M. Jensen and Darlis A. Miller, eds., *New Mexico Women: Intercultural Perspectives* (Albuquerque: University of New Mexico Press, 1986), 101–2, 110; Doris Meyer, *Speaking for Themselves: Neo-Mexicano Cultural Identity and the Spanish Language Press, 1880–1920* (Albuquerque: University of New Mexico Press, 1996), pp. 191-205, 252 note 47; Thomas E. Sheridan, *Los Tucsonenses: The Mexican Community in Tucson, 1854–1941* (Tucson: University of Arizona Press, 1986), 147.

8. Emilio Zamora, "Mutualist and Mexicanist Expressions of a Political Culture in Texas," in Emilio Zamora, Cynthia Orozco, and Rodolfo Rocha, eds., *Mexican Americans in Texas History* (Austin: Texas State Historical Association, 2000), 83–101; Anabelle Oczón, "Bilingual and Spanish-Language Newspapers in Territorial New Mexico," *New Mexico Historical Review* 54 (January 1979), 45–52; Lynne Marie Getz, *Schools of Their Own: The Education of Hispanos in New Mexico, 1850–1940* (Albuquerque: University of New Mexico Press, 1997); Kenneth L. Stewart and Arnoldo De León, *Not Room Enough: Mexicans, Anglos, and Socio-Economic Change in Texas, 1850-1900* (Albuquerque: University of New Mexico Press, 1993), 50–54; Mary Romero, "El Paso Salt War: Mob Action or Political Struggle," *Aztlán* XVI (1985): 119–43; Anselmo Arellano, "The People's Movement: *Las Gorras Blancas,*" in Gonzales-Berry and Maciel, eds., *The Contested Homeland: A Chicano History of New Mexico* (Albuquerque: University of New Mexico Press, 2000), 59–82; Linda Gordan, *The Great Arizona Orphan Abduction* (Cambridge, Mass.: Harvard University Press, 1999); Jerry D. Thompson, ed., *Juan Cortina and the Texas-Mexico Frontier, 1859–1877* (El Paso: Texas Western Press, 1994); Richard Griswold del Castillo, "Joaquin Murrieta: The Many Lives of a Legend," in Richard W. Etulain and Glenda Riley, eds., *With Badges and Bullets: Lawmen & Outlaws in the Old West* (Golden, Colo.: Fulcrum Publishing, 1999), 106–22; Larry D. Ball, *Elfego Baca* (El Paso: Texas Western Press, 1992); Fray Angélico Chávez, *But Time and Chance: The Story of Padre Martínez of Taos, 1793–1867* (Santa Fe, N.M.: Sunstone Press, 1981); Jesús F. de la Teja, ed., *A Revolution Remembered: The Memoirs and Selected Correspondence of Juan N. Seguín* (Austin: Texas State Historical Association, 2002); Elliott Young, *"Libres Fronterizos": Catarino Garza's Revolution on the Texas-Mexico Border* (Durham, N.C.: Duke University Press, 2003); and María González de la Vara, "The Return to Mexico: The Relocation of New Mexican Families to Chihuahua and the Confirmation of a Frontier Region, 1848–1854," in Gonzales-Berry and Maciel, eds., *The Contested Homeland*, 43–57.

9. González, *Refusing the Favor;* Castañeda, "Presidarias y Pobladoras"; Gutiérrez, *When Jesus Came, the Corn Mothers Went Away: Marriage, Sexuality, and Power in New Mexico, 1500–1846* (Stanford: Stanford University Press, 1991); Sarah Deutsch, *No Separate Refuge: Culture, Class, and Gender on an Anglo Hispano Frontier in the American Southwest, 1880–1940* (New York: Oxford University Press, 1987); and Ana Carolina Castillo Crimm, *De León: A Tejano Family History* (Austin: University of Texas Press, 2004 [forthcoming]).

10. For a brief discussion of part of this literature see Griswold del Castillo and De León, *North to Aztlán,* 56–57. Examples of modern academic works that analyze literary sources once "unknown" would be Rosaura Sánchez and Beatrice Pita (edited and with introduction), *The*

Squatter and the Don: María Amparo Ruiz de Burton (Houston: Arte Público Press, 1992); María Herrera-Sobek, *Reconstructing a Chicano/a Literary Heritage: Hispanic Colonial Literature of the Southwest* (Tucson: University of Arizona Press, 1993).

11. Genaro M. Padilla, *My History, Not Yours: The Formation of Mexican American Autobiography* (Madison: The University of Wisconsin Press, 1993); Rosaura Sánchez, *Telling Identities: The California Testimonios* (Minneapolis: University of Minnesota Press, 1995), ix, x, 6, 276–79.

12. Martha Menchaca, *Recovering History, Constructing Race: The Indian, Black, and White Roots of Mexican Americans* (Austin: University of Texas Press, 2001): Lisabeth Haas, *Conquests and Historical Identities in California, 1769–1936* (Berkeley: University of California Press, 1995): Tomás Almaguer, *Racial Faultlines: The Historical Origins of White Supremacy in California* (Berkeley: University of California Press, 1994); Juan Gómez-Quiñones, *Mexican American Labor, 1790–1990* (Albuquerque: University of New Mexico Press, 1994); and Alfredo Mirandé, *Gringo Justice* (Notre Dame: University of Notre Dame Press, 1987).

13. For a brief overview of such episodes, see Griswold del Castillo and De León, *North to Aztlán,* 48–52, 55–58. A new work might be Young's on Catarino Garza, *"Libres Fronterizos."*

14. Betsy Guzmán, *The Hispanic Population: Census 2000 Brief* (Washington D.C.: U.S. Bureau of the Census, 2001), 2, 4 (Table 2: "Hispanic Population by Type for Regions, States, and Puerto Rico: 1990 and 2000"), 7.

15. Ana Carolina Castillo Crimm, "Success in Adversity: The Mexican Americans of Victoria County, Texas, 1800–1880" (Ph.D. dissertation, University of Texas at Austin, 1994), 8–9, 180–81, 216, 219, 288; and Armando Alonzo, *Tejano Legacy: Rancheros and Settlers in South Texas, 1734–1900* (Albuquerque: University of New Mexico Press, 1998), pp. 9, 280, 283, 161–81, 259–70.

16. Alonzo, *Tejano Legacy,* 9, 11, 128–35, 131, 280, 282, 161–81, 259–70.

17. De la Teja, ed., *A Revolution Remembered,* vii; and David R. McDonald and Timothy M. Matovina, eds., *Defending Mexican Valor in Texas: José Antonio Navarro's Historical Writing, 1853–1857* (Austin, Texas: State House Press, 1995), 11–12, 21–26.

18. David L. Torres and Melissa Amado, "The Quest for Power: Hispanic Collective Action in Frontier Arizona," *Perspectives in Mexican American Studies* vol. 3 (Tucson: MASRC, University of Arizona, 1992), 81–90.

19. In a recent assessment of part of the literature that constitutes Chicano history, the historian Manuel G. Gonzales lauded *Foreigners in Their Native Land* for its substance and merit. According to Gonzales, *Foreigners* when published in 1973 "gave much-needed credibility to the emerging field of Chicano history. [Weber] also provided a model of excellence which many Chicano historians have attempted to emulate." In Gonzales considered opinion, *Foreigners* remains a hallmark of historical research, interpretation and writing. Gonzales, *Mexicanos,* pp. 5–6.

Foreword to the First Edition

Scholars in United States history have been writing on immigrant groups for more than a century. Experts who speak for Italians, Jews, Germans, Scandinavians, and others have won national reputations for their books on the newcomers. Ironically, the oldest immigrant people, the descendants of Spaniards and Indians, received almost no scholarly attention until the 1960s. Up to that time, no historian had written a book about the Mexicans and their descendants, and just a handful of popularizers and sociologists had taken note of them. Yet the six million Mexican Americans comprise the second largest ethnic minority in the United States today; in the Southwest, no minority group surpasses them in numbers.

A young generation of Mexican Americans shattered that indifference. Entering colleges and universities in increasing numbers and frequently joining the Chicano movement, which preaches the importance of self-awareness and pride in background, the new students demanded courses that explored their own history. In a few years, in response to these demands, hundreds of classes on Chicano history won the blessings of campus administrators eager to placate a vocal and significant group of Chicanos in Southwestern schools.

Unfortunately, courses on Chicano history confronted two formidable obstacles. Because of the almost total neglect of the Mexican American population by scholars, there were no specialists in the field. Most of the teachers of the new courses had no formal historical training. Further, given the absence of research, the new instructors had to collect their own materials and to rely on less than satisfactory texts. The pioneer pedagogue had to transform himself into a historian and simultaneously assemble sources for teaching an unexplored history.

David Weber's anthology, a collection of Spanish, Mexican, and American writings, represents a bold effort to develop systematically the documentary sources for Mexican American history. The anthology breaks new ground; no comparable documentary collection exists. The documents, personal testimonials by men who lived the history of the Southwest which the new Mexican Americans claim as their heritage, date from 1595, more than a decade before Englishmen settled Jamestown. Weber has translated some of the documents into English for the first time; others appear only in obscure collections previously explored only by connoisseurs of antiquarian history. The documents, written by Spanish and Mexican officials, American businessmen, traders, soldiers, explorers, adventurers, and others, embody a cross section of life in the Southwest. Some describe vividly the joys, laments, and fears of the Spanish-speaking population, and their reactions to foreigners, particularly the Americans who invaded the Southwest after the defeat of Mexico in 1848. The American documents handle the story of the early settlers from another perspective. In some measure, all make the history of Mexican Americans come alive. Weber has chosen his documents with the insight of the professional historian, yet his choices reveal a refreshing sympathy for the Spaniards and Mexicans and their conquered descendants. His anthology documents vividly the rich historical heritage of the Spanish-Mexican Southwest and the dimensions of the conflict between the native peoples and the invaders who followed the American conquest of the Southwest.

As Weber's collection demonstrates, the history of Mexican Americans began more than four centuries ago. Its roots lie deep in the Spanish colonial era. Spanish explorers, priests, and soldiers discovered parts of the Southwest in the sixteenth century. In 1610, just three years after the settlement of Jamestown, Spaniards and mestizos (people of mixed Indian and Spanish blood) settled Santa Fe, New Mexico. Between the beginnings at Santa Fe and the settlement of San Francisco in 1776, Spaniards and mestizos forged a chain of towns and villages stretching from Texas to California. Spain ruled this sprawling region until 1821; officials of the Republic of Mexico governed it until 1848.

The United States won the Southwest from Mexico by force of arms. According to the Treaty of Guadalupe–Hidalgo, Mexico relinquished to the United States half of its national domain, hundreds of towns and villages that were home to a Spanish-speaking population alien by race and culture to the new government. Many of the conquered peoples traced their local origins back more than two centuries. But during that time Spain had not simply built a replica of its own society in the Southwest. Like their Mexican brothers to the south, Californios, Nuevo Mexicanos, and Texanos claimed a mestizo heritage, a blend of Spanish and Indian. Neither Spain nor Mexico had closely supervised the distant provinces, months away by horseback from Mexico City. Distance, official neglect, and the nature of the land, therefore, had stamped the societies of the Southwest with characteristics of their own. The people conquered by the Americans in 1848 were not just Spaniards and Mexicans, but a peculiar breed of Spanish-speaking Southwesterners.

From the Treaty of Guadalupe–Hidalgo to the first decade of the twentieth century, the span covered by this anthology, the vast majority of these Spanish-speaking Catholic people survived in an alien Protestant world. The landowning elite lost its lands; the poor entered the ranks of common laborers. Many retreated to towns along the Mexican border or to isolated mining camps in Arizona, seeking protection from the conquerors. Later in the nineteenth century, as the Southwest—particularly California—developed, descendants of the conquered moved north again, some back to their parents' place of birth. With the coming of the twentieth century and the Mexican Revolution, new immigrants poured into the Southwest from Mexico, mainly into border cities and towns, drastically altering the traditional patterns of old Southwestern communities and reinforcing Mexican ways of life.

Weber's documents record this history and the story of the conflict that raged between Californios, Texanos, and Nuevo Mexicanos on one side and the American conquerors on the other. As the documents testify, it is a vivid history, worthy of study by scholars who seek to master the full historical picture of the American people.

Ramón Eduardo Ruiz
University of California, San Diego
Autumn, 1972

Acknowledgments

In the hope of improving this book I inflicted portions of the manuscript on several of my classes. They deserve my apologies, along with my appreciation for their advice and forbearance. Several students deserve special mention for their help and suggestions: Michael Gonzales, Charles Hughes, Bonnie Royer, and Donna Sandoval. Portions of the manuscript were also read by colleagues who have responded generously with advice and encouragement: Rodolfo Acuña of California State University, Northridge; Pedro Castillo of the University of California, Santa Barbara; José Juárez of the University of California, Davis; Oakah L. Jones of the United States Air Force Academy, Colorado Springs; Ramón Ruiz, of the University of California, San Diego, who also kindly consented to write the foreword for this book; Richard T. Ruetten of California State University, San Diego; Manuel P. Servín of Arizona State University; and Marc Simmons of Cerrillos, New Mexico. I appreciate, too, the careful typing of the manuscript done by Lenora Thomason of San Diego.

Librarians at the universities of Arizona, New Mexico, and Texas have all been kindly and cooperative, but over the long haul I have been most indebted to Irene Wright of the interlibrary loan service at my own university, California State University, San Diego. Very special thanks also go to Juan Gómez-Quiñones of the University of California, Los Angeles, who provided an impetus for this project in early conversations, and who helped me to obtain a welcome grant from the Mexican American Cultural Center at UCLA. Carlos Cortés, of the University of California, Riverside, a former *compañero de clase*, merits a special mention for his sensitive reading of the entire manuscript. My friend and colleague, Dennis Berge, also gave me a helpful critique of the entire manuscript and, as department chairman, has helped to maintain a favorable climate for research, writing, and teaching, despite pressures from an administration that has been preoccupied with the processing of students. Finally, every page underwent the editorial scrutiny of a talented young lady of my acquaintance, to whom this book is lovingly dedicated.

Contents

III. Cultures Collide

IV. All the Rights of Citizens   139

V. Accommodation, Assimilation, and Resistance   203

ILLUSTRATIONS

Introduction

Americans of Mexican descent live in virtually every state of the Union. Although substantial numbers of Mexican Americans live in states such as Illinois, Michigan, and Colorado, the vast majority live in the four Southwestern states adjacent to the United States-Mexican border: California, Arizona, New Mexico, and Texas. The United States census of 1970 indicates that perhaps five million Mexican Americans live in these four Southwestern states alone.[1] Until recently, this sizeable ethnic group had been characterized as "the invisible minority," "a minority nobody knows," or "the forgotten people." From a historian's vantage point, this seems particularly ironic. Of all the European groups that intruded upon the native Americans, Spanish Americans came first. North America had been explored and colonized by Spanish Mexicans well before their Anglo American counterparts arrived on the scene. Being first, however, has proved to be of little advantage. As one writer suggested in 1967, Mexican Americans in the Southwest are

> worse off in every respect than the non-whites (Negroes, Indians, and Orientals), not to mention the dominant Anglos (everybody else). They are poorer, their housing is more crowded and more dilapidated, their unemployment rate is higher, their average educational level is lower (two years below non-whites, four below Anglo).[2]

How can this be explained? The tendency of social scientists has been to suggest that Mexican culture contains serious deficiences which make Mexicans unable to compete in the United States. They say that Mexicans are basically docile, superstitious, fatalistic, present-oriented, emotional, and lacking initiative. Hence, it is argued, Mexicans will remain a disadvantaged group in the United States until they rid themselves of the cultural baggage they brought from Mexico and become "Americanized." Some sociologists have found Mexicans so slow to Americanize that they label Mexicans "unassimilable."[3] These sociologists, then, tend to explain that Mexican Americans themselves are responsible for their own problems in

1

modern America; thus they implicitly exonerate Anglo American culture and institutions. This approach has come under sharp attack in recent years. Mexican American scholars, beginning with Octavio Romano, argue that Anglo American social scientists have perpetuated and legitimized simplistic stereotypes and have allowed their own cultural biases to blind them.[4] Thus far, however, Chicano sociologists have found it easier to say what Mexican American culture *is not*, than to suggest a model for what Mexican American culture *is*. Perhaps this is because Mexican Americans are a highly diverse group—not an "unusually homogeneous ethnic group" as one sociologist has suggested.[5]

For outsiders trying to understand this complex ethnic group, and for Mexican Americans trying to define themselves, history may be more useful than the social sciences, as Octavio Romano has implied. Yet, as one Chicano historian has pointed out: "There is no question but that in studies of Mexicans in the United States the most neglected field is history."[6] Indeed, historians have been criticized more for what they have not said than for what they have said. Not until 1972 did trained historians publish a synthesis of the Mexican American past. Before that, for nearly a quarter of a century, the only published overview of Mexican American history was *North From Mexico: The Spanish-Speaking People of the United States*, by Carey McWilliams, a journalist, attorney, and civil libertarian.[7]

Instead of blaming Mexican Americans for their own plight, McWilliams saw Anglo American discrimination and unique historic circumstances as explanations for the Mexicans' condition in America. McWilliams, like the sociologists before and after him, recognized that Mexican Americans had been slower to assimilate into American culture than had other minorities. The reason, he suggested, is not that Mexicans are slower to accept change than are other ethnics. Rather, it is because Mexican culture continues to be nourished through continuous immigration and constant contact with neighboring Mexico. No other ethnic group in America comes from a country contiguous to the United States. Furthermore, McWilliams suggested that some Mexican Americans never really left their homeland behind. Like American Indians, Mexicans who lived in the Southwest before 1846 found that the United States came to them and conquered them militarily during the Mexican War. In another sense, too, Mexicans who come to the United States do not leave their homeland behind. As McWilliams recently wrote: "Mexicans in moving 'north from Mexico' have always felt that they were moving within an environment that was geographically, culturally, and historically familiar."[8]

One need not be highly observant to see why the American Southwest, where some 85 percent of all Mexican Americans live today, remains familiar territory for emigrating Mexicans. The visitor sees no difference in the landscape as he crosses the border between Sonora and Arizona, or Chihuahua and New Mexico, or Tamaulipas and Texas. Nor do the names on the land seem different as one travels up the Rio Grande from El Paso through Socorro, Albuquerque, and Santa Fe, or as one crosses the Nueces and the Frío rivers on the way from Laredo to San Antonio. Of course, such Anglo names as Pearsall and Truth or Consequences remind the traveler that he has entered the United States. Yet the common use of Mexican architecture, the easy access to Mexican restaurants, movie houses, and music, and, indeed, the presence of entire Mexican American barrios in major cities and villages in the countryside, attest to the long connection the Southwest has had with Spain and Mexico. Those with more than a passing acquaintance with the region come to discover that Mexico has influenced agriculture, mining techniques and laws, water laws, laws pertaining to brands and range, community property laws, settlement patterns, political boundaries, routes for roads, and even language throughout the Southwest.[9]

A study of history, then, may be as useful as sociology or the other social sciences in attempting to understand why Mexican Americans are a unique ethnic group for whom the mythical melting pot has not worked. But what is Mexican American history? First, when does it begin? A few historians suggest that it started in 1848 when the war between Mexico and the United States came to an official end and a significant number of Mexicans became hyphenated Americans—that is, United States citizens.[10] This view seems shortsighted: it is similar to arguing that United States history began in 1783 when the republic became officially independent of England. Just as we recognize that an understanding of our colonial heritage is vital to understanding our history as a nation, so too we need to understand that Mexicans living in the Southwest had a significant heritage before they were militarily conquered and became Mexican Americans.

This brings us to another closely related question. To what extent is Mexican history Mexican American history? To some historians, especially those who specialize in Latin America, Mexican history and Mexican American history are nearly synonomous.[11] That is an unfortunate but understandable point of view. Because most Mexican Americans have come to the United States since World War I, their heritage is linked almost completely to Mexico's past. Mexican history, then, is at least as essential to the understanding of Mexican American history as the history of England is to an understanding of United States history. Indeed, it is probably more essential. Yet, a volume concerning Mexican Americans need not chronicle the history of Mexico any more than a history of the United States need include a history of England. Those seeking to know more about Mexico will find an ample literature elsewhere, for historians have not ignored the subject. Mexican American history, then, should not be viewed as a simple extension of Mexican history. This volume treats only that portion of Mexico which fell under United States control in 1846, where the vast majority of Mexican Americans lived and continue to live. The history of this area of Mexico is, even before 1846, distinctive in many ways from that of the rest of Mexico. The most recent newcomer from Mexico to the Southwest finds that he is entering a milieu whose institutions, traditions, and beliefs have been shaped by a unique historical experience.

If Mexican American history is not synonomous with Mexican history, neither is it synonomous with Indian history. Yet the rhetoric of the Chicano movement seems to be pushing Mexican American history in that direction. Some movement-oriented Chicanos applaud their Indian blood and celebrate the great pre-Columbian civilizations of Mexico while they condemn everything European. The sensitive and gifted poet, Alurista, for example, argues that Nahuatl culture is the heart of Chicano culture—"the heart of Aztlán."[12] The ancestral home of the Aztecs, Aztlán was an area somewhere to the northwest of present-day Mexico City. From Aztlán the Aztecs began a migration which brought them to the valley of Mexico, where they built a great city at Tenochtitlán and then went on to dominate all of central Mexico. A name charged with symbolism, *Aztlán* has become the Chicano name for the Southwest. From this region the Aztecs left to achieve greatness, and to this area the descendants of the Aztecs, Mexican immigrants, have returned. Symbolic and beautiful, the name will serve a useful function in giving a much-needed unity for Southwestern Chicanos who try not to think of themselves as Texans or Californians exclusively.

But the study of Aztec culture, fascinating as it is, should not be confused with Chicano history. Aztlán probably was not in or near the Southwest, and most Mexican Americans are not descended from Aztecs. Rather, Mexican American ancestry lies in the diverse aboriginal population of Mexico, including such groups as Tlascalans, enemies of the Aztecs who cooperated with the Spanish conquerors, and Indians of northern Mexico such as Seris, Yaquis, and Tarahumaras. In the Southwest, Mexicans further mixed their blood with the blood of American Indians.[13]

Reies Tijerina's talk of an Indo-Hispano alliance in present-day New Mexico notwithstanding, there are no historical reasons to suppose that such an alliance ever existed. To suggest that a book of documents on Chicano history ought to include readings on Indians per se, as one writer recently did,[14] is to confuse current rhetoric with historical reality. Although Spain's Indian policy was well intentioned and more carefully conceived than United States policy, and even though there are ample examples of cooperation between Indians and Hispanos,[15] it is also true that "civilized" Indians living at missions revolted against their foreign teachers and that Plains Indians, such as Apaches and Comanches, resisted Hispanization. Moreover, Mexican intruders, always a minority in the Southwest, encroached on Indian lands and frequently showed little sympathy for Indian culture. One Jesuit in Arizona, for example, even expressed doubt that an Indian could have "a rational soul."[16]

If there was little love lost between Indians and Mexicans in the Southwest in general, there was, nevertheless, a good deal of intermixture between individuals of both groups. This continuing process of racial mixture produced a racial and cultural blending in Mexico and the Southwest described best, perhaps, by Simón Bolívar when he wrote of the Americans: "we are . . . neither Indian nor European but a species midway between."[17] Racial mixture is one of the salient features of Chicano ethnicity, for most Mexican Americans remain highly visible. Once a source of shame, even in Mexico, Indian ancestry and dark skin color have become a source of pride for Chicanos who identify themselves as belonging to La Raza de Bronce—the Bronze Race. La Raza, as used by most Chicanos, does not mean the "cosmic" or "final inclusive race" about which Mexican philosopher José Vasconcelos wrote. Rather, some militant members of La Raza see themselves as superior to Anglo Americans. As Chicano historian Mario García has written, such a view "contains elements of racism, but this is unavoidable, for the crisis of the moment demands that Mexican Americans be instilled with racial pride."[18]

This volume is not, then, a study of Indians or of Spaniards, or of Mexico or of the United States. Rather, it seeks to illuminate the experience of Mexicans who lived and continue to live in the area that became the American Southwest in 1848. In isolating the history of Mexican Americans from the rest of the history of Mexico and the United States, this study will, by its very nature, be narrow. Yet, the insight and understanding that comes from studying one thread from the fabric of the past may make it worthwhile to lose sight momentarily of the whole cloth. I have tried to explain the past of the Californios, Arizonenses, Nuevo Mexicanos, and Texanos in all the complexity that space and my own understanding permit. In so doing I have tried to avoid creating villains or heroes, good guys or bad guys.

This study begins in 1540 when explorers from Mexico, then part of the Viceroyalty of New Spain, entered the Southwest. The first chapter looks at today's Southwest during the nearly three centuries that it was under Spanish rule (1540 to 1821), and suggests that the colonists in this region were essentially Mexican, and that the frontier experience made their culture distinctive. The second chapter examines the origins and intensity of anti-Mexican feeling in the United States, which has roots going back at least as far as the period when Spain governed the Southwest. Anti-Mexicanism intensified, however, between 1821, when Mexico became independent of Spain, and 1846, when war broke out between the United States and Mexico. This period of increased contact between Mexicans and Americans saw two major conflicts: the Texas Revolution (1836) and the Mexican War (1846–48). These conflicts are discussed, and their significance for Mexican Americans suggested, in chapter 3. Chapters 4 and 5 treat the period from the signing of the Treaty of Guadalupe-Hidalgo in 1848, which ended the Mexican War, to 1910, when Congress passed legislation to enable the territories of New Mexico and Arizona to become states in the Union, and when the Mexican Revolution got underway, pushing emigrants toward the United States. Chapter 4 examines the treatment that Mexicans in the United States received after the Treaty of Guadalupe-Hidalgo guaranteed them "all the rights of citizens." Chapter 5 surveys the range of responses that Mexican Americans made to their new status as a minority group in an Anglo culture, and finds striking similarities between the activities of Mexican Americans before 1910 and the activities of Mexican Americans in recent years.

Although most Mexicans living in the United States today have come since 1910, events involving those Mexicans who lived in the Southwest before that year are of considerable significance for more recent immigrants. By 1910 many patterns of thought and behavior toward and by Mexican Americans had already become well enough established to endure to the present day. Perhaps no one has stated this idea more forcefully than Yale sociologist Rodolfo Alvarez, when he argues that twentieth-century migrants from Mexico

> were incorporated into an already thoroughly structured, thoroughly defined, social situation. . . . they did not and could not have the individual freedom that other immigrants could have in trying out new roles. It is a travesty to consider post-1900 migration as comparable to immigration by other people into the United States without a careful historical or intellectual understanding of the unique pre-1900 creation of the Mexican-American people.[19]

Nonetheless, the pre-twentieth-century period of Mexican American history has received slight attention. As historian Juan Gómez-Quiñones has recently noted: "The need for a critical evaluation of periods prior to the twentieth century is urgent and long overdue."[20] "The nineteenth century," historian Jesús Chavarría has written, "is the crucible for the Chicano in the Southwest."[21] It is this neglected but important period that the essays and sources in this volume focus upon.

Mexican American history of any era is a young field of study with a scanty historical literature of its own. Yet, much has been written about the scene of Mexican American history—the Southwest. The literature on the period of Spanish control, 1540 —1821, is especially rich. The eminent historian Charles Gibson has suggested that "it is probable that no other part of Colonial Latin America has stimulated so extensive a program of research."[22] Although plentiful, historical writing on the Southwest has not dealt with many of the questions that are now being raised about the Mexican American past. Many of these new questions focus on the role of the masses who, as Pierre Goubert has told us, are far more difficult to study than the elites.[23] Thus, answers to new questions will require the use of new and sophisticated techniques such as quantification, prosopography, and psychology, as well as reliance on primary sources such as newspapers, public records, private correspondence, diaries, and oral interviews.

In piecing together this brief overview of Mexican American history I have consulted primary sources when necessary, relying almost entirely upon those that have been published, and using secondary accounts whenever possible. My debt to other historians is acknowledged in the notes to each chapter, which might serve as a modest guide to further reading. The surface of Mexican American history, of course, has hardly been scratched. As serious work is done, gaps in our knowledge will be filled, current generalizations will give way to increasing subtlety and complexity, new interpretations will emerge, and a work such as this will become outdated. In the meantime, these essays offer a brief summary of the literature to date and, it is hoped, suggest directions that future research might take.

This volume evokes some of the spirit of the times by reprinting primary sources at the end of each chapter. Unlike many "readers," this collection does not attempt to create forced controversies or set up strained dichotomies for students to puzzle over. Rather, the readings have been selected to illustrate themes within each chapter. Opposing points of view are presented only if they were significant to contemporaries. Each of the five chapters in this volume is preceded by an introductory essay which outlines the period under consideration and points the reader toward the primary sources that follow. Each reading is preceded by a brief explanatory note, for documents seldom speak for themselves. Most of the readings in this volume have been written by Mexican Americans or their predecessors; those written by Anglo Americans were selected because they provide insight into their attitudes or because they offer a different perspective on Mexican Americans.

Nearly every book on Mexican Americans needs to devote some space to defining terms, and this one will be no exception. Since Mexican Americans are a diverse group, no label can be found which will be pleasing to all. Indeed, that may not even be desirable.[24] The very name *Mexican American,* for example, is offensive to two substantial groups of Americans of Mexican descent. First, there are those of Mexican descent who have completely assimilated into American culture (or think they have), and prefer to be known as "Americans, just like everyone else." Since this group has abandoned the very culture which made them a distinctive ethnic group, it seems only logical to agree with them that they are not Mexican Americans, but Americans of Mexican descent. Ethnicity is, after all, a cultural, not a racial condition. The second group that finds the term *Mexican American* offensive is that which prefers the name *Chicano*. Chicanos assert that Anglos view "hyphenated Americans" as second-class citizens who are in the process of becoming Americanized (when Chicano historians do use the term *Mexican American* they generally write it without a hyphen). Chicanos reject the necessity for Americanization and argue that a unique culture already exists in the Southwest which is neither totally American nor totally Mexican. This culture requires its own name if it is to find its identity. *Chicano*, judging from its widespread popularity, serves that purpose well. Much energy has been expended in the search for the etymology of Chicano, while the real meaning of the word has been often overlooked. Ruben Salazar, a talented reporter for the *Los Angeles Times*, put it best a few months before his tragic death in August 1970: "A Chicano," he wrote, "is a Mexican-American with a non-Anglo image of himself."[25]

Although its popularity is increasing, the term *Chicano* is still far from receiving universal acceptance. Regional differences continue to prevail. In northern New Mexico, for example, *Spanish American* and *Hispano* remain popular, while in Texas some Mexican Americans prefer to be known as *Latin American*. Each of these terms denies Mexican Americans their *mexicanidad*—their "Mexicanness"—and is essentially defensive, dating to the second and third decades of this century when older Mexican American families did not want to be mistaken for newly arrived Mexicans. In California, where older families are "Spaniards," this defensive distortion of names dates back at least to the gold-rush era, which saw the first large-scale immigration of Mexicans to the Golden State.

In these essays I have employed *Mexican American* as the term which perhaps offends the least number of people, and have avoided such affectations as *Hispanoid*. In the nineteenth century, regional terms such as *Californios, Nuevo Mexicanos, Arizonenses, Texanos,* and *Hispanos* were commonly used, along with *Anglos, Yankees, Greasers,* and *Gringos*. To retain the flavor of the period, I have used all of those terms as well. *Anglo*, short for *Anglo American*, refers to one who has accepted the dominant life-style of a United States citizen; no other ethnic or racial connotation is intended. An Italian American or a Negro might be an *Anglo*, then, from a Mexican point of view.

Finally, although I acknowledge that all citizens of the Western Hemisphere are *Americans*, I have used the term for convenience sake to mean citizens of the United States. Latin American intellectuals may bristle at the preemption of "American" by the Yankees, but the fact remains that in the language of the street in Latin America, *Americano* invariably means a citizen of the United States. Moreover, what other term can one use? "United Statesian" is ridiculous. *Norteamericano,* or North American, has won widespread acceptance in Latin America as a synonym for a citizen of the United States (most people who use it forget that it includes Mexicans and Canadians), and was so used in the nineteenth century. Thus, I have occasionally used *norteamericano* in that sense, too.

David J. Weber
La Mesa, California
Autumn 1972

I.

New Spain's Far Northern Frontier

Editor's Introduction

From 1540, when intensive exploration north from Mexico got under way, until 1821, when Mexico became independent of Spain, today's Southwestern states of California, Arizona, New Mexico, Texas, Nevada, Utah, and much of Colorado formed part of the wealthy Spanish colony of New Spain, as Mexico was then called. Spain had only a nominal hold over this vast territory; permanent colonies were established in coastal California, southern Arizona, the Rio Grande Valley of New Mexico, and in Texas. Yet, the years of Spanish control over the Southwest left remnants of Spanish culture firmly stamped on the area: "This is an imprint," one Spaniard recently wrote, "that nothing and nobody can erase, for history is ineradicable, though it is all too often forgotten by many."[1]

What is most often forgotten is that this colonial period in today's Southwest belonged as much to Mexico and Mexicans as it did to Spain and Spaniards. Although the leaders of Spain's exploring and colonizing expeditions were usually persons born in Spain, the rank and file of those groups consisted of persons born in Mexico, usually of mixed blood, whose culture combined Indian and Spanish elements. These "Spanish" pioneers were neither Indian nor Spanish, but Mexican. Even though this chapter treats a period in which Spain controlled the Southwest, those colonists who entered the region are referred to as *Mexicans* or *Spanish Mexicans*, terms which correspond to *American* and *Anglo American*.

I

Beginning in 1513 when Juan Ponce de León landed on the shores of Florida, Spain's explorers were the first Europeans to explore the area that is now the United States. By the 1520s Spanish maritime explorers had cruised along the northern shore of the Gulf of Mexico, becoming the first Europeans to see Alabama, Mississippi, and Texas, while others sailed up the Atlantic coast to the Carolinas. Between 1539 and 1541 Hernando De Soto led a large, well-equipped expedition into the interior of North America on an agonizing and unsuccessful search for mineral wealth that took his men through today's states of Florida, Georgia, South Carolina, Alabama, Mississippi, Arkansas, Louisiana, Texas, and perhaps Tennessee and Oklahoma.

In 1540, while De Soto tramped through these southern states, Francisco Vásquez de Coronado set out on an equally impressive and equally unsuccessful expedition through the Southwest in search of the mythical Seven Cities of Cíbola and other wealth. In their quest for another Mexico, Coronado's men trekked through Arizona (where they became the first Europeans to see the Grand Canyon), New Mexico, Texas, Oklahoma, and Kansas.

Meanwhile, the Pacific Coast was not neglected. To take supplies to the Coronado party, Hernando de Alarcón sailed up the Gulf of California and steered three ships into the treacherous mouth of the Colorado, sailing upriver to the area of present-day Yuma. By 1543, Juan Rodríguez Cabrillo and Bartolomé Ferrelo had edged two small ships along the coast of the Californias; Ferrelo reached the area of the Rogue River, in present-day Oregon, before turning back.

Thus, only fifty years after Columbus first sighted land in the New World, Spaniards had explored much of the coastline of the United States and had taken a good look at its interior. They did not like what they saw. They had discovered no strait through North America to the fabled Orient. They had found no wealthy Indians to rival the Aztecs or Incas, and had made no important mineral discoveries. Why stay when Spain had richer colonies to enjoy? Colonization, then, did not immediately follow exploration. Spain's subjects needed other incentives to abandon affluent New Spain and settle the remote and arid areas to the north.

When Spain's subjects reentered the Southwest toward the end of the sixteenth century they had goals different from those of the first explorers. Although they never abandoned the hope that rich minerals would be found, converting Indians to Christianity and safeguarding the frontier against encroachment by other powers came to be the most important inducements for Spain to plant the first European settlements in what is now the United States.

New rumors of mineral wealth in the lands Coronado had discovered again brought explorers north from Mexico to the Rio Grande Valley in 1580. This initial probing led to a government-sponsored party, headed by wealthy Juan de Oñate, which began the permanent European occupation of New Mexico in 1598.

Yet, the province had no strategic value at this time, and when the
Spanish crown learned that no minerals had been found, it ordered
New Mexico to be abandoned in 1608. Franciscans, however, had
already begun to baptize Pueblo Indians. Rather than see them revert
to their "pagan" native religion, the crown permitted the Franciscans
and the colonists to stay. Missions became New Mexico's sole reason
for existence. Santa Fe, founded in 1610, became the third permanent
European settlement in the present-day United States, after St.
Augustine (1565) and Jamestown (1607). Connected to the rest of New
Spain only by the lengthy, hazardous trail to Chihuahua, the isolated
colony grew slowly. The nonaboriginal population of New Mexico
probably numbered no more than 2,800 by 1680. That year, in a rare
display of unity prompted by the leadership of Popé, and a black man,
Domingo Naranjo,[2] the Pueblos launched a counterattack, forcing the
intruders from Mexico to flee southward to El Paso del Norte
(present-day Ciudad Juárez). Nevertheless, by 1694 the Spanish
Mexicans had regained control of the province. The eighteenth
century saw New Mexico grow steadily, despite heavy attacks from
Apaches and Comanches which drastically reduced the number of
Pueblo Indians and kept the European population confined, in the
main, to the Rio Grande Valley. By 1821 New Mexico was the most
populous province on the edge of the frontier, with a population of
some 40,000. About a quarter of these were Pueblo Indians, and
among those counted by the census takers as "Spanish and other
classes" were many Indians who had become Hispanized.[3]

Arizona, the next area of the present United States to be penetrated
by missionaries coming north from Mexico, was part of the large
province of Sonora and was not a separate administrative entity
during the Spanish period. Beginning in 1691, with the work of the
famous Eusebio Francisco Kino, the Jesuits extended their mission
chain across what would eventually be the international border. Their
achievements in southern Arizona, however, remained insignificant.
Marauding Apaches and the area's lack of strategic value hindered
further missionary expansion and discouraged mining and ranching.
Thus, despite the best efforts of the Jesuits (and Franciscans after
1767), at the end of the colonial period Arizona contained only a
sparse Mexican population centered in the Santa Cruz Valley. There
was no Mexican settlement north of the presidio of Tucson, founded
in 1776, and much of the rugged plateau country north of the Gila
River remained unexplored.

Although missionaries also led the settlement of Texas and California, in those two areas defense against foreign powers brought about Spanish occupation. Franciscans had urged since the early 1600s, that missions be established in Texas, but not until French colonists, under Robert Cavelier, Sieur de La Salle, built a fort at Matagorda Bay in 1684 did Spain make its first tentative efforts to settle Texas. By 1716, in direct response to heightened French trading activities in Louisiana, permanent missions were established in east Texas near the Neches River. Two years later, in 1718, a mission and presidio were founded at San Antonio as a way station on the trail to east Texas. The chapel of the mission of San Antonio de Valero would become well known as the Alamo.

Besieged by Comanches on horseback, Texas grew slowly, attracting few colonists; its missions failed to expand to the north of San Antonio or to attract substantial numbers of Indian converts. In 1782 Father Juan Morfi reported that the Texas missions contained only 500 neophytes. By 1820 fewer than 2,500 persons of European descent lived in Texas.[4] Only four missions remained active and only three settlements, San Antonio, Nacogdoches, and La Bahía (later called Goliad), had been founded.

Spain colonized California for defensive reasons too, but missions came to dominate the life of the province. Presumed British and Russian threats to the Pacific Coast prompted the sending of the "Sacred Expedition" to Upper California in 1769. Under the leadership of Fray Junípero Serra and Captain Gaspar de Portolá, the expedition established the first mission and presidio in Upper California at San Diego in 1769. By the time of Serra's death in 1784, Franciscans had completed eight more coastal missions; the northernmost was at San Francisco, where a presidio was also constructed. Working among a dense and diverse population of relatively peaceful aborigines, the Franciscans met with more success than they had in Texas. The California missions numbered twenty-one by 1823. Still, the settlers unwittingly brought new diseases, such as smallpox and influenza, that spread quickly in the close mission quarters, causing California's Indian population to decline dramatically during the Spanish period.

Despite its flourishing missions and salubrious climate, distant California attracted few colonists. Anxious to populate the province, the Spanish government had to offer material rewards to encourage colonization, and it even sent some convicts as colonists. After the

Yuma Indian revolt of 1781 closed the only known overland route to California, the area remained dependent upon occasional ships from New Spain for additional colonists, supplies, and news of the outside world. Largely through natural increase, then, rather than colonization, the non-native population of California reached about 3,000 by 1821. A few of these pioneers lived in isolated ranches, but most settled in pueblos scattered along the coast. California had only three self-governing municipalities by 1821: San José, Los Angeles, and Branciforte (Santa Cruz). Yet settlements developed near some of the missions, too, such as those at San Luis Obispo and San Juan Capistrano. Settlements governed by military commanders also grew up at each of the four ill-equipped presidios that had been built by 1821: San Diego, Santa Bárbara, Monterey, and San Francisco.

II

By 1821, pioneers from Mexico had probed their far northern frontier, planting colonies in four areas which would one day fall within the boundaries of the United States: coastal California; southern Arizona; the Rio Grande Valley of New Mexico; and Texas, especially around San Antonio. Each of these provinces developed in isolation from the others, for throughout the period of Spanish sovereignty over Mexico, no lateral lines of communication crossed the Southwest. All roads led to Mexico City. Yet, the society that developed on New Spain's northern frontier never became an exact copy of the society of central Mexico. Rather, it resembled other frontiers of Spanish America, such as those of Chile or Argentina. In these areas, the colonists found no mineral wealth, so settlements grew slowly and the need for Indian labor remained less intense than in wealthier areas of Spain's empire. The nature of Indian societies also explains why Hispanic society developed differently on the far northern frontier. With the major exceptions of the Pueblos in New Mexico and some of the California tribes,[5] Spanish Mexicans found few agriculturally oriented, non-nomadic Indians who could be easily incorporated into Hispanic society and whose labor could be exploited. The encomienda and repartimiento systems, through which Spaniards exploited Indian labor in much of the New World, were used only briefly and unsuccessfully in today's Southwest (in seventeenth-century New Mexico).[6] Thus, Mexicans who came to the far north as conquerors remained as colonists, and necessity frequently forced them to work their own land and raise their own livestock.

In place of the encomienda and repartimiento, other institutions developed in response to frontier conditions. The mission, of limited utility elsewhere, served on the frontier to pacify and Hispanize Indians as well as to save their souls. Garrisons or presidios were established to protect nearby missions from Indians whom the Spaniards termed "barbarous" (indios bárbaros).

Just as Hispanic institutions adapted to the frontier, so too did they become modified by variations within the frontier environment. Although it may be convenient, it is not historically sound to view the Mexican frontier as a homogeneous region. Local conditions led to variations in economic life, land tenure patterns, and cultural developments. Even such a seemingly immutable institution as the mission was not immune. In California and Texas, for example, missionaries found it necessary to congregate seminomadic Indians into villages in order to Christianize and civilize them, and so the padres became involved in countless details of secular life. Yet the kind of missions that worked reasonably well among California Indians failed among the mounted, highly mobile Plains Indians of Texas and eastern New Mexico. In central New Mexico, on the other hand, Pueblos had lived in an urban culture since before the arrival of Europeans. Hence, the missions there functioned apart from the villages, which the Franciscans had the good sense to leave intact.

Most of the soldiers and settlers who journeyed to the far northern frontier were mestizos. In its narrowest sense, a mestizo was one-half Indian and one-half Spaniard. In practice, the term came to apply to mixed bloods generally, whatever proportion of Indian and Spanish blood they might have. Indeed, many mestizos in Mexico also had Negro ancestry.

Blacks were imported as slaves or servants, and it appears that more blacks than Spaniards entered Mexico during the colonial period.[7] They did not remain a distinctive minority, however, for they blended with Indian and Spanish stocks, and their descendants lost their racial identity. In 1822 one Anglo American visitor to Mexico City saw so few Negroes that he thought that the race was "nearly extinct in Mexico."[8] Yet throughout the colonial period, blacks and their offspring participated in the earliest explorations of the Southwest and comprised a sizeable percentage of the earliest "Spanish" pioneers. Jack D. Forbes has conservatively estimated that one-fifth of the Californios in 1790 were part Negro.[9]

The rigid class system based on racial distinctions and wealth, which was firmly rooted in central Mexico, was not as well established on the frontier. Racial mixture continued on the frontier, where Indians formed the majority of the population and where the scarcity of new European immigrants made it nearly impossible for the old families to keep bloodlines pure (only a few could legitimately make this claim). Furthermore, the scarcity of Indian labor on the frontier prevented all but a few families from attaining great wealth and made it all the more difficult to maintain social distinctions and appearances. Of course, some pure-blooded government officials and clergy viewed themselves as superior to the mixed-bloods, which prompted Mexican settlers, in turn, to "whiten" themselves by denying their Indian or Negro ancestry when possible. Yet, being of mixed blood does not seem to have been a serious handicap on the frontier. In California, for example, mixed-bloods were able to obtain land grants and came to form the ranchero class, which, ironically, considered itself Spanish by the Mexican period.[10] Thus, although racial prejudice existed on New Spain's far northern frontier, discrimination—the frequent result of prejudice—was probably less noticeable than in central Mexico, and certainly less important than in the United States, during the same period. Although these questions deserve further research, it seems safe to say that frontier society was more fluid than society in central Mexico, permitting mixed bloods greater social mobility. Of course, a small exploitative aristocracy based on family, wealth, and government service existed, but as France V. Scholes has written of colonial New Mexico:

> Life on the frontier put men on their own, and if a mestizo made a good soldier, he was a welcome member of the community. Many of them attained high military rank, and some became alcaldes mayores or members of the cabildo of Santa Fé.[11]

The cultural level of New Spain's northernmost provinces, as measured by such things as literary output, music, and elaborateness of the arts, remained low compared to the attainments of Mexicans in the viceregal capital of Mexico City, or of Anglos on the eastern seaboard. It seems unlikely, however, that this was due to the "laziness of the citizens" as some writers have suggested.[12] Instead, the explanation probably lies in the hardships imposed by isolation,

Indian hostilities, and the rigorous environment of much of the region. Then, too, the tiny population on the frontier provided an insufficient market to stimulate industry or large-scale agriculture, and great distances discouraged trade with the rest of New Spain.[13] Still, the charge of laziness has been leveled so frequently, not only by Anglos, but by Mexicans who visited the frontier, that further inquiry is necessary. Research into the motives and value system of those (mainly clerics and government officials) who charged Mexican frontiersmen with laziness might be revealing. The question is discussed further in chapter 2.

Although some observers viewed the Mexican pioneers as ne'er-do-wells, others regarded them as hardy groups which had developed a resilient culture.[14] The Californios went so far as to consider themselves superior to their fellow citizens in the rest of New Spain. As Ygnacio Sepúlveda recalled, the Californios "did not have the best of feelings towards those who had not had the fortune of being born in California."[15] Despite their alleged laziness, Mexicans on the far northern frontier developed commendable folk cultures and maintained themselves remarkably well in an area where literacy and education could be viewed only as luxuries until more elemental needs were met.[16] Indeed, as we gain more knowledge of the activities of Mexican pioneers we may discover that their energy and inventiveness was remarkable, given the odds against them. One recent study, for example, describes how a Corporal Antonio Luis discovered a cure for scurvy by using cactus fruit in 1603, and argues that this knowledge was used subsequently by Jesuits in the borderlands.[17]

III

Those familiar with United States expansion into the Far West in the nineteenth century will find that the American frontier invites comparison with the Spanish Mexican frontier. Although there were many similarities between the two frontiers' cultures, the differences usually seem most striking. These helped set the stage for future conflict between Mexicans and Americans in North America.

Some of the differences between the Mexican and Anglo American frontiers can be explained by environment. As Donald J. Lehmer has written,

> Environmental factors made the log cabin, the birchbark canoe, and the long rifle the trademarks of the Anglo-American frontiersman. Different environmental factors made the horse, the mine shaft, and the adobe house the trademarks of the Spanish frontier.[18]

In arid northern Mexico large landholdings become vital for raising cattle, and irrigated farming became a necessity. To maintain irrigation canals and defend fields from Indian attack required such a degree of cooperation among colonists that communal property-holding developed in some areas, especially in New Mexico. This stands in marked contrast to the general Anglo American frontier experience.

Also, different policies and attitudes toward Indians helped to mold two distinct frontier cultures. Spanish Mexicans exploited aborigines for their labor and attempted to save their souls for God. They viewed Indians as a valuable asset whose lives needed to be preserved and who, when they became Christians, were entitled to certain civil rights. Although Mexicans tended to view people of color as inferior, racial mixture was tolerated. Intermarriage between Mexicans and Indians was exceedingly common, especially among the lower classes who were already of mixed blood, and these unions further hastened the acculturation of Indians. Anglo Americans, on the other hand, were less tolerant of white-Indian marriages. Nor did Anglo Americans pause in their exploitation of the material resources of the West to exploit its human resources. Instead of utilizing aborigines and incorporating them into society, Anglo Americans either exterminated them or segregated them on reservations. Yet a caveat seems necessary. As Sherburne F. Cook has written:

> In comparing the objective effects wrought by the Ibero-American and Anglo-Saxon civilizations on the native population, it must not be supposed that the differences . . . were absolute, for human nature is much the same everywhere, despite policies and tradition. The Spanish at times certainly resorted to barbaric physical violence, and the Americans frequently treated their Indians with humanity and justice. Nevertheless, the broad tendencies were apparent and were reflected in the details of the two types of racial contact.[19]

Unlike the Anglo American West, New Spain's far northern frontier was not settled because of population pressures or because of the lure of free land.[20] Rather, Spain regarded the frontier, especially Texas and California, as critical to the defense of New Spain and so encouraged colonization and Hispanization of Indians in order to populate and hold the area. There was less opportunity for the growth of democratic institutions, local autonomy, or for individual initiative on the Spanish Mexican frontier. During most of the colonial period, officials in faraway Mexico City or Madrid generally made important decisions, and local authorities had only to carry them out.[21] Laws and regulations from the central government covered nearly all aspects of political and economic life, including such matters as the laying out of towns, treatment of Indians, methods of irrigation, land tenure, and maintenance of presidios. Commerce, too, was tightly regulated, and trade with foreigners remained illegal until the end of the colonial period. Spain's mercantilistic system thus intensified the isolation of the frontier provinces. With the exception of Texas, the far north remained untouched by foreign influences and the changes that swept across much of Spanish America after the American and French revolutions.

The orderly way in which Spanish Mexicans settled and governed their northern frontier, then, stands in contrast to the haphazard way in which Anglo Americans moved into their Far West. The advance guard of United States civilization was frequently the solitary trapper, the yeoman farmer, or the miner, whose geographical discoveries and building of settlements were only incidental to his main task. In far northern New Spain, however, explorers and colonizers were usually military men and missionaries operating under specific instructions from the crown. The Church worked closely with the state to introduce civilization, whereas on the American frontier churches played a minor role in the initial phase of exploration and settlement (a church was proverbially constructed in a town only after several saloons had been built). Instead of being attracted by self-interest, settlers on New Spain's far northern frontier were often induced to go there by attractive offers of land, seed, tools, titles, exemption from taxes, and military protection. This was the case with both the pioneers who came to San Antonio in 1731 and the founders of Los Angeles in 1781. Although the frontier environment affected both westward-moving Americans and northward-moving Mexicans, the differences in the cultures of the two groups assured the development of dissimilar frontier societies.

IV

By 1821, when Spain lost its hold on Mexico, a distinctive culture had developed on the far northern frontier, with regional variations in California, Arizona, New Mexico, and Texas. Originally Spanish, but modified by exposure to Mexican and Southwestern Indians and tempered by geography and isolation, this frontier society had become truly Mexican. New Mexico, where sixteenth-century customs and language were transmitted most directly from Spain, remained the most "Spanish" of the frontier provinces, but there too, modification of Spanish customs and institutions occurred, and considerable mixture with Indian blood took place.

All of this might be of little consequence if it were not for what Carey McWilliams has termed "the fantasy heritage"; "an absurd dichotomy between things *Spanish* and things *Mexican*,"[22] which both Anglo American and Mexican American in the Southwest have come to accept. Anglos who glorify the region's Spanish heritage while they discriminate against Mexicans are suffering from McWilliams's fantasy. Mexican Americans who prefer to be called Spanish, Hispano, or Latin American in order to disassociate themselves from more recent arrivals from Mexico are also deluded by the fantasy that their ancestors and heritage are Spanish.

The fantasy heritage has manifested itself in the myth that Spain's rule over the Southwest was a bucoloic, romantic period when pastoral life was simple, beautiful, and virtuous. Paradoxically accompanying this romanticization of the period of Spanish domination of the Southwest has been the notion that Spain's failure to build strong, prosperous provinces in the Southwest resulted from despotism, Catholicism, and the mixture of the races: the notion that Spain, an inept colonizing power, had populated the Southwest with inferior peoples of mixed blood and had equipped them with inferior institutions. Each of these viewpoints, of course, fails to allow for the complexities of life on the frontier of New Spain. More tragic, however, these twin delusions rob Mexican Americans of their rich colonial heritage in what is today the American Southwest.

1. Church and State   Luis de Velasco, 1595*

The Spanish crown exhibited considerable concern for detail in administering the exploration and settlement of its far-flung New World possessions, thereby minimizing the decision-making powers of local officials. Even on the remote northern frontier of New Spain colonization was to follow specific procedures which were spelled out in laws or formal instructions. Church and state were to cooperate in settling the frontier, and the welfare of the church was an important responsibility of the officers of the state. Although this did not always occur in practice, the intent of the crown is well illustrated in the following instructions which the king's chief political official in New Spain, Viceroy Luis de Velasco, gave to Don Juan de Oñate upon appointing him to colonize New Mexico.

Don Luis de Velasco, my viceroy, has made a contract with you, the said Don Juan de Oñate, for this project and you have accepted it on the conditions and stipulations which will be delivered to you, signed and attested by notary, so that in conformity with them and the said ordinances that deal with new discoveries and pacifications and other regulations I command that a copy of it be delivered to you for keeping and observing them. I approve and confirm these capitulations, as I have considered it well. Wherefore, trusting that you, in Christian manner and with all fidelity, will make the said discovery and pacification in the form and manner that the said viceroy has agreed and contracted with you, I name you as my governor and captain general, chief, discoverer, and pacifier of the said provinces of New Mexico and its immediate environs so that, as such, in my royal name, you may enter them with the colonists and soldiers, baggage, belongings, munitions, and other necessary things that you would bring for this purpose, in all peace, friendship, and good treatment, which is what I particularly charge you. You should try to bring the natives of these provinces to you and to induce them to hear the word of the holy gospel, that they may receive and accept

*Luis de Velasco, "Oñate's Appointment as Governor of New Mexico," trans. George P. Hammond, *New Mexico Historical Review* 13, no. 3 (July 1938): 246–48. Reprinted by permission of the *New Mexico Historical Review*.

it, converting them to our holy Catholic faith, causing them to understand, by means of interpreters of their languages, if you are able to get them, so that in the various tongues they may be able to communicate and undertake their conversion, or as it may best suit the present occasion or when the priests find it convenient. You shall hold them in personal respect and reverence like ministers of the gospel so that the Indians may attend and revere them and listen to their sermons and instruction, for experience has shown that this is very important. You shall take care that the people who might go in your company shall proceed quietly and peacefully, without committing any excesses or setting a bad example or causing those you wish to draw to you to be angered or feel differently than is just.

You shall order everything for the best and principal end, as stated, for you see it is a matter of importance. You shall arrange all things regarding it wisely and harmoniously, always ordering everything for the glory of God and the increase of our holy Catholic faith. You shall prepare with prudence for the events that may arise, so that neither by carelessness, neglect, nor remissness the Indians lose their zeal and enthusiasm, keeping but not overstepping the instructions of my viceroy that shall be committed to you with this. I order the soldiers, colonists, and servants who may go and remain with you that they shall consider you as their governor and captain general and keep and fulfill whatever you command them and respect your authority under the penalties that you may mete out to them. You shall be prepared to punish any rebels and proceed against those who overstep the bounds of authority, punishing them according to the usages of war, and do anything which may be appropriate in this regard and use the said charges and offices of governor and captain general, chief, discoverer, and pacifier of the said provinces and their immediate environs, conduct and enlist people and name and summon captains and other offices necessary for it and remove and re-appoint as may seem fitting to you. I give you the full power which may rightfully be required in such cases and order my governors, alcaldes mayors, corregidores, and other justices in whatever places they may be in order that for the above they give and do you the favor and aid that you might ask of them and that may be necessary, including carts, little carts, droves of animals, supplies, provisions, and other things which you may request of them in my royal name, under penalty of loss to their offices and a fine of 2,000 ducats for my royal chamber. From this moment I condemn those who violate these orders.

Given in Mexico, October 21, 1595. Don Luis de Velasco. I, Martín López de Gaona, chief notary of New Spain for the king, our lord, transcribed the above at the command of the viceroy in his name. Corrected. Juan Serrano (rubric).

2. Frontier Military   Antonio Martínez, 1817*

Fear of attack by Plains Indians dominated the lives of most colonists from Arizona to Texas. Despite the personal bravery and self-sacrifice of many soldiers and citizens, and notwithstanding periods of respite won by diplomacy or warfare, Indian attacks on Spanish settlements continued until the end of the colonial period. This happened largely because Spain could not adequately arm, equip, or pay presidial soldiers or militia. Some soldiers were convicts condemned to fight on the frontier with shoddy guns, tattered uniforms, and, of course, low morale. As late as 1817 the governor of Texas, Antonio Martínez, begged higher officials for the most minimal supplies for the presidio of Béxar at San Antonio. Across the northern frontier, including California, where Indians were also troublesome, the condition of the presidios was much the same.

I took charge of this government on the 28th of the present month of May, and I duly notify you thereof for your information and in expectation of the orders you may see fit to give me.

I can do no less than state that in spite of the wise and zealous management of my predecessor, *Señor Don* Manuel Pardo, I found this province in a very deplorable condition with respect to the maintenance of the troops and citizens and also to its defense. Of the 500 *fanegas* of corn that Your Excellency saw fit to allocate to this province I was able to bring with me only 184 because of the lack of mules and freighting equipment, and that amount will not furnish aid

---

*Antonio Martínez to Joaquín de Arredondo, Commandant General of the Eastern Provinces, Béxar, May 30, 1817, in *The Letters of Antonio Martínez, Last Spanish Governor of Texas, 1817–1822*, trans. Virginia Taylor (Austin: Archives Division, Texas State Library, 1957), pp. 1–2.

for the coming month of June. On the 15th the troops and families will be in the same miserable condition in which I found them. It is enough for me to tell you that on my arrival in this city the troops had been living entirely on field roots for several days. The amount of money the paymaster has sent is not sufficient to cover the debts that my predecessor contracted for the temporary maintenance of the troops. For this reason, I could not, nor can I give the least help to these officers and troops. Therefore, I earnestly beg you, in consideration of the unfortunate condition of this province of which you have been informed by my statement and by the petitions made by my said predecessor, to make an effort to have some money, and also some cigars, powder, and iron delivered to the paymaster *Don* Francisco Collantes. The province is in urgent need of these commodities. The warehouse has absolutely no provisions for any slight emergency that may arise, and the iron is very necessary for urgently needed repairs, especially for that of the gun carriages which gradually are becoming useless. Your Excellency must not rely on the 500 *fanegas* of corn provided for the assistance of these troops because a large part of it is being consumed by the muleteers since there is no money to pay the corresponding freight charges and it is necessary to give them corn for their food supply. Therefore, if Your Excellency does not see fit to furnish me with more corn, the needs and afflictions of this town and its garrison cannot be terminated.

After covering the important points in this province and furnishing the indispensable convoys that must be kept on the road to transport corn because of the scarcity of mules, as I have told you, this capital is left alone and helpless before the attacks of the barbarians. This was the reason my predecessor did not obey Your Excellency's command in regard to the return of Captain Muñoz to the presidio of Río Grande with the troops of his company. I have reported this matter to you, and finding myself in the same position, I beg Your Excellency to have sent to this city the same number of individuals in order that they may fill the vacancies that will be left, and likewise to have the soldiers of the other provinces replace those who in this one have deserted their posts and who have been retired on account of sickness. Otherwise the forces of this garrison will keep on scattering as they already are, but, regardless of what I have told you, you will please decide to have the said Captain D. Joaquín Muñoz and his troops removed from this post, and I shall execute your orders promptly. God, etc. [God protect you many years]. Béxar, May 30, 1817.

3. "Contributions are small"

Francisco Martínez de Baeza, 1639*

Pioneers who traveled north from Mexico hoped to find a new Mexico, rich with minerals and sedentary Indians who could be exploited. Their hopes were dashed on both counts. Only the Pueblos in New Mexico had achieved a cultural level that made them valuable for Hispanos. On the frontier, then, the traditional system of forced labor, the *encomienda,* existed only in New Mexico. Under this system Pueblo Indians were entrusted (*encomendar* means to entrust) to colonists who could collect tribute in the form of labor or produce from Indians, in exchange for protecting and Christianizing them. In impoverished New Mexico, however, as Governor Francisco Martínez de Baeza described it in 1639, *encomenderos* (those who were entrusted with Indians) scarcely profited from this arrangement. On the frontier, then, there is little truth to the stereotyped view of Spanish-Mexicans living comfortably off of the labor of their Indian charges. The Pueblo Revolt of 1680 destroyed all encomienda arrangements in New Mexico and, with but one exception, no new ones were granted thereafter.

Most Excellent Sir: I, General Francisco Martínez de Baeza, former governor and captain-general of the provinces of New Mexico, in fulfillment of what was ordered by your Excellency in a decree of the nineteenth of January of this year—in which you direct and command me in view of what is contained in a royal cedula of his Majesty, to make a report concerning whether it will be advisable to divide bishoprics and to establish reductions and *doctrinas* among the natives of the provinces of New Mexico and Sinaloa and to require them to pay tithes and some tributes [also to report concerning] the character and fertility of the said provinces and the desirability of paying in money, rather than in clothing, the soldiers and religious who are at those missions—am of the opinion that what is best for the services of the majesties, human and Divine is as follows:

....

*Petition of Francisco Martínez de Baeza, Mexico, February 12, 1639, in Charles Wilson Hackett, ed. and trans., *Historical Documents Relating to New Mexico, Nueva Vizcaya, and Approaches Thereto, to 1773* (Washington, D.C.: 1937), 3:118–20. Reprinted by permission of the Carnegie Institution of Washington.

The provinces of New Mexico are distant four hundred leagues, a little more or less, from this city—two hundred of them [containing] settlements of Spaniards and of peaceable Indians, [and extending] until one reaches the mines of El Parral, which is the last settlement. The other two hundred leagues, traveling always toward the north, [extend] through unsettled country. It is a land that is very cold in winter and very hot in summer, [that is,] until one reaches the first settlement of the said provinces, which is the pueblo of San Antonio de Senecú. It is distant from the villa of Santa Fé, the capital of these provinces, fifty leagues—all settled with Indians reduced to our holy faith. In this distance there are ten or twelve farms of Spaniards, who plant wheat and maize by irrigating with water which is obtained from the Río del Norte. In the villa of Santa Fé, where the governors live, there are few more than fifty inhabitants, with established homes and families, who form a moderate-sized settlement. In it is the principal convent of Señor Saint Francis. . . .

There are perhaps in the entire [province?] and its settlements two hundred persons, Spaniards and *mestizos,* who are able to bear arms, as they do in defense of the converted Indians, who frequently suffer injuries from the neighboring Apaches. These are war-like and, as barbarians, make unexpected attacks upon them. To their defense the governors and [Spanish] inhabitants repair, punishing the Apaches severely. As a result the Apaches restrain themselves and the converted Indians are saved, for the Apaches see that the Spaniards defend them and that those are punished who disturb them. The said religious and the governors in all things do their part, each one in his own way, like good ministers and subjects of his Majesty.

The land is very productive of wheat, maize, and other grains native to it. They raise cattle and sheep as in Spain. There are many kinds of fruits from Spain and some native ones. The [Spanish] settlers and not the natives [Indians] pay tithes of wheat, maize, cattle, horses, mules, sheep, and goats to the custodian of Saint Francis. In my opinion they will amount to fifteen hundred pesos, a little more or less. Because all those of whom I have spoken sow grain and raise cattle for their own sustenance, a *fanega* of wheat is worth a peso; a *fanega* of maize, four *reales.* Calves, colts, and mules are priced according to their ages, and goats and sheep at four *reales.* Because of not having money, the pay is computed in buffalo hides, deer skins, cotton blankets, and other products of the country. With reference to the reduction and division of *doctrinas,* his Majesty will do what is suitable to the service of God. The governors, through *cedulas* [orders] of his Majesty, apportion in *encomienda* the reduced Indians among the inhabitants, for their protection and better preservation, taking care that they may be given in *encomienda* according to the merits and services [of the said inhabitants] and in recognition of the many hardships and inconveniences they are enduring in holding the country. Each Indian repairs once a year to his *encomendero* with a *fanega* of maize, which is worth four *reales*, one cotton blanket a vara and a half square, which is valued at one peso, or, in lieu thereof, a raw buffalo hide or deer skin, either of which has the same value.

Each house is counted as a tributary, and, even though there may be a number of Indians in it, collection is made for but one. For this reason the contributions are small. His Majesty being pleased, in view of the land being very poor and the Indians reduced to his rule having neither a ranchería [village] nor property, it seems to me that it would be conducive to his royal service to release them from paying the tributes. In that way they will be kept in their settlements long enough so that those that may be born in the future will regard their pueblos as their native land and may be inclined to acquire property. Furthermore the newly converted Indians may lose their attachment for their heathen state and may bestow it upon our holy faith. They will be very efficacious means toward this if they are released from new tributes and from any payments to his royal grandeur. This is what seems well to me, and thus I swear it before God and the holy cross, in due form before the present notary. Mexico, February 12, 1639. FRANCISCO MARTINEZ DE BAEZA. He signed before me and I swear that I know him. GERONIMO DE CASTILLO, notary for his Majesty.

4. A Communal Land Grant

Lorenzo Marquis & Antonio José Ortiz, 1794*

Contrary to popular misconceptions, land ownership in the
Southwest in the Spanish period was not confined to the rich
alone. Humble pioneers also received title to private and
common lands. Each colonist usually held private title to a
garden plot (*suerte*) and the site of his adobe home (*solar*), but
pasture, woodlands, and farmlands belonged to all as common
land, or ejidos. Communal grants were most extensive in New
Mexico where survival required a common effort to construct a
townsite, defend lands from hostile Indians, and maintain a
network of acequias (irrigation ditches). The petition and grant
which follow are for the community of San Miguel del Bado,
built on the Pecos River where the Santa Fe Trail would later
cross.

Original Petition for the San Miguel
Del Bado Land Grant

I, Lorenzo Marquis, resident of this town of Santa Fe, for myself
and in the name of 51 men accompanying me, appear before your
excellency and state that, in consideration of having a very large
family, as well myself as those accompanying me, though we have
some land in this town it is not sufficient for our support, on account
of its smallness and the great scarcity of water, which owing to the
great number of people we cannot all enjoy, wherefore we have
entered a tract of land on the Rio Pecos, vacant and unsettled, at the
place commonly called El Vado, and where there is room enough, not
only for us, the 51 who ask it, but also for everyone in the province
not supplied. Its boundaries are on the north the Rio de la Baca from
the place called the rancheria to the Agua Caliente, on the south the
Canon Blanco, on the east the Cuesta with the little hills of Bernal,
and on the west the place commonly called the Gusano—which tract
we ask to be granted us in the name of our Sovereign, whom may God

---

*Translated in Olen E. Leonard, *The Role of the Land Grant in the Social Process of a
Spanish-American Village in New Mexico* (M.A. thesis, Louisiana State University, 1943,
lithographed by Edwards Brothers, Inc., Ann Arbor, Michigan, 1948), pp. 143–45. Published
under the same title by Calvin Horn, Publisher (Albuquerque, 1970), pp. 167–70. Reprinted by
permission of Olen E. Leonard.

preserve, and among these 51 men petitioning are 13 Indians, and among them all there are 25 firearms, and they are the same persons who appear on the subjoined list, which I present in due form, and we unanimously and harmoniously as one person do promise to enclose ourselves in a plaza well fortified with bulwarks and towers, and to exert ourselves to supply all the firearms and ammunition that it may be possible for us to procure. And as we trust in compliance with our petition we request and pray that your Excellency be pleased to direct that we be placed in possession, in the Name of his Royal Majesty our Sovereign, whom may God preserve, and we declare in full legal form that we do not act with dissimulation.

Lorenzo Marquis
For himself and the Petitioners

Original Decree for the San Miguel Del Bado Land Grant

On the 26th of the month of November, One Thousand Seven Hundred and Ninety-Four, I, Antonio José Ortiz, Captain in the militia and principal alcalde of the town of Santa Fe, in pursuance of the order of Lieutenant Colonel Fernando Chacon, Knight of the Order of Santiago and civil and military Governor of this kingdom, before proceeding to the site of El Vado, I, said principal alcalde, in company with two witnesses who were Xavier Ortiz and Domingo Santiestevan, the 52 petitioners being present, caused them to comprehend the petition they had made, and informed them that to receive the grant they would have to observe and fulfill in full form of law the following conditions:

First—That the tract aforesaid has to be in common, not only in regard to themselves but also to all settlers who may join them in the future.

Second—That with respect to the dangers of the place they shall have to keep themselves equipped with firearms and bows and arrows in which they shall be inspected as well at the time of settling as at any time the alcalde in office may deem proper, provided that after two years settlement all the arms they have must be firearms, under the penalty that all who do not comply with the requirement shall be sent out of the settlement.

Third—That the plaza they may construct shall be according as expressed in their petition, and in the meantime they shall reside in the Pueblo of Pecos where there are suffiient accommodations for the aforesaid 52 families.

Fourth—That to the alcalde in office in said pueblo they shall set apart a small separate piece of land for him to cultivate for himself at his will, without their children or successors making any objection thereto, and the same for his successor in office.

Fifth—That the construction of their Plaza as well as the opening of ditches, and all other work that may be deemed proper for the common welfare shall be performed by the community with that union which in their government they must preserve.

And when this was heard and understood by each and all of the aforementioned persons, they accordingly unanimously responded that they understood and heeded what was communicated to them. Wherefore, I took them by the hand and announced in clear and intelligible words that in the name of His Majesty (God preserve Him) and without prejudice to the Royal interest or that of any third party. I led them over said lands, and they plucked up grass, cast stones and shouted "Long Live the King," taking possession of said land quietly and peaceably, without any objection; pointing out to them the boundaries, which are, on the North the Rio de la Baca from the place called the Rancheria to the Agua Caliente, on the South the Canon Blanco, on the East the Cuesta with the little hills of Bernal, and on the West, the place commonly called the Gusano, notifying them that the pastures and watering places are in common.

And that in all time it may so appear, I, acting by appointment, for want of a notary, there being none in this jurisdiction, signed this with my attending witnesses, with whom I act, to which I certify.

                                                                                        Antonio José Ortiz

5. Mestizaje   The First Census of Los Angeles, 1781*

Despite the enduring myth that "Spaniards" settled the borderlands, it is quite clear that the majority of the pioneers were Mexicans of mixed blood. In New Spain the three races of mankind, Caucasian, Mongol, and Negro, blended to form an infinite variety of blood strains, and this blending continued as Mexicans settled among aborigines in the Southwest. Thus *mestizaje*, or racial mixture, was so common that today the vast majority of all Mexicans are of mixed blood. Yet until this century the Mexican upper class viewed mestizos as inferior and placed a high value on their own *pureza de sangre* (purity of blood). This view endures among some Mexicans and Mexican Americans today.

The first census of El Pueblo de Nuestra Señora la Reina de los Angeles del Río de Porciúncula, taken in the year of its founding, 1781, reveals the truly *Mexican* origins of that pueblo's pioneer settlers. Only two of them claimed to be Spanish. The remainder were Indian, mestizo (in its narrowest sense, the child of an Indian and a Spaniard), mulatto (the child of a Negro and a Spaniard), Negro, *coyote* (the child of a mestizo and an Indian), and chino (the child of an Indian and a *salta-atras*—a person with Negroid features born of apparently white parents). Notice also, the paternalistic nature of Spanish government so evident in this census report.

First Census of Los Angeles
Peninsula of California

Census of the population of the City of the Queen of the Angels, founded September 4th, 1781, on the banks of Porciúncula River, distant 45 leagues from the Presidio of San Diego, 27 leagues from the site selected for the establishment of the Presidio of Santa Barbara, and about a league and a half from the San Gabriel Mission; including the names and ages of the residents, their wives and children. Also an

*"First Census of Los Angeles," trans. Thomas Workman Temple II, in *Historical Society of Southern California: Annual Publications*, 15, Part 2 (1931): 148–49. Reprinted by permission of the Historical Society of Southern California.

account of the number of animals and their kind, as distributed; with
a note describing those to be held in common as sires of the different
kinds, farming implements, forges, and tools for carpenter and cast
work, and other things as received.

(1)	Lara, Josef de, Spaniard,	50
	Maria Antonio Campos,	
	india sabina,	23,
	Josef Julian,	4,
	Juana de Jesus,	6,
	Maria Faustina,	2.
(2)	Navarro, Josef Antonio,	
	mestizo,	42,
	Maria Rufina Dorotea,	
	mulata,	47,
	Josef Maria,	10,
	Josef Clemente,	9,
	Maria Josefa,	4.
(3)	Rosas, Basillio, indian	67,
	Maria Manuela Calixtra,	
	mulata,	43,
	Jose Maximo,	15,
	Carlos,	12,
	Antonio Rosalino,	7,
	Josef Marcelino,	4,
	Juan Esteban,	2,
	Maria Josefa,	8.
(4)	Mesa, Antonio, negro	38,
	Ana Gertrudis Lopez,	
	mulata,	27,
	Antonio Maria,	8,
	Maria Paula,	10.
(5)	Villavicencio, Antonio,	
	Spaniard,	30,
	Maria de los Santos	
	Seferina, indian,	26,
	Maria Antonio Josefa,	8.
(6)	Vanegas, Josef, indian	28,
	Maria Maxima Aguilar,	
	indian,	20,
	Cosme Damien,	1.

    (7) Rosas, Alejandro, indian   19,
         Juana Rodriguez, coyote
           indian   20.
    (8) Rodriguez, Pablo, indian,   25,
         Maria Rosalia Noriega,
           indian,   26,
         Maria Antonia,   1.
    (9) Camero, Manuel, mulato,   30,
         Maria Tomasa, mulata,   24.
    (10) Quintero, Luis, negro,   55,
         Maria Petra Rubio,
           mulata   40,
         Josef Clemente,   3,
         Maria Gertrudis,   16,
         Maria Concepcion,   9,
         Tomasa,   7,
         Rafaela,   6.
    (11) Moreno, Jose, mulato,   22,
         Maria Guadalupe
           Gertrudis,   19.
    (12) Rodriguez, Antonio
         Miranda, chino,   50,
         Juana Maria,   11.

Note

That in addition to the cattle, horses, and mules, distributed to the first 11 settlers, as set forth, they were granted building lots on which they have constructed their houses, which for the present are built of palisades, roofed with earth; also 2 irrigated fields for the cultivation of 2 fanegas of corn to each settler; in addition, a plow share, a hoe and an axe: and for the community, the proper number of carts, wagons, and breeding animals as set forth above, for which the settlers must account to the Royal Exchequer at the prices fixed: with the corresponding charges made against their accounts, as found in the Book of Poblacion, wherein are also to be found the building lots, planting fields, farming utensils, and animals belonging to the settler, Antonio Miranda Rodriguez, which will be granted to him, as soon as he appears at said Pueblo.

San Gabriel, November 19, 1781.

6. "Most hardy subjects"

Zebulon M. Pike, 1807*
Miguel Ramos de Arizpe, 1812**

The struggle for survival on the remote northern frontier of New Spain profoundly affected Mexican pioneers. Zebulon Montgomery Pike, a United States explorer who had been taken captive in 1807 by troops from Santa Fe, here describes the beneficial effects of the frontier on the Nuevo Mexicanos. In central Mexico, where Pike also traveled during his captivity, he was less impressed with Mexicans.

Echoing Pike's feeling that the frontier produced hardier citizens was Miguel Ramos de Arizpe, a resident of Coahuila, a state bordering Texas. Educated to the clergy and the law, Ramos de Arizpe knew Mexico City as well as the frontier and so, like Pike, could make comparisons. The selection which follows is from Ramos de Arizpe's report to the Spanish *cortes* or parliament of 1812 and is designed to show the Eastern Interior Provinces of New Spain, which included Texas, in the most favorable light. A man of considerable integrity, who spent six years in jail for expressing liberal views which offended Ferdinand VII, it seems likely that Ramos de Arizpe's exaggerations were only slight.

Zebulon M. Pike, 1807

Being frontier, and cut off, as it were, from the more inhabited parts of the kingdom, together with their continual wars with some of the savage nations who surround them, render them [the New Mexicans] the bravest and most hardy subjects in New Spain; being generally armed, they know the use of them. Their want of gold and silver renders them laborious, in order that the productions of their

---

*"Pike's Observations on New Spain," from *The Journals of Zebulon Montgomery Pike: With Letters and Related Documents,* edited and annotated by Donald Jackson. 2 vols. (Norman, Okla.: 1966), 2:58. Copyright 1966 by the University of Oklahoma Press. Reprinted by permission of the publisher.

**Report that Dr. Miguel Ramos de Arizpe . . . Presents to the August Congress on the Natural, Political and Civil Condition of the Provinces of Coahuila, Nuevo León, Nuevo Santander, and Texas . . .* , trans. and ed. Nettie Lee Benson (Austin: 1950), pp. 16–17. Reprinted by permission of the University of Texas Press.

labor may be the means of establishing the equilibrium between them and the other provinces where those metals abound. Their insolated [*sic*] and remote situation also causes them to exhibit, in a superior degree, the heaven-like qualities of hospitality and kindness, in which they appear to endeavor to fulfill the injunction of the scripture, which enjoins us to feed the hungry, clothe the naked, and give comfort to the oppressed in spirit, and I shall always take pleasure in expressing my gratitude for their noble reception of myself and the men under my command.

Miguel Ramos de Arizpe, 1812

The salubrious air, the agreeable climate, the exceedingly rich soil—all nature invites man to reap the benefit of the easiest and most solid prosperity by means of agriculture, the source of the true wealth of nations. This is, Sir, the most common occupation of the inhabitants of these vast and rich provinces. Agriculture has in general formed their character; and as they have been employed day and night in the honest and systematic cultivation of the soil, from which alone they derive their sustenance, they are truly inflexible to intrigue, virtuously steadfast, haters of tyranny and disorder, justly devoted to true liberty, and naturally the most inclined toward all the moral and political virtues. They are very much devoted also to the liberal and mechanical arts.

These provinces, being by their location the natural bulwark of all the kingdom of Mexico, are in consequence on a frontier exposed to the barbarous Indian nations. Their inhabitants, therefore, are obliged to serve not only as militiamen but even as common soldiers. They are all soldiers; and in Coahuila and Texas, each month they are required to present their arms for inspection. This necessity, otherwise deplorable, has formed in them an extremely commendable character of integrity, honor, and subordination. They are extraordinarily long-suffering under the severest labor and much accustomed to the greatest privations. At times they even live upon the leather of their saddles and knapsacks without deserting nor as much as murmuring. With this combination of such excellent qualities, which result from the celestial climate and are cultivated by such honest occupations, each citizen becomes a worker, each worker a soldier, and each soldier a hero that is worth a hundred ordinary soldiers.

7. "There were no paupers"

José Agustín de Escudero, 1827*

Although debt peonage was commonplace and an elite class developed in colonial New Mexico, it appears that rigid social classes, based on race, broke down on the northern frontier more quickly than in central Mexico. The frontier, where the gulf between the material possessions of the rich and the poor was not immense, seemed to offer greater opportunity for social mobility. More research needs to be done on this subject, however, before any definitive statement can be made.

José Agustín de Escudero, a lawyer from Chihuahua who visited New Mexico in 1827, here describes how the *partido* system of sheep raising, which frequently led to peonage, could also serve to lessen class differences. Escudero's observation that there was no poverty in New Mexico was confirmed by the earlier *Exposición* of Pedro Bautista Pino, written in 1812. Born and raised in New Mexico, Pino wrote "we do not have the vagrants or beggars that swarm like ants in the viceroyalty of Mexico. I had never seen this condition until I had occasion to cross the viceroyalty."[1] In California a similar tradition existed. Spaniard José Arnaz, who knew California in the 1840s, remembered the abundance of beef that was available even to the poor and claimed that "poverty or hunger was unknown in the country."[2]

It can be asserted that there were no paupers in New Mexico at that time, nor could there be any. At the same time, there were no large-scale stockmen who could pay wages or make any expenditure whatever in order to preserve and increase their wealth in this branch of agriculture. A poor man, upon reaching the age when one generally desires freedom and sufficient means to subsist and start a family, would go to a rich stockman and offer to help him take care of one or more herds of sheep. These flocks were composed of *a thousand* ewes and *ten* breeding rams, which were never separated from the herd as

*H. Bailey Carroll and J. Villasana Haggard, trans. and ed., *Three New Mexico Chronicles* (Albuquerque: 1942), pp. 41–42. Reprinted by permission of the Quivira Society.

1. Pedro Bautista Pino, in *Three New Mexico Chronicles*, trans. and ed. H. Bailey Carroll and J. Villasana Haggard (Albuquerque: 1942), pp. 27–28.

2. José Arnaz, "Memoirs of a Merchant," trans. and ed. Nellie Van de Grift Sánchez, *Touring Topics* 20, no. 9 (September 1938): 17.

is the practice of stock raisers in other countries. Consequently, in each flock, not a single day would go by without the birth of two or three lambs, which the shepherd would put with the ewe and force the female to suckle without the difficulties which he would have had with a larger number of offspring. The shepherd would give the owner ten or twenty per cent of these sheep and an equal amount of wool, as a sort of interest, thus preserving the capital intact.

From the moment he received the flock, the shepherd entered into a contract in regard to the future increase, even with his own overseer. As a matter of fact, he usually contracted it at the current market price, two reales per head, the future increase to be delivered in small numbers over a period of time. With this sum, which the shepherd had in advance, he could construct a house, and take in other persons to help him care for and shear the sheep, which was done with a knife instead of shears. The milk, and sometimes the meat, from the said sheep provided him sustenance; the wool was spun by his own family into blankets, stockings, etc., which could also be marketed, providing an income. Thus the wealth of the shepherd would increase until the day he became, like his overseer, the owner of a herd. He, in turn, would let out his herds to others after the manner in which he obtained his first sheep and made his fortune. Consequently, even in the homes of the poorest New Mexicans, there is never a dearth of sufficient means to satisfy the necessities of life and even to afford the comfort and luxuries of the wealthiest class in the country.

8. "Backward" New Mexico

Pedro Bautista Pino, 1812*

> After more than two hundred years of Spanish occupation, New Mexico remained an isolated, sparsely populated frontier province whose trade was strangled by merchants in Chihuahua and by Spanish commercial regulations. New Mexico's secular and religious problems were largely ignored by Spain. In 1812, when Pedro Bautista Pino traveled to Spain to represent New

*H. Bailey Carrol and J. Villansana Haggard, trans. and ed., *Three New Mexico Chronicles* (Albuquerque: 1942), pp. 50–51, 363–67, 94. Reprinted by permission of the Quivira Society.

Mexico in the newly formed cortes, or parliament, he wrote a
graphic description of New Mexico's problems. According to
Pino, even the Church, whose influence had helped to maintain
New Mexico as a colony, could not serve the New Mexicans
well. Since Pino was trying to obtain more financial aid for New
Mexico he made his case as strong as possible, describing only
the problems of his province. Pino's suggestion that the area
needed to be strengthened in order to resist foreign aggression
(in this case from the United States) has a very modern ring to it.

Ecclesiastical government.—The twenty-six Indian pueblos and the
102 settlements of Spaniards, which constitute the population of the
province of New Mexico, are under the spiritual supervision of the
diocese of Durango. These pueblos and settlements are served by
twenty-two missionaries of the order of Saint Francis from the
province of Mexico. In only one pueblo of the district of El Paso and
in the capital are the parish priests secular clergymen. All of the
missionaries and the priests receive an income from the treasury,
excepting those of the villas of Albuquerque, Santa Cruz de la
Cañada, and the capital, who have no income other than the offerings
at the altar.

It is noteworthy that the distance from the [Indian] pueblos, in
which the missionaries reside, to the Spanish settlements range[s]
from eight to ten leagues. In view of such long distances, therefore,
not all the parishioners can go to one town to hear mass, nor can the
parish priests say mass in two towns on the same day; it is also
impossible to have vicariates, because the income or allotment
assigned the missionaries for the spiritual administration of those
towns is itself insufficient. The present allotments were made at an
early date without considering the 102 settlements which have been
established since the year 1780 for the preservation of the province.

For more than fifty years no one has known that there was a bishop;
nor has a bishop been seen in the province during this time.
Consequently, the sovereign provisions and the instructions of
ecclesiastical discipline have not been fulfilled. The misfortunes
suffered by those settlers are infinite because of the lack of a primate.
Persons who have been born during these fifty years have not been
confirmed. The poor people who wish, by means of a dispensation, to
get married to relatives cannot do so because of the great cost of
traveling a distance of more than 400 leagues to Durango. Conse-

quently, many people, compelled by love, live and rear families in adultery. The zeal of the ministers of the church is unable to prevent this and many other abuses which are suffered because of the aforesaid lack of ministers. It is truly grievous that in spite of the fact that from 9,000 to 10,000 duros are paid by that province in tithes, for fifty years the people have not had an opportunity to see the face of their bishop. I, an old man, did not know how bishops dressed until I came to Cádiz [Spain].

General means of making the provinces prosper.—Agriculture, industry, and commerce are the three bases of all prosperity. The province of New Mexico has none of these because of its location, because of the neglect with which the government has looked upon it up to the present time, and because of the annual withdrawal of the small income that it is able to derive from its products and manufactures. It has already been stated that the annual importation into the province of products for its consumption amounts to 112,000 pesos, and that its annual income is only 60,000 pesos. Therefore, there is an annual deficit of 52,000 pesos. The salaries paid by the treasury to the governor of the province, to his assistants, and to the 121 soldiers may be said to be the only income that keeps money in circulation. This income is so small, as we have previously stated, that until recently the majority of its inhabitants had never seen money.

Who would believe that such conditions exist in North America? And what means are available to improve this miserable condition of the province? One can resort to those resources that nature has placed at the province's disposal: the great abundance of furs and their low cost is undeniable. There are, however, no present means of exporting them without great freighting costs. The seaports of San Bernardo, on the North Sea, and the port of Guaimas, on the South sea invite us to make exports to Europe and to Asia. Likewise, through the same ports, articles might be imported without the necessity of paying overland freight for more than 900 leagues, from Vera Cruz or Acapulco. The province would thus double its consumption; the increase of Spanish traders would then be sufficient to overpower the wild Indian tribes; some of which, the most courageous and numerous, already show unmistakable tendencies toward recognizing our government. Once the wild tribes are reduced, the number of our troops can be diminished without danger; there would be new consumers of merchandise, *new defenders of Spanish territory* against aggressions of the United States; the income of the public treasury would be increased by import duties collected at the seaports; in brief, the possible results are inconceivable for one who is unfamiliar with the potential wealth of the province of New Mexico.

The scarcity of professional men.—The province of New Mexico does not have among its public institutions any of those found in other provinces of Spain. So backward is it in this matter that the names of such institutions are not even known. The benefit of primary letters is given only to the children of those who are able to contribute to the salary of the school teacher. Even in the capital it has been impossible to engage a teacher and to furnish education for everyone. Of course there are no colleges of any kind. This condition gives rise to expressions of discouragement by many people who notice the latent scientific ability of the children in this province. For a period of more than two hundred years since the conquest, the province has made no provision for any of them in any of the literary careers, or as a priest, something which is ordinarily done in other provinces of America.

There are no physicians, no surgeons, and no pharmacies. I repeat, in the entire province there is only one surgeon, and he is supported by the 121 soldiers whose salaries are paid by the treasury. Whenever this surgeon makes medical visits to other towns, he has to be paid for them by the person who calls him. If he falls sick, one is obliged to try to find another doctor 300 leagues away. Imagine the condition of a person, gravely wounded, by the time the doctor arrives! The settlers who engage in campaigns at their own expense do not even have the comfort of a doctor to dress the wounds they received in action. And how is it possible for one man to take care of the needs of all the people in a territory consisting of 3,500 square leagues? I am leaving this matter to the consideration of your majesty.

9. The "wretched village" of San Antonio

Juan Agustín Morfi, 1778*

In 1777—78 Fray Juan Agustín Morfi, a Franciscan, accompanied Commandant Teodoro de Croix on an inspection tour of
northern New Spain. This area had become a separate administrative unit in 1776, called the Interior Provinces of New Spain. A
careful observer who took notes as he went along, Morfi would
eventually write a history of Texas. When the party reached San
Antonio, then called the Villa of San Fernando, Morfi felt he had
seen all there was to see of Texas:

> The entire European population of so vast and fertile a
> province is reduced to the villa of San Fernando, which,
> together with the presidio of San Antonio de Béxar,
> constitutes a town so miserable that it resembles a most
> wretched village.

He went on to describe the "capital" of the province of Texas
with its not-yet-famous mission of San Antonio de Valero, the
Alamo.

Villa de San Fernando and Presidio de San Antonio de Béxar. On
the west bank of the San Antonio river, about a league from its source,
above the point where San Pedro creek joins the river, is situated the
villa of San Fernando and the presidio of San Antonio de Béxar, with
no other division between them than the parochial church. To the
west of the presidio is San Pedro creek, in such a manner that the villa
and the presidio are both situated within the angle formed by the
juncture of the two streams. The church building is spacious and has a
vaulted roof, but the whole is so poorly constructed that it promises
but a short life. The town consists of fifty-nine houses of stone and
mud and seventy-nine of wood, but all poorly built, without any
preconceived plan, so that the whole resembles more a poor village
than a villa, capital of so pleasing a province. Its population is made
up of islanders [*isleños*, Spaniards from the Canary Islands, who came
in 1731] and families from the country [New Spain]. The former have
acquired control of practically the whole city government [*regimien-
to*]. They are indolent and given to vice, and do not deserve the

---

*Fray Juan Agustín Morfi, *History of Texas, 1673–1779*, trans. and ed. Carlos Eduardo
Castañeda (Albuquerque: 1935), pp. 92–94. Reprinted by permission of the Quivira Society.

blessings of the land. The soldiers' quarters, originally built of stone and adobe, are almost in ruins. The establishment of this villa, independently of the presidio, has cost the king more than eighty thousand pesos. The streets are tortuous and are filled with mud the minute it rains. The presidio is surrounded by a poor stockade on which are mounted a few swivel guns, without shelter or defense, that can be used only for firing a salvo. There is no other trade than that required to supply the needs of the commissary for the garrison and the meager wants of the wretched settlers. The parish priest looks after the [garrison of the] presidio, there being no chaplain, and receives a small pension for his services. The governor used to live in what was the jail or guard house, which afforded a poor residence at best.

San Antonio de Valero. On the east bank of the San Antonio, about two gunshots' distance from the villa, is the mission of San Antonio de Valero. It consists of a small convent fifty varas square with an arched gallery around the court [patio] on the first and second floors, around which are built the necessary rooms for the missionaries with the corresponding porter's lodge, refectory, offices, and kitchen. On the second patio [backyard] there is a large room with four looms and the necessary spinning wheels to weave cotton cloth for shawls, and ordinary coarse cotton and woolen cloth for the Indians. Two other rooms, in which the raw materials and the tools are kept, adjoin the workshop.

The church [chapel] was ruined through the ignorance of the builder, but a new one, simple, roomy, and well planned, is being erected on the same place, though it is not finished. In the meantime services are held in the sacristy, which is a small room, but very tidy and neat, with a small, new, golden altar on which is venerated a handsome image of the titular Saint Anthony.

The Indian quarters form a square about the mission with attractive porticoes, the whole being watered by a beautiful irrigation ditch bordered by various kinds of trees. Besides this, a well was dug to forestall the lack of water in case of being besieged by the enemy. To safeguard it the door [leading to it] is fortified. At the entrance to the convent a small watchtower was built, with loopholes for three swivel guns which, with other firearms and the corresponding ammunition, are carefully guarded.

This mission was founded with Xaraname, Payaye, Zanas, Ypanis, Cocos, Tops, and Karancawa Indians and from the time of its erection

[1718] to the end of the year 1761, there were 1972 persons baptized, 1247 were administered the holy sacraments at their death, 454 were married, and there were at that time 76 families [at the mission], numbering 275 persons in all. But since that time their number has been greatly reduced and today [1778] it scarcely has enough [neophytes] to cultivate the fields, and the looms have been abandoned [for lack of workers].

10. The Romantic Frontier

Guadalupe Vallejo, 1890*
George Wharton James, 1914**

Despite the hardships that many pioneers had endured on the Mexican frontier, during the last third of the nineteenth century old timers came to romanticize the Spanish and Mexican periods in the Southwest. Both Mexican Americans and Anglo Americans, prompted perhaps by the complexity of life in an increasingly urban and industrialized America, looked back longingly at the simplicity of "Days of the Dons." This was especially common in California, the Southwestern state which was most affected by modernization and which probably had the most idyllic past to look back toward.

Mexican Americans who wrote about the "good old days" in California were almost invariably members of the upper class and naturally wrote from that perspective. The distortion inherent in such elitist writings is apparent to us today as we attempt to understand the past "from the bottom up." Yet most works on the Spanish and Mexican periods have used elitist memoirs such as those of Guadalupe Vallejo to reconstruct the past, for written reminiscences of the lower class do not exist. Vallejo was the niece of wealthy Mariano Guadalupe Vallejo of Sonoma, a key figure in the Mexican and early statehood periods. Notice the role of the lower class in his pretty picture of early California, and his use of the term "Spanish Californians."

Anglo writers, perhaps taking a cue from the California elite, also romanticized Hispanic California. Especially culpable was George Wharton James who here describes the founding of the first mission and presidio at San Diego.

---

*Guadalupe Vallejo, "Ranch and Mission Days in Alta California," *The Century Magazine* 41, no. 2 (December 1890): 183, 184, 189, 191–92.

**George Wharton James, *California: Romantic and Beautiful* (Boston: 1914), pp. 50, 51, 54.

Guadalupe Vallejo, 1890

It seems to me that there never was a more peaceful or happy people on the face of the earth than the Spanish, Mexican, and Indian population of Alta California before the American conquest. We were the pioneers of the Pacific coast, building towns and Missions while General Washington was carrying on the war of the Revolution, and we often talk together of the days when a few hundred large Spanish ranches and Mission tracts occupied the whole country from the Pacific to the San Joaquin. No class of American citizens is more loyal than the Spanish Californians, but we shall always be especially proud of the traditions and memories of the long pastoral age before 1840. Indeed, our social life still tends to keep alive a spirit of love for the simple, homely, outdoor life of our Spanish ancestors on this coast, and we try, as best we may, to honor the founders of our ancient families, and the saints and heroes of our history since the days when Father Junipero planted the cross at Monterey.

The leading features of old Spanish life at the Missions, and on the large ranches of the last century, have been described in many books of travel, and with many contradictions. I shall confine myself to those details and illustrations of the past that no modern writer can possibly obtain except vaguely, from hearsay, since they exist in no manuscript, but only in the memories of a generation that is fast passing away. My mother has told me much, and I am still more indebted to my illustrious uncle, General Vallejo, of Sonoma, many of whose recollections are incorporated in this article.

....

No one need suppose that the Spanish pioneers of California suffered many hardships or privations, although it was a new country. They came slowly, and were well prepared to become settlers. All that was necessary for the maintenance and enjoyment of life according to the simple and healthful standards of those days was brought with them. They had seeds, trees, vines, cattle, household goods, and servants, and in a few years their orchards yielded abundantly and their gardens were full of vegetables. Poultry was raised by the Indians, and sold very cheaply; a fat capon cost only twelve and a half cents. Beef and mutton were to be had for the killing, and wild game was very abundant. At many of the Missions there were large flocks of tame pigeons. At the Mission San José the fathers' doves consumed a cental of wheat daily, besides what they gathered in the village. The doves were of many colors, and they made a beautiful appearance on the red tiles of the church and the tops of the dark garden walls.

The houses of the Spanish people were built of adobe, and were roofed with red tiles. They were very comfortable, cool in summer and warm in winter. The clay used to make the bricks was dark brown, not white or yellow, as the adobes in the Rio Grande region and in parts of Mexico. Cut straw was mixed with the clay, and trodden together by the Indians.

In the old days every one seemed to live out-doors. There was much gaiety and social life, even though people were widely scattered. We traveled as much as possible on horseback. Only old people or invalids cared to use the slow cart, or *carreta*. Young men would ride from one ranch to another for parties, and whoever found his horse tired would let him go and catch another. In 1806 there were so many horses in the valleys about San José that seven or eight thousand were killed. Nearly as many were driven into the sea at Santa Barbara in 1807, and the same thing was done at Monterey in 1810. Horses were given to the runaway sailors, and to trappers and hunters who came over the mountains. . . .

Nothing was more attractive than the wedding cavalcade on its way from the bride's house to the Mission church. The horses were more richly caparisoned than for any other ceremony, and the bride's nearest relative or family representative carried her before him, she sitting on the saddle with her white satin shoe in a loop of golden or silver braid, while he sat on the bear-skin covered *anquera* behind. The groom and his friends mingled with the bride's party, all on the best horses that could be obtained, and they rode gaily from the ranch house to the Mission, sometimes fifteen or twenty miles away. In April and May, when the land was covered with wildflowers, the light-hearted troop rode along the edge of the uplands, between hill and valley, crossing the streams, and some of the young horsemen, anxious to show their skill, would perform all the feats for which the Spanish-Californians were famous.

In these days of trade, bustle, and confusion, when many thousands of

people live in the Californian valleys, which formerly were occupied
by only a few Spanish families, the quiet and happy domestic life of
the past seems like a dream. We, who loved it, often speak of those
days, and especially of the duties of the large Spanish households,
where so many dependents were to be cared for, and everything was
done in a simple and primitive way.

There was a group of warm springs a few miles distant from the old
adobe house in which we lived. It made us children happy to be
waked before sunrise to prepare for the "wash-day expedition" to the
Aqua Caliente. The night before the Indians had soaped the clumsy
carreta's great wheels. Lunch was placed in baskets, and the gentle
oxen were yoked to the pole. We climbed in, under the green cloth of
an old Mexican flag which was used as an awning, and the
white-haired Indian *ganan*, who had driven the carreta since his
boyhood, plodded beside with his long *garrocha*, or ox-goad. The great
piles of soiled linen were fastened on the backs of horses, led by other
servants, while the girls and women who were to do the washing
trooped along by the side of the carreta. All in all, it made an
imposing cavalcade, though our progress was slow, and it was
generally sunrise before we had fairly reached the spring.

We watched the women unload the linen and carry it to the upper
spring of the group, where the water was best. Then they loosened the
horses, and let them pasture on the wild oats, while the women put
home-made soap on the clothes, dipped them in the spring, and
rubbed them on the smooth rocks until they were white as snow. Then
they were spread out to dry on the tops of the low bushes growing on
the warm, windless, southern slopes of the mountain. There was
sometimes a great deal of linen to be washed, for it was the pride of
every Spanish family to own much linen, and the mother and
daughters almost always wore white. I have heard strangers speak of
the wonderful way in which Spanish ladies of the upper classes in
California always appeared in snow-white dresses, and certainly to do
so was one of the chief anxieties of every household. When there were
no warm springs the servants of the family repaired to the nearest
arroyo, or creek, and stood knee-deep in it, dipping and rubbing the
linen, and enjoying the sport.

To me, at least, one of the dearest of my childish memories is the family expedition from the great thick-walled adobe, under the olive and fig trees of the Mission, to the *Agua Caliente* in early dawn, and the late return at twilight, when the younger children were all asleep in the slow carreta, and the Indians were singing hymns as they drove the linen-laden horses down the dusky ravines.

George Wharton James, 1914

The mission and presidio were duly founded and the news sent by special courier to the Viceroy in Mexico. It took this man a month and a half to ride from Monterey to Todos Santos (on the peninsula), allowing for a four days' stop at San Diego. From thence the letters were sent by launch to San Blas, and so on to Mexico City.

It is almost impossible for us to-day to understand the excitement this news caused both in Mexico and Spain. Cathedral bells were rung, and Court and people all attended solemn high mass in token of thanksgiving. The Viceroy issued a proclamation reciting the facts so that all in New Spain might know the glad tidings. Thus the romance of the missions grew and hearts beat high in Mexico, and later in Old Spain itself as the news of the progress of California was spread.

Yet the romance was but begun. There was to be an uprising of the Indians in San Diego; one of the padres was to be slain; Serra was to live to see eight missions established before his death; his successors were to carry on the work until a chain of buildings extended, a day's journey apart, from San Diego on the south, to San Francisco on the north, and later even as high as Sonoma. There were to be struggles with the Indians, some of the missions were to be seized and held in rebellion, some were to be set on fire and partially destroyed, and the romance of converting a whole native population of barbarians into workers at every then-known industry accomplished. The remarkable mission buildings themselves were to arise, built by these Indians under the guidance of the padres.

What is more romantic than to see—even though it be only in the retrospect—the domination of the inferior mind by the superior. And not one over a few, but one over a thousand or more. At each of the missions this domination was soon apparent. The hitherto free, wild,

untamed Indian, roaming where his own sweet will dictated, free to
come or go as he chose, knowing nothing of concentrated effort
except as he doggedly followed his prey in the hunt until it was his,
was soon subject to the larger mind. By the score, in fifties, hundreds,
thousands, they were gathered around the mission establishments,
which immediately became hives of industries. At the ringing of the
morning bell the sleeping *rancheria*—the near-by collection of Indian
kishes or huts where the married Indians lived—sprang into life; the
smoke of a hundred fires ascended, and each dusky woman prepared
the morning meal for her family. But during the process the "Call to
Prayers" bell was heard, and instantly all work ceased, all bowed in
reverence, and these aboriginal men and women prayed with their
lips, even if their hearts only vaguely grasped the significance of the
words they uttered.

With priests for architects, contractors, builders, gang bosses,—and
there were never more than two priests to a Mission to have charge of
all the spiritual labours as well as of the varied industries here
outlined,—the Indians dug and laid the foundations, built the walls,
set the forms for the arched corridors, elevated the heavy roof beams
and tied them in place with their rawhide strips, securely covered
them with tiles—made and baked by their fellows near by—and then
plastered the walls inside and out, whitewashed them, and finally
decorated and adorned altar and sanctuary, sacristy and choir loft.

Oh, the romance and wonder of it all. It fairly thrills the
imagination to reconstruct these scenes of a not far bye-gone day.

II. Yankee Infiltration and the Hardening of Stereotypes

Editor's Introduction

In 1821 Mexico broke free from Spain's crumbling colonial system. The far northern frontier, effortlessly and with little show of enthusiasm, became independent along with the rest of Mexico, thus beginning a period of Mexican sovereignty over the present-day Southwest which would last until Mexico and the United States went to war in 1846. Yet any hopes that an independent Mexico would bring about dramatic changes on the isolated northern frontier were destined to be disappointed as Mexico fell into internal discord and even anarchy. Areas far removed from the capital received little attention. Frustration with the ineffectual and short-lived governments at Mexico City grew so intense that leading citizens in outlying provinces, from Yucatán to California and Texas, talked of separating their regions from the nation. Even though Mexico was too weak to effect significant changes on her northern frontier, change came, nevertheless, when she opened her borders to foreigners.

In 1821, for the first time, foreigners were permitted to live and work in Mexico. With them came new ideas, abundant and inexpensive manufactured goods, and prosperity for the Mexican upper class who traded with the foreigners. Settling on the northern frontier in ever-increasing numbers after 1821, these foreigners—chiefly Americans—unwittingly prepared the area for the eventual United States conquest. Many frontier Mexicans became convinced that it was possible to live and work with Yankees and that a more progressive government might bring greater economic gains to their region. Of equal importance, the meeting of Anglo Americans and Mexicans on the Mexican frontier during these years contributed to shaping stereotypes in Mexico and in the United States which made war between the two nations nearly unavoidable by 1846. The barbarities of war, in turn, reinforced negative stereotypes so strongly that some remain with us today.

The Mexican period, then, which saw American infiltration and the hardening of stereotypes, was a transitional period in Mexican-American history. Yet both of these tendencies, infiltration and stereotyping, had modest beginnings before 1821.

I

Separated by Indians, Frenchmen, and an uncharted wilderness, Spanish Mexican colonists who eked out a living on Mexico's northern frontier and the Anglo American colonists who clung to the Atlantic seaboard lived in isolation from one another throughout most of the colonial period. In the last half of the eighteenth century, however, events brought these peoples closer together. In 1763, when France ceded Louisiana to Spain after the disastrous Seven Years War, Spanish and English colonies in North America came together at the Mississippi. Forty years later, in 1803, the young republic of the United States acquired the vast Louisiana Territory, with its undetermined western border, and moved even closer to the heartland of Mexico.

From 1803 until the western limit of Louisiana was established by treaty in 1819, Spanish officials worried about the expansionist Americans. Indeed, by claiming that Louisiana included most of Texas, the United States government gave Mexico good reason for concern. Official United States exploring parties which ventured into the disputed territory gave Mexican officials evidence of Americans' seemingly sinister designs. From the expedition of Lewis and Clark (1804–06) to that of Stephen H. Long (1820), officials on Mexico's northern frontier remained vigilant. On two occasions viceregal troops turned back United States parties. In 1806 Francisco Viana intercepted Thomas Freeman, who had been sent by Thomas Jefferson to locate the sources of the Red River of Texas. That same year, officials in New Mexico were alerted to the approach of Zebulon Montgomery Pike, whose official instructions were to explore the headwaters of the Red and Arkansas rivers. Pike strayed, probably accidentally, into the Rio Grande Valley and was taken as a prisoner to Santa Fe, then marched to Chihuahua before being released. Pike returned to the United States to publish a detailed report of the country he had seen. Appearing in 1810, Pike's widely read *Journals* became the first introduction to Mexico for many Americans. Pike was one of the first prominent Americans to suggest that Mexico could be easily liberated and that Mexicans would welcome United States assistance.

Although United States-sponsored explorations of the West were worrisome, the unofficial activities of private United States citizens caused Spanish officials even greater concern. In 1800, Philip Nolan led twenty-four men into Texas to round up wild horses. Texas officials suspected Nolan of spying and of planning to conquer the province with the aid of Indian allies. Spanish troops, sent to find Nolan, stopped the party near present-day Waco, killed Nolan and several others in the skirmish that followed, and took ten of his men prisoner. Spanish officials executed one prisoner as a punishment that they hoped would be exemplary. Yet, if this discouraged further intrusions by Americans, it also enraged public opinion in the United States against the "barbarity" of Spaniards. Similar incidents were to follow.

In 1810 Father Miguel Hidalgo y Costilla led an abortive movement for Mexican independence which unleashed a decade of turbulence for Mexico and gave legitimacy to adventurers, or filibusterers, who invaded Mexico from United States soil for the ostensible purpose of liberating Mexico. The first of these invasions was led by Bernardo Gutiérrez de Lara in 1812 and 1813. A former associate of Hidalgo, Gutiérrez raised a motley crew of adventurers in the United States, apparently with the blessing of the United States government,[1] and nearly succeeded in "liberating" Texas. Texas was again the scene of filibustering attempts in 1819 and 1821 when a self-styled "General," James Long, led attacks on Texas. He failed each time. Long was convinced that Texas should have become a territory of the United States in the Treaty of 1819, and his conviction was shared by many frontiersmen who continued to covet Texas.

Other Americans, with less lofty ambitions than "General" Long, tried to enter northern Mexico to trade, trap, or hunt sea otter along the California coast. These ventures were illegal, however, for Spain, anxious to preserve a commercial monopoly over the area, prohibited trade with foreigners. Otter hunters managed to operate successfully on the unguarded California coast, but American merchants and trappers who ventured too close to the New Mexico settlements had their merchandise or furs confiscated and were detained by officials, in some cases for years.

Although Anglo Americans were prohibited from crossing onto the Spanish frontier, they did so anyway. Their behavior enraged Spanish officials. Spain's minister, Luis de Onís, who negotiated the Treaty of 1819, characterized the "arrogant and audacious" Americans as a people who believed themselves "superior to all the nations of Europe," and who were convinced "that their dominion is destined to extend, now, to the isthmus of Panama, and hereafter, over all the regions of the New World."[2] The image of the aggressive, grasping, lawless American was already being formed. At the same time, reports of high-handed treatment of Americans in Mexico helped to reinforce American images of the cruel, inhumane Spaniard. Upon returning to the United States, these first American visitors to northern Mexico told of abundant cattle in California and Texas, of rich silver mines, of a large market starved for manufactured goods, and of weak Spanish defenses, and so served to whet the appetite of others of their countrymen.

II

Agustín de Iturbide's success in severing Mexico from Spain in 1821 brought with it an abrupt change in treatment of foreigners on the frontier. From Texas to California, foreigners were welcomed to trade by Mexicans who had long paid outrageous prices for Spanish manufactures, and who revealed little apprehension about trading with Anglo Americans. Indeed, to some thinkers in newly independent Mexico, the United States seemed to have done extraordinarily well in throwing off its mother country, forming a republic, and remaining independent. Hence, the United States offered much to admire and emulate. The Mexican Constitution of 1824, for example, copied large portions of that of its northern neighbor. Other Mexicans, however, as early as 1821, distrusted the United States and feared that it would expand at Mexico's expense. Along the frontier, though, ideology and diplomacy were not nearly as important as low-cost merchandise and the end of isolation.

In New Mexico, for example, three groups of United States traders were welcomed to Santa Fe within a few months after news of Mexican independence had arrived. Spanish-born Governor Facundo Melgares revealed an admirable adaptability to change by permitting the foreign merchants to trade. As a lieutenant, in 1806, Melgares had been sent onto the plains in a fruitless search for Zebulon Pike. Now, with a change of governments, Melgares summoned the ayuntamiento, or town council, of Santa Fe, swore loyalty to independent Mexico, and welcomed the "gringos."

With Mexican independence, regularized trade developed over the trail between Santa Fe and Missouri. New Mexicans traded bullion, horses, and mules for American manufactured goods, becoming economically dependent upon the Americans. Simultaneously, American trappers entered the area and used New Mexico as a base for trapping in the southern Rockies. Many of these trappers and merchants made New Mexico their permanent home, settling especially at Taos or Santa Fe, becoming Roman Catholics and citizens, learning Spanish, and marrying or living with New Mexican women. Best known among these newcomers were Kit Carson, Antoine Robidoux, James Magoffin, Charles Bent, and Ceran St. Vrain. As the first United States citizens to settle in the area, they often served unconsciously as the advance guard of American Manifest Destiny. New Mexicans learned that the "gringos," although often unpleasant, were not devils and that American rule over the territory would not be intolerable. At the same time, the Americans learned enough of local customs and of the power structure to serve as an effective fifth column when war erupted between the United States and Mexico in 1846.[3]

New Mexicans, of course, were not blind to this infiltration of United States citizens. As early as 1827 Governor Manuel Armijo had told his government that "every day the foreigners are becoming more influential over the miserable inhabitants of this Territory," and warned of an "evil of great consequence" should the foreigners not be dealt with.[4] But when it became apparent that the government in Mexico City lacked the resources to stop the influx of foreigners, even nationalists like Armijo joined them. He formed a trading partnership with an American and imported goods from the United States over the Santa Fe Trail. Other New Mexico oligarchs did likewise.[5] Few Nuevo Mexicanos remained as outspokenly anti-American as the fiery padre of Taos, Antonio José Martínez, who protested against "gringos" acquiring land grants in New Mexico, and against their construction of trading posts where, he argued, the Yankees demoralized Indians with alcohol and incited them against the Mexicans.[6]

Like the Nuevo Mexicanos, Californios welcomed foreign commerce as soon as news of independence reached them. The spring of

1822 saw the arrival of ships from Boston and from Britain, and California's lucrative hide and tallow trade got under way. Hides and tallow were traded for manufactured goods with the foreigners, and the import duties collected from them paid for running California's government. Meanwhile, beginning with Jedediah Smith in 1826, American mountain men in pursuit of beaver fur found their way across the continent to Calfornia. Despite the efforts of Governor José María Echeandía to stop these foreign trappers, they continued to arrive.

Most trappers and traders returned to the United States after conducting their business in California. Just as in New Mexico, however, some stayed on to become citizens, marry local girls, receive land grants, and merge into the California upper class. Jacob Leese of Sonoma, Oliver Larkin of Monterey, William G. Dana of Santa Barbara, Abel Stearns of Los Angeles, and John Warner of San Diego fit this pattern. These men, who settled in California in the 1820s and 1830s, lived comfortably in Mexican society and did not at first favor annexing California to the United States. When in the 1840s they began to work toward independence for California, they proceeded cautiously, trying to win over to their cause California oligarchs such as Mariano Vallejo of Sonoma. But glowing reports of California brought large-scale immigration from the United States in the 1840s. These impatient overland pioneers, many of whom settled in the Sacramento Valley, favored carrying out a coup d'etat by themselves, as soon as their number became sufficient, and annexing California to the United States. That time had arrived by 1845, on the eve of the war with Mexico, when a British naval officer was said to have exclaimed: "A Yankee! A Yankee! Is there nothing but Yankees here?"[7]

Whereas California and New Mexico at first attracted mainly foreign merchants, Texas from the outset attracted colonists who came to stay. On the eve of Mexican independence, in January 1821, Moses Austin had received permission from the *comandante general* at Monterrey, José Joaquín Arredondo, to settle 300 Louisiana families in Texas. Austin, who had lived for a few years as a Spanish subject in Louisiana, became an empresario, receiving a generous grant of land on the Brazos in exchange for bringing Catholic colonists to Texas. The prospect of adding more citizens to sparsely populated Texas pleased Governor Antonio Martínez, who argued that "admitting foreigners would be the easiest, least costly, and most expeditious method of enlarging the population."[8] It proved far more costly than Martínez imagined.

After Mexico became independent of Spain, many native Texans continued to view foreign colonization as desirable, most notably José Erasmo Seguín, a close friend of Moses Austin's son, Stephen. Seguín often boarded young Austin at his home in San Antonio, always refusing payment, it was said. In 1824, when Seguín represented Texas in the National Congress, he worked to bring about the passage of the Colonization Law of that year, which opened Texas to a flood of foreign settlement. According to this legislation, which was elaborated on by the State of Coahuila-Texas, a foreigner who settled in Texas received a liberal grant of land in exchange for developing it, becoming a Mexican citizen and a Roman Catholic, and obeying the law.

Although new arrivals from the United States quickly outnumbered the Texanos, many natives did not view the Americans as a threat. Rather, the immigrants seemed to hold the key to prosperity for their long-neglected region. Hence, natives and newcomers frequently worked together for their mutual interests. When the central government abolished slavery in 1829, for example, José Antonio Navarro wrote to Stephen Austin of "the stupid law which the President has issued concerning the liberation of slaves! . . . the best men of the state are opposed to such a law. It violates justice and good faith."[9] Mexicans in Texas sought to keep low tariffs on goods imported from the United States, and when the central government prohibited further immigration from the United States in 1830, Mexicans living in the area of San Antonio urged that the law be rescinded.

Not all Mexicans in Texas, however, cooperated with the newcomers or took a sanguine view of their increasing influence. Significantly, it was at San Antonio, where the American population was smallest, that Mexicans remained most favorably disposed toward the foreigners. In East Texas, on the other hand, where American immigrants vastly outnumbered Mexicans, conflict between the two cultures was intense. As early as 1828, when General Mier y Terán visited the Texas-Louisiana border, it seemed clear that Texas was in danger of becoming Anglicized and absorbed by the United States. The clash that Mier y Terán foresaw was, in many respects, a clash of cultures. Mexicans and Americans in Texas and across the northern frontier had found much to dislike about one another.[10] In a way, they had always known they would.

III

Even before Mexicans and Americans came into contact with one another in the borderlands, they had formed negative impressions of each other inherited from their respective mother countries, Spain and England. Seventeenth-century New Englanders such as Samuel Sewall and Cotton Mather, for example, who had little direct contact with Spain or Latin America, took a jaundiced view of Catholic Latin America, based largely on what they had read in literature from England. Sewall believed that Mexican culture was doomed to fall before a triumphant Protestantism and hoped that Mexico would hasten the process by revolting against Spain. Mather took the trouble to learn Spanish in order to write a missionary tract for Spaniards in the New World which was designed "to open their eyes and be converted . . . away from Satan to God."[11]

Anti-Spanish views inherited from England were far more complex than simple anti-Catholicism, however. The English colonists also believed that Spanish government was authoritarian, corrupt, and decadent, and that Spaniards were bigoted, cruel, greedy, tyrannical, fanatical, treacherous, and lazy. In responding to these charges, Spanish historians have found it convenient to give them a pejorative label: The Black Legend. In defending themselves from the blackening effect of this "legend," Spaniards have often gone to the other extreme of whitewashing Spain of all faults, giving rise to what Spain's detractors called a White Legend. This, of course, remains a danger for Mexican American scholars today, as they attempt to refute the traditional social-science views of Mexican American culture and construct a new model.

The origins of the Black Legend are complex. Some of its roots lie in the New World, where Spanish conquistadores have been viewed as the apotheosis of evil. Interestingly, Spain's detractors drew much of their material from self-critical writings of Spaniards themselves, most notably Bartolomé de las Casas, who was widely read in England and its American colonies. For our purposes, however, suffice it to say that Mexicans inherited the bad reputation of their Spanish forefathers. As Philip Wayne Powell recently put it, "We [Americans] transferred some of our ingrained antipathy toward Catholic Spain to her American heirs."[12] In making this transfer, Anglo Americans found an additional element to despise in Mexicans: racial mixture. American visitors to the Mexican frontier were nearly unanimous in commenting on the dark skin of Mexican mestizos who, it was generally agreed, had inherited the worst qualities of Spaniards and Indians to produce a "race" still more despicable than that of either parent.

Even before Anglo Americans came into significant contact with Mexicans, then, they thought they knew what Mexicans would be like. Not surprisingly, their expectations were fulfilled. Only the most unschooled American, such as trapper James Ohio Pattie, "expected to find no difference between these people and our own, but their language." Pattie expressed "surprise and disappointment" when he discovered that he was mistaken and that there was "not one white person among them."[13]

The Mexicans whom Americans had the most occasion to meet lived on the frontier, where culture, as we saw in the previous chapter, was less developed than in central Mexico. If Americans found these frontier Mexicans ignorant and economically backward, it was because schools scarcely existed and because the frontier was too isolated to enter fully into the economic life of the rest of the nation. Yet, predisposed to view the Catholic Church and Spanish government as regressive, Hispanic peoples as lazy, and mixed bloods as inferior, Anglos failed to realize that conditions on the Mexican frontier closely resembled those of the American frontier. Anglos generalized about frontier society, assuming that it typified all of Mexico. At the same time, upper-class visitors from Mexico City also deplored the backwardness of their own frontier.[14]

North Americans, then, combining their inherited belief in the Black Legend with racism and their exposure to frontier Mexican culture, came to the conclusion that Mexican people were inferior. They were contemptuous of Mexican government and of Catholicism, and they viewed Mexicans as indolent, ignorant, bigoted, cheating, dirty, bloodthirsty, cowardly half-breeds.[15] Often those Americans who had least contact with Mexicans denounced them most virulently. Mexican women, it should be noted, were usually exempt from such remarks. Francis Parkman, the famed historian who journeyed to the Far West in 1846 as a young man, distinguished between the sexes by referring to Mexican women as "Spanish" and to men as "Mexican."[16] Perhaps the only accomplishment which Yankees uniformly admired in Mexican men was their horsemanship.

The Mexicans, in turn, did not fail to notice and comment on the Anglo Americans' feelings of superiority. Especially evident to

Mexicans was the Americans' attitude toward people of color—Indians and Negroes. The "fanatical intolerance" of the Americans, as one Mexican editor put it, was evident in many ways. John Randolph, for example, argued on the floor of the United States Senate that because some Latin Americans had Negro ancestors they were not the equal of Anglo Americans. United States newspapers circulated in Mexico reported this, and other episodes which made it clear that Americans viewed Mexico's "primitive inhabitants" as no better than American Indians and that Mexico deserved to be conquered because it was less industrious and efficient than the United States.[17]

In small ways the Americans' behavior seemed to exhibit disrespect toward Mexicans. In 1832, for example, Miguel Sena, a member of the Santa Fe town council, or ayuntamiento, complained that the Americans mocked the system of justice and acted shamefully in the courtroom: "As soon as they enter, they stretch themselves or recline on the seats, and if they are not ordered to stand, they give their answers in that position, and with their hats on their heads." The following year the ayuntamiento of Santa Fe found it necessary to require that Americans close their shops on Sundays "to avoid public scandal, and to keep the Day of the Lord with due respect."[18]

Surely not all Americans were contemptuous of Mexicans, and not all Mexicans were contemptuous of Americans. Some liberal Mexicans who were not disturbed by Protestantism or Republicanism found much to admire in the young United States. On the far northern frontier some Mexicans probably did view the Anglo Americans as "ingenious men" who "knew everything" and who "can all read and write like priests," as one contemporary American observer vainly supposed.[19] Yet, the more common view seems to have been that the "gringos" were arrogant, aggressive, unscrupulous racists who endangered the very existence of Mexico as a nation. So intense had anti-Americanism become by 1846 that many Mexicans were willing to fight a war to protect their homes, religions, language and customs from the odious "Anglo-Saxon race" which seemed to threaten to enslave all Mexicans.[20] By 1846 the two cultures had already clashed in Texas, and the shedding of blood had excited tempers on both sides to a fever pitch. This conflict of cultures will be discussed in the next chapter.

1. "Calculating the profit"

Carlos Dehault Delassus, 1804*

Even before the United States acquired Louisiana, officials in New Spain had worried about westward-moving Anglo Americans. Concern about United States aggression heightened after Louisiana became a United States territory in 1803. In August 1804, the former Spanish lieutenant governor of Upper Louisiana, Carlos Dehault Delassus, was still at St. Louis, although it was under American control. In a letter to the Marqués de Casa Calvo, a Spanish boundary commissioner, Delassus revealed considerable insight into the ambitious plan of United States merchants. His warning about the plans of Captain Lewis refers, of course, to the Lewis and Clark expedition.

Reservada [confidential].

I do not regret that circumstances require me to remain in this post much longer than I expected since it facilitates my observing the movements and listening to the conversations of the Americans as a result of the retrocession of this province to France and the cession by the latter to the United States.

It is clearly to be seen that the general opinion of this latter named nation is that its limits will extend to Mexico itself, extending their boundary lines to the Río Bravo, penetrating into the said kingdom at different points adding [following] other small rivers. So general is this persuasion that I believe that beforehand many are thinking of obtaining a great advantage from those lands, and, as I see it, they are already calculating the profit which they will obtain from the mines. Their conversations support this belief.

I am informed that they are disposed to send troops to the Upper Missouri, although at this moment I am not very certain of this information. There is no doubt that this news is rumored here and if they do not carry out this plan soon it will be because of the few troops which they have now, but it is not necessary to overlook that

---

*Delassus to Casa Calvo, St. Louis, August 10, 1804, in A. P. Nasatir, ed., *Before Lewis and Clark: Documents Illustrating the History of the Missouri, 1785–1804* (St. Louis: 1952), 2:742–45. Reprinted by permission of the Historical Documents Foundation, St. Louis, Mo.

they will approach that Kingdom as soon as it is possible. At least appearances indicate that.

The officials who are commanding here are continually informing themselves from the Indians of the Missouri and the white hunters and traders, whether they know the shortest routes to New Mexico or to Santa Fé. I know positively that in the month of July of this year merchants left here in some embarcations for that purpose.

I believe that Your Excellency knows that one can go from here to Mexico in less than two months. This can be done it is true with hard work and is exposed to meeting with various Indian Nations who are making war and exposed to being defeated by those parties, but by taking arms and some presents one can succeed in pacifying them and with continually seeing the Americans pass through those districts they [those barbarians] will very soon accustom themselves to trading with them and will facilitate them on their voyages. Perhaps it will result that those Indians who are friends of the Spaniards [now] will become enemies, incited by the Americans.

At present this post abounds in dry goods of all sorts and many of the finest. There is a surplus here of more than three-fourths for the consumption of this district, and more are arriving every day. I do not doubt that it is for the purpose of sending them to the frontiers of Mexico. I am of the opinion that if the greatest precautions are not taken to stop this contraband, within a short time, one will see descending the Missouri, instead of furs, silver from the Mexican mines [which will] arrive in this post in abundance.

It is also said that the voyage of Captain Lewis (of which I have informed Your Excellency at the time) is directing itself towards New Mexico; that his plan to discover the Pacific Ocean was no more than a pretext. This I doubt because the preparations which he made here before leaving did not indicate any other object than a very long voyage such as was announced, although it would not be impossible to verify it [what was said].

> May God Keep Your Excellency many years.
> St. Louis, Illinois, August 10, 1804.
> Carlos Dehault Delassus [rubric]

2. "Indications are very dangerous"

Joaquín del Real Alencaster, 1807*

In New Mexico, Delassus's warning seemed prophetic, for as early as 1804 American merchants began to arrive at Santa Fe, and by 1806 reports reached New Mexico of the expedition of Zebulon Montgomery Pike (spelled "Paike" in the following document). In early 1807, when Pike strayed, probably by accident, into Spanish territory, he was arrested under orders from New Mexico Governor Joaquín del Real Alencaster and taken prisoner to Santa Fe. Told by one of Pike's men that a rescue party was on the way from the United States (a pure fabrication), Real Alencaster made plans to defend New Mexico from American attack. In the report which follows, Real Alencaster described these preparations. In doing so, he also made a rare assessment of the loyalty of New Mexicans and their attitude toward the Yankees. At this early date New Mexicans had little fear of a United States conquest if this report is reliable.

I have . . . given orders for all able-bodied men to be ready to take arms, and, having examined and reinforced the points of defense in case of serious occurrences, and made preparation for the greatest possible force to be opposed [to an invader], I shall present my person wherever indicated, without my attacks [of ill health] being the slightest obstacle, so as to carry out my duty and reflect credit on my discharging of my obligation.

I repeat that, in spite of the precautions which I have taken, I still doubt that anything extraordinary will occur; but still, the character of the Anglo-American, his pride and ambition, and the exceedingly weak forces on which I can count for defense, all make my vigilance very important; and I consider it necessary for Your Exc. to be informed about it all, both so that Your Exc. may be good enough to send me reinforcements as you think necessary and possible, and so you may indicate to me the orders and commands suitable for success

*Real Alencaster to Nemesio Salcedo, Commanding-General of the Interior Provinces of New Spain, Santa Fe, April 15, 1807. From *The Journals of Zebulon Montgomery Pike: With Letters and Related Documents,* edited and annotated by Donald Jackson. 2 vols. (Norman, Okla.: 1966), 2:199–200. Copyright 1966 by the University of Oklahoma Press. Reprinted by permission of the publisher.

in carrying out my mission, and finally to avoid evils which, if they are not very near, may be considered not very remote.

With regret I find it necessary to report Your Exc. a sad observation which I have made; especially since the arrival of Paike, the citizens of this Prov. have received with extreme affection and hospitality both the citizens of Louisiana who have come here and the Anglo-Americans, first the Soldier Basquez and then the Tailor Nicolas Coleé, American, have been pardoned [?] for their ambition, their hardness of temperament and the many requirements and charges which they impose upon the citizenry; and since the arrival of the [Pike] party, I have had very highly surreptitious information and have overheard the conversation of the people about whether the Anglo-Americans will come and the possibility that they may make themselves masters of this Province, without observing any displeasure among these people or hearing them express animosity or willingness to risk their lives to guard their Homes; and they speak with the greatest insipidity and timidity—which indications are very dangerous to us, and I can envision myself in the situation of having to struggle to prevent the horrible results, which it seems to me impossible for Your Exc. to realize completely.

I ask nothing of Your Exc. insistently, for you know about [the small quantity of] troops, arms and munitions which exist in this command.

....

Joaquín del Rl. Alencaster

3. California "would fall without an effort"

William Shaler, 1808*

Spanish officials in New Mexico were not the only ones to become alarmed at Anglo American intruders. Beginning in the 1790s, Anglo Americans also began showing up in Texas and California. Among the earliest Anglo American visitors to Spanish California was William Shaler, captain of a ship that in 1803 traded for sea otter skins with willing Californios.

---

*William Shaler, *Journal of a Voyage between China and the North-Western Coast of America made in 1804* (Claremont, Calif.: 1935), pp. 59–60, 75–78.

In a work first published in 1808, Shaler revealed himself to be one of the earliest proponents of an idea that came to be associated with Manifest Destiny by the mid-1840s. California, Shaler argued, would prosper under a more progressive government and that, in itself, would justify its seizure by the United States. Shaler also predicted that California's weak defenses would make it easy to conquer. Here he spoke with considerable authority since his ship had successfully fled from the harbor at San Diego, sailing directly in front of the shore battery without being seriously hit. Stories of the weak defenses of the north Mexican provinces continued to circulate. When the United States government sent troops into the area during the Mexican War, it did so with considerable confidence that victory would be easy.

The Spanish population of the Californias is very inconsiderable; by the best information I could obtain, it hardly exceeds 3000 souls, including the garrisons, among which, even the latter, the officers excepted, there are very few white people: it principally consists of a mixed breed. They are of an indolent, harmless disposition, and fond of spirituous liquors. That they should not be industrious, is not surprising; their government does not encourage industry. For several years past, the American trading ships have frequented this coast in search of furs, for which they have left in the country about 25,000 dollars annually, in specie and merchandize. The government have used all their endeavors to prevent this intercourse, but without effect, and the consequence has been a great increase in wealth and industry among the inhabitants. The missionaries are the principal monopolizers of the fur trade, but this intercourse has enabled the inhabitants to take part in it. At present, a person acquainted with the coast may always produce abundant supplies of provisions. All these circumstances prove that, under a good government, the Californias would soon rise to ease and affluence.

The mutual jealousies and selfish policy of the great European powers have been the causes that some of the most beautiful regions of the universe have long languished under the degrading shackles of ignorance and superstition; and the Spanish monarchy has been so long left to the quiet enjoyment of the finest part of the new world, that they have been at full liberty to extend their conquests there in every direction, without any other obstacle than the feeble opposition of the native savages. Any of the great maritime powers that should determine to give independence to New Spain, or wrest it from the Spanish dominion, would naturally seek to establish themselves in California, from whence, as a place of arms, they might carry on their operations against that defenceless kingdom with a certainty of success. This the Spaniards have doubtless foreseen, and been before hand in occupying it, with a view of forming a barrier to those possessions. The foregoing shows that what they have yet done has had a directly contrary effect. They have, at a great expence and considerable industry, removed every obstacle out of the way of an invading enemy; they have stocked the country with such multitudes of cattle, horses, and other useful animals, that they have no longer the power to remove or destroy them; they have taught the Indians many of the useful arts, and accustomed them to agriculture and civilization; and they have spread a number of defenceless inhabitants over the country, whom they never could induce to act as enemies to those who should treat them well, by securing to them the enjoyments of liberty, property, and a free trade, which would almost instantaneously quadruple the value of their actual possessions: in a word, they have done everything that could be done to render California an object worthy the attention of the great maritime powers: they have placed it in a situation to want nothing but a good government to rise rapidly to wealth and importance.

The conquest of this country would be absolutely nothing; it would fall without an effort to the most inconsiderable force; and as the greatest efforts that the Spanish government would be capable of making towards its recovery would be from the shores of New Spain, opposite the peninsula, a military post, established at the bay of Angels, and that of San Diego fortified and defended by a competent body of troops, would render such an attempt ineffectual. The Spaniards have few ships or seamen in this part of the world; the arsenal of San Blass [sic] would be their only resource on such an occasion, and that might be very easily destroyed. But, admitting that the inactivity of the invaders should permit them to transport troops over to the peninsula, those that come from New Spain could not be very formidable, either in point of numbers or courage, and they would have to penetrate through Lower California, where they would not find even water in their march: all the other resources of that desolate country could be easily removed out of their way. They could not march round the head of the gulf: the natural obstacles of such an expedition would be very numerous; and they must besides force their way through many warlike nations of savages.

An expedition by sea to Upper California would be equally difficult for them: the bad weather they must encounter in winter, and the great length of the passage in summer, on account of the prevailing north-west winds, would render it a very precarious undertaking. In a word, it would be as easy to keep California in spite of the Spaniards, as it would be to wrest it from them in the first instance.

4. The Black Legend   William Robertson, 1777*

Even before Anglo Americans such as Shaler entered New Spain, their attitudes towards Spaniards were probably conditioned by books they had read or heard about. Literature which placed Spaniards in an unfavorable light was readily available to Anglo Americans: works in translation by Spaniards such as Las Casas, and Jorge Juan and Antonio de Ulloa, and the writings of Englishmen such as Thomas Gage, Richard Hakluyt, and William Robertson.

Robertson's *History of America,* a portion of which is excerpted here, was first published in 1777 and received wide circulation in the United States. It went through many editions, including a cheap paperback printing, and was frequently serialized in popular magazines. Writers such as Robertson led their readers to believe that cruel, rapacious Spaniards came to the New World in search for treasure, mines, and to live in idleness on the toil and sweat of exploited Indian laborers. Implicitly, if not explicitly, these writers contrasted avaricious and indolent Spaniards to the English colonists, who supposedly came to the New World to build homes, farm, and work with their own hands.

Some historians have long recognized that this dichotomy, "between the Spanish pick and the English hoe," to use Herbert Bolton's phrase, is "somewhat fanciful and has been greatly overworked."[1] Nonetheless, Robertson's writing may still sound

---

*William Robertson, *The History of America*, 2 vols. (Albany, 1822), 2:50, 202–5.

1. Herbert E. Bolton, "Defensive Spanish Expansion and the Significance of the Borderlands," in John Francis Bannon, ed., *Bolton and the Spanish Borderlands* (Norman, Okla.: 1964), p. 33.

2. See Philip Wayne Powell, *Tree of Hate: Propaganda and Prejudices Affecting United States Relations with the Hispanic World* (New York, 1971), pp. 131–44.

convincing to modern readers because many textbooks continue to portray the Spanish conquest and colonization of
America in Black Legend clichés.[2] Robertson may also sound
convincing because there is a kernel of truth behind the Black
Legend. Some Spaniards were cruel, indolent, treasure-hungry
adventurers. So, too, were some Englishmen.

In almost every district of the Mexican empire, the progress of the
Spanish arms is marked with blood, and with deeds so atrocious, as
disgrace the enterprising valour that conducted them to success. In
the country of Panuco, sixty caziques or leaders, and four hundred
nobles, were burnt at one time. Nor was this shocking barbarity
perpetrated in any sudden sally of rage, or by a commander of inferior
note. It was the act of Sandoval, an officer whose name is entitled to
the second rank in the annals of New Spain, and executed after a
solemn consultation with Cortes; and to complete the horror of the
scene, the children and relations of the wretched victims were
assembled, and compelled to be spectators of their dying agonies. The
example of Cortes and his principal officers encouraged and justified
persons of subordinate rank to venture upon committing greater
excesses.

. . . In all those extensive regions, the original race of inhabitants
wasted away; in some it was totally extinguished. In Mexico, where a
powerful and martial people distinguished their opposition to the
Spaniards by efforts of courage worthy of a better fate, great numbers
fell in the field; and there, as well as in Peru, still greater numbers
perished under the hardships of attending the Spanish armies in their
various expeditions and civil wars, worn out with the incessant toil of
carrying their baggage, provisions, and military stores.

But neither the rage nor cruelty of the Spaniards were so
destructive to the people of Mexico and Peru, as the inconsiderate
policy with which they established their new settlements.—The
former were temporary calamities, fatal to individuals; the latter was
a permanent evil, which, with gradual consumption, wasted the
nation. When the provinces of Mexico and Peru were divided among
the conquerors, each was eager to obtain a district, from which he
might expect an instantaneous recompense for all his services.
Soldiers, accustomed to the carelessness and dissipation of a military

life, had neither industry to carry on any plan of regular cultivation, nor patience to wait for its slow but certain returns. Instead of settling in the vallies occupied by the natives, where the fertility of the soil would have amply rewarded the diligence of the planter, they chose to fix their stations in some of the mountainous regions, frequent both in New Spain and in Peru. To search for mines of gold and silver, was the chief object of their activity. . . . In order to push forward those favourite projects, so many hands were wanted, that the service of the natives became indispensably requisite. They were accordingly compelled to abandon their ancient habitations in the plains, and driven in crowds to the mountains. This sudden transition from the sultry climate of the vallies to the chill penetrating air peculiar to high lands in the torrid zone; exorbitant labour, scanty or unwholesome nourishment, and the despondency occasioned by a species of oppression to which they were not accustomed, and of which they saw no end, affected them nearly as much as their less industrious countrymen in the islands. They sunk under the united pressure of those calamities, and melted away with almost equal rapidity. In consequence of this, together with the introduction of the small-pox, a malady unknown in America, and extremely fatal to the natives, the number of people both in New Spain and Peru was so much reduced, that in a few years the accounts of their ancient population appeared almost incredible.

....

The Spanish monarchs, far from acting upon any such system of destruction, were uniformly solicitous for the preservation of their new subjects. . . .

. . . But the avarice of individuals was too violent to be controlled by the authority of laws. Rapacious and daring adventurers, far removed from the seat of government, little accustomed to the restraints of military discipline while in service, and still less disposed to respect the feeble jurisdiction of civil power in an infant colony, despised or eluded every regulation that set bounds to their exactions and tyranny. The parent state, with persevering attention, issued edicts to prevent the oppression of the Indians; the colonists, regardless of these, or trusting to their distance for impunity, continued to consider and treat them as slaves. The governors themselves, and other officers employed in the colonies, several of whom were as indigent and rapacious as the adventurers over whom they presided, were too apt to adopt their contemptuous ideas of the conquered people; and instead of checking, encouraged or connived at their excesses. The desolation of the New World should not then be charged on the court of Spain, or be considered as the effect of any system of policy adopted there. It ought to be imputed wholly to the indigent and often unprincipled adventurers, whose fortune it was to be the conquerors and first planters of America, who, by measures no less inconsiderate than unjust, counteracted the edicts of their sovereign, and have brought disgrace upon their country.

5. "Degenerate inhabitants of New Mexico"

Rufus B. Sage, 1846*

> After Americans were permitted to trade and settle in Mexico in 1821, their condemnation of Mexicans took on the authority of firsthand experience. Generally, however, those North Americans with the least acquaintance with Mexicans were most intemperate in their writings. Such a one was Rufus B. Sage, a newspaperman turned Rocky Mountain trapper, who was born and raised in Connecticut. Sage visited the remote village of Taos in northern New Mexico briefly in 1842. His observations about New Mexicans are based entirely on his visit to Taos and nearby settlements.
>
> Containing elements of the Black Legend, anti-Catholicism, and racism, Sage's view of Mexicans was commonplace for an Anglo American in the 1840s. *Scenes in the Rocky Mountains,* from which this selection is taken, was first published in 1846 when anti-Mexican feeling ran high in the United States. By ridiculing Mexicans on the eve of war with Mexico, Sage did little to diminish the popularity of his book. One wonders whether writers such as Sage were as staunchly anti-Mexican as their writing indicates, or whether they were simply playing to the prejudices of their readers.

---

*LeRoy R. and Ann W. Hafen, eds., *Rufus B. Sage: His Letters and Papers, 1836–1847, With an Annotated Reprint of His "Scenes in the Rocky Mountains . . . . ,"* 2 vols. (Glendale, Calif.: 1956), 2:82–87. Reprinted by permission of the Arthur H. Clark Company.

The mountains are rich in minerals of various kinds. Gold is found in considerable quantities in their vicinity, and would doubltless yield a large profit to diggers, were they possessed of the requisite enterprise and capital. At present these valuable mines are almost entirely neglected,—the common people being too ignorant and poor to work them, and the rich too indolent and fond of ease.

The Mexicans possess large *ranchos* of sheep, horses, mules, and cattle among the mountains, which are kept there the entire year, by a degraded set of beings, following no business but that of herdsmen, or *rancheros.*

This class of people have no loftier aspirations than to throw the *lasso* with dexterity, and break wild mules and horses.

They have scarcely an idea of any other place than the little circle in which they move, nor dream of a more happy state of existence than their own. Half-naked and scantily fed, they are contented with the miserable pittance doled out to them by the proud lordlings they serve, while their wild songs merrily echo through the hills as they pursue their ceaseless vocations till death drops his dark curtain o'er the scene.

There are no people on the continent of America, whether civilized or uncivilized, with one or two exceptions, more miserable in condition or despicable in morals than the mongrel race inhabiting New Mexico. In saying this, I deal in generalities; but were I to particularize the observation would hold good in a large majority of cases.

Next to the squalid appearance of its inhabitants, the first thing that arrests the attention of the traveller on entering an [*sic*] Mexican settlement, is the uninviting mud walls that form the rude hovels which constitute its dwellings.

These are one story high and built of *adobies* [*adobes*], with small windows, (like the port-holes of a fortification,) generally without glass. The entrance is by an opening in the side, very low, and frequently unprotected by a door. The roof is a terrace of sod, reposing upon a layer of small logs, affording but poor protection from the weather.

The interior presents an aspect quite as forbidding;—the floors are simply the naked ground,—chairs and tables are articles rarely met with. In case of an extra room, it is partitioned off by a thin wall of mud, communicating with its neighbor through a small window-shaped aperture, and serves the double purpose of a chamber and store-house.

A few rags, tattered blankets, or old robes, furnish beds for its inmates, who, at nightfall, stow themselves away promiscuously upon the ground or in narrow bins, and snooze their rounds despite the swarms of noxious vermin that infest them, (companions from which they are seldom free, whether sleeping or waking,—and afford them, perhaps, in greater number and variety of species than any other known people.)

During the winter months, these filthy wretches are seen, day after day, basking at the sunny side of their huts, and bestowing upon each other certain friendly offices connected with the head, wherein the swarming populace of the pericranium are had in alternate requisition.

The entire business of the country is in the hands of the rich, upon whom the laboring classes are mainly dependent for support; and, as a natural consequence, the rich know no end to their treasures, nor the poor to their poverty.

The common laborer obtains only from four to six dollars per month, out of which he must feed and clothe himself. In case he runs in debt beyond his means, he is necessitated by law to serve for the required amount, at two dollars per month;—thus, once in debt, it is almost impossible ever to extricate himself.

Having faintly depicted the real condition of a large majority of the degenerate inhabitants of New Mexico, it will be expected of me to say something of their intelligence and morality; and here a still more revolting task awaits my effort.

Intelligence is confined almost exclusively to the higher classes, and the poor "*palavro*" comes in for a very diminutive share.

Education is entirely controlled by the priests, who make use of their utmost endeavors to entangle the minds of their pupils in the meshes of superstition and bigotry. The result of this may be plainly stated in a few words:

Superstition and bigotry are universal,—all, both old and young, being tied down to the disgusting formalities of a religion that manifests itself in little else than senseless parade and unmeaning ceremony,—while a large majority can neither read nor write.

These conservators of intelligence and morals are often as sadly deficient in either as those they assume to teach. Gambling, swearing, drinking, Sabbath-breaking, and sundry other vices, are the too frequent concomitants of their practice;—under such instructors, who can fail to foresee the attendant trains of evils? The abject condition of the people favors the impress of unsound instruction and deteriorating example, reducing public morals to a very low ebb.

Property and life are alike unsafe, and a large proportion of the whole community are little other than thieves and robbers. Profanity is their common language. In their honesty, integrity, and good faith, as a general thing, no reliance should be placed. They are at all times ready to betray their trust whenever a sufficient inducement is presented.

With the present of a few dollars, witnesses may be readily obtained to swear to anything; and a like bonus placed in the hands of the *Alcaldi* [*alcalde*] will generally secure the required judgment, however much at variance with the true merits of the cause.

Thus, justice becomes a mere mockery, and crime stalks forth at noon-day, unawed by fear of punishment, and unrebuked by public opinion and practice.

But fear, in most cases, exercises a far more controlling influence over them than either gratitude or favor. They may be ranked with the few exceptions in the family of man who cannot endure good treatment. To manage them successfully, they must needs be held in continual restraint, and kept in their place by force, if necessary,—else they will become haughty and insolent.

As servants, they are excellent, when properly trained, but are worse than useless if left to themselves.

In regard to the Mexican women, it would be unfair to include them in the preceding summary.

The ladies present a striking contrast to their countryman in general character, other than morals. They are kind and affectionate in their disposition, mild and affable in their deportment, and ever ready to administer to the necessities of others. But, on the score of virtue and common chastity, they are sadly deficient; while ignorance and superstition are equally predominant.

One of the prime causes in producing this deplorable state of things may be attributed to that government policy which confines the circulating medium of the country within too narrow limits, and thus throws the entire business of the country into the hands of the capitalist.

A policy like this must ever give to the rich the moneyed power, while it drains from the pockets of the poor man and places him at the mercy of haughty lordlings, who, taking advantage of his necessity, grant him but the scanty pittance for his services they in tender compassion see fit to bestow.

The higher classes have thus attained the supreme control, and the commoners must continue to cringe and bow to their will. In this manner the latter have, by degrees, lost all ambition and self-respect, and, in degradation, are only equalled by their effeminacy.

Possessed of little moral restraint, and interested in nothing but the demands of present want, they abandon themselves to vice, and prey upon one another and those around them.

A few miles to the southeast of Taos, is a large village of Pueblos, or civilized Indians. These are far superior to their neighbors in circumstances, morals, civil regulations, character, and all the other distinguishing traits of civilization.

6. "Blood . . . as ditch water"

Walter Prescott Webb, 1931 & 1935*

Accounts such as Sage's may lead the reader to reflect that virulent anti-Mexicanism, although lamentable, is a thing of the past. The writings of the late Walter Prescott Webb, Texas's renowned historian, demonstrate how stereotypes have lingered on in modern historical scholarship. Mixing the Black Legend with racism, Webb repeated stereotypes which echo those of the nineteenth century. In his classic *Great Plains,* Webb put forth a racist explanation for Spain's failure to hold the frontier against nomadic Indians in the latter part of the eighteenth century. Even Webb's premise is in error, however, for, beginning in 1786, Spanish military policy actually succeeded in bringing a calm to the northern frontier which lasted

*Walter Prescott Webb, *The Great Plains,* copyright 1931, 1959 by Walter P. Webb. Published by Xerox Corporation. All rights reserved. Reprinted by permission of the publisher. *The Texas Rangers: A Century of Frontier Defense.* Foreword by Lyndon B. Johnson (Austin: 1935; 2nd ed., 1965), pp. 13–14, reprinted by permission of the University of Texas Press.

1. Llerna B. Friend, "W. P. Webb's Texas Rangers," *Southwestern Historical Quarterly* 74, no. 3 (January 1971): 294, 321.

until the Wars for Independence disturbed Mexico in 1810. It should be remembered that Comanches and Apaches were no pushover for United States forces, who enjoyed superior technology, a century later.

Webb repeated this racist argument in *The Texas Rangers,* a portion of which also follows. In fairness to Webb it should be noted that before his death in 1963 he expressed a wish to revise his work on the Rangers, especially in regard to Mexican Americans.[1]

Webb: *The Great Plains,* 1931

In the beginning the Spanish military exploring campaigns were usually successful. The early *conquistadores* had at their heels the daring and courageous sons of Spain, pure Spaniards brought up in the school of chivalry, with high ideals of personal valor. Coronado had three hundred "gentlemen on horseback" who lacked nothing in reckless daring; in fact, they were considered good riddance by Mendoza, the viceroy of Mexico, because they were making him trouble. But as time went on, the novelty of the *entradas* wore off, and since no gold was found on the northern frontier the best men of Spain were no longer drawn there. There were always a few good men on the edge of civilization and beyond, but sometimes the best were recruited from other nations, such as the Frenchman De Mézières. If this northern frontier was to be held, it must be held by men of iron and steel, and these in turn must be supported by a sturdy population able to protect their homes and their property. A homogeneous European society adaptable to new conditions was necessary. This Spain did not have to offer in Arizona, New Mexico, and Texas. Its frontier, as it advanced, depended more and more on an Indian population and on the mixture that resulted from the mingling of the blood of Spaniards, Negroes, and Indians, with the Indians predominating: Spaniards, Indians, Negroes, mestizos, mulattoes, and many other combinations, referred to by Rubí as "so-called Spaniards."

This mixture of races meant in time that the common soldiers in the Spanish service came largely from pueblo or sedentary Indian stock, whose blood, when compared with that of the Plains Indians, was as ditch water. It took more than a little mixture of Spanish blood and the mantle of Spanish service to make valiant soldiers of the timid pueblo Indians, who were born in fear of the raiders from the Plains.

So it happened that in the beginning, as the Spanish frontier advanced, it cut like a blade of Damascus steel; but as the frontier came northward the temper was gradually taken out of it, and when it reached the Apachería and Comanchería, where the best metal was imperative, it crumbled and fell away. In the end the frontier had to be upheld by a handful of courageous leaders supported by ineffective presidials. The task was too heavy for them. The result was that from the middle of the eighteenth century to the end of the Spanish régime the Apache and Comanche warriors ripped and shredded the frontier at will, leading Rubí, after his inspection in 1766, to distinguish sharply between the imaginary frontier of Spain and the real one, to recommend that the Spaniards fall back to the south, in places hundreds of miles, and to reverse completely the policy pursued by Spain at a time when she had no actual European rival on her northern frontier.

Webb: *The Texas Rangers,* 1935

The Mexican nation arises from the heterogeneous mixture of races that compose it. The Indian blood—but not Plains Indian blood—predominates, but in it is a mixture of European, largely Latin. The result is a conglomerate with all gradations from pure Spanish to pure Indian. There are corresponding social gradations with grandees at the top and peons at the bottom. The language is Spanish, or Mexican, the religion Catholic, the temperament volatile and mercurial. Without disparagement it may be said that there is a cruel streak in the Mexican nature, or so the history of Texas would lead one to believe. This cruelty may be a heritage from the Spanish of the Inquisition; it may, and doubtless should, be attributed partly to the Indian blood. Among the common class, ignorance and superstition prevail, making the rabble susceptible to the evil influence of designing leaders. Whatever the reasons, the government of Mexico has ever been unstable, frequently overturned by civil war, and changed but seldom improved by revolution. This constant political ebullition has made any governmental policy, however good it might be, impossible of realization, and transitory.

The Mexican warrior, like the Indian, was a horseman, and in the northern part of the country mainly a *ranchero.* He loved gay attire, both for himself and horse; the braided trousers, the broad sombrero, the gay *serape*, the silver spurs, and the embossed and inlaid saddle exhibit a facet of his character.

He carried the lance for show, and was most skillful and devastating with the knife. As a warrior he was, on the whole, inferior to the Comanche and wholly unequal to the Texan. The whine of the leaden slugs stirred in him an irresistible impulse to travel with rather than against the music. He won more victories over the Texans by parley than by force of arms. For making promises—and for breaking them—he had no peer.

7. "An ill opinion of the Mexicans"

José María Sánchez, 1828*

Americans frequently made generalizations about all of Mexico based on impressions of the frontier society they encountered in Texas, New Mexico, and California. Yet educated Mexicans living on the frontier, and some visitors from more cultured centers of the Mexican interior, also deplored the backwardness of their own frontier and expressed painful awareness of many of the ills that the Anglo Americans identified. Mexicans, however, generally had greater understanding of the reasons for their problems than did the foreigners. The following selection is from the diary of José María Sánchez, a sublieutenant of the artillery corps, who journeyed to the Texas frontier with a special investigative committee sent from Mexico City under the direction of Manuel Mier y Terán. Sánchez was clearly unimpressed with the Texanos who lived in the area of San Antonio (San Fernando de Béjar) and in East Texas near Nacogdoches. He described them in terms similar to those used by Rufus Sage.

In 1730, the missions of Concepción, San José, and San Francisco were moved from the frontier of Texas and rebuilt in the vicinity of the Mission of San Antonio. In the same year the *Villa de San Fernando* was founded on the opposite bank of the river and was

*José María Sánchez, "A Trip to Texas in 1828," trans. Carlos E. Castañeda, *Southwestern Historical Quarterly*, 29, no. 4 (April 1926): 257–60, 283. Reprinted by permission of the Texas State Historical Association.

joined to the settlement of the *presidio* or Mission of the Alamo by a
bridge of trees that was built, the two making one place, as one might
say, through the middle of which runs the aforementioned river. The
streets are not exactly straight, for they curve at various points, and
the buildings, though many are of stone, show no beauty, nor do they
have any conveniences. There are two squares, almost joined together, being divided merely by the space occupied by the parochial
church, but neither one is worthy of notice. The commerce, which is
carried on by foreigners and two or three Mexicans, is very
insignificant, but the monopoly of it is very evident. I could cite many
instances to prove by assertion, but I do not wish to be accused of
ulterior motives. Although the soil is very rich, the inhabitants do not
cultivate it because of the danger incurred from Indian attacks as soon
as they get any distance from the houses, as the Indians often lurk in
the surrounding country, coming in the silence of the night without
fear from the troops, for by the time the latter notice the damage
done it is already too late. No measures can be taken for the
maintenance of a continuous watch on account of the sad condition of
the troops, especially since they lack all resources. For months, and
even years at times, these troops have gone without salary or supplies,
constantly in active service against the Indians, dependent for their
subsistence on buffalo meat, deer, and other game they may be able to
secure with great difficulty. The government, nevertheless, has not
helped their condition in spite of repeated and frequent remon-
strances. If any money arrives, it disappears instantly, for infamous
hands are not lacking to take it and give the poor soldiers goods at
double their normal value in exchange for what they have earned,
suffering the inclemencies of the weather while these inhuman tyrants
slept peacefully in their beds. I am not exaggerating; on the contrary,
I keep silent about many worse things I could say. The character of
the people is care-free, they are enthusiastic dancers, very fond of
luxury, and the worst punishment that can be inflicted upon them is
work. Doubtless, there are some individuals, out of the 1,425 that
make up the total population, who are free from these failings, but
they are very few. . . . The missionaries undertook the reduction of
the gentiles with their accustomed zeal, but in our day the glamor of
learning has come upon us so suddenly that it has blinded some of the
very few persons of judgment [in Bejar], property owners in the main,
who clamored loudly: "Out with the friars, out with the
good-for-nothings." Thus they abolished the missions and divided

among themselves the lands they have not known how to cultivate and which they have left in a sad state of neglect.

....

The Americans from the north have taken possession of practically all the eastern part of Texas, in most cases without the permission of the authorities. They immigrate constantly, finding no one to prevent them, and take possession of the *sitio* [location] that best suits them without either asking leave or going through any formality other than that of building their homes. Thus the majority of inhabitants in the Department are North Americans, the Mexican population being reduced to only Bejar, Nacogdoches, and La Bahía del Espíritu Santo, wretched settlements that between them do not number three thousand inhabitants, and the new village of Guadalupe Victoria that has scarcely more than seventy settlers. The government of the state, with its seat at Saltillo, that should watch over the preservation of its most precious and interesting department, taking measures to prevent its being stolen by foreign hands, is the one that knows the least not only about actual conditions, but even about its territory.

....

The population [of Nacogdoches] does not exceed seven hundred persons, including the troops of the garrison, and all live in very good houses made of lumber, well built and forming straight streets, which make the place more agreeable. The women do not number one hundred. The civil administration is entrusted to an *Alcalde*, and in his absence, to the first and second *regidores*, but up until now, they have been, unfortunately, extremely ignorant men more worthy of pity than of reproof. From this fact, the North American inhabitants (who are in the majority) have formed an ill opinion of the Mexicans, judging them, in their pride, incapable of understanding laws, arts, etc. They continually try to entangle the authorities in order to carry out the policy most suitable to their perverse designs.

....

The Mexicans that live here are very humble people, and perhaps their intentions are good, but because of their education and environment they are ignorant not only of the customs of our great cities, but even of the occurrences of our Revolution, excepting a few persons who have heard about them. Accustomed to the continued trade with the North Americans, they have adopted their customs and habits, and one may say truly that they are not Mexicans except by birth, for they even speak Spanish with marked incorrectness.

8. "Lazy people of vicious character"

José María Sánchez, 1828*

Although unimpressed by the Texanos, Sánchez also took a dim view of Anglo American frontiersmen living in Texas. Sánchez's description of Americans on the Texas frontier should be compared with Shaler's and Sage's descriptions of New Mexicans and Californians.

Villa de Austin [San Felipe de Austin], April 27.—We continued along hills without trees, the ground being wet and muddy, until we arrived at a distance of four or five leagues from the settlement of San Felipe de Austin, where we were met by Mr. Samuel Williams, secretary of the empresario, Mr. Stephen Austin; and we were given lodging in a house that had been prepared for the purpose.

This village has been settled by Mr. Stephen Austin, a native of the United States of the North. It consists, at present, of forty or fifty wooden houses on the western bank of the large river known as *Rio de los Brazos de Dios*, but the houses are not arranged systematically so as to form streets; but on the contrary, lie in an irregular and desultory manner. Its population is nearly two hundred persons, of which only ten are Mexicans, for the balance are all Americans from the North with an occasional European. Two wretched little stores supply the inhabitants of the colony: one sells only whiskey, rum, sugar, and coffee; the other, rice, flour, lard, and cheap cloth. It may seem that these items are too few for the needs of the inhabitants, but they are not because the Americans from the North, at least the greater part of those I have seen, eat only salted meat, bread made by themselves out of corn meal, coffee, and home-made cheese. To these the greater part of those who live in the village add strong liquor, for

°José María Sánchez, "A Trip to Texas in 1828," trans. Carlos E. Castañeda, *Southwestern Historical Quarterly* 29, no. 4 (April 1926): 270–71, 273–74, 281. Reprinted by permission of the Texas State Historical Association.

they are in general, in my opinion, lazy people of vicious character. Some of them cultivate their small farms by planting corn; but this task they usually entrust to their negro slaves, whom they treat with considerable harshness. Beyond the village in an immense stretch of land formed by rolling hills are scattered the families brought by Stephen Austin, which today number more than two thousand persons. The diplomatic policy of this empresario, evident in all his actions, has, as one may say, lulled the authorities into a sense of security, while he works diligently for his own ends. In my judgment, the spark that will start the conflagration that will deprive us of Texas, will start from this colony. All because the government does not take vigorous measures to prevent it. Perhaps it does not realize the value of what it is about to lose.

May 12.—Our beasts of burden not being used to this climate suffered a great deal because of the bad forage. For this reason the general ordered that I should go to Mr. Groce, an American, to buy corn; and Mr. Chovell, wishing to accompany me, we started on our mission with a corporal and four soldiers through plains covered with grass and flowers, but at the same time so full of water that it seemed as if we were traveling through lakes, so deep did the horses sink in the bog. At about three in the afternoon we arrived at Groce's place and secured the corn we were to take back. We asked for some food, and it was given to us in the house, consisting, as is customary among Americans, of bacon, milk, and coffee; and when we had finished, we were taken upstairs to see Mr. Groce who was in bed and unable to move. Our visit was very short because we could not understand each other. After a short while, Mr. Groce's son came out with a doctor who appeared to be a pedant, and another young man, the son-in-law of Mr. Groce, all of them Americans, and by signs and sentences in Latin written with pencil they carried on a conversation with us, trivial in the main, but they did not deign to offer us shelter in the house, even though they saw us camping under the trees. Later, they asked us into the house for the sole purpose of showing us the wealth of Mr. Groce and to introduce us to three dogs called Ferdinand VII, Napoleon, and Bolívar. The indignation at seeing the name of the Colombian Liberator thus debased, cause Mr. Chovell to utter a violent oath which the impudent fellows did not understand or did not wish to understand. We returned immediately to our camp and went

9. Yndio, y Chino, Albarazado.

10. Yndio, y Negro, Sambaigo.

1. The census taker took special pains to determine the racial mixture of New Spain's inhabitants, and to give each its proper designation. Painting by Pedro Alonso O'Crouley, from *A Description of the Kingdom of New Spain* (1774), reproduced by permission of John Howell–Books.

2. Exaggerated accounts of Spanish cruelty to Indians circulated widely in the American colonies (see chapter II). This engraving by Theodore De Bry, which appeared in a 1598 edition of Bartolomé de las Casas's *Brief History of the Destruction of the Indies,* shows Spaniards forcing Indian women to work in the fields and Indian men to work in the mines. The Spaniards punished lagging workers by whipping them and dripping hot grease on their wounds.

3. The stereotype of Mexicans as sinister characters is well illustrated in this engraving from Colonel Frank Triplett's *Conquering the Wilderness,* published in 1883. This illustration was entitled "Greasers"; a nearby illustration carried the caption "Murderous Mexicans."

4. Rufus Sage (see chapter II) was typical of Anglo Americans who viewed adobe homes as "rude hovels" made of "uninviting mud walls." Because they were familiar only with wood frame houses, Anglo Americans were slow to appreciate the beauty of adobe and to understand its practical value in areas where wood was scarce. Pictured in this 1879 Santa Fe scene is a building said to be the oldest inhabited adobe in the country.

5. Some of California's most illustrious "Spanish" pioneers had Negro ancestry. This is Pío Pico, last Mexican governor of California, 1845–46. Pico's grandmother was a *mulata* according to the 1790 census. Some of Pío Pico's correspondence appears in chapter III. Photo courtesy of the Los Angeles County Museum of Natural History.

6. Mexicans disagreed about the best policy to adopt toward the incoming "gringo" immigrants and merchants (see chapter III). Men such as Governor Manuel Armijo of New Mexico warned the Mexican government that the Americans would be dangerous, but men such as José Antonio Navarro, pictured here, welcomed American immigrants. Navarro was one of three Mexicans who signed the Texas Declaration of Independence in 1836. Reproduction courtesy of the Institute of Texan Cultures.

7. Illustrative of the mythology that surrounds the Alamo is Henry McArdle's "Dawn at the Alamo." Measuring seven feet high and twelve feet wide, this painting was completed in 1883 after eight years of labor. The detail reproduced here shows Davy Crockett, in the lower right-hand corner, in an especially valiant pose. Above him is the cool and noble figure of Colonel William B. Travis, about to be dispatched by a sinister, grinning Mexican soldier. Reproduced courtesy of the Archives Division, Texas State Library.

8. Some Mexicans resisted United States military occupation of the Southwest, but others probably agreed with Angustias de la Guerra Ord, who said that the conquest "did not bother the Californians, least of all the women." An excerpt from her reminiscences appears in chapter III.

9. Luis de la Rosa, Mexico's minister in Washington, showed his government's concern for the welfare of its former citizens by protesting that their rights under the Treaty of Guadalupe-Hidalgo (see chapter IV) were violated in the California mines in 1849.

10. Artist A. F. Harmer expressed his vision of the bucolic "Days of the Dons" in this painting, c. 1885, showing Don Antonio F. Coronel and his wife, Doña Mariana. Coronel's reminiscences of the California mines appear in chapter IV. Reproduction courtesy of the Los Angeles County Museum of Natural History.

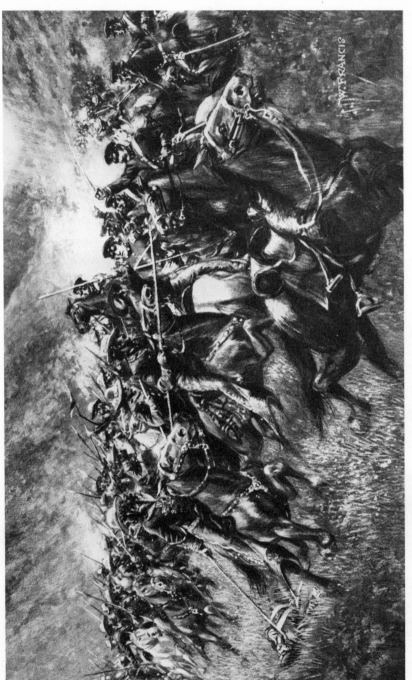

11. The United States occupation of the Southwest met staunch resistance among some Mexicans. In California, at San Pascual, Andrés Pico's mounted lancers routed Stephen Kearny's force, as shown in this painting, done in about 1909, "The Battle of San Pascual," by Walter Francis. Reproduced by permission of the Bancroft Library, University of California, Berkeley.

to bed without supper because we could not get anything. Groce is a man of 45 or 50 years of age; he came from the United States to establish himself on the eastern bank of the Brazos River in order to avoid paying the numerous creditors that were suing him. He brought with him 116 slaves of both sexes, most of which were stolen. These wretched slaves are the ones who cultivate the corn and cotton, both of which yield copious crops to Mr. Groce. Likewise, he has a great many head of cattle, innumerable hogs, and a great number of horses; but he is a man who does not enjoy his wealth because he is extremely stingy, and he treats his slaves with great cruelty.

June 2.—After the rays of the sun had found their way through the thick woods of Texas, we started again, and after crossing the Neches, whose flood waters were beginning to subside, we traveled over wooded and rolling country, troubled by the mosquitoes and a burning thirst occasioned by the excessive heat. We came across a poor house occupied by two children, ten or eleven years old, pale and dirty, signs that plainly indicated the poverty of this family of solitary Americans. We heard that the mother was in Nacogdoches. How strange are these people from the North! We halted at about three in the afternoon on the western bank of the Angelina River at the house of a poor American who treated us with considerable courtesy, a very rare thing among individuals of his nationality.

9. "Industrious, honest North American settlers"

Ayuntamiento of San Antonio, 1832*

Not all Mexicans took as jaundiced a view of the Yankees as José María Sánchez. Upper-class Mexicans, in particular, saw advantages for themselves and their provinces in increased commercial contact with *norteamericanos.* The ayuntamiento of San Antonio, in a special meeting in December 1832, expressed dissatisfaction with the neglect Texas had received from the Mexican government and urged that Texas remain

*Translated in Eugene C. Barker, "Native Latin American Contributions to the Colonization and Independence of Texas," *Southwestern Historical Quarterly* 46, no. 3 (January 1943): 328–29. Reprinted by permission of the Texas State Historical Association.

open to continued Anglo American immigration which would
benefit the area. The ayuntamiento was, of course, composed of
the elite of San Antonio, men such as Erasmo Seguín, José
Antonio Navarro, and Francisco Ruiz. How the lower class
viewed continued Yankee immigration cannot be easily determined. Although Texas may have become more prosperous as a
result of the influx of Yankees, neither Mexico nor the Texanos
benefited in the long run from the policy of liberal immigration
which set the stage for conflict in 1836.

What shall we say of the law of April 6, 1830? It absolutely
prohibits immigrants from North American coming into Texas, but
there are not enough troops to enforce it; so the result is that desirable
immigrants are kept out because they will not violate the law, while
the undesirable, having nothing to lose, come in freely. The industrious, honest North American settlers have made great improvements
in the past seven or eight years. They have raised cotton and cane and
erected gins and sawmills. Their industry has made them comfortable
and independent, while the Mexican settlements, depending on the
pay of the soldiers among them for money, have lagged far behind.
Among the Mexican settlements even the miserable manufacture of
blankets, hats and shoes has never been established, and we must buy
them either from foreigners or from the interior, 200 or 300 leagues
distant. We have had a loom in Béxar for two years, but the
inhabitants of Goliad and Nacogdoches know nothing of this ingenious
machine, nor even how to make a sombrero.

The advantages of liberal North American immigration are innumerable: (1) The colonists would afford a source of supply for the
native inhabitants. (2) They would protect the interior from Indian
invasions. (3) They would develop roads and commerce to New
Orleans and New Mexico. (4) Moreover, the ideas of government held
by North Americans are in general better adapted to those of the
Mexicans than are the ideas of European immigrants.

It is unquestionable that the lack of a government which shall feel
directly the needs of Texas and understand the means necessary to
multiply its population and protect its welfare has been, is, and will
continue to be the chief source of our sufferings.

10. "Waiting the result"   Thomas O. Larkin, 1846*

Although Mexico acted belatedly to close Texas to American settlers, it did not do so in New Mexico and California where foreign immigration was smaller. In these areas foreigners never became numerically dominant as they did in Texas. Nevertheless, they exerted considerable influence before, during, and after the Mexican War. Here, Thomas Oliver Larkin, United States consul at Monterey, assesses the influence and mood of the foreigners in California in April 1846, on the eve of war with Mexico. Note especially his judgment of the attitudes of the Californios toward a United States take-over of California. By 1846 Yankee infiltration of far northern Mexico had severed Texas from Mexico, and it was fully expected that California would follow the same pattern. Over two decades of contact between Mexicans and Anglo Americans on the Mexican frontier had prepared some people on each side for a transfer of sovereignty, even while alarming others.

There is from one thousand to twelve hundred Foreigners (including their families) in California, a majority of them residing in the Bay of San Francisco and on the Sacramento River. One third of the men are Citizens of this Country. Many of them never expect to speak the prevailing language of the Country. At this early period a knowledge of the English language is to a Merchant of more importance, than the Spanish.

In 1832 there was in the whole department two or three hundred Foreigners. There is now some eight or ten, who have resided here twenty-five years. They were sailors, now Farmers, entrapped from their vessels by the former Spanish Government. The first arrival of American settlers on the Sacramento, has been since 1840. Three fourths of the whole number of Foreigners in this country are Americans. Of the remaining fourth the subjects of Great Britain predominate. Of this fourth a majority are in expectation of being under the Government of the United States. Probably all are willing in preference to remaining as they now are. For the last five years the

*Thomas Oliver Larkin, "Description of California," Monterey, California, April 20, 1846, in George P. Hammond, ed., *The Larkin Papers* (Berkeley: 1953), 4:306–7. Originally published by the University of California Press; reprinted by permission of the Regents of the University of California. (For greater clarity I have taken the liberty of modernizing Larkin's spelling).

largest proportion of the Emigrants have arrived at New Helvetia
(Captain Sutter's establishment). Excepting a few of them from
"Oregon," they left Independence (Missouri) which is the starting
point every April or May, arriving on the Pacific in September or
October. Soon after their arrival at New Helvetia, they scatter over
the River Sacramento and the Bay of San Francisco, asking for Farms
from the Government, or settling on private grants by the owner's
consent. Some have arrived at the Pueblo de los Angeles (Town of the
Angels) near San Pedro, Via Santa Fe, some of whom had married at
the latter place. A few arrive by water from Valparaiso, Callao and
the Sandwich Islands.

A person traveling from San Diego to San Francisco, or Bodega can
stop at a Foreigner's farm house almost every few hours, and travel
without any knowledge of the Spanish language. Among the Emigrants from Independence, there are several German families, who
have resided in the United States, and are attached to her institutions.
A majority of them are from the Western States, Farmers, Mechanics
and labourers. Others are young men from the New England or
Middle States who left home seeking a fortune in the Western States,
and from thence to this country. The Emigration in 1845 amounted to
from four to five hundred. From the United States Newspaper reports
of 1845 from one to two thousand are expected to arrive this August
or October.

Many Foreigners now hold land under the expectation of being
under the flag of the United States. This idea already enhances the
value of land. No one league has yet brought one thousand dollars. On
the Sacramento four fifths of the farms are unoccupied, would not
bring two hundred dollars *per* league (five thousand seven hundred
and sixty acres). An unoccupied piece of land, of average quality
without any Horses or Cattle on it, sixty miles above New Helvetia of
four leagues on the River, by two leagues back (twelve miles by six or
forty-six thousand acres) sold this year under one thousand dollars by a
Californian to an English purchaser living in Monterey. The latter
now values it at two thousand dollars. A considerable portion of the
Californians are well aware, that their land and property would
increase in value, by change of Flags! Some are quietly waiting the
result. Some are indifferent on the subject, and others against it. Two
years after the safe and sure possession by the United States, . . .
they would object to returning to their present state and situation.

III.

Cultures Collide

Editor's Introduction

With increased contact between Americans and Mexicans after 1821, stereotypes hardened on both sides and opportunities for conflict increased. At the root ot this potential conflict was North American expansionism. Convinced of their cultural and racial superiority over Mexicans, Americans thought that territorial conquest would not only be easy, it would be justified; superior Anglo American institutions and stock would help to redeem the degenerate Mexicans. American frontiersmen had made no secret of their interest in Texas, even while it was still under Spanish rule. In 1821 the first Mexican diplomatic representative to the United States had predicted that the aggressive Americans would "be our sworn enemies . . . and there is no doubt that the object of their ambitious plans is the province of Texas."[1] Fifteen years later, in 1836, Mexico lost Texas. A decade after that, in 1846, the Mexican War—known in Mexico as *La guerra de '47* or *La invasión norteamericana*—got under way, and Mexico lost still more territory to the United States in a humiliating defeat.

These years of overt hostility between Mexicans and Americans are of considerable significance for Mexican Americans. The Texas Revolution and the Mexican War cost Mexico half of her national territory, and Mexicans living in this lost territory became the first substantial group of Mexican Americans. Years of bloodshed intensified existing prejudices into deep hatreds which lingered long after the fighting was forgotten, especially in Texas, where the most blood had been spilled.

I

Mexico's colonization law of 1824, designed to promote immigration, was extraordinarily successful in sparsely populated Texas. Juan N. Almonte, who wrote a statistical report on Texas based on an 1834

88

visit, estimated that North Americans outnumbered Mexicans in Texas by four to one (17,000 Americans, including 2,000 slaves, had come into Texas; the Mexican population he thought to be 4,000). His estimate of the number of Americans may be low.[2] Despite their numerical majority in Texas, the Americans had little political power because Texas was part of the state of Coahuila-Texas. Since Coahuila contained nine-tenths of the state's population, it dominated the legislature, and that rankled Texans who wanted more control over their own affairs.

To achieve greater autonomy, Anglo Americans, as well as some Texanos, favored separation of Texas from Coahuila. Americans, especially, wanted local self-government in order to protect those "inalienable rights" which they had brought from the United States. Most Americans in Texas had conveniently forgotten that they had become Mexican citizens and had given up such "rights" as public worship for Protestants (although the law requiring them to convert to Catholicism was never enforced), and trial by a jury of their peers. Mexican justice, which was slow, inefficient, and subject to *personalismo* in remote Texas, was especially annoying to the newcomers. Derived from Roman and Spanish tradition, Mexican law placed the state above the individual and assumed guilt until innocence was proven. Laws in Texas were sometimes made by the same alcaldes who administered and interpreted them. Customs duties, designed to make American immigrants trade more with Mexico than the United States, seemed ruinously high, and their enforcement hindered American smuggling. Even property rights were not sacrosanct in Texas. When President Vicente Guerrero liberated all slaves in Mexico in 1829, Americans in Texas (some 75 percent of whom were Southerners) were outraged at this violation of their "private property" without their consent—and this by a people who practiced *de facto* slavery in the form of debt peonage.

All of these grievances—and there were others—reflected deep cultural differences which formed an essential cause of conflict that led to the Texas Revolution in 1836.[3] Cultural differences manifested themselves most clearly in political issues which affected relations between Texas and Mexico. Yet within Texas itself, Samuel Lowrie, in his classic monograph *Culture Conflict in Texas*, found that "on the whole the relations between the Mexicans of Texas and the Anglo-American settlers were friendly." The two groups, Lowrie suggested, had mutual interests which led to cooperation, and they did

not come into frequent contact with one another.⁴ A minor
exception was in Haden Edward's empresario grant in East Texas,
where older Mexican families found their titles to land called into
question and protested to the Mexican government.

In 1826, after Mexican officials revoked this grant, Haden Edwards
called for a revolt and declared the entire state of Texas the
independent Republic of Fredonia. Although Edwards's revolt was
put down with the help of loyal American colonists under Stephen
Austin, it quite naturally contributed to Mexican fears that American
immigrants could be dangerous. To get a firsthand report on the
extent of the danger, the central government sent General Manuel
Mier y Terán to Texas in 1827. Alarmed that the Americans were not
assimilating, but instead traveling "with their political constitutions
in their pockets,"⁵ Mier y Terán made recommendations which led to
the passage of the Law of April 6, 1830. This closed Texas to further
United States immigration and attempted to reorient Texas commerce toward Mexico.

Although the Law of April 6, 1830 was not effective, tensions in
Texas seemed to subside by 1833, when Antonio López de Santa Anna
assumed the presidency of Mexico. Heading a liberal administration,
Santa Anna allowed greater regional autonomy and seemed ready to
alleviate many of the grievances of the Texans. The next year,
however, to save his tottering regime, Santa Anna thought it was
necessary to dissolve his own congress, abolish state governments, and
put himself at the head of a centralized dictatorship. From then on
relations between Santa Anna's administration and areas such as
Yucatán, Zacatecas, California, and Texas deteriorated steadily,
leading to revolts against the government. Due to its distance from
the capital and its proximity to the United States as a source of
supplies and manpower, the revolt in Texas was the most successful.

Hostilities began in the coastal town of Anáhuac in June 1835,
when a group of Texans, angered at the central government's efforts
to collect customs duties and curtail smuggling, captured a garrison
under Captain Antonio Tenorio. By autumn of 1835, partly in reprisal
for this act of defiance, Mexican troops under General Martín
Perfecto de Cós were on their way to Texas. Although sentiment for
independence was strong and growing, some Texans hoped for a reconciliation with the central government and others hoped to buy time
to obtain aid from the United States. Thus, Texas delegates who met
in a convention at San Felipe de Austin in early November of 1835 did
not vote for independence. Instead, they swore loyalty to the Mexican

Constitution of 1824, which had allowed considerable local autonomy, and resolved to resist the approaching centralist army. With the help of Texas Mexicans from Victoria, led by Captain Plácido Benavides, the Texans defeated Martín Perfecto de Cós at San Antonio. This initial victory brought only a slight reprieve; by February 1836 Santa Anna himself had reached the Rio Grande at the head of a formidable force.

Santa Anna's first objective in Texas was San Antonio de Béxar, the stronghold of Texas's Mexican population which, he thought, "could be relied upon to lend that cooperation which can be expected only of friends."[6] Leading Texas resistance at San Antonio was a desultory force composed chiefly of Anglo Americans. Although they had ample warning of Santa Anna's approach, the Texas forces allowed themselves to be caught by surprise. Colonel Juan N. Seguín, organizer of the Second Regiment of Texas Volunteers had sent Blas Herrera, one of his scouts, to the Rio Grande. When Herrera brought back word that Santa Anna was on his way, the Anglos in San Antonio refused to take a Mexican's warning seriously. Much of the local Mexican population, however, began to evacuate the town.[7] When Santa Anna arrived on February 23, the rebels holed up in the Alamo, a former mission built in 1718 that had been converted to a military barracks and fort. With reinforcements arriving daily, Santa Anna stormed the Alamo on March 6, killing all able bodied men—some 175.

As it is usually retold in the United States, the story of Santa Anna's victory at the Alamo makes heroes of Americans and villains of the Mexicans.[8] In reality, there was little heroism or villainy on either side. That was especially true for Texas Mexicans, most of whom were caught in the middle of the struggle, although some took sides. A few fought in the Alamo alongside Americans and died: Juan Abamillo, Juan Antonio Badillo, Carlos Espalier, Gregorio Esparza, Antonio Fuentes, and Andrés Nava—all from San Antonio—and Galba Fuqua of Gonzales.[9] Juan N. Seguín and Antonio Cruz would also have died in the Alamo had they not been sent on a dangerous ride through enemy lines to seek help from Colonel James Fannin at Goliad. Some Texas Mexicans had entered the Alamo during the first days of Santa Anna's siege but left when the cause appeared hopeless. The decision to fight with the Americans against fellow Mexicans must have been an agonizing one in the first place. The issue even divided families. Gregorio Esparza, for example, who died defending the Alamo, had a brother, Francisco, who fought on the Mexican side.

Like any residents of a war-torn land, most of the San Antonio

Texanos seem to have looked after their families' safety first, fighting on neither side and cooperating with the group in charge.[10] Many, of course, remained loyal to Santa Anna's regime, covertly if not overtly. Five weeks before Santa Anna's arrival, one American termed Texanos "the Mexican Tory party," and characterized them as the "internal enemy."[11] Colonel William B. Travis, who took command of the Alamo when Bowie fell ill, suspected that native informants had revealed his strategy to Santa Anna. In his last communication from the Alamo on March 3, Travis wrote that those Mexicans "who have not joined us in this extremity should be declared public enemies, and their property should aid in paying the expenses of the war."[12] Although Travis died in the Alamo, his attitude toward Mexicans lived on long after the revolution and affected even those Mexicans who fought for Texas, so deeply did hatreds run. Mexicans who fought on the Texas side, for example, found it harder to collect land bounties after the war ended than did their Anglo American counterparts.[13]

Although those Anglo Americans who died at the Alamo knew nothing of it, delegates from all over Texas had gathered at Washington-on-the-Brazos and signed a declaration of independence on March 2, 1836. The arrival of Santa Anna's army on Texas soil had turned public opinion in favor of a complete break with Mexico. Among the fifty-eight signatories of the Declaration of Independence were three Mexicans: Lorenzo de Zavala, José Antonio Navarro, and Francisco Ruiz. Flooded streams prevented Juan Antonio Padilla, delegate from Victoria, from reaching the convention. Lorenzo de Zavala would soon be elected vice-president of the Texas Republic.

On March 8 the commander in chief of the Texas army, Sam Houston, learned from two Mexicans that the Alamo had fallen but refused to believe them. A few days later the news was confirmed, and Houston began a judicious retreat across Texas with Santa Anna in pursuit. News of the Alamo, and Santa Anna's execution of nearly four hundred Texas prisoners at Goliad, helped to rally Texans to Houston's side. Although Houston's army had grown and Santa Anna's had diminished because he had divided his force, Santa Anna still held numerical superiority when he and Houston came to their final confrontation at San Jacinto on April 21. Confident that Houston would not attack, Santa Anna relaxed his guard, and Houston gained the element of surprise. What followed would be more accurately described as a slaughter than a battle, as Texans, with revenge for

Goliad and the Alamo on their minds, killed hundreds of Mexican soldiers.[14] Fighting alongside the victorious Texans at the Battle of San Jacinto was Juan N. Seguín's regiment of Texas Mexicans. Santa Anna himself was taken prisoner and forced to sign the Treaties of Velasco on May 14, which, among other things, ended hostilities, and ordered all Mexican troops to withdraw to the Mexican side of the Rio Grande. Although Mexico never ratified the treaties, which Santa Anna signed under obvious duress, Texas independence was virtually assured.

From the outbreak of hostilities to the Battle of San Jacinto, some Texas Mexicans had fought alongside the "gringos" against Santa Anna's government. In doing so they became traitors, despised by Mexico. They also came to be forgotten by most Americans in Texas, who viewed all Mexicans as bad Mexicans. Reflecting on the question in 1936, a century later, Texas writer Rubén Rendón Lozano wrote: "I do not think that the Saxon leaders of that era, who are justly praised, would approve of the manner in which the deeds of their Latin brothers have been ignored and neglected. To them, the Latin-Texans were . . . comrades in arms. . . . In all fairness, the latter should share equally in the glory that properly belongs to all heroes of the Texas War of Independence."[15] Rendón Lozano is correct, but Texas Mexicans ought not be remembered only as Texas patriots. It is more realistic to remember that most Mexicans in Texas found themselves caught in a struggle between two cultures, not knowing whether to remain loyal to Mexico or become loyal to Texas—whether to be traitors to Mexico or traitors to Texas. The Texano community divided over this question. Texas Mexicans, then, were caught squarely in the middle, just as they have been ever since.

II

The Mexican War of 1846 seemed to grow inexorably out of the struggle between Texas and Mexico, which did not come to an end with the Texans' successful revolt. Declining to recognize Texas independence, Mexico threatened to retake its lost province. For nearly a decade the boundary between Mexico and the Lone Star Republic remained aflame.

Conditions along the border were at their worst in 1842. That year

Mexican forces took Refugio and Goliad, and twice occupied San Antonio. These were raids, rather than attempts at occupation, however, for Mexico's internal problems prevented her from raising an army large enough to effectively reoccupy Texas. On their part, Texans sent an ill-disguised military expedition across the plains to Santa Fe in 1841, in an unsuccessful attempt to "liberate" New Mexico. The Texas "merchants" were captured, marched to Mexico City, and imprisoned. In retaliation, Texans preyed on Mexican merchants along the Santa Fe Trail, killing one prominent trader, Antonio José Chávez, in United States territory. In 1843 the Mexican government ordered the Santa Fe Trail closed. A group of Texans also crossed the Rio Grande to invade Mexico in 1842, but were captured at the town of Mier. Texas prisoners from the Mier and Santa Fe expeditions were marched to Mexico City and imprisoned in Perote Castle. Stories of their captors' cruelty circulated widely after some of the men were released, and this further enraged public opinion against Mexicans in both Texas and the United States. Texas Mexicans, some of whom had helped to resist the raiders from Mexico,[16] found increasingly that any Mexican in Texas was considered a bad Mexican. That issue, however, belongs to the next chapter.

Tensions between Mexico and Texas soon escalated into war between Mexico and the United States. Some Mexican officials had attributed the success of the Texas revolt to the American government, which had allowed its citizens to continue to cross freely into Texas and which had sent an ominous military force to the Texas border, ostensibly to chastize Indians. In 1836 Mexico warned that if the United States annexed Texas, Mexico would view it as a belligerent act. Until 1845 the United States restrained itself from annexing Texas, more because of northern opposition to adding another slave state than because of the threat of war with Mexico. Meanwhile, American expansionists set their sights beyond Texas to the Pacific Coast.

Since 1835, when President Andrew Jackson attempted to buy San Francisco Bay, the United States government had made no secret of its interest in acquiring California.[17] Thomas ap Catesby Jones, commander of the American Pacific squadron, provided a graphic demonstration of this interest in 1842 when he briefly captured California's capital, Monterey, on the mistaken notion that Mexico and the United States had gone to war.

In 1845 President James K. Polk, newly elected on an expansionist platform, took positive steps to acquire California. In the fall of 1845 Polk sent a secret message to Thomas Larkin, United States consul at Monterey, suggesting that Larkin persuade the Californios to secede from Mexico as Texans had done. California, Polk said, would be welcome to annex itself to the United States. Although some Californios thought well of the plan, Larkin did not have time to put it into operation. Meanwhile, that same autumn, Polk sent John Slidell to Mexico City with instructions to buy Upper California and New Mexico for up to $25 million (and more of northern Mexico if possible).

Slidell's task was particularly delicate, for Mexico had broken diplomatic relations with the United States. In March 1845 the Polk administration had invited a willing Texas to join the Union. The Mexican ambassador, who had warned that annexation would be regarded by his government as tantamount to an act of war, left Washington immediately. Still, Mexico did not declare war. President José Joaquín de Herrera, along with other influential leaders, believed that war would be unwise. Yet public opinion in Mexico demanded that the national honor be vindicated. Especially galling to Mexicans was the United States' claim that on the basis of the Treaties of Velasco Texas extended to the Rio Grande. Historically, the Texas boundary had been farther north at the Nueces River. John Slidell carried instructions to settle the Texas boundary question, to obtain payment of claims of United States citizens against Mexico, and to purchase more Mexican territory, but he had no opportunity. Bowing to popular opinion, the Mexican government refused to deal with Slidell.[18]

On January 13, 1846, the day after he received news of Slidell's rejection, Polk dispatched a force under General Zachary Taylor into the disputed area between the Nueces and the Rio Grande. Taylor took a position near the mouth of the Rio Grande, across from Matamoros, began building a fort, and blockaded the river—an act of war under international law.

On May 11, 1846, the United States declared war on Mexico, using as a pretext a skirmish between American and Mexican forces in the disputed area between the Rio Grande and the Nueces. In a war message to Congress, President Polk solemnly declared that "Mexico has passed the boundary of the United States, has invaded our territory and shed American blood upon American soil." "War exists," Polk said, "notwithstanding all our efforts to avoid it."

Although the war was popular in many quarters in the United States, the cynicism of Polk's declaration was not lost on all Americans. Abraham Lincoln, a new member of the House of Representatives, introduced to Congress his famous "Spot Resolutions," which demanded that the precise spot on which blood had been shed be identified. American blood, Lincoln recognized, had not been shed on American soil, but on disputed soil. That, of course, would not have sounded convincing in a war message.

In retrospect, the cynicism of Polk's message seems even clearer. Most historians now know that if Polk had failed to accomplish his objectives peacefully, he would have declared war on Mexico even without a convenient pretext. Indeed, Polk's private diary makes it plain that he and his cabinet had agreed to declare war on Mexico on May 9, a few hours *before* news reached Washington of the shedding of American blood on the Rio Grande.[19]

Until recently, Mexican Americans who looked into United States historical literature to understand the causes of the Mexican War have found it depicted as a struggle between a righteous, vigorous democracy and a series of backward, corrupt, and petty regimes in Mexico. Certainly most American historians have acknowledged United States expansionism as a cause of conflict. Nevertheless, they have implied that a pretentious and haughty Mexico brought on hostilities by refusing to give up its northern borderlands and accept the reality of America's Manifest Destiny. In recent years, however, historians have tended to place responsibility for the war more squarely on the United States, and to display greater insight into Mexico's reasons for resisting United States expansion.[20]

Some Mexican leaders refused to surrender Texas, choosing instead to fight Americans in what might be a losing war, because they believed that Texas was the first line of defense for the rest of the nation. The expansionist *Norteamericanos*, who talked openly of exporting their institutions and Anglo-Saxon blood to the "backward" peoples of the continent, had to be stopped before they swallowed up more of Mexico and more Mexicans. The war with the United States would not be a mere struggle for territory, but, as one high-ranking Mexican official wrote in 1840, it would be a struggle "of race, of religion, and of customs."[21] Thus, the clash of cultures which had contributed to the Texas revolt also helped to bring on the Mexican War. Americans, believing in their cultural superiority, thought that war with Mexico would be easy and quick, as well as profitable.

Mexicans knew that not only their territory was threatened, but their way of life, their *mexicanidad*, and this hardened their will to resist.[22]

III

When war was declared, Zachary Taylor's men won a series of victories in northern Mexico, while Colonel Stephen W. Kearny led the Army of the West over the Santa Fe Trail to seize New Mexico effortlessly in August 1846. New Mexico Governor Manuel Armijo had probably been bribed to surrender by James Magoffin, a Missouri merchant with long experience in New Mexico. Yet, even before he could have been bribed, Armijo had decided to leave New Mexico, thereby enabling Kearny to enter the province without resistance. Armijo has often been accused of cowardice, yet it should be remembered that he had sounded the tocsin against the Americans as early as 1827 and that the odds against him in 1846 were considerable. In the end, Armijo appears to have been both pragmatic and nationalistic.[23]

Kearny quickly created a civil government in New Mexico, wisely retaining Hispanos in most local offices. He placed two New Mexicans in high offices—Donaciano Vigil became territorial secretary and Antonio José Otero filled one of three territorial judgeships. Charles Bent, a longtime resident of Taos who was at home in both Mexican and American society, became governor.

The ease of the conquest was illusory. Most New Mexicans seemed determined to resist their conquerors. George F. Ruxton, an Englishman traveling through New Mexico in late 1846, found "the most bitter feeling and most determined hostility" against the Americans. The *patrona* of one family, he said, expressed relief upon discovering that he was an Englishman and exclaimed: *"Gracias á Dios,* a Christian will sleep with us tonight, and not an American!"[24] This hostility toward Americans, which some observers thought a result of the drunken, brawling, boasting, bullying conduct of American troops, soon manifested itself in guerrilla resistance. A Yankee in Santa Fe, for example, reported that American soldiers were "found beaten to death with rocks [,] no one knows by whom."[25]

New Mexicans' hostility toward their conquerors became most apparent when it was learned that some of the territory's leading citizens, men such as Diego Archuleta, Tomás Ortiz, Agustín Durán, and Padre Antonio José Martínez, had organized a revolt. Scheduled for Christmas Eve, 1846, the rebellion was thwarted when the wife of one of the conspirators, fearful of bloodshed, warned the Americans. Although some of the leaders of the resistance movement fled to Chihuahua, the planned insurrection did not come to an end. It was only delayed. On January 19, 1847, disaffected Mexicans joined with Pueblo Indians at Taos to rise up against their conquerors. This Taos Rebellion ended only when the United States Army besieged the Pueblo of Taos and killed many of the rebels. Rumors of still another rebellion by Mexicans at Taos persisted, necessitating the maintenance of an army garrison there until 1851.[26] Opposition to the American conquest of New Mexico seems to have been more widespread than most writers have suggested.[27]

Like the New Mexicans, Californians also revolted against the Americans after an apparently peaceful conquest. In June 1846, even before news of war between Mexico and the United States reached California, disaffected American immigrants had led a revolt to "free" California from Mexico. Following the Texas model, these "Bear Flaggers" established an independent republic, but their revolt merged into the bigger war when a United States naval force occupied Monterey in July. American forces met no resistance in occupying California. The territory's two most important political leaders, Commandant General José Castro and Governor Pío Pico, announced that resistance was futile without support from their government and left for Mexico. They hoped, however, that aid from Mexico would arrive and permit a reconquest.

Help from Mexico did not materialize, but by September the high-handed military leadership of Lieutenant Archibald Gillespie at Los Angeles provoked Californios in the South to revolt. Led by such men as José María Flores, Andrés Pico, and José Antonio Carrillo, the Californios won two notable victories and for a brief time held southern California from Santa Barbara to San Diego. At Los Angeles they defeated Gillespie's forces in the "Battle of the Old Woman's Gun." Ironically, Gillespie had earlier remarked that "Californians of Spanish blood . . . have a holy terror of the American rifle, and will never expose themselves to make an attack."[28] At San Pascual, some thirty-five miles north of San Diego, mounted lancers led by Andrés Pico routed Kearny's newly arrived force from New Mexico. At the Battle of San Pascual, described by one historian as "the largest armed conflict ever to occur within the boundaries of California,"[29]

Pico did not follow up his victory and capture Kearny's force. By January 1847 the Californios' resistance had been broken at Los Angeles by a better equipped American army, but the fact that the Californios had fought back seems to have raised many Americans' estimation of them. As Kearny put it: "They have been most cruelly and shamefully abused by our people. . . . Had they not resisted they would have been unworthy [of] the name of men."[30]

Rumors persisted that the Californios were plotting another revolt, and the conquerors remained uneasy. In February 1848 three suspects, Antonio Chávez, Francisco Rico, and Gabriel de la Torre, were required to post bonds of $5,000 each and to swear not to commit any hostile act against the government.[31] "The native sons," wrote one observer in June 1848, "have hope that the Americans will tire of a long and stubborn war and that in some time they will be left to live in their land in peace and tranquility."[32] That, of course, would not come to pass.

The initial lack of military resistance by New Mexicans and Californians during the war did not indicate that they welcomed American conquest. On the contrary, a significant number of Mexicans in each area opposed the gringos openly or covertly. Some Mexicans, of course, especially in the upper class, had become convinced that they could not prosper under Mexican government; they stood to profit from the new arrangement. Men such as Mariano Vallejo in California and Donaciano Vigil in New Mexico collaborated openly with the enemy. Since history is usually written by the winning side, such collaborators have won a dominant place in literature on the Southwest.

The reaction of the Mexican community in the Southwest—including much of the upper class—to the coming of the gringos was a mixed one, just as during the Texas revolt. Some collaborated with the enemy, some resisted, and others remained indifferent. The subject needs further research before clearer conclusions can be drawn.

IV

Despite the American seizure of California and New Mexico and Taylor's victories in northeastern Mexico, Mexicans refused to come to the bargaining table. They did so only after the "gringos" occupied Mexico City itself, which Winfield Scott did in September 1847 after days of bitter fighting—this in spite of Mexico's internal political discord. Even then, the Mexican negotiators did not sign the Treaty of Guadalupe Hidalgo, which ended the war, until February 1848.

The North American Invasion cost Mexico one-third of its territory (one-half, counting Texas). It could have been worse. Some United States senators, such as Sam Houston, did not want to ratify the Treaty of Guadalupe Hidalgo, arguing that the United States should take still more of northern Mexico. "The Mexicans," Houston said in a speech in 1848, "are no better than Indians, and I see no reason why we should not go on in the same course now and take their land."[33] A vocal group of senators also wanted to take less of Mexico than the treaty provided for, but they constituted a clear minority. Indeed, a movement to take *all* of Mexico had gained broad support among politicians and journalists. Some of these ultraexpansionists, especially Southerners, abandoned the idea of taking all of Mexico when they reflected on the prospect of having to absorb Mexico's people along with its territory. Thus the American sense of cultural and racial superiority that contributed to bringing on war with Mexico contributed also to bringing it to a judicious conclusion. In May, the United States Senate finally approved the Treaty of Guadalupe Hidalgo and settled for a third of Mexico (coincidentally the third with the fewest Mexicans). There remained, however, those who agreed with the *New York Herald* when it argued on February 25, 1848: "We will take a large portion [of Mexico] now, and the balance at a more convenient season."[34]

Conflicts between Mexicans and Americans continued into the 1850s, as private American citizens led filibustering expeditions from United States soil. Filibusters such as William Walker, who invaded Baja California in 1853–54, and Henry Alexander Crabb, who entered Sonora in 1857, kept tension high along the border. Along the Rio Grande, international cattle thieves kept Southwest Texas in turmoil until the 1880s.

The breakdown of relations between Mexicans and Americans on the international level had its counterpart in relations between Mexican Americans and Anglo Americans in the Southwest. Years of violent conflict left deep wounds on both sides, wounds which would not heal rapidly after the fighting stopped. Mexicans who had become Americans as a result of the Texas Revolution and the Mexican War knew well the depth of those wounds.

1. "I am warning you"

Manuel Mier y Terán, 1828* & 1829**

Well before the tensions in Texas climaxed in open rebellion, some farsighted officials expressed fear that the growing influence of the North Americans would result in the loss of Texas. Among those officials was General Manuel Mier y Terán, a hero of the Mexican war for independence.

In the fall of 1827, President Guadalupe Victoria dispatched Mier y Terán at the head of a special commission charged with inspecting the Texas-United States boundary and making recommendations for a policy which would assure that Texas remain part of Mexico. The commissioners reached Laredo in February 1828, then crossed Texas, going by way of San Antonio and Austin's colony at San Felipe. They reached Nacogdoches in East Texas in early June 1828. There, on June 30, Mier y Terán wrote a personal letter to President Victoria, describing the extent of Anglo influence in East Texas and voicing his fears for the future of Texas. A year later, in November 1829, as military commander of Mexico's eastern interior provinces, Mier y Terán expressed his sentiments even more strongly in a letter to the Mexican minister of war. Portions of these two letters follow. Mier y Terán's report prompted passage of the Law of April 6, 1830, which closed the Mexican border to further American immigration.

Manuel Mier y Terán, 1828

. . . As one covers the distance from Béjar to this town, he will note that Mexican influence is proportionately diminished until on arriving in this place he will see that it is almost nothing. And indeed, whence could such influence come? Hardly from superior numbers in population, since the ratio of Mexicans to foreigners is one to ten; certainly not from the superior character of the Mexican population, for exactly the opposite is true, the Mexicans of this town comprising

---

*Mier y Terán to Guadalupe Victoria, Nacogdoches, June 30, 1828, in Allaine Howren, "Causes and Origin of the Decree of April 6, 1830," *Southwestern Historical Quarterly* 16, no. 4 (April 1913): 395–98. Reprinted by permission of the Texas State Historical Association.

**Mier y Terán to Minister of War, Pueblo Viejo, November 14, 1829, from Ohland Morton, *Terán and Texas: A Chapter in Texas-Mexican Relations* (Austin: 1948), pp. 99–101. Reprinted by permission of the Texas State Historical Association.

what in all countries is called the lowest class—the very poor and very ignorant. The naturalized North Americans in the town maintain an English school, and send their children north for further education; the poor Mexicans not only do not have sufficient means to establish schools, but they are not of the type that take any thought for the improvement of its public institutions or the betterment of its degraded condition. Neither are there civil authorities or magistrates; one insignificant little man—not to say more—who is called an *alcalde*, and an *ayuntamiento* that does not convene once in a lifetime is the most that we have here at this important point on our frontier; yet, wherever I have looked, in the short time that I have been here, I have witnessed grave occurrences, both political and judicial. It would cause you the same chagrin that it has caused me to see the opinion that is held of our nation by these foreign colonists, since, with the exception of some few who have journeyed to our capital, they know no other Mexicans than the inhabitants about here, and excepting the authorities necessary to any form of society, the said inhabitants are the most ignorant of negroes and Indians, among whom I pass for a man of culture. Thus, I tell myself that it could not be otherwise than that from such a state of affairs should arise an antagonism between the Mexicans and foreigners, which is not the least of the smoldering fires which I have discovered. Therefore, I am warning you to take timely measures. Texas could throw the whole nation into revolution.

The colonists murmur against the political disorganization of the frontier, and the Mexicans complain of the superiority and better education of the colonists; the colonists find it unendurable that they must go three hundred leagues to lodge a complaint against the petty pickpocketing that they suffer from a venal and ignorant *alcalde*, and the Mexicans with no knowledge of the laws of their own country, nor those regulating colonization, set themselves against the foreigners, deliberately setting nets to deprive them of the right of franchise and to exclude them from the *ayuntamiento*. Meanwhile, the incoming stream of new settlers is unceasing; the first news of these comes by discovering them on land already under cultivation, where they have been located for many months; the old inhabitants set up a claim to the property, basing their titles of doubtful priority, and for which there are no records, on a law of the Spanish government; and thus arises a lawsuit in which the *alcalde* has a chance to come out with some money. In this state of affairs, the town where there are no magistrates is the one in which lawsuits abound, and it is at once evident that in Nacogdoches and its vicinity, being most distant from the seat of the general government, the primitive order of things should take its course, which is to say that this section is being settled up without the consent of anybody.

In spite of the enmity that usually exists between the Mexicans and the foreigners, there is a most evident uniformity of opinion on one point, namely the separation of Texas from Coahuila and its organization into a territory of the federal government. This idea, which was conceived by some of the colonists who are above the average, has become general among the people and does not fail to cause considerable discussion. In explaining the reasons assigned by them for this demand, I shall do no more than relate what I have heard with no addition of my own conclusions, and I frankly state that I have been commissioned by some of the colonists to explain to you their motives, notwithstanding the fact that I should have done so anyway in the fulfillment of my duty.

They claim that Texas in its present condition of a colony is an expense, since it is not a sufficiently prosperous section to contribute to the revenues of the state administration; and since it is such a charge it ought not to be imposed upon a state as poor as Coahuila, which has not the means of defraying the expenses of the corps of political and judicial officers necessary for the maintenance of peace and order. Furthermore, it is impracticable that recourse in all matters should be had to a state capital so distant and separated from this section by deserts infected by hostile savages. Again, their interests are very different from those of the other sections, and because of this they should be governed by a separate territorial government, having learned by experience that the mixing of their affairs with those of Coahuila brings about friction. The native inhabitants of Texas add to the above other reasons which indicate an aversion for the inhabitants of Coahuila; also the authority of the *comandante* and the collection of taxes is disputed.

That which most impressed me in view of all these conditions is the necessity of effective government in Nacogdoches at least, since it is the frontier with which the Republic is most in contact. Every officer of the federal government has immense districts under his jurisdiction, and to distribute these effectively it is necessary to give attention to economy as well as to government and security. The whole population here is a mixture of strange and incoherent parts without parallel in our federation: numerous tribes of Indians, now at peace, but armed and at any moment ready for war, whose steps toward civilization should be taken under the close supervision of a strong and intelligent government; colonists of another people, more progressive and better informed than the Mexican inhabitants, but also more shrewd and unruly; among these foreigners are fugitives from justice, honest laborers, vagabonds and criminals, but honorable and dishonorable alike travel with their political constitution in their pockets, demanding the privileges, authority and officers which such a constitution guarantees.

Manuel Mier y Terán, 1829

The department of Texas is contiguous to the most avid nation in the world. The North Americans have conquered whatever territory adjoins them. In less than half a century, they have become masters of extensive colonies which formerly belonged to Spain and France, and of even more spacious territories from which have disappeared the former owners, the Indian tribes. There is no Power like that to the north, which by silent means, has made conquests of momentous importance. Such dexterity, such constancy in their designs, such uniformity of means of execution which always are completely successful, arouses admiration. Instead of armies, battles, or invasions, which make a great noise and for the most part are unsuccessful, these men lay hands on means, which, if considered one by one, would be rejected as slow, ineffective, and at times palpably absurd. They begin by assuming rights, as in Texas, which it is impossible to sustain in a serious discussion, making ridiculous pretensions based on historical incidents which no one admits—such as the voyage of La Salle, which was an absurd fiasco, but serves as a basis for their claim to Texas. Such extravagant claims as these are now being presented for the first time to the public by dissembling writers; the efforts that others make to submit proofs and reasons are by these men employed in reiterations and in enlarging upon matters of administration in order to attract the attention of their fellow-countrymen, not to the justice of the claim, but to the profit to be gained from admitting it. At this stage it is alleged that there is a national demand for the step which the government meditates. In the meantime, the territory against which these machinations are directed, and which has usually remained unsettled, begins to be visited by adventurers and *empresarios;* some of these take up their residence in the country, pretending that their location has no bearing upon the question of their government's claim or the boundary disputes; shortly, some of these forerunners develop an interest which complicates the political administration of the coveted territory; complaints, even threats, begin to be heard, working on the loyalty of the legitimate settlers, discrediting the efficiency of the existing authority and administration; and the matter having arrived at this stage—which is precisely that of Texas at this moment—diplomatic maneuvers begin: They incite uprisings in the territory in question and usually manifest a deep concern for the rights of the inhabitants.

2. "The two people cannot mingle together"

Committee of Vigilance and Public Safety for the Municipality of San Augustín, 1835*

Mier y Terán had read the signs correctly. The Americans in Texas would use concern for their political rights as a justification for revolt. The American point of view toward Mexico and Mexicans is well illustrated in the following resolution drawn up by a citizens committee in San Augustín. Both in its language and procedure, it is decidedly Anglo-Saxon.

In attempting to secure their "rights," Americans in Texas had formed municipal committees of safety and correspondence, borrowing a technique from their revolutionary forefathers. First tried in Texas during a time of crisis in 1832, the committees of correspondence had elected delegates to a statewide convention. This manner of bringing citizens together outside of legal channels disturbed some of the Texas Mexicans, such as Ramón Músquiz, *jefe político* in San Antonio, who sympathized with the Americans' goals. Committees of correspondence, such as that of San Augustín, were formed again in 1835 and became an

---

*Resolution of December 22, 1835, published in the *Telegraph and Texas Register* (San Felipe de Austin), January 23, 1836, pp. 102–3.

important vehicle for bringing on the declaration of independence. It is significant that the San Augustín committee, after discussing its political grievances, concluded by arguing that Mexicans and Americans were culturally unsuited to live together.

"Shall the next Convention make a Declaration of Independence, and form a Republican Government for Texas?"

This committee, after much reflection, and after viewing this momentous subject . . . cannot but take the affirmative of the proposition. And in discussing it before the people of Texas, they feel peculiar pleasure in their knowledge of the fact, that they are addressing themselves to the unbiased intelligence of a high minded, patriotic, and enlightened community. . . . They are duly sensible that facts and reason are all that ought or will be listened to.

This proposition naturally divides itself into two parts:
First. Has Texas the moral and political right to declare herself independent of the Mexican government?
On this first part of the proposition, the reasons assigned in the declaration of the Convention appear to this committee conclusive. To wit,
That as Santa Anna, &c. had, by force of arms, overthrown the federal institutions of Mexico, and dissolved the social compact which exists between Texas and the other members of the Mexican confederacy, Texas was no longer morally or civilly bound by the compact of union.
This correct and sensible declaration of the late Convention, is an elemental part of national law, and is broadly recognized and enforced by the standard writers on that law.
It was the foundation of the English revolution of 1688, which banished the Stuart family from the throne . . .

Second. If the people of Texas have the moral and political right to declare themselves independent of the Mexican government, is it expedient for them now to exercise that right?

In order to illustrate this part of the proposition, the committee propose[s] to take a rapid review of the past.

In the year of eighteen hundred and twenty-one, Texas was an uninhabited wilderness, infested by hostile Indians, from the Sabine river to San Antonio; not excepting Nacogdoches itself. Encouraged by the invitation of the colonization laws, the settlement of the wilderness was commenced, and continued by individual enterprises, entirely unaided by succors of any kind from the government; the settlement of the country has not cost the government one cent. The emigrants dared to settle an unreclaimed wilderness, the haunt of wild beasts, and the home of the daring and hostile savages; and in so doing, poured out their blood like water. . . . In the successful progress of the settlement of the country, and in the midst of the enactment of the flood of laws proffering protection to the persons and property of the emigrants, General [Vicente] Guerrero came to the office of the presidency of the republic. He and his friends spoke of liberty as a goddess, before whose shrine they were wont to worship; and the inviolable sacredness of person and property; friendship to the emigrants, &c.

Among the first acts of his administration, was one to free all the negroes: this he said, was to give splendor to his official career, and make an epoch in the history of the republic. . . .

To Guerrero, succeeded [Anastacio] Bustamente, the vice-president. The latter was considered the antipode of the former. Under his rule was enacted the law of the sixth of April, 1830, the eleventh section of which prohibited the emigration of natives of the United States of the north [into Texas], but none other: this totally separated many of the first emigrants from their relatives and friends, who intended to have removed to the country, and had disposed of their property to do so. Families, and the nearest ties of kindred and friendship were thus severed.

Bustamente was displaced by Santa Anna, who was extolled as the great apostle of equal rights. He was represented as standing in the portico of the temple of Mexican liberty, with his brows bound with a patriot's wreath, unrolling and vindicating the constitution and laws of his country.

Him, the first Convention memorialised, petitioned, we will not say supplicated: he answered all their prayers with the silence of contempt.

The second Convention again petitioned and memorialised this man, and "to make assurance doubly sure, and take a bond of fate," sent one of their most respectable and influential citizens [Stephen F. Austin] on to the city of Mexico, to solicit in person in behalf of the rights of the people of Texas. This distinguished citizen . . . Santa Anna . . . without ceremony thrust into prison, and continued his dark and gloomy durance for perhaps more than eighteen months; and then only released him to administer to his own wants. Enough. Fellow-citizens, what are we contending for? Can true reconciliation ever grow where roots of hatred have struck so deep? His guaranty, what would it avail before the god of his devouring ambition?

The Anglo-Americans and the Mexicans, if not primitively a different people, habit, education and religion, have made them essentially so. The two people cannot mingle together. The strong prejudices that existed at the first emigrations, so far from having become softened and neutralised contact, having increased many fold. And as long as the people of Texas belong to the Mexican nation, their interests will be jeopardised, and their prosperity cramped. And they will always be more or less affected by the excitements of that revolutionary people.

Of all the times for Texas to declare herself independent, the present is perhaps the most exquisitely appropriate. The causes will fully justify the act before the enlightened world, and win its approbation.

....

Then, fellow-citizens, let us instruct our delegates to the next convention to pass a *Declaration of Independence* with one loud and unanimous voice. . . .

3. "Their decision irrevocably sealed their fate"

Antonio López de Santa Anna, 1837*

It seems safe to suggest that the events of March 6, 1836 at the Alamo have contributed more to Mexican American school children's loss of self-esteem than any other historical episode. Children learn that thousands of Mexicans needlessly and wantonly slaughtered some 175 Americans who courageously chose to die.

The story of the Alamo was never so simple. We have seen that not all of the defenders of the Alamo were Yankees. Nor did they choose to die. Although Colonel Travis's slogan was "Victory or Death," he clearly expected victory. "I believe this place can be maintained," he wrote, and from his first call for help, on February 23, through March 3, Travis expected more men to come to his assistance. At the beginning of the siege, Santa Anna had only some 600 troops. By the end of the siege, some 2,400 had arrived, not the 6,000 sometimes suggested. Most of the Mexican soldiers were bewildered Indian conscripts who did not even speak Spanish. Woefully ill-equipped, they were no match for superior Texas artillery and long rifles. Travis, then, had reason to remain confident of victory until toward the end when it became clear that no help from fellow-Texans would be forthcoming.[1]

In the document that follows, Santa Anna explains his side of the battle of the Alamo. Writing to defend his own actions, Santa Anna naturally tries to put himself in the best possible light. He probably minimizes his losses at the Alamo, for example, and his explanation for the necessity of storming it was later questioned by some of his own officers. It is easy to suggest in retrospect that Santa Anna, who considered his victory at the Alamo "but a small affair," committed errors in judgment; it is more important to remember that there was another side to the Alamo which Santa Anna here presents.

---

*"Manifesto which General Antonio López de Santa-Anna Addresses to his Fellow Citizens Relative to his Operations During the Texas Campaign and his Capture 10 of May 1837" (Vera Cruz, 1837), trans. and ed. Carlos E. Castañeda, *The Mexican Side of the Texas Revolution* (Dallas: 1928), pp. 13–14, 18–19. Reprinted by permission of Graphic Ideas, Inc.

1. Walter Lord, "Myths and Realities of the Alamo," *The American West* 5, no. 3 (May 1968): 18–25, provides a succinct summary of myths about the Alamo and their origins.

The enemy fortified itself in the Alamo, overlooking the city. A siege of a few days would have caused its surrender, but it was not fit that the entire army should be detained before an irregular fortification hardly worthy of the name. Neither could its capture be dispensed with, for bad as it was, it was well equipped with artillery, had a double wall, and defenders who, it must be admitted, were very courageous and caused much damage to Béxar. Lastly, to leave a part of the army to lay siege to it, the rest continuing on its march, was to leave our retreat, in case of a reverse, if not entirely cut off, at least exposed, and to be unable to help those who were besieging it, who could be reenforced only from the main body of the advancing army. This would leave to the enemy a rallying point, although it might be only for a few days. An assault would infuse our soldiers with that enthusiasm of the first triumph that would make them superior in the future to those of the enemy. It was not my judgment alone that moved me to decide upon it, but the general opinion expressed in a council of war, made up of generals, that I called even though the discussions which such councils give rise to have not always seemed to me appropriate. Before undertaking the assault and after the reply given to Travis who commanded the enemy fortification, I still wanted to try a generous measure, characteristic of Mexican kindness, and I offered life to the defendants who would surrender their arms and retire under oath not to take them up again against Mexico. Colonel Don Juan Nepomuceno Almonte, through whom this generous offer was made, transmitted to me their reply which stated that they would let us know if they accepted and if not, they would renew the fire at a given hour. They decided on the latter course and their decision irrevocably sealed their fate.

On the night of the fifth of March, four columns having been made ready for the assault under the command of their respective officers, they moved forward in the best order and with the greatest silence, but the imprudent huzzas of one of them awakened the sleeping vigilance of the defenders of the fort and their artillery fire caused such disorder among our columns that it was necessary to make use of the reserves. The Alamo was taken, this victory that was so much and so justly celebrated at the time, costing us seventy dead and about three hundred wounded, a loss that was also later judged to be avoidable and charged, after the disaster of San Jacinto, to my incompetence and precipitation. I do not know of a way in which any fortification, defended by artillery, can be carried by assault without the personal losses of the attacking party being greater than those of the enemy, against whose walls and fortifications the brave assailants can present only their bare breasts. It is easy enough, from a desk in a peaceful office, to pile up charges against a general out on the field but this cannot prove anything more than the praiseworthy desire of making war less disastrous. But its nature being such, a general has no power over its immutable laws. Let us weep at the tomb of the brave Mexicans who died at the Alamo defending the honor and the rights of their country. They won lasting claim to fame and the country can never forget their heroic names.

4. "Texians! render every possible assistance"

Juan Nepomuceno Seguín, 1836*

Although Santa Anna had been defeated at San Jacinto and had signed the Treaties of Velasco ending the war, Texans continued to fear another invasion from Mexico. In June, 1836, when further trouble seemed imminent, Colonel Juan N. Seguín received instructions to evacuate the inhabitants of San Antonio, who were chiefly Mexicans. Seguín, a native of San Antonio who had fought on the side of the Anglo Americans throughout the Texas revolution, had become military commander and provisional mayor of San Antonio. In the document that follows, published originally in a newspaper at Columbia, the *Telegraph and Texas Register,* Seguín appealed to fellow Texanos to prove their loyalty to independent Texas by abandoning their homes and moving eastward.

Seguín's warning, which turned out to be a false alarm, went unheeded by the Mexican residents of San Antonio. At the very least, the incident illustrates division within the Mexican community. It is not possible, however, given the present state of research, to say why Mexicans did not evacuate San Antonio. Perhaps some remained loyal to Mexico; perhaps some had little confidence in Seguín's predictions; more likely, they did not want to abandon their homes and preferred to take their

---

*Juan N. Seguín, *Telegraph and Texas Register,* September 21, 1836. *Telegraph and Texas Register,* November 9, 1836.

chances with Mexican troops. To some Anglo Americans, however, the San Antonians' failure to move was taken as a sign of disloyalty to Texas. Months later, in October 1836, when Mexican forces entered San Antonio and drove off some cattle, the *Telegraph and Texas Register* expressed unrestrained delight at the San Antonians' bad fortune.

Telegraph and Texas Register, September 21, 1836

We judge that the following authentic articles will be perused with satisfaction, as they afford proofs of the services and patriotism of Lieut. Col. John N. Seguin, who has persevered in his attachment to the cause of liberal principles, and whose gallantry at San Jacinto, was conspicuous. Col. Seguin, was a "Liberal" among the Mexicans, and is so among the Texians: a conduct which reflects on him the greatest credit, because some of his countrymen, who from friends have become our enemies, appear to have identified their *principles* with their *party*, condemning in *Independent* Texas the same doctrines she had proclaimed as an integral part of the Mexican Republic. We would insert the articles mentioned, in their original Spanish; but the want of a printer able to compose in that language prevents our doing so.

John N. Seguin, Lieut. Colonel of the Army of Texas, to the inhabitants of Bexar.

Fellow Citizens: Military movements compel me to repair to Head Quarters. I have in consequence to evacuate this town, but previous to doing so, I require your aid to carry off the cattle and place them where the enemy cannot make use of them. I have no doubt that you will assist cheerfully in this measure, thereby furnishing to the supreme government of Texas a proof of your attachment to the just cause, and the beloved liberty we are contending for. If, on the contrary, you fail to render this slight service, your disaffection will be manifest; and although a matter of regret to the said supreme government, yet it can then no longer treat you as Texians, but, perhaps, as enemies. Be not deceived with the idea that we have not forces wherewith to repel force—time will show to the contrary, and will convince you that Texas must be free.

Fellow Citizens: your conduct on this day is going to decide your fate before the general government of Texas. If you maintain your post as mere lookers-on; if you do not abandon the city and retire into the interior of Texas, that its army may protect you, you will, without fail, be treated as real enemies, and will suffer accordingly. My ties of birth and the friendship I entertain towards you, cause me to desire your happiness, and I therefore address you in that spirit of truth which in me is characteristic.

TEXIANS! render every possible assistance, and soon shall you enjoy your liberty and your property, which is the wish of your country man and friend,

John N. Seguin
Bexar, 21st June, 1836

Telegraph and Texas Register, November 9, 1836

We learn from Col. Seguin, that a company of the enemy, some three weeks since, entered San Antonio, their object being to drive off cattle, and to annoy that portion of the Mexican citizens, favorable to our cause. Should our Mexican friends receive harm from these predatory excursions of the enemy, they will, perhaps, in future, better appreciate the advice and orders of our friend, Col. Seguin, who cautioned them of the danger of remaining in Bejar, and urged the necessity of their assisting him in driving off the stock, and removing eastward, which would be proof to our government, of their attachment to the just cause in which we were engaged. But the good advice and admonition of Col. Seguin, were little attended to; and we shall be truly glad, if the enemy and our pretended friends in Bejar, do not save us the trouble of securing the stock and other property west of the Guadaloupe.

Our enemy, no doubt, are doing what we should have done some time since. It is well enough to have assistance in effecting an object, and in short time, we shall not be put to the trouble of driving stock, or taking care of Spanish cattle.

5. "War . . . our final salvation"

José María Tornel y Mendívil, 1837*

The end of the Texas revolution found Mexico anxious to retake Texas and deeply suspicious of the motives of the United States. Divided and troubled at home, Mexico was ill-equipped to reconquer Texas. Yet, many Mexicans, subscribing to a domino or containment theory, correctly forecasted that the United States must be stopped at Texas or it would take still more of Mexico.

Such a prediction was made by José María Tornel y Mendívil, who served as secretary of war during the Texas Revolution. Tornel y Mendívil was convinced that American diplomacy for the previous two decades had been designed to take Mexican territory and that the sending of United States troops to the Texas border in 1836 to chastise Indians was "a pretext for intervention." The real object of their presence, Tornel y Mendívil argued, "was to help the rebels *in case of necessity.*" The necessity never arose. The Anglo Americans, he wrote, "look upon us as pigmies, objects deserving of their pity. They consider our possessions but a fair prize of their greed." What choice, then, had Mexico but to go on the offensive and retake Texas, or lose more of Mexico?

From the state of Maine to Louisiana a call has been made in the public squares to recruit volunteers for the ranks of the rebels in Texas.

Everywhere meetings have been held, presided over, as in New York, by public officials of the government, to collect money, buy ships, enlist men, and fan that spirit of animosity that characterizes all the acts of the United States with regard to Mexico. The newspapers, paid by the land speculators, without excepting the *Globe* of Washington, which is doubtless an official organ, have sponsored the insurrection of Texas with the same ardor they would have supported the uprising of 1776. Our character, our customs, our very rights have been painted in the darkest hues, while the crimes of the Texans have

---

*José María Tornel y Mendívil, "Relations Between Texas, The United States of America and the Mexican Republic" (Mexico, 1837), trans. and ed. Carlos E. Castañeda, *The Mexican Side of the Texas Revolution* (Dallas: 1928), pp. 358–61, 370–71. Reprinted by permission of Graphic Ideas, Inc.

been applauded in the house of the President, in the halls of the capitol, in the marts of trade, in public meetings, in small towns, and even in the fields. The President of the Mexican republic was publicly executed in effigy in Philadelphia in an insulting and shameful burlesque. The world has witnessed all these incidents, of which we have become aware through the shameful accounts in the newspapers of the United States. Could greater insults, outrages, or indignities be offered us by an open declaration of war? Let national indignation answer the question.

The Anglo-Americans, not content with having supplied the rebels with battleships to prey upon our commerce, to deprive us of our property and to commit all the abuses of piracy upon the high seas and on our defenseless coast, have protected them with their fleet and have captured the ships of the Mexican squadron that have tried to prevent contraband trade in Texan waters. It is such acts that make our blockade ineffective. . . . On September 1, 1835, our schooner *Correo* was captured by a vessel of the United States. The papers and belongings of its commander and officers were pillaged and the men were taken to New Orleans and locked in the public jails of the city. Would not the United States have protested with unexcelled indignation if the schooner *Grampus,* or any other of their war vessels, had been captured by the *Correo* and brought at once with its entire crew to a Mexican port? . . .

All nations have respected this inherent right of sovereignty of our country except the United States, who escort all ships going to the Texas coast with their Florida fleet. This enables such vessels to carry contraband of war such as arms, munitions, and volunteers for our enemies. Yet this nation demands of us the fulfillment of treaties so shamefully violated by herself!

The Texas question . . . has given the cabinet of the United States, every opportunity desired for the increase of her territory. Relying upon the inability of the Mexican republic to assemble the necessary resources for a definite and successful attempt to recuperate her lost territory and to vindicate her honor, nothing will be easier for the Americans than to add one more star to their flag.

....

. . . The loss of Texas will inevitably result in the loss of New Mexico and the Californias. Little by little our territory will be absorbed, until only an insignificant part is left to us. Our destiny will

be similar to the sad lot of Poland. Our national existence, acquired at
the cost of so much blood, recognized after so many difficulties, would
end like those weak meteors which, from time to time, shine fitfully in
the firmament and disappear. It is for this reason that General Terán
wrote the government, "Whoever consents to and refuses to oppose
the loss of Texas is a despicable traitor, worthy of being punished with
a thousand deaths."

Such is the opinion of all good Mexicans. The general who to-day
holds in his hands the destinies of the nation is guided by this same
conviction. The resources of the country now available are more than
sufficient to humble the pride of those who, not knowing how to
defend their territory, obtained a victory at San Jacinto by a mere
whim of fortune, that fickle goddess that seems to rejoice in
disappointing those who place too much confidence in her favors.
Five thousand infantry and 500 cavalry would be enough, more than
enough, to put an end to the high hopes of the Texans, to drive them
to the banks of the Sabine, and to reconquer the favors of destiny. The
superiority of the Mexican soldier over the mountaineers of Kentucky
and the hunters of Missouri are well known. He knows how to endure
all privations with serene calmness, and how to overcome hunger and
conquer death herself. Veterans, seasoned by twenty years of wars,
cannot be intimidated by the presence of an enemy, ignorant of the
art of war, incapable of discipline, and renowned for insubordination. . . .

The fear that we will find ourselves involved in a war against the
United States if we refuse to subscribe to the terms demanded is not
without foundation. If their diplomacy has been dictated by a
preconceived plan,—and this cannot be doubted by those who have
observed the skill with which the cabinet in Washington directs its
affairs—it is obvious that their aim has been to acquire possession of
the disputed territory by force if necessary. This will involve us in
more serious difficulties than even those presented by the Texas
question itself. War with the United States, however, need not be
feared, for our final salvation may depend upon it.

6. "The sacrificial goat"   Pío Pico, 1846–48*

The following excerpts from Governor Pío Pico's official correspondence reveal the desperate situation of a California official who wanted to remain loyal during the Mexican War. In May 1846, even before he learned of the outbreak of war with the United States, Governor Pico warned his home government that hostilities seemed imminent and that reinforcements were needed if the Californios were to defend themselves. Help failed to arrive, however, and by August, Pico had fled to Baja California, exhorting his countrymen to resist and to have faith. Mexico would eventually send help.

Pío Pico remained in exile for a year and a half, begging the central government for help and proclaiming the loyalty of the Californios. By March 1848 even the staunchly patriotic Pico had lost faith in Mexico. None of his letters had been answered by the foreign minister. Embittered, Pico returned to California in July 1848, making a pathetic attempt to regain his office of governor. Clearly, loyalty had not paid.

Pío Pico to the Minister of Foreign Relations,
Los Angeles, May 25, 1846.

Excellent Sir:

The uncertainty in which we find ourselves in this Department concerning the true state existing at this date in the political affairs between our Government and the Republic of the United States of the North, the excessive introduction of armed adventurers from the Nation, leaves us no doubt of the war that we shall have with the North Americans. The critical situation in which we find ourselves constrains me more and more to politely arouse His Excellency the President through Your Excellency's mediation so that he may take care of us efficaciously; providing us with the necessary resources for an honorable resistance, that may serve as a warning to the depraved plans of that piratical Nation.

*George Tays, ed. and trans., "Pío Pico's Correspondence with the Mexican Government, 1846–1848," *California Historical Quarterly* 13, no. 2 (June 1934): 103–4, 122–23, 114, 148–49. Reprinted by permission of the California Historical Society.

The Departmental Treasury is exhausted and there is no hope whatever of pecuniary aid.

May it please Your Excellency to make the contents of this note known to His Excellency the President, to whom equally with Your Excellency I offer my obedience and esteem.

God and Liberty, Los Angeles, May 25, 1846.

Pío Pico

Pío Pico to the People of California,
Los Angeles, August 10, 1846.

The Constitutional Governor of the Department of California, to the people under his rule.

Fellow Citizens: For many years now the United States of America has given an inkling of the drift of their ambitions to dismember the Mexican Territory, and to effect the spoliation of the most fertile and valuable parts of it. And with that motive they have omitted no means whatsoever to put into operation their sinister ends. Texas presents to us the details of the whole body of ills produced by its generous hospitality in sheltering the foes that some day were to tear the bosom of the Fatherland.

Compatriots: Our Department finds itself today invaded by powerful forces of the United States of America. The efforts which have been made by the Departmental Government to provide for the national defence are well known, and my compatriots will do me the justice of believing that if they have not achieved their purpose, it has been not because of omissions, but due to the unfortunate and difficult situation in which the Department finds itself, completely lacking in all resources to carry on a war.

Mexicans: The Commander of the invasion has put into practice (perhaps to wash away the crime he has committed) means of seduction, wishing by flattery and shameless promises to have us declare our independence under the starry flag: or if we do not, he will attack the Department as an integral part of Mexico. Such a declaration should justly anger our hearts whether we consider the first or the second of his proposals, because being all of us true Mexicans, never, oh never, must we commit an act of treason.

Inhabitants of California: Your Governor being placed in the hard alternative of ignominy or migration, has chosen the latter and from today he separates himself from you, taking with him the acute sorrow that he leaves you in the power of the unjust conqueror. I order you and beg you never to be taken in by flattery, cunning and false promises of the cringing enemy. Prove to the nation and the whole world, that your difficult situation, and not your consent, make you bear the oppressive chain of the usurper. Conserve ever in your bosoms the sacred fire of liberty, and without shame the glorious name of good Mexicans.

Californians all: Have confidence in the high National Government; it has sworn to perish or to save the Republic of all domination, and there is no doubt that this will be accomplished. Be persevering, and be not dismayed even in the face of torture. Let *Mexico* be your motto. The Supreme Being that guards over the future destiny of nations, will provide us the glorious day in which we shall again see our dear Fatherland free and happy. That will be for me, beloved Compatriots, the fulfillment of all my happiness and the only thing to which my heart aspires; in the midst of the bitter sorrow that it feels in telling you Good bye!

Your fellow citizen and friend. Angeles. August 10, 1846.

Pío Pico

Pío Pico to the Minister of Foreign Relations,
Molegé [Mulegé], Baja California, October 27, 1846.

I can assure Your Excellency that in all the inhabitants of that Department there burns an intense anger against its invaders, encouraged by a great enthusiasm to sacrifice themselves in its defence, awaiting some small opportunity to contribute to the reconquest of that part of the Republic, as soon as they see themselves supported by the aid of troops sent to them by the Supreme Government.

. . . All the Californians and other Mexicans residing there are held in the unhappy state of prisoners of war, a forced neutrality having been demanded of them.

I do not believe it superfluous to place in Your Excellency's Superior knowledge, that the enemy daily wisely invents a thousand means of seduction in order to win the Californians, with the object that they may demand their independence from Mexico, attaching themselves to the United States undoubtedly in order to have some shield by which to defend their usurpation; which they have been unable to obtain notwithstanding that they find themselves aided by the influence enjoyed by two or three Mexicans who traitorously embraced the enemy's cause in dishonour of the Mother Country, they being Don Juan Bandini, deputy of the Most Excellent Assembly, Don Pedro C. Carrillo, receiver of the Custom-house of San Diego, and the 2nd Ensign of the Presidial Company of San Diego, Don Santiago E. Arguello, who is now in that port exercising the functions of civil official and of Military Commandant of that post, under the Government of the United States as your Excellency will learn by the note which I attach . . . this officer came to the frontier of Lower California in my pursuit and to raise the enemy flag, trampling that of Mexico on September 23 last.

Pío Pico to the Minister of Interior and Foreign Relations,
Hermosillo, Sonora, March 29, 1848.

I do not wish to detract Your Excellency's attention with my complaints, but allow me to say this, that for three years I have served the office of Governor of California without having seen during all that time one single *real* of my salary; furthermore, I have paid out of my private purse the salaries of the Secretary of my Administration, the cost of stationery, and various other expenses that have been necessary in my emigration. In my country I possess some wealth, and now with all communications cut between this State and that of my birth I am unable to furnish myself with resources of any kind. This has forced me to request, from Guaymas, that that Ministry might furnish me with some amount on account of my credit, but it has already been seen that no notice has been taken of my request.

I now entreat from His Excellency the President permission to return to my country, since I am not permitted to be of any use or service here, and that I be allowed to withdraw in a way honorable alike for me and for the people whom I have had the honor of governing.

California will undoubtedly cease to belong to the Mexican family, it seems as if Fate has thus decreed it, but let the rest of the Republic take leave of it with decorum, and let it not be delivered to its new brothers, the States of the North, as if it were a flock of sheep or a band of horses. Let its Governor be treated, and in his person the people of California, with dignity. We want and have always wanted to be nothing if not Mexicans, and we have given brilliant proofs of our affection, but let not our cup of sorrow that our separation naturally brings us be embittered more by humiliating and scorning us.

If our dismemberment is necessary for the health of the rest of our brothers, let us be the victim, the sacrificial goat that shall pay for all the sins of the people. Providence undoubtedly wishes that it shall be thus; but although separated, we would like to conserve some remembrances of past relations and not to remember only that we have been objects of scorn abandoned to misery.

This occasion gives me for the last time the opportunity to offer Your Excellency the expressions of my highest consideration and esteem.

God and Liberty, Hermosillo, March 20, 1848.

Pío Pico

7. "We would have made some kind of resistance"

Report of the Citizens of New Mexico to the President of Mexico, Santa Fe, September 26, 1846*

Like Pío Pico, New Mexico Governor Manuel Armijo also withdrew to Mexico at the outbreak of hostilities. Armijo's departure, however, was more notorious than Pico's, because it led to the abandoning of New Mexico's defenses and Kearny's easy occupation of Santa Fe.

While awaiting a court martial in Chihuahua, Armijo defended his decision to flee New Mexico on the grounds that his troops refused to fight. Quite a different story was told by both the New Mexico assembly, and by a group of 105 citizens, whose report to the president of Mexico follows. Their version of the failure to defend Santa Fe is probably more correct than Armijo's, for there is evidence, albeit inconclusive, that Armijo

---

*Trans. and ed. Max L. Moorhead, in "Notes and Documents," *New Mexico Historical Review* 26, no. 1 (January 1951): 69–75. Armijo's version of these events appears in the same source. Reprinted by permission of the *New Mexico Historical Review*.

was bribed to abandon New Mexico, and that he had earlier decided that defense of the province was doomed to failure.

It can at least be said with certainty that many New Mexicans did not welcome the Americans in 1846. Rather, many New Mexicans volunteered to fight. After New Mexico fell, some New Mexicans lamented that they had not offered greater resistance and began to plan a revolt against their conquerors.

Report of the Citizens of New Mexico to the President of Mexico
Santa Fe, September 26, 1846

Very Excellent Señor Presidente:

We, the citizens of New Mexico, desiring that a circumstantial relation of the manner and means by which the North American Republic took possession of this country be made known to Your Excellency, have deemed it our duty to make an exact report to Your Excellency of what happened. . . .

More than four thousand men—mounted, armed, and supplied with ammunition as best they could at their own expense—presented themselves to His Excellency [Armijo] to aid in the defense of the country. For sixty leagues around from this city these masses rushed in at the call of their government, abandoning their families and property. These they left exposed to the incursions of the savages, who, not losing the opportunity offered them, attacked several points on the frontier, stealing what they could, killing several families, and carrying off some women and children as prisoners.

On the 16th Sr. Armijo left this city with his dragoons and the remaining residents for the said Cañon de Pecos, where the other inhabitants were waiting encamped. They carried four pieces of artillery of 4- and 6-calibre narrow-taper. He also issued an order for the members of the very excellent Departmental Assembly and the principal residents of this city and the surrounding country who were present to accompany him. This was carried out in part. Having camped in the said canyon and having convened the members of the honorable Assembly there, His Excellency invited them to advise him whether to defend the Department or enter into negotiations with the enemy. To this one of the gentlemen replied that such was not the place for deliberations; that they had gathered there not as members of the very excellent corporation, although they were proud of belonging to it, but as soldiers; that it behooved them to act as such, doing as they were ordered. Thereupon His Excellency assembled the militia officers and the leading inhabitants and consulted with them on the course he should follow under the circumstances. The only one who spoke said that they had been gathered in the field to fight, that they should and wished to do so. His Excellency then replied that he would not risk facing battle with people lacking military training, and that he would do whatever seemed fitting to him and with his [regular] troops. After that he ordered them [the militia and civilians] to return to their homes. Then he assembled the officers of the regular troops and consulted with them on the measures to be taken, the enemy being then five leagues away. They replied that they would advance and give battle. When this decision was heard by the troops, it was received with simultaneous *vivas* and spontaneous acclamation. His Excellency then said he [too] was resolved to press forward. But as soon as the citizenry retired, instead of advancing he and the dragoons and artillery retreated.

On leaving this city, Sr. Armijo left the political and military command of the Department in charge of the Secretary of Government [Juan Bautista Vigil y Alarid]. . . .

This Very Excellent Sir, is what happened in the Department of New Mexico and to its inhabitants. . . .

As a result, the troops of the United States occupied this city on August 18th without the slightest resistance.

Very Excellent Sir, we wish that the conduct of our governor and commandant-general, Don Manuel Armijo, had been other than it was as we are all interested in the good name and reputation of the Mexican Republic and the honor of its army. There was not lacking those who would have advised His Excellency as a last resort in those anxious circumstances to send an official communication to the North American general saying that he was retiring with his military forces to the right bank of the Río Bravo del Norte until the Mexican government should give him further orders, as they were not sufficient to give battle; that he would protest before the entire world, before God and men, that he did not recognize this Department as territory of the United States, as it had never been a part of Texas; but that, obliged by the circumstances, he was beginning a military retreat, declaring with the greatest solemnity that the Department of New Mexico was not surrendering to the republic of North America. But he did not wish to adopt this measure. It would have saved his military reputation and in some measure covered his responsibility.

Since the middle of last June His Excellency Sr. Armijo knew beyond doubt that the [American] expedition would arrive this year. He also received definite news of the said expedition on July 10th, through the four merchants from this Department whom we have mentioned. Very early in August, Sr. Don Pío Sambrano arrived at this city and he, too, told him that the said expedition was on the road. If he had mustered the citizenry in July which he gathered later; if he had marched with it and his troops to meet the enemy then, not at the gateway of the city as he did, but at the greatest possible distance from it; if he had not allowed the more than fifty thousand pesos entering the frontier customs house of this city in July to be invested in other than the organization of the country's defense; if he had raised and trained companies for that purpose, as he had more than enough men with arms, horses, and their own equipment; if the money he collected from exempting some individuals from the campaign had been put to the same use; if he also had designated the same purpose for that collected by voluntary subscription in this city and for that which he received from the municipal funds; if he had arranged in time for the production of munitions of war, for which there was more than enough powder and lead in the Department; if he had purchased some food supplies to have in reserve; if he had taken advantage of the good disposition which all the citizens exhibited at the junta which he convoked in this city, in which they offered him their lives and property; if he had accepted the generous offers of the same which the visiting vicar and various other wealthy residents of the Department had made him; and finally, if he had personally marched to the frontier with the forces which he could have had at his disposal: without doubt we would have fought the invaders, firing at them day and night. We would have managed to surprise them and seize their horses, to ambush them in the waterless deserts, to burn their pasturage, to take advantage of the almost inaccessable mountain passes which they had to cross, and, finally, we would have made some kind of resistance. It would be a great deal for us to venture that victory would have crowned our efforts, but at least we would have had the honor of having tried. Nothing, absolutely nothing was done. And Sr. Armijo can say full well: *I have lost everything, including honor.*

More than four thousand men are witness to the deeds which we have related. The entire Department is convinced of the truth of our assertions, and our honor, more than any other consideration, has obliged us to send Your Excellency this repetitious manifesto so that at no time may it be believed that we have been a disgrace to the Mexican nation, with which we are bound by so many ties. We offer Your Excellency our most distinguished respects and attentive considerations.

God and Liberty. Santa Fe. September 26, 1846.

8. "Keep yourselves quiet"   Donaciano Vigil, 1847*

Widespread discontent with the United States occupation surfaced in New Mexico in January 1847 with the Taos Rebellion. Led by Antonio María Trujillo, Pablo Montoya, Manuel Cortés, a Pueblo Indian named Tomasito, and others, the rebels struck on January 19 in several places in northern New Mexico. At Taos, the rebels killed Governor Charles Bent, along with other Americans. The plan of the rebels, according to one United States officer, seemed to be "to put to death every American and every Mexican who had accepted office under the American government."[1] The revolutionary army quickly secured the allegiance of nearly every town in northern New Mexico and prepared to march on Santa Fe. Two rebel leaders, Juan Antonio García and Pedro Vigil, issued a circular "To the Defenders of their Country," urging New Mexicans to take up arms against the Americans.

In the midst of this rebellion Donaciano Vigil, acting as governor in place of the murdered Charles Bent, sent out the following circular exhorting New Mexicans to remain loyal to the United States. That was, he argued, the only sensible thing to do; he portrayed the revolutionaries as rabble and the loyalists as "honest and discreet men." Along with other Mexicans who took the American side during the war, Vigil illustrates the traditional split in the Mexican community in the Southwest. No documents from the defeated rebels remain to illuminate their side of the argument.

---

*Vigil's proclamations appear in Ralph Emerson Twitchell, *The Leading Facts of New Mexico History*, 2 vols. (Cedar Rapids, Iowa: 1912), 2:248–49, and in Sen. Doc. 442, 56th Cong., 1st Sess. I have relied heavily on Twitchell's account of the rebellion.

1. Colonel Sterling Price to the Adjutant General of the Army, Santa Fe, February 15, 1847, quoted in E. Bennett Burton, "The Taos Rebellion," *Old Santa Fe* 1, no. 2 (October 1913): 187.

Fellow Citizens: Your regularly appointed governor had occasion to go on private business as far as the town of Taos. A popular insurrection headed by Pablo Montoya and Manuel Cortéz, who raised the cry of revolution, resulted in the barbarous assassination of his excellency, the governor, of the greater part of the Government officials, and some private citizens. Pablo Montoya, whom you already know, notorious for his insubordination and restlessness, headed a similar insurrection in September, 1837. Destitute of any sense of shame, he brought his followers to this capital, entered into an arrangement, deserted, as a reward for their fidelity, the unfortunate Montoyas, Esquibel and Chopon, whose fate you know, and retired himself well-paid for his exploits to his den at Taos. The whole population let the weight of their execration fall on others and this brigand they left living on his wits—for he has no home or known property, and is engaged in no occupation. Of what kind of people is his gang composed? Of the insurgent Indian population of Taos, and of others as abandoned and desperate as their rebellious chief. Discreet and respectable men are anxiously awaiting the forces of the Government in order to be relieved from the anarchy in which disorder has placed them and this relief will speedily be afforded them. In the year 1837 this mischievous fool took, as a motto for his perversity, the word "Canton," and now it is "the re-union of Taos!" Behold the works of the champion who guides the revolution! And can there be a single man of sense who would voluntarily join his ranks? I should think not.

Another of his pretended objects is to wage war against the foreign government. Why, if he is so full of patriotism, did he not exert himself and lead troops to prevent the entry of American forces in the month of August, instead of glutting his insane passions and showing his martial valor by the brutal sacrifice of defenseless victims, and this at the very time when an arrangement between the two governments, with regard to boundaries, was expected? Whether this country has to belong to the government of the United States or return to its native Mexico, is it not a gross absurdity to foment rancorous feelings toward people with whom we are either to compose one family, or to continue our commercial relations? Unquestionably it is.

To-day or to-morrow a respectable body of troops will commence their march for the purpose of quelling these disorders of Pablo Montoya, in Taos. The government is determined to pursue energetic measures toward all the refractory until they are reduced to order, as well as to take care of and protect honest and discreet men; and I pray you that, harkening to the voice of reason, for the sake of the common happiness and your own preservation, you will keep yourselves quiet and engaged in your private affairs.

The term of my administration is purely transitory. Neither my qualification nor the ad interim character, according to the organic law in which I take the reins of government, encourage me to continue in so difficult and thorny a post, the duties of which are intended for individuals of greater enterprise and talents; but I protest to you, in the utmost fervor of my heart that I will devote myself exclusively to endeavouring to secure you all the prosperity so much desired by your fellow-citizen and friend.

Donaciano Vigil
January 22, 1847

9. Reactions to Defeat

Juan Bautista Vigil y Alarid, 1846*
Juan Bautista Alvarado, 1876**
Angustias de la Guerra Ord, 1878***

Facing almost certain defeat at the hands of a logistically superior United States force, some upper-class Mexicans in California and New Mexico recognized the futility of resistance and acknowledged that a liaison with the government of the United States might be more beneficial to them than Mexican government had been. Yet the elite felt considerable loyalty to Mexico and so greeted the conquest with mixed emotions. The reaction of lower-class Mexicans, who left no written records, cannot be easily determined.

---

*Quoted in Ralph Emerson Twitchell, *The History of the Military Occupation of the Territory of New Mexico, From 1846 to 1851, By the Government of the United States* (Danville, Ill.: 1909), pp. 74–75.

**Juan Bautista Alvarado, "History of California," 1876 (MS, Bancroft Library), 5:219–22. Reproduced by permission of the Director, the Bancroft Library, University of California, Berkeley, Calif.

***Angustias de la Guerra Ord, *Occurrences in Hispanic California*, trans. and ed. Francis Price and William H. Ellison (Washington, D.C.: 1956), p. 59. Reprinted by permission of the Academy of American Franciscan History.

Juan Bautista Vigil y Alarid, who served as acting governor of New Mexico when Manuel Armijo fled before Kearny's forces, probably expressed the ambivalence of many New Mexico politicians in a public speech he made to General Kearny, just after the occupation of Santa Fe. Years later, in 1876, a former governor of California, Juan Baustista Alvarado, reflected on the Californios' reaction to the conquest more candidly than did Vigil. At the same time, there were members of the aristocracy who openly welcomed the American conquest. Such a one was Angustias de la Guerra, daughter of José de la Guerra y Noriega of Santa Barbara. Dictating her reminiscences in 1878, the sixty-two-year-old wife of Dr. James L. Ord professed to speak for the women of California.

[see the correction on the bottom of p. 131, DJW, 2003]

Juan Bautista Vigil y Alarid, 1846

General:—The address which you have just delivered, in which you announce that you have taken possession of this great country in the name of the United States of America, gives us some idea of the wonderful future that awaits us. It is not for us to determine the boundaries of nations. The cabinets of Mexico and Washington will arrange these differences. It is for us to obey and respect the established authorities, no matter what may be our private opinions.

The inhabitants of this Department humbly and honorably present their loyalty and allegiance to the government of North America. No one in this world can successfully resist the power of him who is stronger.

Do not find it strange if there has been no manifestation of joy and enthusiasm in seeing this city occupied by your military forces. To us the power of the Mexican Republic is dead. No matter what her condition, she was our mother. What child will not shed abundant tears at the tomb of his parents? I might indicate some of the causes for her misfortunes, but domestic troubles should not be made public. It is sufficient to say that civil war is the cursed source of that deadly poison which has spread over one of the grandest and greatest countries that has ever been created. To-day we belong to a great and powerful nation. Its flag, with its stars and stripes, covers the horizon of New Mexico, and its brilliant light shall grow like good seed well cultivated. We are cognizant of your kindness, of your courtesy and that of your accommodating officers and of the strict discipline of your troops; we know that we belong to the Republic that owes its origin to the immortal Washington, whom all civilized nations admire and respect. How different would be our situation had we been invaded by European nations! We are aware of the unfortunate condition of the Poles.

In the name, then, of the entire Department, I swear obedience to the Northern Republic and I tender my respect to its laws and authority.

JUAN BAUTISTA VIGIL y ALARID (Rubric)

Governor.

Santa Fé, August 19, 1846.

Juan Bautista Alvarado, 1876

Commodore Sloat . . . whenever he had occasion to speak in public always showed himself disposed to protect the rights of all the inhabitants of the country, irrespective of which language they spoke, the religion they professed or their place of birth. At the same time, however, that Commodore Sloat expressed his satisfaction with the behavior of the inhabitants of Monterey, he complained very bitterly of the political and judicial authorities who, instead of remaining steadfastly at their posts and trying to preserve order, had fled to the hills and were trying to gather men together to rescue the capital from the hands of the enemy. In regard to the conduct of the Monterey authorities, Commodore Sloat used to say,

> Everyone has a perfect right to work out his own happiness and that of his country when there is a probability at all of succeeding in an enterprise, but in these circumstances I consider it criminal for judges and alcaldes to try and rouse the people against me. These people have suffered all sorts of injustices and have nevertheless borne with resignation all the ills with which luck and Fate have visited them. I came with

good intentions; I bring wealth and a brilliant future; and they do not appreciate those gifts. Truly, this procedure is more that of insane people than of persons in their right minds, because if they used common sense they would understand that I am too strong to allow myself to be forced to give up what I have acquired.

· It may be that this reasoning was in accord with the way of thinking of a nation whose creed is summed up in the phrase "time is money," but we, who from youth up had been reared in the school of adversity, and who loved our country most dearly because we had only been able by dint of immense sacrifices to maintain it at the level of contemporary civilization, felt very differently from that which characterized the thoughts of the renowned Sloat. Even though we knew that nothing short of a Divine miracle would enable us to force the frigate *Savannah* and her consorts to abandon the port of Monterey, not even for this reason would we desist from making a supreme effort to show the world that although we had strong motives for complaint against Mexico, which had for so many years been the bane of our existence and had robbed us unmercifully, we, ever generous, were not willing to take advantage of an occasion when the Mexican Republic was engaged in a foreign war to settle our family differences; nor were my fellow citizens and I who had read the papers and knew the constitution of the United States, unaware that Alta California stood to gain a great deal by the change in flag, for it was well-known that the enterprising spirit of the North Americans, who had filled the East Indies with wooden nutmegs, and the island Jamaica with wooden hams would know how to make their influence felt on California soil and make towns grow where there had been only rocks before. Although we knew all of the advantages which would accrue to us from the new alliance which Commodore Sloat was proposing, we preferred the life of privation, uncertainty and snares which we expected to continue until the mother country had come out defeated or victorious in the unequal contest to which she had rashly provoked her powerful neighbor. Our resistance was not motivated by the hatred we had for the North Americans, or their government and institutions, but was dictated by a conscience which aspired to fulfilling as far as possible our duties as Mexican citizens. As was to be supposed, our efforts were without effect. Victory chose to rest in the enemy camp, and a majority of those of us who were taken prisoners had to bow our proud heads before the might of the North

American government and its valiant marines. Take notice that I say marines and not soldiers, because, had it only been a question of the soldiers accompanying General Kearny to California, we should not have delayed a day in giving them passports to the Elysian Fields, had they refused to surrender unconditionally.

Angustias de la Guerra Ord, 1878

Finally the memorable 7th of July arrived. On the morning of that day, I well remember, there were in Monterey harbor 3 American warships, one which flew the ensign of Comm. Sloat.

During the morning the preparations could be seen. Many armed boats, filled with men, came ashore and took possession without any interference. There was no garrison, and I believe that the only Mexican officer present was old Captain Mariano Silva.

The conquest of California did not bother the Californians, least of all the women.* It must be confessed that California was on the road to the most complete ruin. On one hand the Indians were out of hand, committing robberies and other crimes on the ranches, with little or nothing being done to curb their depredations. On the other hand were the differences between the people of the north and of the south, and between both against the Mexicans and other bands. But the worst cancer of all was the plundering which was carried on generally. There had been such looting of the resources of the government, that the treasury chest was "scuttled." General Castro maintained a corps of officers sufficient for an army of 3,000 men; all good or bad, drew their salaries, more to satisfy their partisans. Of these officers, few offered their services when the hour came to defend the country against the foreign invasion. The greater part performed no more service than the figurehead of a ship.

---

*Correction, added in 2003, DJW. This sentence was mistranslated in the published English-language edition of her memoirs. In Spanish, the document actually says: "*La toma del país no nos gustó nada a los californios, y menos a las mujeres.*" Loosely translated, Angustias de la Guerra Ord means that the seizure of California by the United States "gave absolutely no pleasure to the Californians, least of all the women." Genaro M. Padilla, *My History, Not Yours: The Formation of Mexican American Autobiography* (Madison, 1993), 149–50, correctly chided me for "carelessly" relying on this translation. As Rosaura Sánchez points out, however, "The gist of the sentence is not too far from the mistranslation, as Ord seems to suggest that given the ruinous conditions she stipulates anything would be better." Sánchez, *Telling Identities. The Californio testimonios* (Minneapolis 1995), 324n.40. See, too, "Ocurrencias en California [excerpt]" by Angustias de la Guerra de Ord, in *Nineteenth Century California Testimonials*, ed. by Rosaura Sánchez, Beatrice Pita, and Barbara Reyes. *Crítica* Monograph Series (San Diego, 1994), 71.

10. "A duty before God"
William P. Rogers, 1846*
Robert F. Stockton, 1847**

Once war with Mexico got under way, some Americans began to analyze the nation's motives for fighting. Neither military victory nor territorial gain seemed to be sufficient reasons for war. Instead, the United States had a higher obligation—to bring the superiority of its institutions to the backward Mexicans. War would "redeem" the Mexicans and rescue them from themselves.

Those who rationalized the war in this way could hardly escape the conclusion that if the United States had an obligation to redeem Mexicans, its duty should extend beyond those few Mexicans in California and New Mexico to include all of Mexico. Thus, American Manifest Destiny was accompanied by an idealistic moral imperative which historians know as Mission.[1]

The idea of Mission had broad support, as illustrated by the two following documents. The first is an entry of November 10, 1846 from the diary of William P. Rogers. A twenty-six-year-old Georgia-born lawyer, Rogers was a captain of a volunteer company that served under Zachary Taylor. The second document is a portion of a speech given in Philadelphia on December 30, 1847, by Commodore Robert F. Stockton, recently returned as commander of United States naval forces in California.

William P. Rogers

I have heard it intimated that it may probably become policy of our government to conquer not only a peace with Mexico but to annihilate its government. I can not now say that this would be morally right but there is much to induce the opinion that it would be

---

*Eleanor Damon Pace, ed., "The Diary and Letters of William P. Rogers, 1846–1862," *Southwestern Historical Quarterly* 32, no. 4 (April 1929): 268. Reprinted by permission of the Texas State Historical Association.

**Niles' Register* 73 (January 22, 1848): 335.

1. The best discussion of this theme is Frederick Merk, *Manifest Destiny and Mission* (New York: 1963). Albert K. Weinberg's *Manifest Destiny: A Study of Nationalist Expansionism in American History* (Baltimore: 1935), remains valuable.

promotive of humanity and the cause of freedom and religion. It is true it will lead to a great deal of bloodshed but it will greatly improve the condition of the poor Mexican, besides it will subject one of the most delightful countries on earth to an intelligent people, who will cultivate and improve its soil. The question is then whether the good will overbalance the evil. I think it will. The whole country wherever I have been bears striking evidence of the degradation of the people. The former fields are not cultivated—their houses and villages are decaying, the people as a mass are ignorant and rude in their manners. There is not as much wealth here as there was a few years ago, for in some of their towns there are some buildings that must have cost a great deal. Everything indeed is indicative of a gradual decline of the nation. They profess to live in a republic and yet their laws are more oppressive and more onerous than those of any civilized monarchy. Two fifths of what they make is given to the church and one half of the remainder to the extensive land proprietors of the nation. Rascality too is one of the prime characteristics of their public functionaries—Alcaldes and the like. . . .

Robert F. Stockton

Mexico is poor and wretched. Why? Misgovernment—insatiable avarice—unintermitted wrong unsparing cruelty and unbending insolence—these have inflicted their curse on the unhappy country, and made her what she is. But as the darkest hour is that which just precedes the advent of the morning sun, so let us hope that a better and happier day is now about to dawn upon fortunate Mexico. Be it ours, now to forgive her all her trespasses, and returning good for evil, make her free and happy!—[enthusiastic applause which lasted several minutes.]

If I were not the sovereign authority as I was once the viceroy—[laughter]—I would prosecute this war for the express purpose of redeeming Mexico from misrule and civil strife. If, however, such a treaty were offered me as that offered to the government of the United States, before God, I would consider it my bounden duty to reject it. [Loud applause.]—I would say to them, we can pay the indemnity ourselves. But we have a duty before God which we cannot—we must not evade. The priceless bond of civil and religious liberty has been confided to us as trustees—[cheers]—I would insist, if the war were to be prolonged for fifty years, and cost money enough to demand from us each year the half of all that we possess, I would still insist that the inestimable blessings of civil and religious liberty should be guaranteed to Mexico. We must not shrink from the solemn duty. We dare not shrink from it. We cannot lose sight of the great truth that nations are accountable as well as individuals, and that they too must meet the stern responsibilities of their moral character—they too must encounter the penalty of violated law in the more extended sphere adapted to their physical condition.

Let the solemn question come home to the bosom and business of every citizen of this great republic: "What have I done—what has this generation done for the advancement of civil and religious liberty!" —[Applause.]

It is in view of this responsibility—of our obligations to the infinite source of all our peace, prosperity and happiness—of our duty to fulfill the great mission of liberty committed to our hands, that I would insist, cost what it may, on the establishment of a permanent, independent republic in Mexico—[Cheers.] I would insist that the great principle of religious toleration should be secured to all—that the Protestant in Mexico should be guaranteed the enjoyment of all the immunities and privileges enjoyed by Mexicans in the United States. [Loud cheers.] These great and benevolent objects I would accomplish by sending into Mexico a force adequate to maintain all the posts which we now occupy, to defend them against any assaults that might be made against them, and to keep open our communications. I would seize upon Paredes, Arista, and other military chieftains, and send them to St. Helena, if you please. [Laughter and applause.] I would declare an armistice; and the executive should be called upon to issue a proclamation, and send six or more commissioners to meet Mexico in a liberal and generous spirit.

We have vanquished Mexico. She is prostrate at our feet—we can afford to be magnanimous. Let us act so that we need not fear the strictest scrutiny of the Christian and civilized world. I would with a magnanimous and kindly hand gather these wretched people within the fold of republicanism. [Loud applause.] This I would accomplish at any cost.

11. "The Government of a white race"

John C. Calhoun, 1848*

Those who wanted to redeem all of Mexico found a powerful opponent in Senator John C. Calhoun of South Carolina. Calhoun had been an expansionist, and had worked to bring about the annexation of Texas in 1845. Yet he opposed the Mexican War and opposed annexing more of Mexico. In a speech before the United States Senate on January 4, 1848, Calhoun argued that absorbing hostile Mexicans into the Union would be impossible. His comparisons with Ireland and French Canada have a surprisingly contemporary ring. Calhoun further argued that "colored races" were incapable of democratic government; Mexicans would make inferior United States citizens.

The racist sentiments of Calhoun's argument have been repeated in the twentieth century, in updated versions employing the language of the social sciences.

. . . It is without example or precedent, either to hold Mexico as a province, or to incorporate her into our Union. No example of such a line of policy can be found. We have conquered many of the neighboring tribes of Indians, but we never thought of holding them in subjection—never of incorporating them into our Union. They have either been left as an independent people amongst us, or have been driven into the forests.

I know further, sir, that we have never dreamt of incorporating into our Union any but the Caucasian race—the free white race. To incorporate Mexico, would be the very first instance of the kind of incorporating an Indian race; for more than half of the Mexicans are Indians, and the other is composed chiefly of mixed tribes. I protest against such a union as that! Ours, sir, is the Government of a white race. The greatest misfortunes of Spanish America are to be traced to the fatal error of placing these colored races on an equality with the white race. That error destroyed the social arrangement which formed the basis of society. . . .

Sir, it is a remarkable fact, that in the whole history of man, as far

---

*U.S., Congress, Senate, *The Congressional Globe*, 30th Cong., 1st sess., 1848, pp. 98–99.

as my knowledge extends, there is no instance whatever of any
civilized colored races being found equal to the establishment of free
popular government, although by far the largest portion of the human
family is composed of these races. And even in the savage state we
scarcely find them anywhere with such government, except it be our
noble savages—for noble I will call them. They, for the most part, had
free institutions, but they are easily sustained amongst a savage
people. Are we to overlook this fact? Are we to associate with
ourselves as equals, companions, and fellow-citizens, the Indians and
mixed race of Mexico? Sir, I should consider such a thing as fatal to
our institutions.

....

I come now to the proposition of incorporating her into our Union.
Well, as far as law is concerned, that is easy. You can establish a
Territorial Government for every State in Mexico, and there are some
twenty of them. You can appoint governors, judges, and magistrates.
You can give the people a subordinate government, allowing them to
legislate for themselves, whilst you defray the cost. So far as law goes,
the thing is done. There is no analogy between this and our Territorial
Governments. Our Territories are only an offset of our own people, or
foreigners from the same regions from which we came. They are small
in number. They are incapable of forming a government. It would be
inconvenient for them to sustain a government, if it were formed; and
they are very much obliged to the United States for undertaking the
trouble, knowing that, on the attainment of their majority—when they
come to manhood—at twenty-one—they will be introduced to an
equality with all the other members of the Union. It is entirely
different with Mexico. You have no need of armies to keep your
Territories in subjection. But when you incorporate Mexico, you must
have powerful armies to keep them in subjection. You may call it
annexation, but it is a forced annexation, which is a contradiction in
terms, according to my conception. You will be involved, in one word,
in all the evils which I attribute to holding Mexico as a province. In
fact, it will be but a Provincial Government, under the name of a
Territorial Government. How long will that last? How long will it be
before Mexico will be capable of incorporation into our Union? Why,
if we judge from the examples before us, it will be a very long time.
Ireland has been held in subjection by England for seven or eight
hundred years, and yet still remains hostile, although her people are

of kindred race with the conquerors. A few French Canadians on this continent yet maintain the attitude of hostile people; and never will the time come, in my opinion, Mr. President, that these Mexicans will be heartily reconciled to your authority. They have Castilian blood in their veins—the old Gothic, quite equal to the Anglo-Saxon in many respects—in some respects superior. Of all nations of the earth they are the most pertinacious—have the highest sense of nationality—hold out longest, and often even with the least prospect of effecting their object. On this subject also I have conversed with officers of the army, and they all entertain the same opinion, that these people are now hostile, and will continue so.

But, Mr. President, suppose all these difficulties removed; suppose these people attached to our Union, and desirous of incorporating with us, ought we to bring them in? Are they fit to be connected with us? Are they fit for self-government and for governing you? Are you, any of you, willing that your States should be governed by these twenty-odd Mexican States, with a population of about only one million of your blood, and two or three millions of mixed blood, better informed, all the rest pure Indians, a mixed blood equally ignorant and unfit for liberty, impure races, not as good as the Cherokees or Choctaws?

We make a great mistake, sir, when we suppose that all people are capable of self-government. We are anxious to force free government on all; and I see that it has been urged in a very respectable quarter, that it is the mission of this country to spread civil and religious liberty over all the world, and especially over this continent. It is a great mistake. None but people advanced to a very high state of moral and intellectual improvement are capable, in a civilized state, of maintaining free government; and amongst those who are so purified, very few, indeed, have had the good fortune of forming a constitution capable of endurance.

IV.

All the Rights of Citizens

Editor's Introduction

The ratification of the Treaty of Guadalupe-Hidalgo by Mexico and the United States in the spring of 1848 brought the Mexican War to an end and gave the United States additional territory amounting to roughly a third of Mexico (a half, counting Texas, which was annexed in 1845). It was, of course, the least populated third, with clusters of Mexican settlements only along the California coast and in the upper Rio Grande Valley of New Mexico. Extending north to the 42d parallel, which forms the northern boundary of California today, the newly conquered territory also included areas where no permanent Mexican settlement existed: part or all of today's Nevada, Utah, Wyoming, Colorado, Kansas, Oklahoma, and Arizona above the Gila River. Southern Arizona, where Mexican settlement centered in the Santa Cruz Valley, remained Mexican territory until 1853. Then Antonio López de Santa Anna, once again President of Mexico, sold southern Arizona and the Mesilla Valley of southwestern New Mexico to the United States, through its minister, James Gadsden. Convinced that the purchase would provide the most level route for a transcontinental railroad, the United States Senate ratified the Gadsden Treaty in 1854.

The Spanish-speaking population of this vast area acquired from Mexico between 1845 and 1854 was about 75,000, according to most estimates: 60,000 Nuevo Mexicanos, 7,500 Californios, about the same number of Texanos, and less than 1,000 Mexicans living around the presidios of Tucson and Tubac in what would eventually become Arizona.[1] These people constituted a unique new ethnic bloc in the United States. Quickly conquered, subjected to an alien political system in an alien culture, the fact that they were guaranteed all the rights of citizens did not prevent them from becoming foreigners in their native land.

140

I

The conquered Mexicans had heard promises from the very outset of the war—from Commodore John D. Sloat in California, and General Stephen Watts Kearny in New Mexico—that their lives, property, and religion would be protected and that the new government would be better than the old. The most binding promise came in the form of articles 8 and 9 of the Treaty of Guadalupe Hidalgo, as finally ratified. Although the Supreme Court declared that the treaty did not apply to Texas (*McKinney* vs. *Saviego*, 1855), it did apply to the Gadsden Purchase territory.

The Treaty of Guadalupe Hidalgo is the key document of Mexican American history, for through it Mexicans living in the Southwest became Americans and were guaranteed "all the rights of citizens of the United States." Yet the treaty remains relatively unknown in the United States. In Mexico, on the other hand, since losers have a longer memory than victors, the treaty is still remembered with bitterness. The treaty "imposed on Mexico was one of the harshest in modern history," a Mexican historian wrote in 1965.[2] In the United States the treaty has come to public attention in recent years due to the Chicano movement and to the efforts of Reies López Tijerina of New Mexico, who won considerable publicity by trying to get the Mexican government to investigate violations of the treaty and to bring those violations before the United Nations with the help of Cuba.

As important as the Treaty of Guadalupe Hidalgo is for Mexicans, the question of implementing both the letter and the spirit of the treaty is more important than the treaty itself. There has been an almost naive faith since the treaty was signed that the guaranteeing of rights in writing should be equivalent to guaranteeing them in practice. For example, when news of the ratification of the Treaty of Guadalupe Hidalgo reached California on August 6, 1848, Governor Richard B. Mason declared: "There will be a firm and stable government, administering justice with impartiality. . . . Americans and Californians will now be one and the same people, subject to the same laws, and enjoying the same rights and privileges; they should, therefore, become a band of brothers."[3] Governor Mason's optimism quickly proved to be unwarranted. On the other hand, some Mexican politicians charged their government with signing a treaty which "abandoned the inhabitants of California and New Mexico, . . . sacrificed them in its desire to make peace," and "traded them as if they were a group of slaves or a herd of sheep."[4] While such charges had much emotional appeal, we must remember that Mexico signed the treaty under duress, and that it contained specific safeguards for Mexicans living in the ceded territories. Mexican negotiators had insisted that the rights of their "brothers" to the north be protected. If they were not, the blame does not lie so much with the treaty as with those who were charged with its implementation.

Among its guarantees, the treaty permitted those Mexicans who wished to return to Mexico to do so. Those who wished to remain, yet retain their Mexican citizenship, could do so by making a public declaration of their intent within a year after the ratification of the treaty. Those who neither left nor declared their intention to remain Mexican, would automatically become United States citizens when Congress established a civil government for the newly won territory.

How many Mexicans chose to leave the conquered territory or to retain their Mexican citizenship cannot be ascertained with precision. Clearly, the Mexican government did not abandon its subjects like "a herd of sheep," but encouraged them to return to Mexico. On August 19, 1848, the administration of José Joaquín Herrera issued a decree to attract Mexicans back to Mexico. Three commissioners were to arrange the migrations. Mexicans in Alta California were to receive land in Baja California or Sonora; those in New Mexico, land in Chihuahua; and the Texas Mexicans, land in Tamaulipas, Coahuila, or Nuevo León. Twenty thousand pesos were appropriated for the task.[5] Apparently, however, commissioners went only to New Mexico, the most populous of the lost provinces. At Santa Fe in 1849, United States officials blocked the Mexican effort at repatriating its citizens, according to one commissioner, Father Ramón Ortiz. The harassment that Father Ortiz received brought an official protest from the Mexican government. Nevertheless, one United States officer estimated that some one or two thousand Nuevo Mexicanos returned to Mexico by 1850.[6]

There is evidence that well after the war the Mexican government was still trying to repatriate Mexicans. In 1855, for example, Mexicans in California were urged to settle in Sonora with promises of free land as well as political rights they had not enjoyed in the United States. As late as 1878, the Mexican government paid half the steamer passage of Mexicans shipping out of Yuma for the fatherland.[7]

Mexicans who willingly abandoned their homes to resettle in

Mexico were probably those wealthy enough to leave, or those who lived close to the international border. Nuevo Laredo, for example, was founded at this time by Mexicans leaving "old" Laredo.[8] In southern New Mexico, the town of Mesilla was founded on the Mexican side of the Rio Grande about 1851 by residents of the nearby town of Doña Ana, who were driven from their homes on the east side of the river by Anglos who encroached on their lands. In this case, however, efforts to flee the United States were in vain. When Santa Anna sold the Mesilla Valley, the residents of Mesilla found themselves back in the United States again.[9]

Some Mexicans who left the United States for Mexico returned willingly after learning that coexistence with the "gringos" was possible. When United States forces occupied Tucsón in 1856 after the Gadsden Purchase, for example, nearly half of the town's 650 inhabitants fled across the border, according to one observer. Yet many, including former Mexican soldiers and their families, soon returned to work their lands.[10] Thus, any estimate of the number of Mexicans returning to Mexican territory after the Mexican War must be taken with caution.

II

Although the Treaty of Guadalupe Hidalgo promised that Mexicans who stayed in the Southwest would receive "all the rights of citizens of the United States," it seems clear in retrospect that this promise was not fulfilled. At best, Mexican Americans became second-class citizens. At worst, they became victims of overt racial and ethnic prejudices. This occurred, in part, because Mexican Americans had become politically impotent in lands they once governed. In order to protect their civil rights, economic interests, and cultural institutions, Mexican Americans needed to learn a new political game. More important, they needed majorities to win elections. Only in New Mexico did the Hispanos have sufficient numbers to play the Anglo American political game at the state level, and thereby protect their rights as citizens.

In New Mexico, Hispanos remained the numerically dominant group until the 1940s. The territory grew more slowly than other Western states, even after the coming of the railroad in the 1880s. As late as 1912, when New Mexico became a state, Hispanos comprised nearly 60 percent of the population.[11] In the Rio Grande Valley, the most populous area of the territory and the seat of power, the population was overwhelmingly Hispano. Hence, Hispanos played a key role in territorial and local politics in New Mexico where the rights of new citizens, as guaranteed by the Treaty of Guadalupe-Hidalgo, were better protected than in any other area of the Southwest in the latter half of the nineteenth century. We will return to this subject in the next chapter.

Arizona, which formed part of New Mexico until 1863, also remained a territory until 1912. Mexicans constituted the majority of Arizona's population through the 1870s,[12] but, unlike the Hispanos of New Mexico, they did not hold political power on the territorial level. Most of the Spanish-speaking residents of Arizona were newly arrived immigrants from Sonora who held transient jobs on ranches, farms, and, by the 1880s, in mines, smelters, and railroad yards. Subsisting on a wage scale that was below that of Anglo Americans, most struggled to make ends meet and apparently paid little attention to the niceties of becoming United States citizens. Nor were they encouraged to do so. Most Anglo politicians in Arizona feared, as did Sylvester Mowry in 1859, that "American influence will be swallowed up by the great preponderence of the Mexican vote."[13] Only when Arizona desperately needed more citizens in order to qualify for statehood in the 1870s were Mexicans urged to exercise the rights of citizens.[14]

Anglos held firm control of Arizona throughout the territorial period. From 1863 to 1912, no one of Spanish surname served in an important territorial office, either elective or appointive. A few Mexican Americans managed to win election to the legislative assembly, mainly in the years before 1880. These men—Jesús and Juan Elías, Francisco S. León, Esteban Ochoa, Ramón Romano, and Mariano G. Samaniego and others—came chiefly from Tucson.[15] A mercantile center and the only area of Mexican concentration in Arizona before the Gadsden Purchase, Tucson and nearby settlements in the Santa Cruz Valley remained the only part of Arizona where Mexican Americans remained politically influential on the local level. Partly in order to wrest political control of the territory from Hispanos, Anglos had worked to separate Arizona from New Mexico before 1863,[16] then shifted the capital from Tucson to Prescott, in the Anglo-dominated intermontane region of central Arizona. Prescott remained the territorial capital from 1864 to 1887, when the government moved to Phoenix, a young city that had become the commercial center and Anglo stronghold of central Arizona.

Fear of Mexican American domination of the territory remained an important theme in Arizona politics. In 1906, when it appeared that the only way Arizona and New Mexico could become states would be to combine as one large state, Anglo citizens of Arizona opposed the idea, partly because of fear that Hispanos would dominate the new state. One congressman put the question squarely: "Can Arizona as a single state control it better by itself, or shall we join the Mexican greasers [of New Mexico] to Arizona and let them control it?"[17]

Texas, already overwhelmingly Anglo American in 1836, saw its population quadruple in the next decade, from 30,000 in 1836 to 140,000 in 1846. The increase came largely from Anglo immigration, especially into East Texas. Despite some fresh immigration from Mexico during this decade, the Mexican population of some areas of Texas probably decreased. The Texas Constitution of 1836 had declared that any person who refused to participate in the revolution, or who aided the enemy, "shall forfeit all rights of citizenship, and such lands as they may hold in the republic."[18] Since it was difficult to distinguish a loyal Mexican from a disloyal Mexican—especially for Anglo newcomers—it was expedient to assume that all Mexicans were disloyal. Under these circumstances, Texanos had little chance of retaining political power. They were outvoted and intimidated.

Between 1836 and 1845, while Texas was an independent nation, the only Hispano delegates to the Texas Congress came from San Antonio, the one municipality where Texanos retained a majority. These representatives were oligarchs: Juan N. Sequín, Rafael de la Garza, José Antonio Navarro, and his uncle, José Francisco Ruiz.[19] The latter two had signed the Texas Declaration of Independence.

In 1845, when Texas entered the Union, José Antonio Navarro was the only Mexican delegate to the constitutional convention.[20] The convention debates revealed strong racist sentiment among some delegates who thought that Mexicans should not be allowed to vote in Texas. As one delegate put it: "I fear not the Castilian race, but . . . those who, though they speak the Spanish language, are but the descendents of that degraded and despicable race which Cortez conquered." According to another delegate, it had been the custom in some areas of Texas to deny the vote to Texas Mexicans, even though they took the oath of allegiance, simply because "they could not be considered white persons; they were Mexicans."[21] Still, such racist fears did not prevail among the delegates. With José Antonio Navarro arguing that the measure was "odious,"[22] the delegates rejected a motion to limit the vote in Texas to "white persons." In practice, however, Mexican Americans continued to be intimidated from voting in some areas of Texas. In 1850, of the sixty-four members of the state legislature, none was born in Texas or Mexico. By that same year, Mexicans in Texas numbered 11,212, only 5 percent of the state's population.[23] The newcomers clearly held complete control of the state government.

On the local level, too, Texas Mexicans lost political power quickly. Following the Texas Revolution, Mexicans fled from Goliad and Victoria in large numbers. Only in San Antonio did they retain a majority. There they dominated political offices until the mid-1840s when San Antonio also became engulfed by newcomers. By then many upper-class Texano leaders had either fled or become intimidated.[24] The perceptive Frederick Law Olmsted, who visited Texas in 1856, observed that although Mexican Americans could vote, few made use of that right: "Should they do so, they might probably, in San Antonio, have elected a government of their own. Such a step would be followed, however, by a summary revolution."[25]

Mexicans continued to be courted as a voting bloc in San Antonio, but their real numerical strength came to be in the river towns of South Texas, such as Laredo and Brownsville. Along the Rio Grande, Mexican Americans soon formed a majority of the population, but they were unable to hold political power. One specialist in Texas politics recently suggested why: "Mexican vaqueros and laborers along the Rio Grande seemed susceptible because of economic dependence and the language barrier to manipulation by large landowners and their own local leaders."[26] As in Mexico, the ranching economy lent itself to permanent *patrón-peón* relationships and those were often carried over into politics. On the United States side of the border, however, the economically powerful Anglo more often than not became the political patron or "boss." Thus, historical circumstances of economic dependence, language, and Anglo intimidation made it exceedingly difficult for South Texas Mexicans to elect one of their own people to important political office, even though they held a numerical majority. Instead, the Spanish-speaking citizens were "voted," as the saying went, and their votes went to support the

political machines of men such as Jim Wells of Brownsville, and
Bryan Callaghan and his son, "King Bryan II," a two generation
dynasty which took over San Antonio in 1846 and "ruled" it until
1912.[27]

Although the Mexican vote helped political bosses hold power,
there is little evidence to suggest what benefits the Spanish-speaking
people received from this arrangement. More research needs to be
done in this area, however, especially in comparing the bosses of the
lower Rio Grande Valley to the ward bosses of cities in the Northeast
during the same period. Perhaps the most tangible benefit that
Mexican Americans received from political bosses was a payoff at
election time. Charges that politicians bought Mexican American
votes circulated as early as 1853 in San Antonio.[28] In that sense, even
Mexican nationals benefited from elections in Texas, for they were
brought across the river and paid to vote. This practice continued into
the twentieth century despite a constitutional amendment adopted in
1890 which required foreigners to file for citizenship six months
before an election. Political bosses of South Texas opposed the
amendment, with Jim Wells lamenting the loss of the Mexican voters:
"We will sorely need every one of them."[29]

Farther inland from the Rio Grande, where Spanish-speaking voters
were less numerous and therefore less important, dark-skinned
Mexicans might be denied the right to vote on racial grounds. This
practice, which was illegal but apparently commonplace in some
areas, gained legality in the 1890s when "white primaries" became
popular in many Texas counties. Designed chiefly to keep Negroes
from the polls, these primaries were used in counties such as Gonzales
(1902) and Dimmit (1914) to disenfranchise Mexican Americans, too.
In Texas, where the Democratic nominee always won the election,
the primary was, of course, the key election.[30]

A poll tax, adopted in Texas by constitutional amendment in 1902,
also deterred Mexican Americans from voting. Just as the lawmakers
intended, the tax kept "irresponsible" poor people from influencing
the affairs of state. Texas, according to one study, experienced "less
than fifty percent voter participation in primary and state elections
throughout the first half of the twentieth century," and Mexican
Americans along with black Americans, who were the least affluent
groups in the state, were also the least represented in politics.[31]

In California before the gold rush, Mexicans seemed headed toward full participation in American government. Between 1847 and 1849, the United States military governors generally tried to retain Californios in local offices or to find candidates acceptable to them.[32] Yankees in California had no memory of an Alamo or Goliad to keep hatreds alive. On the contrary, since Californios had asserted their independence from Mexico before the conquest and many of them had been cooperative, knowledgeable Americans viewed them as superior to other Mexicans. When a convention met at Monterey in 1849 to draft a constitution for what would become the state of California, eight of the forty-eight delegates were Californios elected by mixed Anglo-Californio constituencies. Setting a pattern that has lingered to the present day, these eight delegates did not vote as a bloc on all issues. Nor did they speak frequently in the convention, apparently because of the awkwardness of using a translator. Most vocal of the eight were José Antonio Carrillo of Santa Barbara, Mariano Vallejo of Sonoma, and his nephew, Pablo de la Guerra of Santa Barbara. Despite their silence on most issues, the Californios spoke effectively on matters which affected their interests. They won approval of a measure to have all state laws and regulations translated into Spanish and prevented the assembly from completely disenfranchising Indians (delegate Manuel Domínguez of Los Angeles was known as a mestizo, and others of the Californio delegates probably had some Indian blood, too).[33]

The state constitution, which took effect in 1850, was, as historian Leonard Pitt has noted, "the only major document of state the Californios ever helped to shape."[34] The momentous discovery of gold at Sutter's Mill on January 24, 1848 (only a week before the signing of the Treaty of Guadalupe-Hidalgo), had attracted adventurers from around the world. By the end of 1849, California's population had soared to some 115,000. By 1850, the state boasted a population of 380,000.[35] Spanish-speaking Californians, who comprised nearly the entire population of California before the Mexican War, constituted only 15 percent of the state's population in 1850 (including those born in Latin America and Spain). By 1870, Spanish-speaking Californians numbered about 4 percent of the state's population. Thus, the growth of the Mexican American community in no way corresponded to the overall growth of the state, and Mexican American political influence declined accordingly.[36]

Thoroughly outnumbered, especially in northern California where most of the gold-seekers settled, the Californios had little chance of winning election to state office. Even such a highly respected leader as Mariano Vallejo of Sonoma found himself unelectable in his home district, and there was open discussion about disenfranchising Mexican Americans.[37] Only four Californios, all from the southern counties, served in the lower house of the legislature from 1850 to 1876.[38] On one occasion a Californio occupied the governor's chair, but that did not reflect the group's political power. In 1875 Romualdo Pacheco of Santa Barbara, who had been elected lieutenant governor in 1871, served out the last year of a governor's term when the governor had gone on to the United States Senate. Pacheco was not renominated by his party. Moreover, he did not achieve his lofty position as a typical Californio or as a representative of his ethnic group. Pacheco had spent his boyhood on the Hawaiian Islands and had forgotten how to speak Spanish by the age of twelve. During his boyhood, his mother was remarried to an Anglo. Although most Spanish-speaking Californians were Democrats, Pacheco was a Republican.[39]

By the 1870s the Mexican American vote had become inconsequential in state elections in California, and the Californios' loss of power on the state level left them vulnerable to legislation which ran contrary to their interests. In 1851, for example, the six southern counties, which made up the Mexican American stronghold in California, had twelve representatives in the state legislature compared to forty-four for the more populous north. Yet, because of taxes on land which fell heaviest on the Spanish-speaking population, the southerners "were paying in taxes thirty-five times more per citizen than the northern counties," according to one study.[40] The 1855 legislature passed laws prohibiting such Sunday amusements as bull, bear, and cock fights, clearly aimed at customs of the Californios. The same legislature passed an antivagrancy act aimed at the Spanish-speaking which was popularly known as the "Greaser Law." The 1855 legislature also refused to provide for the translation of laws into Spanish as required by the state constitution.[41]

Only away from the gold fields, in southern California communities such as Los Angeles and Santa Barbara, did Mexican Americans constitute a majority of the population. There, until the 1870s, they could elect some of their own to local office and even send an occasional reluctant congressmen to the foreign atmosphere of the state capital at Sacramento.[42] In this respect, southern California resembled other bastions of Mexican American political strength such as the Tucson area of southern Arizona, north central New Mexico, and South Texas to some extent. These somewhat exceptional areas will be discussed further in the next chapter.

III

Mexican Americans' loss of political power, which accompanied their relative numerical decline in California, Texas, and Arizona, resulted in a threat to their civil liberties. Without political strength, Mexicans in America could not hope to protect themselves from capricious laws, or from the wrath of Yankee nativists. The Spanish-speaking peoples in the Southwest frequently found that the highly touted American system of justice operated on two levels: one for Mexicans and another for Anglos. This was especially evident in California and Texas, where economic competition between Anglo Americans and Mexican Americans was most fierce.

The influx of Anglo American gold-seekers to California had a greater effect on the Californios than simply making them a minority—it contributed to making them a despised minority unable to obtain equal protection of the law. In 1848, the year that gold was discovered in California, an estimated 1,300 Californios flocked to the mines.[43] The following year they were joined by other Latin Americans, especially from Chile, Peru, and the nearby Mexican state of Sonora. The Californios enjoyed great success in the mines because they were on the scene first. Latin Americans were also generally successful because they had mining experience and skills. Indeed, Hispanic mining tools and techniques, such as the batea (pan), arrastra (mill), and the patio and amalgamation processes, were adopted by Anglo miners. As one student of Western mining has noted: "As late as the 1880s mining men were literally relying on Spanish techniques hooked up to a steam engine."[44] Latin American miners, some observers pointed out, were quite willing to instruct Anglos and Californios alike in mining techniques. Still, the Latins continued to be more successful, perhaps because, in addition to possessing superior skills, they were also harder working and more tenacious.

As it became evident that there was not enough gold in California for everyone, the sight of foreign "interlopers" hauling gold out of United States territory made some American miners envious and furious.[45] In 1849 lynchings, beatings, and institutionalized robbery of foreign miners, most of whom were Mexican and Mexican American, became commonplace. Mining camps could be lawless places for Anglos, too, but those who spoke Spanish or had brown skin might be shot "on general principles," as one miner put it. In addition, there was little risk of being punished for shooting a "greaser." Inequality before the law, one of the most deplorable manifestations of nativism, was all too common in the California mining camps. The situation became so grave that in autumn of 1849 the Mexican minister in Washington, Luis de la Rosa, sent an official protest to the United States secretary of state, condemning the "violent enmity and persecution" of Mexicans in California which, he said, violated the Treaty of Guadalupe-Hidalgo.[46] The United States government responded that the charges were not specific enough and took no action, but the California lawmakers did.

In 1850 the California legislature passed the notorious Foreign Miners' Tax, which required foreigners to pay twenty dollars a month for the privilege of mining. The tax was misnamed, however, for in practice it was more of a "Mexican Miners' Tax." It was collected chiefly from the Spanish-speaking, including Mexican Americans who, although they had become naturalized citizens through the Treaty of Guadalupe-Hidalgo, were still treated as foreigners. Reaction and resistance to the tax was intense, violence in mining camps increased, and a substantial number of Mexican miners returned to Mexico horrified or saddened. The legislature repealed the tax in 1851, when it became clear that cheap labor was needed in the quartz mines, and when merchants complained that the exodus of Mexicans was bad for business. The tax was reduced to a more modest fee, and it remained on the books until 1870.[47] Within a few years the tax was collected mainly from Chinese, who replaced the "greasers" as California's most despised minority. Mexicans and Mexican Americans joined Anglos in abusing Chinese in California; no ethnic group seems to have a monopoly on nativism.[48]

Prior to the wave of anti-Mexicanism provoked by economic conflict in the gold fields, the Californios had enjoyed respect and status among American newcomers who viewed them as superior to other Mexicans. By 1850, however, the Mexican immigrants, or "cholos" as the Californios contemptuously called them, constituted the majority of Spanish-speaking Californians. The older California families found themselves hard pressed to disassociate or distinguish themselves from the cholos, and all Spanish-speaking peoples merged together in the minds of the new Yankee arrivals as "greasers" and "greaseritas." All became foreigners, whether guaranteed citizenship by the Treaty of Guadalupe-Hidalgo or not, except perhaps for the upper-class Californios.[49] Although they had been successful in the mines in 1848, most Californios seem to have abandoned the gold fields in 1849 or 1850 under threats of violence, and returned to their homes convinced that American justice offered little protection for those who spoke Spanish and had dark skin. Violence toward Mexicans in the mines culminated, historian Leonard Pitt has suggested, with the lynching at Downieville on July 5, 1851, of a woman, Juanita, who was accused of stabbing a man. Details of the affair remain unclear, but it is certain that Juanita was one of few women to be lynched on the frontier, and the only one in California. The proceedings were so extraordinary that newspapers at first refused to believe reports.[50]

After the discovery of gold, justice in California for Mexicans and Mexican Americans became inequitable not only in the mining region, but throughout the state. In San Francisco, a newspaper reported in 1854 that "none but Mexicans could be convicted of a capital offense," and three years later Manuel Domínguez, a signer of the California Constitution of 1849, was not permitted to testify in court because of his Indian blood. In Los Angeles in the 1850s, the Spanish-speaking community became increasingly enraged over the prevailing double standard of justice.[51] Francisco P. Ramírez, the young editor of Los Angeles's Spanish language newspaper, *El Clamor Público*, wondered if it was worth the trouble to publish the laws of California in Spanish and English: "What language they may be published in does not matter much—in Kanaka or in Chinese it is the same if we are always to be governed by Lynch Law. Everyone understands perfectly the words 'hang! hang!' "[52]

In Texas, where hatred for Mexicans ran deep, justice for Mexican Americans was more difficult to obtain than in California. To Southern emigrants who pushed westward across Texas, bringing with them a cotton-slave economy, Mexicans were rarely regarded as having the rights of "white folk." Rather, Texas Mexicans were viewed as "yaller niggers,"[53] only a cut above slaves, with whom, it was supposed, they sympathized. In 1856, for example, when a planned slave uprising in Colorado and Matagorda counties was discovered, a local newspaper reported: "Without exception, every Mexican in the county was implicated. They were arrested, and ordered to leave the county within five days, and never again to return, under the penalty of death." No mention was made about due process of law for these "incendiaries." Being of Mexican descent was proof enough of guilt.[54]

Unable to compete with slave labor in East Texas and uncomfortable with Southern prejudices, Texas Mexicans remained concentrated in the ranching country of South Texas, west of the Nueces River. There, near the lawless border where Anglo and Hispano alike indulged in cattle thieving and pillaging, justice was difficult to come by for anyone. Mexican Americans found themselves under attack from two directions: their cattle might be driven across the Rio Grande by Mexican rustlers, or into East Texas by Anglo thieves. As occurred in the mining region of California, those Mexican Americans who successfully competed economically with Anglos were most likely to be harrassed.

This was illustrated in what has come to be known as the "Cart War" of 1857—an incident which sparked official protest from the Mexican minister in Washington. Mexicans and Texas Mexicans had created a successful business of hauling freight from the port of Indianola, Texas, to San Antonio more cheaply and rapidly than their Anglo competitors. Anglos retaliated by murdering Mexican cartmen, driving off their oxen, and destroying oxcarts and freight. Public opinion in the counties involved ran heavily against the "greasers," who were regarded as a "nuisance." According to one contemporary, local authorities "made no efforts whatever either to suppress the crimes or to bring the criminals to justice."[55] Only when the violence began to affect other Anglos were law enforcement officials called in to restore order. The lack of justice for Mexicans in some South Texas counties was notorious.

Justice for Texanos in South Texas may have been lacking, but swift retribution was not. In 1876, for example, when a Mexican murdered Lee Rabb, a Nueces County rancher, his friends took revenge by killing about forty "innocent Mexicans," according to the estimate of one contemporary. One story was that Rabb's mother offered $50 for every pair of Mexican ears brought to her.[56] This Texas tradition of revenge by proxy was kept alive by Texas's finest law enforcement officers, the Texas Rangers. Some Rangers deliberately killed innocent Mexicans in revenge against the guilty. Some Mexicans also died "accidentally" because of the Rangers's tendency to shoot first and ask questions later. Instead of feeling protected by "*los rinches*," Mexicans in Texas came to fear law enforcement officials. Every Ranger, Mexican folklore has it, always carried a rusty old gun so that if he killed an unarmed Mexican, he could place it next to the body and claim that he killed the man in self-defense.[57] Rangers were known to execute their Mexican prisoners on the spot, and on at least one occasion they made their victims dig their own graves. Ranger terrorization of Mexican Americans in Texas continued into the twentieth century amidst pressure to disband the force.[58] In Texas, then, Mexican Americans were victimized not only by lawbreakers, but by law enforcers as well.

Mexican Americans also experienced unequal protection of the law in Arizona and New Mexico, especially in eastern New Mexico, where Texas ranchers came into contact with Hispanos, and in mining districts, where attitudes exported from the gold fields of California were widespread. Yet, despite occasional outbursts of nativism in these two territories, ethnic relations seem not to have reached the consistently low level characteristic of California or Texas in the nineteenth century. The foregoing discussion of injustices toward Mexicans in America is, of course, of more than historical interest. As the United States Commission on Civil Rights recently reported, Mexican Americans continue to be victimized by a double standard of justice in the Southwest.[59] The roots of that double standard run deeper than the commission reported and will not die easily.

IV

It was largely lower-class Mexican Americans whose rights as new citizens were violated by the dual standard of justice operative in much of the Southwest. Upper-class, lighter-complected Hispanos were more secure in their personal rights, but had to fear for the security of their property. Ownership of land, the basic unit of wealth and social status in the agrarian and pastoral economies of Mexico's far northern frontier, came under fire after the United States took control of the area. Across the Southwest, Hispano landowners lost control of private and communal lands as the century wore on. This process evolved at different rates and under different circumstances in each area of the Southwest. It had its beginning in the Republic of Texas in 1836.

At first glance, Texas Mexicans seem to have benefited from the liberal land policies of the Texas Republic. According to the 1836 Constitution, all loyal Texans who lived in Texas when independence was declared on March 2, 1836, and who had not previously owned land, were guaranteed "headrights," grants of land totaling as much as 4,605 acres. In the Bexar land district some 500 Texas Mexicans received these grants. In addition, Texans who served in the army were entitled to "bounties" of land. These went to some 140 Texanos, although they found it more difficult to obtain these grants than did Anglos.[60]

The advantages that Texas Mexicans had in obtaining land in Texas probably existed more in theory than in practice. The Texas Constitution of 1836 stated that persons who refused to fight against Mexico during the revolution, or who had aided the enemy, would lose "such lands as they may hold in the Republic." For those Anglos who coveted the lands of Texas Mexicans, it was convenient to assume that all Mexicans had aided the enemy and should be driven off their property.

In the wave of anti-Mexican hatred that followed the Texas Revolution, many Mexicans, fearful of mindless reprisals, abandoned their lands and fled across the Rio Grande. Towns such as Victoria and Goliad became nearly deserted after the revolution. Many Texas Mexicans who received headrights sold them to speculators (chiefly Anglos, although Texano oligarchs such as Juan Seguín and Francisco de la Garza engaged in this business).[61] Some Texas Mexicans who had been forced off their ancestral lands returned years later when the atmosphere seemed less volatile. They found Anglos living on their property, some claiming headrights and bounties. Overlapping claims resulted, of course, which led to costly litigation, some of which dragged on into the twentieth century.[62]

Lower-class Mexicans in Texas probably lost their lands through force and intimidation, while the upper-class hacendados saw their lands disappear legally through circumstances similar to those in California and New Mexico: expensive and interminable litigation, chicanery of lawyers, overlapping claims, and high taxes based on the alien concept of assessed value of land rather than on what the land produced.[63] Although the state of Texas upheld the validity of most of the Spanish and Mexican grants,[64] a slow but inexorable shift of land ownership of these grants, from Hispano to Anglo, took place. In Nueces County, for example, fifteen grants, all owned by Mexicans, covered the county in 1835. By 1848 Mexicans had lost seven of those fifteen; by 1859, only one of the fifteen remained in the hands of a Texano.[65] In border counties such as Webb, Zapata, and Starr, where slight immigration put little pressure on the hacendados to sell land until after the turn of the century, the process was slower but equally inexorable.[66]

The federal government played no part in these land matters in Texas, for when Texas entered the Union in 1845 it retained control of all its public lands, a situation unique in American history. On the other hand, in New Mexico, Arizona, and California land grants were protected by the Treaty of Guadalupe-Hidalgo which promised that property would be protected "as if the same belonged to citizens of the United States." Thus, responsibility for protecting property rights in the remainder of the Southwest rested with the federal government, which was extraordinarily inefficient in carrying out the task.

Land titles were confirmed most quickly in California, where the demands of gold-seeking American immigrants forced Congress to action. Three years after the signing of the Treaty of Guadalupe-Hidalgo, Congress passed the California Land Act of 1851, which established a cumbersome and controversial machinery for confirming titles of holders of Spanish and Mexican grants. The act put the burden of proof of title upon the claimant, who had to convince the Board of Land Commissioners that his title was legitimate. If title could not be proved, the land entered the public domain. Regardless of the decision of the board, however, either government attorneys or the claimant could appeal the case to the United States district court, and, beyond that, to the Supreme Court. Although the Board of Land Commissioners finished its work by 1856, almost all of the 813 cases that it had heard were appealed to the district court, and 99 were appealed to the Supreme Court. The average time for settlement of a claim in California was seventeen years.[67]

If the process worked slowly in California, it was still preferable to the agonizingly tedious system that Congress devised for Arizona and New Mexico. Not until 1854 did Congress appoint a surveyor-general to investigate the legitimacy of titles in New Mexico, of which

Arizona was a part until 1863. In New Mexico, Congress itself assumed responsibility for final judgment on all claims. Until Congress took action, no land in New Mexico or Arizona would hold a clear title or enter the public domain. By 1880 the surveyor-general had been inundated by over 1,000 claims in New Mexico, but had reported only 150 to Congress. Of those 150, Congress had acted on 71. In Arizona, where there were fewer Spanish and Mexican period grants than in New Mexico, a surveyor-general had examined 15 titles by 1888. Although he had approved 13 of them, Congress had yet to act on any of the Arizona grants.[68] In an effort to speed up this procedure, in 1891 Congress finally established the special Court of Private Land Claims for New Mexico, Arizona, and Colorado. The rules under which this court operated were more legalistic and less receptive to questions of usage and custom than in California four decades earlier. The Court of Private Land Claims finished its work in 1904, over fifty years after the signing of the Treaty of Guadalupe-Hidalgo, and some appeals still remained to be heard by the Supreme Court.[69]

Years of costly litigation in a foreign language, in a judicial system that many only vaguely comprehended, were usually ruinous for the Hispano claimants. In New Mexico, for example, more than 80 percent of the grant holders lost their lands. There, since community grants and communal holdings were more common than individual grants, the slowness of litigation had its greatest impact on small farmers and herders. Across the Southwest, sharp Anglo lawyers divested Hispanos of their grants, sometimes legitimately as payment for services, and on other occasions through outright chicanery—by forging documents or deliberately giving wrong advice. In New Mexico, the land grant business became the territory's major industry, employing numerous lawyers and enabling one, Thomas B. Catron, to obtain two million acres and part-ownership of four million more. Corruption, centering around land matters, flourished in New Mexico, involving public officials at all levels through the notorious Santa Fe Ring, which was composed largely of Anglo Americans.[70]

This is not to suggest, of course, that Hispanos were completely innocent of wrongdoing. Some upper-class Mexican Americans swindled lower-class Mexican Americans. Some pressed claims to grants that they knew had not fulfilled the requirements for clear title under Mexican law, and a few made skillful forgeries of grants. Yet, on the balance, the Yankees, who had the advantage of using their native language and familiar laws and legal procedures, retained the upper hand.

Years of unclear titles frustrated not only the Hispanos, but Anglos, too, who had been in the habit of preempting or squatting on public lands, then eventually receiving title to them. Many Anglos rationalized that large, undeveloped landholdings were immoral, and thus fair game for settlement. Where congressional delay left the line between public land and private land hazy, Anglo squatters also had to spend their meager resources on litigation and grew increasingly restive.[71] In northern California, especially, their frustrations led to violence in the 1850s: Anglo squatters staked off claims on Californios' lands, burned crops, razed orchards, and tormented vaqueros, successfully driving some Californios off their property.[72] In New Mexico, until the turn of the century, settlers attempting to file claims under the Homestead Act of 1872 or the Desert Land Act of 1877 were hindered by the uncertainty of titles. There, too, congressional delay hampered the development of public lands, and Yankees used coercion and violence to divest the Hispanos of their private claims.[73] Thus, congressional slowness did injustices both to Anglo newcomers and to the Mexican American landowners in California and New Mexico, serving to intensify hostility between the two groups.

It seems clear that during the slow process of confirming titles, ownership of land shifted from the hands of the Spanish-speaking to the Anglo newcomers. The question that has engaged historians is: Why? Part of the explanation lies in the complexity of determining what had been clear titles to land under Mexican law. Land had been abundant on Mexico's far northern frontier, and men with legal training were noticeably absent. Hence, there had been little need to have exact boundaries or ironclad titles. Disputes rarely arose. Property descriptions, called *diseños*, often included such perishable landmarks as a cow's skull or a tree stump, or such vague terms as "the skirts of the mountains." Frequently no records existed.

To convert this informal system to Yankee precision, and to verify titles as the federal government required, was costly. Yet in California, Arizona, and New Mexico, Congress failed to furnish sufficient funds for attorneys, for research into Mexican archives, or for surveys. Hence, failure to implement congressional legislation adequately also explains the slowness of procedures. Some historians, however, have asked whether the machinery that the federal government established to validate titles was in itself equitable and whether it met the requirements of the Treaty of Guadalupe-Hidalgo. In response to this question historian Paul Gates, the leading authority on United States federal land policy, has answered an emphatic yes.

Writing about the California Land Act of 1851, Gates argues that the Californios were treated fairly—indeed, too fairly.[74] Many of the California grants, Gates asserts, were illegal under Mexican law, yet the federal courts confirmed them because of leniency and sometimes incompetency. Errors in administering the act usually favored the claimants. The Californios, Gates suggests, had more land than they needed, and that land would have been of little value if the Americans had not taken over California. Moreover, by 1851 non-Mexicans held 42 percent of the 813 claims in California. The Land Act, then, was not prejudicial to any one group. Delays in the system were due largely to the claimants who, Gates says, kept disorderly records, persisted in claiming more land then they had a right to, and profited from delays by renting out lands which would not have been theirs anyway. Loss of the Californios' lands resulted not from the Land Act of 1851, which Gates terms "statesmanlike," but from the recklessness and improvidence of the Californios themselves[75] and from population pressures which demanded more intensive use of land. Taxes, too, put an unaccustomed burden on property owners, frequently forcing them to sell land at low prices or take out usurous loans to raise cash. This, of course, could not be blamed on the Act of 1851.

Most writers, while acknowledging the validity of some of Gates' arguments, have placed heavier responsibility on the federal government for creating a system which forced Hispanos into expensive litigation and obscured their titles.[76] These critics have argued, as did Senator Thomas Hart Benton in 1851, that it would have been preferable to approve all land titles automatically, then allow challenges to be brought before the court on an individual basis. By calling all titles into question, the United States government violated the spirit, if not the letter, of the Treaty of Guadalupe-Hidalgo. Most writers would agree with New Mexico's historian-attorney, William Keleher, that "the promise to protect the future citizens in their property had not been kept."[77] Landowners in the nineteenth century agreed with Keleher, too. Ironically, it was the same Yankees who had been so critical of the slowness of Mexican justice who now subjected Mexican Americans to costly legal delays. Those Yankees had an aphorism that seems applicable to their own procedures: "Justice delayed is justice denied."

Whatever the cause, loss of land had a wide-ranging impact upon the Mexican American community across the Southwest. It eroded the basis of the elite's power, leaving that class preoccupied with its personal economic problems and less able to devote its attention to political affairs or to provide leadership for the community. Small landowners, too, were affected. In New Mexico, in particular, some villages' common grazing and woodlands (ejidos) were lost for lack of a clear title. The repercussions of that are still being felt in New Mexico today, where *La Alianza Federal de Mercedes,* led by fiery Reies López Tijerina, has made headlines since its dramatic attempts to regain federal land in the Carson National Forest in 1966.

The promises of the Treaty of Guadalupe-Hidalgo notwithstanding, it seems clear that not only had Mexican Americans become a minority in America by the end of the nineteenth century, but that many had become second-class citizens. Bereft of political power, subject to a capricious sytem of justice, and pushed off private and communal lands, they had truly become foreigners in their native land. They were not passive witnesses to this process, however, as we will see in the next chapter.

1. "Their property, their persons, their religion"

Stephen Watts Kearny, 1846*

On August 15, General Kearny and his Army of the West reached Las Vegas, the first sizeable Mexican settlement on the road from the East to Santa Fe. From a rooftop overlooking the plaza in the early morning sun, Kearny read a proclamation to the people of Las Vegas. Several local officials occupied the adobe roof with Kearny, and when he was finished reading, he asked them to take an oath of allegiance. The officials did so, eyes downcast. Kearny, not understanding that the Mexicans' downcast eyes symbolized respect, is reported to have said to one official: "Captain, look me in the face, while you repeat the oath of office." In years to come, a similar scene would be repeated in the Southwest between countless Anglo American school teachers and their Mexican American students.

Kearny's proclamation at Las Vegas made strong assurances—even to the point of guaranteeing United States protection against Indians. Kearny was to make similar assurances in the plaza at Santa Fe on August 19 and 22.

Mr. Alcalde, and people of New Mexico: I have come amongst you by the orders of my government, to take possession of your country, and extend over it the laws of the United States. We consider it, and have done so for some time, a part of the territory of the United States. We come amongst you as friends—not as enemies; as protectors—not as conquerors. We come among you for your benefit—not for your injury.

Henceforth I absolve you from all allegiance to the Mexican government, and from all obedience to General Armijo. He is no longer your governor; (great sensation.) I am your governor. I shall not expect you to take up arms and follow me, to fight your own people, who may oppose me; but I now tell you, that those who remain peaceably at home, attending to their crops and their herds, shall be protected by me, in their property, their persons, and their religion; and not a pepper, not an onion, shall be disturbed or taken by my troops, without pay, or by the consent of the owner. But listen! he

---

*Quoted in *Lieutenant Emory Reports*, ed. Ross Calvin (Albuquerque: 1951), pp. 49–50.

who promises to be quiet, and is found in arms against me, I will hang!

From the Mexican government you have never received protection. The Apaches and the Navajoes come down from the mountains and carry off your sheep, and even your women, whenever they please. My government will correct all this. It will keep off the Indians, protect you in your persons and property; and, I repeat again, will protect you in your religion. I know you are all great Catholics; that some of your priests have told you all sorts of stories—that we should ill-treat your women, and brand them on the cheek as you do your mules on the hip. It is all false. My government respects your religion as much as the Protestant religion, and allows each man to worship his Creator as his heart tells him is best. Its laws protect the Catholic as well as the Protestant; the weak as well as the strong; the poor as well as the rich. I am not a Catholic myself—I was not brought up in that faith; but, at least one-third of my army are Catholics, and I respect a good Catholic as much as a good Protestant.

There goes my army—you see but a small portion of it; there are many more behind—resistance is useless.

Mr. Alcalde, and you two captains of militia, the laws of my country require that all men who hold office under it shall take the oath of allegiance. I do not wish, for the present, until affairs become more settled, to disturb your form of government. If you are prepared to take oaths of allegiance, I shall continue you in office, and support your authority.

2. "All the rights of citizens"

The Treaty of Guadalupe Hidalgo, 1848*

When the Treaty of Guadalupe Hidalgo was signed on February 2, 1848, three of its twenty-three articles—VIII, IX, and X—concerned those Mexicans who remained in the conquered territory. Article X was completely eliminated by the United States Senate before it ratified the treaty on March 19, 1848. The

---

*Hunter Miller, ed., *Treaties and Other International Acts of the United States of America* (Washington, D.C.: 1931–32), 5:217–19, 241–43, 254–56, 380–81.

1. Norman F. Graebner, "The Treaty of Guadalupe Hidalgo: Its Background and Formation" (Ph.D. dissertation, University of Chicago, 1950), pp. 417–18.

Senate also revised Article IX, leaving only Article VIII un-
changed. Article X, which had validated all Mexican land grants
in the Southwest, was stricken from the treaty because some
senators feared that old Mexican grants might take precedence
over the later holdings of American settlers in Texas. Article IX
was amended because it implied United States hostility toward
the Catholic church, and because the unresolved slavery
question made senators reluctant to grant rapid statehood to
the newly acquired territory.[1]

In a letter of March 18, 1848 to the Mexican minister of
foreign relations, Secretary of State James Buchanan explained
in diplomatic language the reasons for these changes. An
uneasy Mexican legislature ratified the treaty on May 25, 1848.
To allay Mexican fears, when ratifications of the treaty were
formally exchanged at Querétaro on May 30, 1848, a protocol
was appended to the treaty which provided an official explanation of the changes that the United States had made. Like
Buchanan's letter, the protocol assured Mexico that the altered
wording of the articles would not change the original intent of
the treaty or diminish the rights of Mexicans who might remain
in the occupied territory. The United States never regarded the
protocol as a legally binding part of the treaty, even though
Mexico took it more seriously.

Articles VIII and IX as finally ratified did not affect Mexicans
or Mexican Americans in Texas. In the case of John F. McKinney
versus Manuel Saviego (1855), the United States Supreme Court
ruled that Articles VIII and IX did not apply to Texas, which had
been independent a decade before the Mexican War. The
protection of those articles was extended, however, to Mexicans
absorbed by the Gadsden Purchase. Article V of the Gadsden
Treaty specified that articles VIII and IX of the Treaty of
Guadalupe Hidalgo would apply to Mexicans in the territory
sold by President Santa Anna.

ARTICLE VIII OF THE TREATY AS RATIFIED

Mexicans now established in territories previously belonging to
Mexico, and which remain for the future within the limits of the
United States, as defined by the present treaty, shall be free to
continue where they now reside, or to remove at any time to the
Mexican Republic, retaining the property which they possess in the
said territories, or disposing thereof, and removing the proceeds
wherever they please; without their being subjected, on this account,
to any contribution, tax or charge whatever.

Those who shall prefer to remain in the said territories, may either retain the title and rights of Mexican citizens, or acquire those of citizens of the United States. But they shall be under the obligation to make their election within one year from the date of the exchange of ratifications of this treaty: and those who shall remain in the said territories, after the expiration of that year, without having declared their intention to retain the character of Mexicans, shall be considered to have elected to become citizens of the United States.

In the said territories, property of every kind, now belonging to Mexicans, not established there, shall be inviolably respected. The present owners, the heirs of these, and all Mexicans who may hereafter acquire said property by contract, shall enjoy with respect to it, guaranties equally ample as if the same belonged to citizens of the United States.

ARTICLE IX OF THE TREATY AS RATIFIED

The Mexicans who, in the territories aforesaid, shall not preserve the character of citizens of the Mexican Republic, conformably with what is stipulated in the preceding article, shall be incorporated into the Union of the United States and be admitted, at the proper time (to be judged of by the Congress of the United States) to the enjoyment of all the rights of citizens of the United States according to the principles of the Constitution; and in the mean time shall be maintained and protected in the free enjoyment of their liberty and property, and secured in the free exercise of their religion without restriction.

ARTICLE IX PRIOR TO AMENDMENT BY THE U.S. SENATE

The Mexicans who, in the territories aforesaid, shall not preserve the character of citizens of the Mexican Republic, conformably with what is stipulated in the preceeding Article, shall be incorporated into the Union of the United States, and admitted as soon as possible, according to the principles of the Federal Constitution, to the enjoyment of all the rights of citizens of the United States. In the mean time, they shall be maintained and protected in the enjoyment of their liberty, their property, and the civil rights now vested in them according to the Mexican laws. With respect to political rights, their condition shall be on an equality with that of the inhabitants of the other territories of the United States; and at least equally good as that of the inhabitants of Louisiana and the Floridas, when these provinces, by transfer from the French Republic and the Crown of Spain, became territories of the United States.

The same most ample guaranty shall be enjoyed by all ecclesiastics and religious corporations or communities, as well in the discharge of the offices of their ministry, as in the enjoyment of their property of every kind, whether individual or corporate. This guaranty shall embrace all temples, houses and edifices dedicated to the Roman Catholic worship; as well as all property destined to its support, or to that of schools, hospitals and other foundations for charitable or beneficent purposes. No property of this nature shall be considered as having become the property of the American Government, or as subject to be, by it, disposed of or diverted to other uses.

ARTICLE X PRIOR TO DELETION BY THE U.S. SENATE

All grants of land made by the Mexican Government or by the competent authorities, in territories previously appertaining to Mexico, and remaining for the future within the limits of the United States, shall be respected as valid, to the same extent that the same grants would be valid, if the said territories had remained within the limits of Mexico. But the grantees of lands in Texas, put in possession thereof, who, by reason of the circumstances of the country since the beginning of the troubles between Texas and the Mexican Government, may have been prevented from fulfilling all the conditions of their grants, shall be under the obligation to fulfill the said conditions within the periods limited in the same respectively; such periods to be now counted from the date of the exchange of ratifications of this treaty: in default of which the said grants shall not be obligatory upon the State of Texas, in virtue of the stipulations contained in this Article.

The foregoing stipulation in regard to grantees of land in Texas, is extended to all grantees of land in the territories aforesaid, elsewhere than in Texas, put in possession under such grants; and, in default of the fulfilment of the conditions of any such grant, within the new period, which as is above stipulated, begins with the day of the exchange of ratifications of this treaty, the same shall be null and void.

The Mexican Government declares that no grant whatever of lands in Texas has been made since the second day of March one thousand eight hundred and thirty six; and that no grant whatever of lands in any of the territories aforesaid has been made since the thirteenth day of May one thousand eight hundred and forty-six.

Finally, the relations and communication between the Catholics living in the territories aforesaid, and their respective ecclesiastical authorities, shall be open, free and exempt from all hindrance whatever, even although such authorities should reside within the limits of the Mexican Republic, as defined by this treaty; and this freedom shall continue, so long as a new demarcation of ecclesiastical districts shall not have been made, conformably with the laws of the Roman Catholic Church.

BUCHANAN EXPLAINS:

The second amendment of the Senate is to strike out the 9th Article and insert the following in lieu thereof.

[Here follows the English version of Article 9]

This article is substantially the same with the original 9th article; but it avoids unnecessary prolixity and accords with the former safe precedents of this Government in the Treaties by which we acquired Louisiana from France and Florida from Spain.

....

Under these Treaties with France and Spain, the free and flourishing States of Louisiana, Missouri, Arkansas, Iowa and Florida have been admitted into the Union; and no complaint has ever been made by the original or other inhabitants that their civil or religious rights have not been amply protected. The property belonging to the different churches in the United States is held as sacred by our Constitution and laws as the property of individuals; and every individual enjoys the inalienable right of worshipping his God according to the dictates of his own conscience. The Catholic Church in this country would not, if they could, change their position in this particular.

After the successful experience of nearly half a century, the Senate did not deem it advisable to adopt any new form for the 9th Article of the Treaty; and surely the Mexican Government ought to be content with an article similar to those which have proved satisfactory to the

Governments of France and Spain and to all the inhabitants of Louisiana and Florida, both of which were Catholic provinces.

I ought perhaps here to note a modification in the 9th article, as adopted by the Senate, of the analogous articles of the Louisiana and Florida Treaties. Under this modification, the inhabitants of the ceded territories are to be admitted into the Union, "at the proper time (to be judged of by the Congress of the United States") &c.

Congress, under all circumstances and under all Treaties are the sole judges of this proper time, because they and they alone, under the Federal Constitution, have power to admit new States into the Union. That they will always exercise this power as soon as the condition of the inhabitants of any acquired territory may render it proper, cannot be doubted. By this means the Federal Treasury can alone be relieved from the expense of supporting territorial Governments. Besides, Congress will never lend a deaf ear to a people anxious to enjoy the privilege of self government. Their application to become a State or States of the Union will be granted the moment this can be done with safety.

The third amendment of the Senate strikes from the Treaty the 10th Article.

It is truly unaccountable how this article should have found a place in the Treaty. That portion of it in regard to lands in Texas did not receive a single vote in the Senate. If it were adopted, it would be a mere nullity on the face of the Treaty, and the Judges of our Courts would be compelled to disregard it. It is our glory that no human power exists in this country which can deprive one individual of his property without his consent and transfer it to another. If grantees of lands in Texas, under the Mexican Government, possess valid titles, they can maintain their claims before our Courts of Justice. If they have forfeited their grants by not complying with the conditions on which they were made, it is beyond the power of this Government, in any mode of action, to render these titles valid either against Texas or any individual proprietor. To resuscitate such grants and to allow the grantees the same period after the exchange of the ratifications of this Treaty to which they originally entitled for the purpose of performing the conditions on which these grants had been made, even if this could be accomplished by the power of the government of the United States, would work manifold injustice.

These Mexican grants, it is understood, cover nearly the whole sea coast and a large portion of the interior of Texas. They embrace thriving villages and a great number of cultivated farms, the proprietors of which have acquired them honestly by purchase from the State of Texas. These proprietors are now dwelling in peace and security. To revive dead titles and suffer the inhabitants of Texas to be ejected under them from their possessions, would be an act of flagrant injustice if not wanton cruelty. Fortunately this Government possesses no power to adopt such a proceeding.

The same observations equally apply to such grantees in New Mexico and Upper Calfornia.

The present Treaty provides amply and specifically in its 8th and 9th Articles for the security of property of every kind belonging to Mexicans, whether acquired under Mexican grants or otherwise in the acquired territory. The property of foreigners under our Constitution and laws, will be equally secure without any Treaty stipulation. The tenth article could have no effect upon such grantees as had forfeited their claims, but that of involving them in endless litigation under the vain hope that a Treaty might cure the defects in their titles against honest purchasers and owners of the soil.

And here it may be worthy of observation that if no stipulation whatever were contained in the Treaty to secure to the Mexican inhabitants and all others protection in the free enjoyment of their liberty, property and the religion which they profess, these would be amply guarantied by the Constitution and laws of the United States. These invaluable blessings, under our form of Government, do not result from Treaty stipulations, but from the very nature and character of our institutions.

3. "For me the placers were finished"

Antonio Franco Coronel, 1849*

Accounts of the lack of justice for Mexicans and Mexican Americans in the California mines are abundant, but few were written by the victims themselves. One exception (and perhaps the only one) is the memoir of Mexican-born Antonio F. Coronel, who had come to California as a youth with the Híjar-Padrés colony in 1834. Coronel settled in Los Angeles, where his father, Ignacio, was a school teacher. Following his experience in the mines, Coronel returned to Los Angeles where he served as mayor (1853), on the city council (1846–67), and as state treasurer (1867–71).

Coronel's experience in the mines seems typical. In 1848, when news of the gold discovery reached them, Californios from as far south as Los Angeles and San Diego headed to the gold fields. Among them were Coronel and his companions. By October, they had begun mining at the Placer Seco, or Dry Diggings, and all "achieved brilliant results." Coronel left the mountains when winter set in, journeying to Sonoma to pick up fresh supplies and horses for further mining in the spring. In 1849, however, newcomers flocked to California from all over the world, bringing racial and ethnic tensions to a pitch and changing dramatically the situation for Mexican Americans, as Coronel sorrowfully described it.

. . . I arrived at the Placer Seco [about March, 1849] and began to work at a regular digging.

In this place there was already a numerous population of Chileans, Peruvians, Californians, Mexicans, and many Americans, Germans, etc. The camps were almost separated according to nationalities. All, some more, some less, were profiting from the fruit of their work. Presently news was circulated that it had been resolved to evict all of those who were not American citizens from the placers because it was

---

*Antonio Franco Coronel, "Cosas de California," dictated to Thomas Savage for the Bancroft Library, 1877, pp. 176–84, and published by permission of the Director, the Bancroft Library. Translated by David J. and Carol S. Weber. We have added accents and other punctuation where necessary for clarity and accuracy. A translation of Coronel's complete account of his activities in the mines appears in Appendix A of Richard Morefield, "The Mexican Adaptation in American California, 1846–1875" (M.A. thesis, University of California, Berkeley, 1955), which unfortunately came to our attention only after we had finished our own transcription and translation of this document.

believed that the foreigners did not have the right to exploit the placers.

One Sunday, [notices] appeared in writing in Los Pinos and in several places, that anyone who was not an American citizen must abandon the place within twenty-four hours and that he who did not comply would be obliged to by force. This was supported by a gathering of armed men, ready to make that warning effective.

There was a considerable number of people of various nationalities who understood the order to leave—they decided to gather on a hill in order to be on the defensive in case of any attack. On the day in which the departure of the foreigners should take place, and for three or four more days, both forces remained prepared, but the thing did not go beyond cries, shots, and drunken men. Finally all fell calm and we returned to continue our work. Daily, though, the weakest were dislodged from their diggings by the strongest.

After this agitation had calmed down, a Frenchman named Don Augusto and a Spaniard named Luis were seized—persons with whom I had dealt and who appeared to me to be honorable and of fairly good upbringing. All who had known them had formed the same opinion as I, and this seizure caused great surprise. Some of the most prominent people met together and commissioned me to investigate the reason for these arrests. I went to an American I had known in Los Angeles, one Richard, who had been a cavalry sergeant—I asked him to look into it for me. He answered immediately that they had been accused by an Irish fellow (an old man) of having stolen from him four pounds of gold from the place where he had buried it. I gave an account of my constituents and then, without loss of time, five pounds of gold was gathered from among all of us to see if payment would set these prisoners free. I approached the leader, whose appearance was disagreeable and ferocious. Wanting to vindicate the two men, I presented my plan to him through an interpreter. I told him we knew them as good men who had sufficient resources of their own and no need to appropriate those of another. Nevertheless, I had here five pounds of gold, one more than the old Irishman said they had stolen from him. He took the five pounds of gold and told me that he would go to report to his group—that I should return in the afternoon, some two or three hours later. Before the hour he had indicated to me, we saw the movement of armed men, the major part under the influence of liquor. Afterward we saw a cart leave with our two unfortunates, their arms tied behind their backs. Two men guarded them from on top of the cart, which was followed by a large crowd, some on foot and others on horseback. On the cart there was an inscription, poorly written in charcoal or something similar, which said that whoever might intercede for them would suffer the same punishment. They reached an oak tree where the execution was to take place. When the ropes had been hung around their necks, they asked to write something to their families and to arrange their affairs. For having made this request, one of the men received a slap in the face. Then, suddenly, they moved the cart and the unlucky men were hanged.

This act horrified me and it had the same effect upon many others—in two days I raised camp and headed toward the northern placers.

The reason for most of the antipathy against the Spanish race was that the greater portion was composed of Sonorans who were men accustomed to prospecting and who consequently achieved quicker, richer results—such as the *Californios* had already attained by having arrived first and acquiring understanding of this same art. Those who came later [mainly Anglo Americans], were possessed by the terrible fever to obtain gold, but they did not get it because their diggings yielded but little or nothing, or because their work did not correspond to what they took out. Well, these men aspired to become rich in a minute and they could not resign themselves to view with patience the better fortune of others. Add to this fever that which the excessive use of liquor gives them. Add that generally among so many people of all nationalities there are a great number of lost people, capable of all conceivable crimes. The circumstance that there were no laws nor authorities who could protect the rights and lives of men gave to these men advantages over peaceful and honorable men. Properly speaking, there was no more law in those times than that of force, and finally, the good person, in his own defense, had to establish the law of retaliation.

I arrived at Sacramento with my mules, loaded them, and headed north to the place where I had left my tent in charge of my brother.

Some fourteen miles distant from Sutter's mill, toward the north, I met my brother and the servants, and several others of the Spanish race, coming, fleeing on foot. They told me that a party of armed foreigners had run them out quickly, without permitting them to take either their animals or other things. I returned to the mill where there was a small population—there I had some acquaintances. My aim was to see if I could sell the cargo that I carried, in order to leave the placers. I sold the goods in different places, almost all the mules, etc., at prices so low that I lost two-thirds of the gold they had cost me. These people took advantage of the situation in which I found myself.

At this time, Juan Manso arrived there with some Sonorans, still of the party of Andrés Pico—Ramón Carrillo, with some other companions from Sonoma, came also. Concerning the alternatives of continuing, or of retreating as I had been going to do, one Fisher, a merchant of Sutter's Mill and an old acquaintance of mine from Los Angeles, together with other merchants from the place, began to persuade us that this measure did not represent the feeling of the greater part of the people who lived in these parts and that these acts must have come from some party of highwaymen; because it was published thus, it was understood that the Californians were considered the same as the rest of the Americans; that they would give us a credential signed by the outstanding people from here in which we would be commended as such citizens and worthy of respect. I did not agree, but at the insistence of the others, I acceded to return and set about anew to take out gold from the placers.

....

> Once again Coronel's party found gold and all set to work: Manuel Serrano and his brothers; Dolores Sepúlveda; José de García Feliz; Ramón Carrillo; and other Californians. Nearby were the Bacas, originally from New Mexico and now from Sonoma. Under Coronel's leadership, the Californios adopted a policy of secrecy in order to avoid further incidents. Although the work was hard, the results of the first week's digging were very successful. Then, on Saturday night, an Irishman from Ramón Carrillo's group disappeared. The man had lived in California for some time and was trusted; but he was known to have a weakness for alcohol.

. . . He went to Sutter's Mill, he got drunk, and revealed all of our affair, plans, rules, etc. On the following Monday, we staked out new diggings and proceeded to work them immediately. The work was harder because the gold was much deeper and there was more rock, but on the other hand the gold turned out to be denser and in greater quantity. Almost everyone had to occupy the week working his diggings in order to reach the gold. But, during this time, a large number of armed men gathered daily, taking account as before. They had such complete knowledge of our business that on Saturday of this week armed men began to slip in, making their camp immediately next to ours. Then I thought about the goal of those people and I charged everyone in our camp to be very prudent and moderate so that they not give the others a pretext to bother us.

Now all of us were piling up our dirt, which was rather rich and promised us better results than the first week. About ten in the morning all of these merciless people, numbering more than 100, invaded our diggings at a moment when all of us were inside of them. The invaders were so courteous that they asked who the leader of our party was. When I was pointed out to them, their leader and some eight more surrounded my digging. . . . All of these men raised their pistols [*pistolas fajadas*], their Bowie knives; some had rifles, other pickaxes and shovels.

Their leader spoke to me, introducing himself and two others with pickaxes and shovels in my digging. He led me to understand that this was theirs because before we took the place, one or two months before, he with his men took possession of this same and that a boundary had been marked out from one side of the river to the other. He told me several things in English so that I did not understand him immediately, but all amounted to saying that this was his property. Excited, I answered him harshly, but fortunately he did not understand me. I was able to reflect for a moment that the gold was not worth risking my life in this way.

The rest of the invaders took possession of the other diggings in the same way. My companions ran to our camp before me and armed themselves. I knew their hostile intentions. Already they had ordered that a number of horses be saddled. I arrived where they were and persuaded them to calm down. Indeed, whatever attempt they might make would be fruitless. For me the placers were finished.

We mounted our horses and left the place. The entire party dispersed and I left for Los Angeles without stopping in any place longer than was necessary.

4. "Hanged as suspects"   El Clamor Público, 1857*

Injustice toward Mexican Americans, and the failure of the law to protect them, was not confined to the gold fields of California, but existed throughout the state. When Coronel returned to Los Angeles, he must have discovered that law enforcement had broken down there, too, and vigilante committees were formed to take over where government officials failed. Although some Californios participated in and approved of vigilante justice, more often the Spanish-speaking people of Los Angeles were its victims. Historian Leonard Pitt found that by 1854 "the Spanish-speaking of Los Angeles felt oppressed by a double standard of justice such as some of them had previously experienced in the gold mines." "Every important lynch-law episode and most minor ones involved the Spanish-speaking."[1]

The following letter describes the retaliation made by the good citizens of Los Angeles against a band of thieves who were of Mexican origin. This letter, written from Los Angeles, apparently by an unidentified Frenchman, appeared in the March 4, 1857 issue of Le Phare, a French-language newspaper published in San Francisco. It was translated into Spanish by Francisco P. Ramírez, editor of El Clamor Público of Los Angeles. Ramírez, a man proficient in French, English, and Spanish, believed that the letter accurately reflected events in Los Angeles. What would have resulted if Mexican Americans had been guilty of similar brutality?

                                                    Los Angeles
                                                    February 21
Mr. Editor:

Now you must have learned through the newspapers of our city of the sad events that have occurred in the country during the present month. But these newspapers have omitted many circumstances, in spite of their being well known and of public notoriety. Under no pretext should their silence be excused. Journalism is the advanced sentinel of civilization; its life is a life of continual combat, constantly on the defense. . . .

---

*El Clamor Público, March 21, 1857. Trans. David J. Weber.

1. Leonard Pitt, The Decline of the Californios: A Social History of the Spanish-speaking Californians, 1846–1890 (Berkeley:1968), pp. 160, 154.

For three months a band of thieves has run about the streets and outlying areas of this city by night, abandoning themselves to all kinds of wickedness, including the most refined highway robbery. Various persons have complained to the authorities, but the authorities respond: "Do you have witnesses? Do you want to pay to have them arrested?" And the band continued robbing and killing with all security, by the light of day and in the middle of the city under the chin of the police officials who seem to view this as a comedy. This is not strange; [they say] "the Mexicans are killing each other." . . . Four or five Americans have established a Vigilante Committee, made a call to all the population for the public security, and named captains of a company to go in pursuit of the bandits. Here is where the drama begins with all its horrors, and wrapped in a mystery so strange that one is obliged to believe that the bandits were not the persecuted ones. In a few words, a company (all Americans), its captain Sanford, headed toward the Mission of San Gabriel. All the Mexican residents in that place were arrested and treated with unequalled brutality. Two of these unfortunates had been arrested at the entrance of the Mission. They had to submit to an interrogation of the most provocative sort. Intimidated by the threats, and impelled by the instinct of self preservation, they began to run, especially when they saw the captain draw his pistol. But, ay! at the first movement that they made, a general volley followed. One fell wounded from various shots. The other was able to reach a lake or marsh. He abandoned his horse and concealed himself in the rushes. Vain efforts. The American band arrived, set fire to the marsh, and very soon, among the general cries of gaiety, they discovered the head of the unfortunate above the flames. A second volley and all was done.—I deceive myself. It was not finished so quickly. The body, loaded over a horse, was transported to the Mission in the midst of cries and shouts of joy and gaiety. Here, overtaken by horror, thought stops because it is impossible to find expressions to describe the scene which took place and was related to me by many witnesses worthy of trust. The body was thrown to the ground in the midst of the mob. One being, with a human face, stepped forward with a knife in his hand. . . . With one hand he took the head of the dead man by its long hair, separated it from the body, flung it a short distance and stuck his dagger in the heart of the cadaver. Afterward, returning to the head, he made it roll with his foot into the middle of his band and the rabble, amidst the cries and the hurrahs of the greater number. . . . Is it not horrible? But wait, we have not yet seen all. Another band arrived from another place with two Californios. They had been arrested as suspects, one of them going in search of some oxen, the other to his daily work. They were conducted into the middle of the mob. The cries of "To death! To death!" were heard from all sides. The cutter of heads entered his house, coming out with some ropes, and the two unfortunates were hanged—despite the protests of their countrymen and their families. Once hanged from the tree, the ropes broke and the hapless ones were finished being murdered by shots or knife thrusts. The cutter of heads was fatigued, or his knife did not now cut! Perhaps you will believe that this very cruel person was an Indian from the mountains, one of those barbarians who lives far from all civilization in the Sierra Nevada! Wrong. That barbarian, that mutilator of cadavers, is the Justice of the Peace of San Gabriel! . . . He is a citizen of the United States, an American of pure blood. . . .

Afterwards, two Mexicans were found hanging from a tree, and near there another with two bullets in the head.

On the road from Tejon another company had encountered two poor peddlers (always Mexicans) who were arrested and hanged as suspects.

> The same issue of *El Clamor Público,* which carried the story of indiscriminate retaliation against Mexicans in the Los Angeles area also published the following notice:

Meeting.

We have been informed that all the individuals of *la raza Española,* residents of this county, will hold a meeting in this city for the purpose of asking the competent authorities to take suitable measures to pass sentence upon the Justice of the Peace of the Mission of San Gabriel for horribly murdering three innocent Mexicans, residents of that place.

5. "A foreigner in my native land"

Juan Nepomuceno Seguín, 1858*

In turbulent Texas, political control could be violently wrested from Hispanos, even though they constituted a majority in a settlement. San Antonio is a case point. For a few years after the Texas Revolution few Anglos lived in San Antonio, and Texanos continued to govern their city. This was the situation until 1842, when a Mexican force under General Rafael Vásquez captured the city. Vásquez invited all former Mexicans to return to Mexico and announced that the Mayor of San Antonio, Juan N. Seguín, was still a loyal Mexican.

Vásquez appears to have been deliberately trying to discredit Seguín, and the plan succeeded, for Seguín had Anglo enemies who were eager to believe anything that would remove him from power. Although Seguín demonstrated his loyalty by leading the troops who pursued Vásquez back to the border (as he had done during the Texas Revolution—see chapter 3), Seguín became suspect and was forced into hiding. With their leader in disgrace and Texas Volunteers occupying the city and harrassing them by stealing livestock and corn, many Texas Mexicans decided to leave for Mexico. Some probably did sympathize with Mexico, but most seem to have been driven out of San Antonio by Anglo violence. According to Bishop John Odin, twenty prominent Texano families left San Antonio in 1842, and countless others joined them.

In 1839 there had been 1,500 Mexicans and 250 Anglos in San Antonio. By 1846, after the exodus of Texas Mexicans and an influx of new Anglo immigrants, the population of the city was divided evenly between the two groups at about 750 each. With most of the leading Mexican families gone or intimidated, Americans dominated the political affairs of the city.

Juan Seguín himself resigned as mayor and joined the Texano refugees who fled San Antonio in 1842. Seguín was forced to settle in Mexico, the country he had fought against in the Texas Revolution. He explains why in the following selection from his memoirs.

---

*Personal Memoirs of John N. Seguín, From the Year 1834 to the Retreat of General Woll from the City of San Antonio, 1842 (San Antonio: 1858), pp. iii–iv, 18–32 passim. See also a fine short study, Ray F. Broussard, San Antonio During the Texas Republic: A City in Transition. Southwestern Studies, monograph no. 18 (El Paso: 1967), pp. 14, 28–31.

A native of the City of San Antonio de Bexar, I embraced the cause of Texas at the report of the first cannon which foretold her liberty; filled an honorable situation in the ranks of the conquerors of San Jacinto, and was a member of the legislative body of the Republic. I now find myself, in the very land, which in other times bestowed on me such bright and repeated evidences of trust and esteem, exposed to the attacks of scribblers and personal enemies, who, to serve *political purposes*, and engender strife, falsify historical facts, with which they are but imperfectly acquainted. I owe it to myself, my children and friends, to answer them with a short, but true exposition of my acts, from the beginning of my public career, to the time of the return of General Woll from the Rio Grande, with the Mexican forces, amongst which I was then serving.

....

I have been the object of the hatred and passionate attacks of some few disorganizers, who, for a time, ruled, as masters, over the poor and oppressed population of San Antonio. Harpy-like, ready to pounce on every thing that attracted the notice of their rapacious avarice, I was an obstacle to the execution of their vile designs. They, therefore, leagued together to exasperate and ruin me; spread against me malignant calumnies, and made use of odious machinations to sully my honor and tarnish my well earned reputation.

A victim to the wickedness of a few men, whose imposture was favored by their origin, and recent domination over the country; a foreigner in my native land; could I be expected stoically to endure their outrages and insults? Crushed by sorrow, convinced that my death alone would satisfy my enemies, I sought for a shelter amongst those against whom I had fought; I separated from my country, parents, family, relatives and friends, and what was more, from the institutions, on behalf of which I had drawn my sword, with an earnest wish to see Texas free and happy.

....

Ere the tomb closes over me and my contemporaries, I wish to lay open to publicity this stormy period of my life; I do it for friends as well as for my enemies, I challenge the latter to contest, with facts, the statements I am about to make, and I leave the decision unhesitatingly to the witnesses of the events.

....

The tokens of esteem, and evidences of trust and confidence, repeatedly bestowed upon me by the Supreme Magistrate, General Rusk, and other dignitaries of the Republic, could not fail to arouse against me much invidious and malignant feeling. The jealousy envinced against me by several officers of the companies recently arrived at San Antonio, from the United States, soon spread amongst the American straggling adventurers, who were already beginning to work their dark intrigues against the native families, whose only crime was, that they owned large tracts of land and desirable property.

....

. . . In those evil days, San Antonio was swarming with adventurers from every quarter of the globe. Many a noble heart grasped the sword in the defence of the liberty of Texas, cheerfully pouring out their blood for our cause, and to them everlasting public gratitude is due; but there were also many bad men, fugitives from their country, who found in this land an open field for their criminal designs.

San Antonio claimed then, as it claims now, to be the first city of Texas; it was also the receptacle of the scum of society. My political and social situation brought me into continual contact with that class of people. At every hour of the day and night, my countrymen ran to me for protection against the assaults or exactions of those adventurers. Some times, by persuasion, I prevailed on them to desist; some times, also, force had to be resorted to. How could I have done otherwise? Were not the victims my own countrymen, friends and associates? Could I leave them defenceless, exposed to the assaults of foreigners, who, on the pretext that they were Mexicans, treated them worse than brutes. Sound reason and the dictates of humanity would have precluded a different conduct on my part.

....

On my return to San Antonio [in 1842], several persons told me that the Mexican officers had declared that I was in their favor. This rumor, and some threats uttered against me by Goodman, left me but little doubt that my enemies would try to ruin me.

....

. . . Reports were widely spreading about my pretended treason.

Captain Manuel Flores, Lieutenant Ambrosio Rodriguez, Matias Curbier, and five or six other Mexicans, dismounted with me to find out the origin of the imposture. I went out with several friends, leaving Curbier in my house. I had reached the Main Plaza, when several persons came running to inform me, that some Americans were murdering Curbier. We ran back to the house, where we found poor Curbier covered with blood. On being asked who assaulted him, he answered, that the gunsmith Goodman, in company with several Americans, had struck him with a rifle. A few minutes afterwards, Goodman returned to my house, with about thirty volunteers, but, observing that we were prepared to meet them, they did not attempt to attack us. We went out of the house and then to Mr. Guilbeau's, who offered me his protection. He went out into the street, pistol in hand, and succeeded in dispersing the mob, which had formed in front of my house. Mr. John Twohig [sic] offered me a shelter for that night; on the next morning, I went under disguise to Mr. Van Ness' house; Twohig, who recognised me in the street, warned me to "open my eyes." I remained one day at Mr. Van Ness'; next day General Burleson arrived in San Antonio, commanding a respectable force of volunteers. I presented myself to him, asking for a Court of Inquiry; he answered, that there were no grounds for such proceedings. . . .

I remained, hiding from rancho to rancho, for over fifteen days. Every party of volunteers en route to San Antonio, declared, "they wanted to kill Seguin." I could no longer go from farm to farm, and determined to go on to my own farm and raise fortifications,

Several of my relatives and friends joined me. Hardly a day elapsed without receiving notice that a party was preparing to attack me; we were constantly kept under arms. Several parties came in sight, but, probably seeing that we were prepared to receive them, refrained from attacking. On the 30th of April, a friend from San Antonio sent me word that Captain Scott, and his company, were coming down by the river, burning the ranchos on their way. The inhabitants of the lower ranchos called on us for aid against Scott. With those in my house, and others to the number of about 100, I started to lend them aid. I proceeded, observing the movements of Scott, from the junction of the Medina to Pajaritos. At that place we dispersed, and I returned to my wretched life. In those days I could not go to San Antonio without peril of my life.

Matters being in this state, I saw that it was necessary to take some step which would place me in security, and save my family from constant wretchedness. I had to leave Texas, abandon all, for which I had fought and spent my fortune, to become a wanderer. The ingratitude of those, who had assumed to themselves the right of convicting me; their credulity in declaring me a traitor, on mere rumors, when I had to plead in my favor the loyal patriotism with which I had always served Texas, wounded me deeply.

Seeing that all these plans were impracticable, I resolved to seek a refuge amongst my enemies, braving all dangers. But before taking this step, I sent in my resignation to the Corporation of San Antonio, as Mayor of the city, stating to them, that, unable any longer to suffer the persecutions of some ungrateful Americans, who strove to murder me, I had determined to free my family and friends from their continual misery on my account, and go and live peaceably in Mexico. That for these reasons I resigned my office, with all my privileges and honors as a Texan.

I left Bexar without any engagements towards Texas; my services paid by persecutions, exiled and deprived of my privileges as a Texas citizen, I was in this country a being out of the pale of society, and when she could not protect the rights of her citizens, they were privileged to seek protection elsewhere. I had been tried by a rabble, condemned without a hearing, and consequently was at liberty to provide for my own safety.

After the expedition of General Woll, I did not return to Texas till the treaty of Guadalupe Hidalgo. During my absence nothing appeared that could stamp me as a traitor. My enemies had accomplished their object; they had killed me politically in Texas, and the less they spoke of me, the less risk they incurred of being exposed in the infamous means they had used to accomplish my ruin.

. . . The rumor, that I was a traitor, was seized with avidity by my enemies in San Antonio. Some envied my military position, as held by a *Mexican;* others found in me an obstacle to the accomplishment of their villainous plans. The number of land suits which still encumbers the docket of Bexar county, would indicate the nature of these plans, and any one, who has listened to the evidence elicited in cases of this description, will readily discover the base means adopted to deprive rightful owners of their property.

I have finished my memoirs; I neither have the capacity nor the desire to adorn my acts with literary phrases. I have attempted a short and clear narrative of my public life, in relation to Texas. I give it publicity, without omiting or suppressing anything that I thought of the least interest, and confidently I submit to the public verdict.

Several of those who witnessed the facts which I have related, are still alive and amongst us; they can state whether I have in any way falsified the record.

6. "No justice for the Mexicans in Texas"

Comisión Pesquisadora, 1873*

By the early 1870s violence along the Texas-Mexican border had reached crisis proportions, with dire consequences for Texas Mexicans. The situation was serious enough that in 1872 Congress authorized a three-man commission to investigate crimes along the border. Crime, the commission concluded, was largely the fault of border raiders from Mexico and of Mexican officials who permitted raids to be launched from their soil. Mexico was to blame, they calculated, for $27,859,363.97 worth of damages.

The following year, in 1873, Mexico sent to the border its own *Comisión Pesquisadora*, which concluded that most of the violence and thievery came from within Texas and that Mexicans who stole cattle learned their trade in the United States. Clearly, each of the reports was biased, but as J. Fred Rippy, who made the most detailed study of this period, cautiously concluded, "the truth perhaps corresponds more nearly with the findings of the Mexican commissioners."[1]

The following selection from the report of the Mexican commission describes the unhappy condition of Texas Mexicans, caught in the middle of international conflict. It discusses the Cart War of 1857 and quotes from Texas sources to conclude that there was "no justice for the Mexicans in Texas." Certainly, many Anglos concurred with the Mexican commission. Senator

---

*Comisión Pesquisadora de la Frontera del Norte, *Reports of the Committee of Investigation Sent in 1873 by the Mexican Government to the Frontier of Texas*, trans. from the official edition made in Mexico (New York: 1875), pp. 129–32.

1. J. Fred Rippy, *The United States and Mexico* (New York: 1926), p. 288.

Joseph E. Dwyer, who made a special report on border troubles in 1875, found that "there is a considerable element . . . that think the killing of a Mexican is *no crime.*"[2]

By 1880 some order began to come to the lawless Texas-Mexican border, both because of the efficient, if often brutal, tactics of the Texas Rangers, described in the next reading, and because Mexico had entered a period of rule by a strongman, Porfirio Díaz (1876–1910), who quieted the Mexican side of the border with his own Ranger-like force, the rurales. Yet, despite the veneer of order, Texanos continued to suffer from a dual standard of justice in Texas.

The Commission has already referred to the condition of the Mexicans in Texas subsequent to the treaty of Guadalupe. Their lands were especially coveted. Their title deeds presented the same confusion as did all the grants of land made by the Spanish government, and this became the fruitful source of litigation by which many families were ruined. The legislation, instead of being guided by a spirit of equity, on the contrary tended toward the same end; attempts were made to deprive the Mexicans of their lands, the slightest occurrence was made use of for this purpose, and the supposition is not a remote one, that the cause of such procedure may have been a well settled political principle, leading as far as possible to exclude from an ownership in the soil the Mexicans, whom they regarded as enemies and an inferior race.

At the commencement, and during the disorganization which was prolonged after the Treaty of Guadalupe, robberies and spoliations of lands were perpetrated by parties of armed Americans. It is not extraordinary to find some of them whose only titles consist of having taken possession of and settled upon lands belonging to Mexicans. After these spoliations there came the spoliations in legal forms, and all the resources of a complicated legislation.

At the time the Commission made its report it had not then received various documents to which reference will be made in the proper places by notes. Some of these show the insecurity under which the Mexican population in Texas had labored, and refer to the difficulties known as the cart question.

The residents of Uvalde county, Texas, in September, 1857, passed

---

2. Joseph E. Dwyer to Governor Richard Coke, in U.S. Senate, *Testimony Taken by the Special Committee on Texas Frontier Troubles,* 44th Cong., 1st sess., 1876, H. Rept. 343, ser. 1079, pp. 124–25.

several resolutions, prohibiting all Mexicans from traveling through the country except under a passport granted by some American authority. At Goliad several Mexicans were killed because it was supposed that they had driven their carts on the public road.

On the 14th and 19th of October the Mexican Legation at Washington addressed the United States Government a statement of these facts, adding that it had been informed that in the vicinity of San Antonio, Bexar [County], Texas, parties of armed men had been organized for the exclusive purpose of pursuing the Mexicans upon the public roads, killing them and robbing their property, and that the number of victims was stated to have been seventy-five. That it was also informed that Mexican citizens by birth, residing peaceably at San Antonio, under the protection of the laws, had been expelled from the place, and finally that some of the families of the victims of these extraordinary persecutions had begun to arrive in Mexico on foot and without means, having been obliged to abandon all their property in order to save their lives.

The Secretary of State on the 24th of the same month addressed a communication to Mr. E. M. Pease, the Governor of the State of Texas, in which he says:

> These reports are not exclusively Mexican. The least among the outrages appear to be the violation of rights guaranteed by law, and under treaties, and I have no doubt that you will have adopted speedy and energetic measures to ascertain the truth and punish the aggressors.

Governor Pease on the 11th of November, 1857, sent a message to the Texas Legislature. In it he stated that during the month of September previous, the Executive had received authentic information that a train of carts had been attacked a short distance from Ellana, Carnes County, while peaceably traveling on the public highway, by a party of armed and masked men, who fired upon the cartmen, killing one and wounding three others. That at the same time he had also received notice of another attack which took place the latter part of July, upon a train in Goliad county. That the attack was made at night, and three of the cartmen were wounded. That the killed and wounded in both instances were Mexicans, with the exception of one who was an American. That with these same reports proof had also been received that a combination had been formed in several counties for the purpose of committing these same acts of violence against citizens of Mexican origin, so long as they continued to transport goods by those roads.

The Governor continues by stating the measures adopted by him for suppressing and punishing such outrages. He states that he proceeded to San Antonio for the purpose of ascertaining whether measures had been taken for the arrest of the aggressors and to prevent the repetition of such occurrences, to which end he had conferences with several citizens of Bexar. The result of these conferences convinced him that no measures had been taken or probably would be taken for the arrest of the guilty parties, or prevention of similar attacks. That in fact combinations of the kind mentioned did exist, and that they had been the origin of repeated assaults upon the persons and property of Mexicans who traveled over those roads. That in several of the border counties there prevailed a deep feeling of animosity towards the Mexicans, and that there was imminent danger of attacks and of retaliation being made by them, which if once begun would inevitably bring about a war of races.

The following paragraph of the same message shows how inexcusable these outrages were:

> We have a large Mexican population in our western counties, among which are very many who have been carefully educated, and who have rendered important services to the country in the days of her tribulation. There is no doubt but that there are some bad characters amongst this class of citizens, but the great mass of them are as orderly and law-abiding as any class in the State. They cheerfully perform the duties imposed upon them, and they are entitled to the protection of the laws in any honest calling which they may choose to select.

The condition of the Mexican population residing in Texas has changed but little since 1857. Governor Pease's message to the Texas Legislature that year exposes and explains the reason of revolts such as the one which occurred on the banks of the Rio Bravo under Cortina in 1859.

A large portion of the disturbances which occurred between the Bravo and Nueces rivers is attributable to the persecutions suffered by the Mexicans residing there; persecutions which have engendered the most profound hatred between the races.

Governor Pease, in the message referred to in the foregoing note, gives it to be understood that the Mexicans did not enjoy the protection of the courts and the authorities. He says our laws are adequate to the protection of life and property, but when the citizens and authorities of a county become indifferent to their execution, they are useless. Some remedy must be found for this condition of things, and the only means which suggests itself to me, is that jurisdiction be given to the grand jury, the officers and courts in any adjoining county where an impartial trial may be obtained, to arrest and try the offenders.

This passage shows that there was no justice for the Mexicans in Texas, and with regard to which the complaint has frequently been made.

The Texas Mexicans enjoyed no greater personal security than did their property, and what is remarkable, is that they were wronged and outraged with impunity, because as far as they were concerned, justice and oppression were synonymous. Here is what a Brownsville newspaper says upon the subject:

> We have had occasion frequently to deplore that want of the administration of the law in such manner as to render to all parties the justice to which they were entitled. According to our ideas, when an officer enters upon the discharge of his duties, he should mark out for himself such a line of conduct as would insure the impartial exercise of his duties, laying aside all distinctions of race and persons, and remove from his proceedings everything which would tend to give them the appearance of a farce. Our population is, as is well known, divided into two classes, Americans and Mexicans; the latter are unquestionably more exposed to wrong than the former; their natural timidity makes them inoffensive, and by reason of the difference of language they cannot well understand our laws or fully enjoy their rights. We have heard one of our highest officers state that it would be difficult to find a class of people more obedient to the laws. It is true that among them there are bad characters, and these should be severely punished, but this fact at times gives rise to their all being classed in the same category, and ill-used. We do not address any one in particular, our remarks are general. Americans have at times committed offenses which in them have been overlooked, but which, if committed by Mexicans would have been severely punished. But when election time comes, it is wonderful to behold the friendship existing for

the Mexican voters, and the protection extended to them, the sympathy which until then had remained latent or concealed, suddenly reveals itself in all its plentitude, and many are astonished not to have found until then the amount of kindly feeling professed towards them by their whilom friends. Promises of all kinds are made to them, but scarcely are the promises made, when they are broken. An hour before the election they are fast friends, "—an hour after the election they are a 'crowd of greasers.'" The magistrates are not Pachas or absolute rulers; a certain respect is due to their position, and the consciousness of the responsibility resting upon them should make them feel their duties.—*American Flag*, Brownsville, August 20th, 1856.

The Mexicans, whether they be Texans or whether they preserve their original nationality, have been the victims both of their persons and property, and they have not been fully protected by the laws.

7. "A set policy of terrorizing the Mexicans"

A Texas Ranger, 1875*

Founded officially in 1835 to fight Indians, the Texas Rangers soon became heroes in Texas, but villains to Texas Mexicans. Termed "brave and clean-cut frontiersmen" by J. Frank Dobie,[1] the Rangers (*los rinches*) have been regarded by some Texas Mexicans as the region's Ku Klux Klan.

Hatred of Mexicans had a long tradition among the Rangers. During the Mexican War they formed two special units of volunteers. Their atrocities in the Mexican northeast—the pillaging of farms and the shooting or hanging of innocent peons—led General Zachary Taylor to threaten to jail an entire

---

°N. A. Jennings, *A Texas Ranger*. Foreword by J. Frank Dobie. (Dallas, Tex.: 1930), pp. 65–66, 71–72.

1. J. Frank Dobie, Foreword to Jennings, *A Texas Ranger*, p. viii.

2. Stephen B. Oates, "Diablos Tejanos: The Texas Rangers in the Mexican War," *Journal of the West* 9, no. 4 (October 1970): 487–504. This article stands in refreshing contrast to the usual laudatory accounts of the Rangers, such as Walter Prescott Webb's classic.

3. Affidavit of Jesús Sandoval, May 3, 1875, before F. J. Parker, Clerk, Circuit Court of the U.S., Eastern District of Texas, in U.S. Senate, *Testimony Taken by the Special Committee on Texas Frontier Troubles*, 44th Cong., 1st sess., 1876, H. Rept. 343, ser. 1709, pp. 83–84.

unit. In Mexico City *Los Tejanos Sangrientes* killed children and
old men and raped women, thereby infuriating General Winfield Scott who authorized a plan to get the Rangers out of the
city.[2]

The Rangers were disbanded during the Civil War, then
reestablished in 1874, in two commands. The smaller group,
known as the Special Force, was sent under Captain L. H.
McNelly to the Mexican border to control cattle theft and
brigandage. In the selection that follows, Ranger N. A. Jennings
describes the activities of the Special Force in 1875. Jennings
reveals the extraordinary complexity of ethnic divisions along
the border. At times Rangers defended Mexicans to preserve
order. They even had a Texas Mexican fighting with them, Jesús
Sandoval, whose rancho had been burned by Mexicans. Sandoval hated Mexicans, who accused him of being "americanized
and consequently criminal—a traitor to Mexico."[3]

We went by easy stages across the country to Corpus Christi, the
pretty little old town on the Gulf of Mexico. We were ordered there
because Mexican raiders had come across the Rio Grande and spread
terror throughout that part of Texas.

We arrived at Corpus Christi on the morning of April 22, 1875, and
found the country in the wildest state of excitement. We were told
how large bands of raiders were coming in every direction to lay
waste the country-side and burn the town. The most extravagant
rumors found ready credence from the terrorized people. The civil
authorities seemed helpless. Large parties of mounted and well-armed
men, residents of Nueces County, were riding over the country,
committing the most brutal outrages, murdering peaceable Mexican
farmers and stockmen who had lived all their lives in Texas. These
murderers called themselves vigilance committees and pretended that
they were acting in the cause of law and order.

We remained encamped near the town for two days, to rest our
jaded horses and to try to get a clear idea of the actual condition of
affairs.

It seemed that the excitement had been first caused by a raid made
by Mexicans (from Mexico) in the neighborhood of Corpus Christi.
These raiders had stolen cattle and horses, burned ranch houses,
murdered men and ravished women, and then escaped back to
Mexico. The excitement which followed was seized upon by a
number of white men living in Nueces County as a fitting time to

settle up old scores with the Mexican residents of that and some of the adjoining counties. Many of these Mexicans, it must be admitted, had been making a livelihood by stealing and skinning cattle, and the sheriffs and constables had failed to make any efforts to detect and punish them.

On the evening of April 24th a report was brought in that a party of raiders from Mexico had been seen at La Para, about sixty miles from Corpus Christi. McNelly at once started with the troop to the place and arrived the following day. There we learned that the party reported to be Mexican raiders was really a posse of citizens from Cameron County, under a deputy sheriff, and that they "had come out to protect the people of La Para from further outrages from the citizens of Nueces County," meaning certain lawless bands organized in Nueces County.

McNelly ordered the deputy sheriff to take his posse back and disband it. After some demurring on the part of the posse, this was done. We went into camp and sent scouting parties out in every direction to disband the various vigilance committees and "regulators" which were roaming through the country.

On April 26th two companies of white men, commanded by T. Hynes Clark and M. S. Culver, cattlemen, came to our camp and said they wanted to co-operate with the Rangers.

"We need no one to co-operate with us," said the Captain. "I have heard that some of you men are the very ones accused of a number of outrages committed on Mexican citizens of this State, and you must disband at once and not re-assemble, except at the call and under the command of an officer of the State. If you don't do as I say, you will have us to fight."

The Texans didn't like this high-handed way of talking and were disposed at first to dispute McNelly's authority, but the Captain showed them very quickly that he meant business and they disbanded.

....

. . . We paid frequent visits to Matamoras after nightfall. We went there for two reasons: to have fun, and to carry out a set policy of terrorizing the Mexicans at every opportunity. Captain McNelly assumed that the more we were feared, the easier would be our work of subduing the Mexican raiders; so it was tacitly understood that we were to gain a reputation as fire-eating, quarrelsome dare-devils as quickly as possible, and to let no opportunity go unimproved to assert ourselves and override the "Greasers." Perhaps everyone has more or less of the bully inhert [inherent] in his make-up, for certain it was that we enjoyed this work hugely.

"Each Ranger was a little standing army in himself," was the way Lieutenant Wright put it to me, speaking, long afterward, of those experiences. The Mexicans were afraid of us, collectively and individually, and added to the fear was a bitter hatred.

Half a dozen of the boys would leave camp after dark and make their way over the river to Matamoras by way of the ferry. If we could find a *fandango,* or Mexican dance, going on, we would enter the dancing-hall and break up the festivities by shooting out the lights. This would naturally result in much confusion and, added to the reports of our revolvers, would be the shrill screaming of women and cursing of angry Mexicans. Soldiers would come running from all directions. We would then fire a few more shots in the air and make off for the ferry, as fast as we could go.

Usually, at such times, we would be followed—at a safe dis-tance—by a company or two of soldiers. Sometimes we would fire back, over their heads, and sometimes they would shoot at us; but we always got back safely to the Texas side. When we reached Brownsville, we would hunt another *fandango*—there were always some of these dances going on every night—and proceed, as in Matamoras, to break it up.

The news of our big fight with the raiders reached everyone's ears, and none was so bold as to attempt to resist our outrages upon the peace and dignity of the community, for such they undoubtedly were. But we accomplished our purpose. In a few weeks we were feared as men were never before feared on that border, and, had we given the opportunity, we should undoubtedly have been exterminated by the Mexicans, but there was "method in our madness," and we never gave them the chance to get the better of us.

8. "Parceled out to Mexicans"

The Tucson Citizen, 1904*

Among the more bizarre examples of injustice toward Mexican Americans in the Southwest was an episode involving forty light-skinned orphan children from New York who were placed in the homes of persons of Mexican descent in the mining district of Clifton-Morenci, in Arizona Territory. As described in the following newspaper articles, this action aroused the wrath of the Anglo community. The Anglos claimed that the children had been adopted by parents who were too poor to care properly for them. Yet the fact that these same Anglo citizens referred to the Mexican parents as "half breeds" who made the children sick with strange foods (such as watermelon), leave little doubt that ethnic and racial differences were at the root of the Anglos' ire.

An Anglo vigilante group forced the Mexicans to surrender the newly adopted children. The Mexican families had no chance of regaining the children through court action. Such was the nature of justice in Arizona that even the New York orphanage that had brought the children to the territory was unable to get them back again from the Anglo families who had seized them. In a popular decision, the Arizona Supreme Court winked at the vigilantes, regarding them as "committees" rather than mobs.[1]

ORPHANS AND FOUNDLINGS AT CLIFTON-MORENCI
FORTY CHILDREN BROUGHT FROM NEW YORK AND
DIVIDED UP AMONG MEXICAN LABORERS
ALMOST CAUSES A RIOT.

Morenci, Ariz., Oct. 5.—Last Saturday night a special car attached to the regular train, brought into Clifton forty foundlings and orphans, of both sexes, ranging in age from two and a half years to five years. They were shipped from New York City under auspices of the nuns in

---

* *The Tucson Citizen*, October 5, 1904; October 19, 1904.

1. The story has been told in Raymond A. Mulligan, "New York Foundlings at Clifton-Morenci: Social Justice in Arizona Territory, 1904–05," *Arizona and the West* 6, no. 2 (Summer 1964): 104–18; and more fully in A. Blake Brophy, *Foundlings on the Frontier: Racial and Religious Conflict in Arizona Territory, 1904–1905* (Tucson: 1972).

charge of the Foundlings' Home, ostensibly to be placed in good homes among Catholic families.

They were under the charge of G. Whitney Swayne and were accompanied by three nuns and three nurses named Miss Reynolds, Miss Dixon, and Miss Bowen.

By previous arrangement made through the Catholic priest, Father Mandin, who had charge of the Morenci-Clifton parish, the children had all been promised to Mexican families. The American families, it seems, were in entire ignorance of the disposition to be made of the children and did not become enlightened until eighteen of the little tots had been parceled out to Mexicans, and the balance of twenty-two had been taken to Morenci in stages.

Upon the arrival at Morenci of the contingent destined for that place, the children were divided up among Mexicans with whom prior arrangements had been made. As the children were all apparently Americans born in New York, the American people here became highly excited at the disposition of the children and there was much talk of tar and feathers and lynching. The excitement grew as the matter continued to be agitated and several hundred people gathered at both Morenci and Clifton to take action regarding the matter. At Morenci the excitement abated somewhat upon the promise of the priest and Mr. Swayne to immediately take the children away from the Mexicans. This was finally accomplished before midnight, and the priest and Swayne were then taken to Clifton by Clifton officers to meet and make explanations to a crowd of about 350 people who were awaiting them. What is regarded here as the strangest part of the whole proceedings was the refusal to give any of the children to American families even though they were of the Catholic religion.

It has been ascertained that a number of prominent families in good standing, with comfortable homes, applied for the guardianship of some of the children but met with refusal and instead the children were given to Mexicans, many of whom could not even support their own children, some of these being of the poorest class of laborers residing in shacks.

It is charged that several Americans saw money given to the priest by people who secured the children and the rumor spread that the little fair-haired orphans were being sold. It was subsequently explained by the priest that this money was for the purpose of providing ample clothing for the children, according to a previous arrangement, and he declared he could prove this by several storekeepers.

The children were mostly of the blond type with fair hair and blue eyes and appeared to be in good health. The turning over of these to the lowest type of Mexican laborers drove the Americans to the extreme of excitement.

The priest narrowly escaped violence both at Morenci and Clifton. As it was, he received several punches in the ribs and was jostled about roughly by the excited crowd. Some of the more hot-headed openly advocated lynching him, while not a few demanded that he be tarred and feathered. The officers from Clifton, however, held back the crowd and protected the priest from serious violence.

It is understood that an arrangement had been reached for the immediate return of the forty children to New York. The people, however, will not permit the removal of the children until Swayne gives satisfactory assurances that they will be taken back from whence they came. Many people here regard it as simple traffic in children.

The priest was ordered yesterday morning to leave the community, or in the vernacular of the town, to "hit the trail and keep going until he was out of the county." He left on a trail at once very much frightened and it was said that he had gone to Tucson. The priest is a Frenchman and has only been in this country about seven or eight months. Swayne has telegraphed to New York and when the people here get satisfactory assurances that the children will be well cared for they will be permitted to depart. In the meantime the little ones are being tenderly cared for in Clifton and Morenci.

CLIFTON FOUNDLING SCANDAL TOLD IN NEW YORK
THE SISTERS AND NURSES RELATE A TALE OF WOE . . .

New York, Oct. 19.—Mentally and physically exhausted, having been delayed enroute four days by washouts on the railroads, three Sisters and four nurses of the New York Foundlings' Hospital returned from Arizona last night and told of their terrifying experience with mobs that threatened their lives because the children they sought to place with families in the Territory were taken to the homes of Catholic Mexicans.

The Sisters had gone to Clifton and Morenci, Ariz., to deliver forty foundlings to Mexican families under the authority of the priest of that district. At Morenci a mob drove them from their hotel and threatened to shoot them.

Dr. G. W. Swain [Swayne], agent of the hospital, narrowly escaped lynching, and the priest was driven from the county.

The Foundling Hospital will appeal to the Federal authorities to recover from the residents of these towns nineteen children who were torn from the arms of the nurses. One Sister, relating her experiences to a reporter today said:

> At Clifton we left sixteen children, and the others at Morenci, eighteen miles distant, and over a hard mountain road. Some of the children were taken to refined, gentle, prosperous Spanish people, whose homes were neat and clean.
>
> On Sunday night we were called from the rooms of our hotel in Morenci. In the street a sheriff sat on horseback, with a revolver, like the other men. Women called us vile names, and some of them put pistols to our heads. They said there was no law in that town; that they made their own laws. We were told to get the children from the Spaniards and leave by Tuesday morning. If we did not we would be killed. We got the children, but nineteen of the twenty-four were taken from the nurses by force and put, I understand, into the families of Americans.
>
> When we reached Clifton we were compelled to take once more that trying journey to Morenci and obtain the five children left there. When we left Arizona we had twenty-one children, who were taken by Dr. Swain [Swayne] into Illinois, where we had many applications for them.

9. "Compelled to sell, little by little by little"

Antonio María Pico, et al., 1859*

As Californios found themselves embroiled in costly and time-consuming litigation to confirm titles to their land, they did not stand by as passive witnesses to their demise. Rather, they fought back by any means possible, legal or illegal, to retain their property. As this forcefully argued petition to the United States Congress shows, the Californios understood well the forces working against them. Here they criticize high taxes, which they found ruinous, and the Land Act of 1851. They suggest that the Land Act was unnecessary and that it violated their rights as citizens under the Treaty of Guadalupe Hidalgo.

Although historian Paul Gates has found that 346 of the 813 claims for Spanish and Mexican period land grants in California were made by non-Mexicans, it is interesting that nearly all of the fifty signatures on this petition belonged to Hispanos. The Spanish-speaking landowners seem to have had greater difficulty than Anglos in adapting to United States judicial procedures.

TO THE HONORABLE SENATE AND
HOUSE OF RESPRESENTATIVES OF THE
UNITED STATES OF AMERICA

We, the undersigned, residents of the state of California, and some of us citizens of the United States, previously citizens of the Republic of Mexico, respectfully say:

That during the war between the United States and Mexico the officers of the United States, as commandants of the land and sea forces, on several occasions offered and promised in the most solemn manner to the inhabitants of California, protection and security of their persons and their property and the annexation of the said state of California to the American Union, impressing upon them the great

---

*Petition of Antonio María Pico *et al.*, to the Senate and House of Representatives of the United States. Manuscript HM 514 in the Huntington Library, San Marino, California. Reprinted by permission of the Huntington Library. This item has previously been published in the appendix to Robert Glass Cleland, *Cattle on a Thousand Hills: Southern California, 1850–1880*, 2nd. ed. (San Marino, Calif.: 1951), 238–43.

advantages to be derived from their being citizens of the United States, as was promised them.

That, in consequence of such promises and representations, very few of the inhabitants of California opposed the invasion; some of them welcomed the invaders with open arms; a great number of them acclaimed the new order with joy, giving a warm reception to their guests, for those inhabitants had maintained very feeble relations with the government of Mexico and had looked with envy upon the development, greatness, prosperity, and glory of the great northern republic, to which they were bound for reasons of commercial and personal interests, and also because its principles of freedom had won their friendliness.

When peace was established between the two nations by the Treaty of Guadalupe Hidalgo, they joined in the general rejoicing with their new American fellow countrymen, even though some—a very few indeed—decided to remain in California as Mexican citizens, in conformity with the literal interpretation of that solemn instrument; they immediately assumed the position of American citizens that was offered them, and since then have conducted themselves with zeal and faithfulness and with no less loyalty than those whose great fortune it was to be born under the flag of the North American republic—believing, thus, that all their rights were insured in the treaty, which declares that *their property shall be inviolably protected and insured;* seeing the realization of the promises made to them by United States officials; trusting and hoping to participate in the prosperity and happiness of the great nation of which they now had come to be an integral part, and in which, if it was true that they now found the value of their possessions increased, that was also to be considered compensation for their sufferings and privations.

The inhabitants of California, having had no choice but to dedicate themselves to the rural and pastoral life and allied occupations, ignorant even of the laws of their own country, and without the assistance of lawyers (of whom there were so few in California) to advise them on legal matters, elected from among themselves their judges, who had no knowledge of the intricate technical terms of the law and who were, of course, incompetent and ill-fitted to occupy the delicate position of forensic judicature. Scattered as the population was over a large territory, they could hardly hope that the titles under which their ancestors held and preserved their lands, in many cases for over half a century, would be able to withstand a scrupulously critical examination before a court. They heard with dismay of the appointment, by Act of Congress, of a Commission with the right to examine all titles and confirm or disapprove them, as their judgment considered equitable. Though this honorable body has doubtless had the best interests of the state at heart, still it has brought about the most disastrous effects upon those who have the honor to subscribe their names to this petition, for, even though all landholders possessing titles under the Spanish or Mexican governments were not forced by the letter of the law to present them before the Commission for confirmation, nevertheless all those titles were at once considered doubtful, their origin questionable, and, as a result, worthless for confirmation by the Commission; all landholders were thus *compelled de facto* to submit their titles to the Commission for confirmation, under the alternative that, if they were not submitted, the lands would be considered public property.

The undersigned, ignorant, then, of the forms and proceedings of an American court of justice, were obliged to engage the services of American lawyers to present their claims, paying them enormous fees. Not having other means with which to meet those expenses but their lands, they were compelled to give up part of their property, in many cases as much as a fourth of it, and in other cases even more.

The discovery of gold attracted an immense number of immigrants to this country, and, when they perceived that the titles of the old inhabitants were considered doubtful and their validity questionable, they spread themselves over the land as though it were public property, taking possession of the improvements made by the inhabitants, many times seizing even their houses (where they had lived for many years with their families), taking and killing the cattle and destroying their crops; so that those who before had owned great numbers of cattle that could have been counted by the thousands, now found themselves without any, and the men who were the owners of many leagues of land now were deprived of the peaceful possession of even one vara.

The expenses of the new state government were great, and the money to pay for these was only to be derived from the tax on property, and there was little property in this new state but the above-mentioned lands. Onerous taxes were levied by new laws, and if these were not paid the property was put up for sale. Deprived as they were of the use of their lands, from which they had now no lucrative returns, the owners were compelled to mortgage them in order to assume the payment of taxes already due and constantly increasing. With such mortgages upon property greatly depreciated (because of its uncertain status), without crops or rents, the owners of those lands were not able to borrow money except at usurious rates of interest. The usual interest rate at that time was high, but with such securities it was exorbitant; and so they were forced either to sell or lose their lands; in fact, they were forced to borrow money even for the purchase of the bare necessities of life. Hoping that the Land Commission would take quick action in the revision of titles and thus relieve them from the state of penury in which they found themselves, they mortgaged their lands, paying compound interest at the rate of from three to ten per cent a month. The long-awaited relief would not arrive; action from the Commission was greatly delayed; and, even after the Commission would pronounce judgment on the titles, it was still necessary to pass through a rigorous ordeal in the District Court; and some cases are, even now, pending before the Supreme Court of the nation. And in spite of the *final* confirmation, too long a delay was experienced (in many cases it is still being experienced), awaiting the surveys to be made by the United States Surveyor-General. The general Congress overlooked making the necessary appropriations to that end, and the people were then obliged to face new taxes to pay for the surveys, or else wait even longer while undergoing the continued and exhausting demands of high and usurious taxes. Many persons assumed the payment of the surveyors and this act was cause for objection from Washington, the work of those surveyors rejected, and the patents refused, for the very reason that they themselves had paid for the surveys. More than 800 petitions were presented to the Land Commission, and already 10 years of delays have elapsed and only some 50 patents have been granted.

The petitioners, finding themselves unable to face such payments because of the rates of interest, taxes, and litigation expenses, as well as having to maintain their families, were compelled to sell, little by little, the greater part of their old possessions. Some, who at one time had been the richest landholders, today find themselves without a foot of ground, living as objects of charity—and even in sight of the many leagues of land which, with many a thousand head of cattle, they once had called their own; and those of us who, by means of strict economy and immense sacrifices, have been able to preserve a small portion of our property, have heard to our great dismay that new legal projects are being planned to keep us still longer in suspense, consuming, to the last iota, the property left us by our ancestors. Moreover, we see with deep pain that efforts are being made to induce those honorable bodies to pass laws authorizing *bills of review,* and other illegal proceedings, with a view to prolonging still further the litigation of our claims.

The manifest injustice of such an act must be clearly apparent to those honorable bodies when they consider that the native Californians were an agricultural people and that they have wished to continue so; but they have encountered the obstacle of the enterprising genius of the Americans, who have assumed possession of their lands, taken their cattle, and destroyed their woods, while the Californians have been thrown among those who were strangers to their language, customs, laws, and habits.

. . . It would have been better for the state, and for those newly established in it, if all those titles to lands, the *expedientes* of which were properly registered in the Mexican archives, had been declared valid; if those holders of titles derived from former governments had been declared perpetual owners and presumptive possessors of the lands (in all civilized countries they would have been acknowledged legitimate owners of the land); and if the government, or any private person or official who might have pretensions to the contrary, should have been able to establish his claim only through a regular court of justice, in accordance with customary judicial procedure. Such a course would have increased the fame of the conquerors, won the faith and respect of the conquered, and contributed to the material prosperity of the nation at large.

San Francisco, February 21, 1859.
Antonio María Pico [and forty-nine others]

10. "A denial of justice"
Public Land Commission, 1880*

It was not only claimants who complained about the slowness of governmental procedures in investigating land titles.
Government officials, too, knew that the system worked poorly.
That was especially evident in New Mexico, where delays in
confirming titles were so extraordinarily slow that the Public
Land Commission, appointed by Congress in 1879 to investigate
the situation, charged that congressional slowness led to
injustices. Some of the reasons for delay, and its effects, are
described in the following excerpt from the land commission's
report. Yet, awareness of the problem did not lead to a quick
solution. Titles remained cloudy in New Mexico for two
decades after this report was published.

The Public Land Commission appointed under acts of March 3,
1879, and June 16, 1880, in their preliminary report of February 24,
1880, after careful review of the subject, and having before it the
testimony of a score of witnesses as to the necessity for legislation,
made the following suggestions (see H. Ex. Doc. No. 46, Forty-sixth
Congress, second session, together with testimony taken, 690 pages):

In California, Congress, by the acts of March 3, 1851, June 14, 1860,
July 1, 1864, and July 23, 1866, provided machinery for the
ascertainment and settlement of these claims, which has resulted in
their final confirmation or rejection and in their subsequent segrega-
tion from the adjacent public lands. Questions of title were settled by
the Federal courts, and authority to segregate claims judicially
confirmed was vested in the proper executive officers of the United
States.

But in the remainder of the territory derived from Mexico a
different mode from [sic] settling private land claims was prescribed.
The basis of such settlement is the eighth section of the act of July 22,

---

*U.S. Congress, *Recommendation of the Public Land Commission for Legislation as to Private
Land Claims*, 46th Cong., 2nd sess., 1880, H. Exec. doc. 46, pp. 1116–17.

1854, which made it the duty of the surveyor-general to "ascertain the origin, nature, character, and extent of all claims to lands under the laws, usages, and customs of Spain and Mexico," and to report his conclusions to Congress for its direct action upon the question of confirmation or rejection. The law was singularly defective in machinery for its administration, and it imposed no limitation of time in the presentation of claims, and no penalty for failure to present. Its operation has been a failure amounting to a denial of justice both to claimants and to the United States. After the lapse of nearly thirty years, more than one thousand claims have been filed with the surveyor-general, of which less than one hundred and fifty have been reported to Congress, and of the number reported Congress has finally acted upon only seventy-one. Under the law, only copies of the original title papers were submitted to Congress, and it is not presumed that its committees are so constituted as to make safe judicial findings upon the validity of titles emanating from foreign Governments, nor to measure the era of claims whose boundaries rest exclusively upon meager recital of natural objects in term of very general description. As a consequence the committees of Congress have naturally been reluctant to act with insufficient data upon questions which involved the functions of the judge rather than of the legislator, and as these claims have heretofore pertained to a semi-foreign population in a comparatively unsettled portion of our Territories, business of more importance to the general welfare of the nation has been permitted to exclude these local matters from regular consideration. In the limited number of cases finally confirmed, Congress has been compelled to confirm by terms of general description, which have usually proved to include much greater areas of land than Congress would knowingly have confirmed. The established rule of area under the Mexican colonization law was a maximum of eleven leagues to a claimant, being a little less than 50,000 acres; but as illustrations of the natural result of confirmation without proper judicial investigation, one confirmation by Congress to two claimants has proved to embrace 1,000,000 acres and another about 1,800,000 acres.

The time has arrived when the States and Territories containing these treaty claims are no longer on the frontier, and they have ceased to be populated exclusively by a foreign population. Lines of transcontinental railroads are piercing them in every direction; the restless activity of American civilization is spreading towns and farms over the plains, and has exposed the hidden treasures of the mountains; emigration is flowing in with magical rapidity, and industry and thrift are exploring every avenue for development and investment. But at the foundation of all permanent growth lies the security and certainty of land titles, and no discussion is required to prove that this is unattainable in communities covered with claims to title of foreign derivation and of unascertained boundaries. Even the Government is ignorant of the line of demarkation between its public lands and these treaty claims, and uncertainty and insecurity taint the titles of its purchasers.

V. Accommodation, Assimilation, and Resistance

Editor's Introduction

During the last half of the nineteenth century, Mexican Americans saw a steady erosion of their political influence and their economic status, and faced threats to their political rights, their institutions, and their culture. As might be expected, they responded to these adverse circumstances in a variety of ways: a very few, living in rural and isolated areas in the Southwest, remained almost completely untouched by the winds of change; some lashed out in angry violence; some used violence to attain political or economic ends; many accommodated themselves pragmatically to the new culture, working within the system while yet retaining their ethnic identity; others tried to assimilate completely into the dominant culture.

The Mexican American community actively, energetically, and often painfully made adjustments to the cultural environment of its conquerors. Any response that Mexican Americans made, however, was tempered by two circumstances which, when taken together, made the Mexican American past distinct from that of any other ethnic group in the United States. First, Anglo Americans retained prejudices toward Mexican Americans based on racial as well as cultural grounds. A Mexican American with dark skin and Indian features could never completely assimilate into Anglo culture. It was generally the lighter-skinned elite who found it easiest to assimilate, and who were most willing to do so. Second, fresh immigration from geographically contiguous Mexico—sometimes a trickle and sometimes a flood—continued throughout the nineteenth century and down to the present day, constantly nourishing Mexican culture in the Southwest.

I

Violence was the most extreme and probably the least common response of outraged Mexican Americans to Anglo domination. Many writers have suggested that those Mexicans who turned to banditry did so as a form of nonverbal protest against the inequities of new Anglo institutions, and as a response to the social upheaval that characterized the abrupt transition from Mexican to American society. The so-called bandidos fit British historian Eric J. Hobsbawm's model of a social bandit—ideally a young, unmarried peasant who commits an act which the state regards as criminal, but which most of his peers regard as justifiable or heroic. The social bandit, according to Hobsbawm's analysis, might take the form of "the noble robber of Robin Hood, the primitive resistance fighter or guerrilla unit . . . and possibly also the terror-bringing avenger." Social banditry, says Hobsbawm, "is most likely to become a major phenomenon when . . . traditional equilibrium is upset, . . . or at the moments when the jaws of the dynamic modern world seize the static communities in order to destroy and transform them."[1] Not surprisingly, banditry was most prevalent in California and Texas, the areas of the Southwest that underwent the most profound economic and social dislocations after the United States occupation of 1846.

In California, bandidos first achieved prominence in the 1850s in the socially chaotic mining region. Bandits, of course, came from all ethnic groups, but a disproportionate number were of Mexican ancestry. Leonard Pitt found that "16 to 20 percent of San Quentin inmates from 1854 to 1865 were Mexicans or Californians," which represented a much higher proportion of Hispano prisoners than the proportion of Hispano residents of California.[2] The foremost student of banditry in California, Joseph Henry Jackson, made an interesting distinction between the motives of Anglos and Mexicans who turned to crime. The unemployed Americans did so, Jackson said, in order to make a living, while Mexicans did so in order to get revenge.[3] Perhaps that explains why the Spanish-speaking badmen in Jackson's study seem to commit bloodier crimes than their Anglo counterparts. In any event, without using the term, Jackson too suggested that California's Spanish-speaking badmen were social bandits.

Joaquín Murrieta has come to be the prototype bandido and one of California's most enduring legends. Unfortunately for the student of history, little can be said with certainty about Joaquín, even if he existed. By 1853, a "Joaquín" had become the scourge of the mining country. Whenever an unknown Mexican committed a crime the blame seems to have fallen on Joaquín. At one point Joaquín was reported to be in Placerville in the north and in San Diego in the south, simultaneously. To confuse matters there was no agreement as to his surname, at least five of which were suggested: Botilleras, Carrillo, Ocomoreña, Valenzuela, and Murrieta. In the spring of 1853 when the state legislature considered offering a reward for the capture of Joaquín, Assemblyman José María Covarrubias of Santa Barbara suggested that the plan was illegal. Joaquín had not been convicted of any crime, and no one knew what he looked like. Nevertheless, the governor put a price on Joaquín's head (heads?), and the legislature authorized a party of rangers to get the "robbers commanded by the five Joaquíns." The rangers, not surprisingly, got their man. But which man? To collect their reward the rangers brought back a head preserved in whisky which a number of citizens swore was that of Joaquín Murrieta. Yet, there were widespread rumors that the rangers had killed an innocent Mexican in order to collect the reward.[4]

Joaquín Murrieta achieved fame after his death, chiefly because of the publication in 1854 of a semifictional biography by John Rollin Ridge. A Cherokee Indian, Ridge was able to empathize with an oppressed minority. He presented Joaquín as a Robin Hood, a man driven to a life of crime by an evil Anglo society. Whether the story is true or not is of little importance; the fact that it was widely believed is significant. After several popular novels, countless magazine articles, and a few movies based on the Ridge account, Murrieta as a symbol has become more important than Murrieta the man.

Social banditry in California was not confined to the mining camps or the gold-rush era. It spread to the coastal towns and the southern ranchos and continued into the 1870s, by which time a second generation of bandidos came on the scene. Among the new crop of Spanish-speaking badmen were the sons of some illustrious California families: Castros, Lugos, Sepúlvedas, and Vallejos.[5] These second-generation Mexican Americans felt uncomfortable with the culture of their fathers, which they knew Anglos scorned and despised. At the same time they met formidable obstacles to complete assimilation into Anglo society. Thus, these young Mexican Americans were alienated from both cultures, and as cultural "outs" they found it an easy step to life outside the law. There is some evidence that Spanish-speaking outlaws in California enjoyed the sympathy and support of their own people, a requisite for social banditry. That support, however, was not universal. The "better element" of Californios frequently participated in posses and vigilante groups to help round up Mexican American badmen, and so earned the gratitude of the Anglo community. That, of course, occurred in other areas of the Southwest, too.

Although some California bandidos were driven to a life of crime by societal pressures, none articulated his protest as well as Juan Nepomuceno Cortina of Texas, who may be more accurately described as a social revolutionary than as a social bandit. In 1859 Cortina raided the city of Brownsville, touching off months of panic among Anglos. Cortina's War, as this event came to be called, was not designed for plunder or murder. Cortina spelled out the reasons for his fighting in two proclamations, issued during the "war." After his raid on Brownsville, Cortina took refuge at his family's ranch, defeating both the Brownsville militia and a party led by Texas Rangers who had been sent to dislodge him. With the arrival of the United States cavalry, however, Cortina fled across the Rio Grande to Mexico. Throughout the hostilities, most Anglos regarded Cortina as a murderous villain, while Mexican Americans clearly identified with him. As one cavalry officer complained: "The feeling against Americans made it impossible to obtain reliable information of Cortina's plans."[6] Cortina's reputation as a bandit to some and a hero to others led José T. Canales, a Brownsville attorney and a distant relative of Cortina, to make the following observation in 1951: "Whether a man is called a 'bandit' or a 'hero' often depends just upon one word—SUCCESS; for very often a successful bandit turns out to be a real hero and true patriot, such as . . . [George] Washington."[7] It was Cortina's bad fortune to lose his war, but some Anglos recognized the justice of his cause. As Sam Houston, no lover of Mexicans, acknowledged, the Cortina War had "grown out of local abuses."[8] Frederick Law Olmsted, traveling in Texas a few years before Cortina's War, provided a clear explanation for social banditry. Since Mexicans in Texas had been "rendered furious by wholesale injustice," he wrote, "it is no wonder if they should take to the very crimes with which they are [falsely] charged."[9]

Violent resistance to Anglo domination did not depend solely upon dynamic individuals such as Murrieta or Cortina. The entire Mexican American community took action when its vital interests were threatened. This was demonstrated dramatically in the El Paso "Salt War" of 1877. The Guadalupe Salt Lakes, situated about one hundred miles east of El Paso, had been available for public use since the Spanish period. They were heavily utilized after 1868, when Mexican residents of El Paso cleared a wagon road to them. In 1877, when one

Charles H. Howard attempted to monopolize the salt deposits by charging a fee for their use, he aroused Mexicans on both sides of the border into a well-organized revolt. At first, Mexicans "arrested" Howard and forced him to sign a paper renouncing his claim to the salt and agreeing to leave the city. But Howard left only briefly. When he returned to El Paso to protect his claim, supported by some Texas Rangers, the Mexicans responded bitterly. The war over salt turned into a race war with rumors spreading that all "gringos" would die (of the 5,000 inhabitants of El Paso, fewer than 100 were Anglos). The Mexican community executed Howard and forced the Rangers to surrender—the only such occasion in Ranger history. When the fighting was over, Ranger reinforcements arrived, after the nick of time. They killed some "escaping" Mexicans, raped a woman, and committed other atrocities in revenge. Curiously, no Mexicans were ever brought to trial for their role in the Salt War, but in the long run they lost the war. All, eventually, had to pay for salt.[10]

In New Mexico, the Mexican American community employed violence to protect its lands. Forming a secret society called the Gorras Blancas, or White Caps, Hispanos fought a guerrilla war in Mora, Santa Fe, and San Miguel counties that reached its peak in 1890. The White Caps cut miles of fences, destroyed railroad ties, severed telegraph lines, and burned ranches to the ground in their fight against the "land-grabbers," who were usually Anglos.

The movement died as White Caps ran out of fences to cut, and as their leaders turned to politics, attempting to work within the system. The People's Party, which seemed to represent White Cap aspirations, enjoyed only brief success at getting its candidates elected, especially in San Miguel County.[11] In the long run, the violent tactics of the White Caps may have been more successful than the methods of the politicians, for violence awakened many moderates to the need for reform of the land laws in New Mexico. The *Las Vegas Optic*, originally thoroughly opposed to the White Caps, editorialized on August 18, 1890: "While fence-cutting is wrong, in the eyes of the law a heinous crime, still the crime of grabbing land, fencing up pasturage, water, wood and road-ways from the people to whom the privilege of access belongs, is still a greater crime."

Cortina's War, the El Paso Salt War, and the activities of persons such as Murrieta and the Gorras Blancas represent only the highlights of Mexican American resistance and reaction to Anglo provocations. In subtle and unspectacular ways, Mexican Americans also used force to defend themselves, and it may be that as more research is done in this area, parallels will be found between Mexican resistance to Anglo domination and black resistance to slavery.[12] Even with our present limited knowledge, however, it seems clear that Mexican Americans did not respond passively to Anglo provocations, as popular stereotypes suggest.

II

Most Mexican Americans rejected violence as a solution to their problems, except in times of intense social upheaval or crisis. Instead, they either accommodated themselves to Anglo society or else tried to assimilate into it entirely. Assimilation (the gradual adoption of the characteristics of another group), occurred across the Southwest, but especially in areas where Hispanos formed such a tiny minority that they could not protect or reinforce their culture; they began to feel ill at ease and "different" when speaking Spanish, practicing Mexican customs, or eating Mexican food in the presence of Anglos. Accommodation (the process of adapting to another culture rather than adopting it entirely) occurred most successfully in those areas where Hispanos were numerous enough to maintain political influence and in turn protect their culture and institutions.

In southern California, southern Arizona, South Texas, and the Rio Grande Valley of north central New Mexico, Hispanos had maintained some degree of political influence for decades after the Mexican War. In these pockets of Mexican American political strength, leadership came principally from the elite, who were not united on all issues, and sometimes did not even belong to the same party. Loyalty to family often transcended loyalty to party or to issues,[13] and Mexican American upper-class politicos were as capable of exploiting their own lower class as any other group of politicians. Nevertheless, when their vital interests were affected, Mexican American politicos displayed considerable unity. Their political influence, however, depended on tenuous alliances with the Anglo oligarchy which lasted only until they were outnumbered by the Anglos. That generally coincided with the coming of the railroad. Southern California provides a good example.

Californios retained a numerical majority in the southern part of the state (excepting San Diego) into the 1870s, holding such local offices as tax assessor, justice of the peace, city councilman, and even mayor. Antonio Coronel, for example, served as superintendent of schools for Los Angeles in 1852 and became mayor of the city the following year. In towns such as Santa Barbara, where few Yankees resided, Mexican American control of local politics was nearly complete. In Los Angeles, on the other hand, with its steadily growing Anglo population, upper-class Californios cooperated with the newcomers to control politics. The *ricos* could deliver the vote, usually in exchange for patronage. Votes could be purchased from lower-class Californios, and Anglos as well, who valued a vote less for its abstract value than for its tangible value—a dollar in the 1850s.

Cooperation between Anglos and Mexican American oligarchs in southern California, as throughout the Southwest, was probably based more on mutual economic interests than on mutual self-respect. The latter, of course, may have been an outgrowth of the former. So long as their goals coincided with those of the Anglos, the Hispanos, held at least the illusion of power. Rancheros in southern California, for example, resented the control that the populous northern counties had over the state legislature and the high taxes which fell heavily on large landowners. Beginning in 1850 Californio and Anglo oligarchs agitated to divide the state in half in order to achieve greater autonomy. Their efforts nearly succeeded. In 1859 Andrés Pico of Los Angeles introduced a joint resolution in the state assembly asking for the formation of the "Territory of Colorado," to be composed of the five southernmost California counties. The ideas was approved in a statewide referendum, but died in Washington in the politics of the oncoming Civil War.

The Californios, then, played Yankee politics in order to protect their own interests. The first serious blow to their power in the southern counties came from nature itself. Floods in the winter of 1862, followed by two years of extraordinary drought, devastated the ranchos. With the great cattle herds nearly extinguished, rancheros fell into debt, and many lost their property because they were unable to pay taxes. Still, the Californios survived this blow, remaining politically influential. The death knell for Mexican American influence in the politics of southern California came not from nature, but from the railroad. In 1876 the Southern Pacific entered Los Angeles; a decade later, in 1887, the Santa Fe connected Los Angeles and San Diego to the eastern United States. The arrival of the railroad brought the "boom of the 80s" to southern California—an era of unprece-

12. Colonel Juan Nepomuceno Seguín fought for Texas independence in 1836 on the side of the Anglo Americans, and urged other Texanos to do the same. Later, Seguín's loyalty to Texas was called into question (as described in chapter IV), and he wrote that he had become "a foreigner in my native land." Reproduction courtesy of the Archives Division, Texas State Library.

13. An articulate young spokesman for the Californios, Francisco P. Ramírez was editor of the Spanish-language newspaper *El Clamor Público* from 1855 to 1859. Ramírez deplored the lynchings of Mexicans in California. In an editorial he suggested that it did not matter if laws were published in Spanish in California because "everyone understands perfectly the words 'hang! hang!'" An article from Ramírez's newspaper is among the readings in chapter IV. Photo courtesy of the Los Angeles County Museum of Natural History.

14. A distinguished Californio and one of the signers of the state's first constitution in 1849, Manuel Domínguez was not permitted to testify in a San Francisco courtroom in 1857 because of his Indian ancestry.

15. In communities such as Los Angeles, pictured here in 1886, the rapid influx of Anglo American immigrants overwhelmed Mexican culture and institutions. Photo courtesy of the Los Angeles County Museum of Natural History.

16. In places such as Santa Fe, pictured here in the 1880s, where fewer Americans settled, Mexican Americans held onto their culture much longer.

17. Some bandidos in the Southwest probably turned to crime because, as Tiburcio Vásquez, shown here, explained, they felt "unjustly and wrongfully deprived of [their] social rights." An interview with Vásquez appears in chapter V. Photo courtesy of the Los Angeles County Museum of Natural History.

18. Juan Nepomuceno Cortina (see chapter V), while governor of Tamaulipas, Mexico.

19. One of the founders of *La Alianza Hispano-Americana* (see chapter V) was Ignacio Calvillo, pictured here, who said that the Alianza was formed in 1893 to "protect and fight for the rights of Spanish-Americans in Tucson." Photo courtesy of the Arizona Historical Society.

20. Mexican Americans in New Mexico enjoyed greater political power than in any other area of the Southwest (see chapter V). In 1897 Miguel Antonio Otero, pictured here, was appointed territorial governor; he held that office until 1906.

dented economic expansion and Yankee immigration. The effect on the Californios was similar to that which the gold rush had had in the northern counties three decades earlier. Vastly outnumbered by the end of the 1880s, Californios ceased to play an important role in the politics of the southern counties.[14]

The situation in southern Arizona was strikingly similar. From 1863, when Arizona Territory was formed, Anglos dominated Arizona politically, economically, and socially. Yet in and around Tucson, which had been the center of Arizona's tiny Mexican population before the Gadsden Purchase, Hispanos and Anglos enjoyed political and social equality. From 1863 until about 1880, according to a study by James Officer, "the Mexican and Anglo upper classes of the community were indistinguishable."[15] This harmonious situation arose out of the necessity of cooperating against a common and more numerous enemy of both groups—the Apaches. Also, a severe shortage of Anglo women in Tucson (in the 1870 census, there were only thirty-seven, some of whom were nuns) resulted in closer interethnic relationships. Finally, Tucson's trade was oriented toward the neighboring state of Sonora, and the necessities of dealing with Mexican merchants and freighters enhanced ethnic understanding. Indicative of this close relationship with Mexico is the fact that pesos were the dominant currency in Tucson until the 1870s, and Mexican freighting and mercantile firms, such as that of Esteban Ochoa, were as well known as those of Anglos such as Michael Goldwater.[16] This ethnic harmony ended with changing demographic and economic circumstances.

The arrival of the railroad in the 1880s ended southern Arizona's dependence on Mexican trade routes and Mexican merchants. Moreover, Anglo women entered the territory on the train as the region became more "civilized" and danger from Apaches declined. The 1880s also saw military posts close as their usefulness diminished, and the resultant exodus of soldiers from the territory brought a severe depression to Tucson. As jobs became scarce and competition grew more intense, ethnic relations deteriorated too. The *Tucsonenses* did not accept these changes passively. Instead, Mexican American community leaders formed organizations in the 1890s to fight social and economic discrimination and to place more of their members in key political posts. There is evidence that by 1910 they had achieved some success, but the days when mutual interests forced Anglo and Mexican Americans to cooperate had come to an end. Tucson entered a period described by Officer as "stabilized pluralism," in which Anglos were dominant but tolerant—at least until the depression of the 1930s created economic conflicts which heightened ethnic tensions again. By 1910, Officer says, Tucson's "Anglo and Mexican sub-societies were quite clearly separated except at the very top levels, where a handful of successful businessmen was managing to keep a foot in either camp."[17]

The Lower Rio Grande Valley of South Texas was similar to southern Arizona in some ways. Isolated from the rest of Texas, this area was culturally and economically tied to Mexico until a railroad line, completed in 1904 with Mexican labor, connected Brownsville and the valley to the rest of Texas. The arrival of low-cost transportation made irrigated farming practical, and South Texas underwent a transformation from a ranching to an agricultural economy. With larger amounts of capital at its disposal, as well as technological advantages and political leverage, an Anglo elite supplanted the Mexican American elite, but Anglos never outnumbered Mexicans in the Lower Rio Grande Valley. The increased farm production which resulted from the arrival of the railroad in 1904 increased the demand for cheap labor, and so the valley continued to attract Mexican immigrants and to remain predominantly Mexican American.[18] Yet in the period from 1848 to 1912, Mexican Americans in South Texas were never as politically influential as their counterparts in southern Arizona, for reasons suggested in the previous chapter.

Mexican Americans were most successful at protecting their culture and institutions in the Rio Grande Valley of northern New Mexico. There Mexican culture had its deepest roots and was best prepared to resist the shock of Anglo cultural impact. There, too, Mexican Americans remained the numerically dominant group throughout the nineteenth century, putting Anglos on the cultural defensive. Anglo newcomers, frequently hostile toward Mexicans at first, tended to develop tolerance and understanding when they were outnumbered.[19] Thus, in north central New Mexico, as in southern Arizona, mixed marriages were common, and Anglo business and professional men learned Spanish and formed partnerships with Nuevo Mexicanos if they were to succeed.[20] Also, as in southern Arizona, Anglos and Hispanos in New Mexico faced a common enemy in Indians (Apaches and Navajos in this case), who forced them to cooperate. Not until the 1870s were Indians brought under Anglo-Hispano control.

Mexican culture remained vigorous and expansive in New Mexico. As Indians lost control of their ancestral lands, Hispanos advanced their settlements onto new frontiers east and west of the Rio Grande Valley into Texas and Arizona, and north into southern Colorado.[21] Moving onto the eastern plains, however, Hispano sheepmen and farmers came into contact with westward-moving Anglo cattlemen, chiefly Texans and Southerners who had contempt for the "greasers." At these points of contact the Hispano advance slowed down and made painful adjustments. The usual antipathy between sheepmen and cattlemen in the West, intensified by ethnic hatreds, led to violent clashes, the best known being the Lincoln County War (1876–78), in which Billy the Kid gained notoriety. Contemporaries were well aware that these range wars manifested ethnic tensions. The *Santa Fe New Mexican*, for example, referred to troubles in Lincoln County in 1874 as "the unfortunate war . . . between the Texans and the Mexicans."[22]

Southeastern New Mexico, especially, came to be dominated by Anglo ranchers by the 1890s, and to be known as "Little Texas." This area took pride in its "development, enlightenment, progress and power," which resulted, one local paper boasted, from "the magic wand of the Anglo-Saxon," as opposed to the culture of the "greaser [who] is too lazy to keep up; and smells too badly to be endured."[23] Residents of this Anglo area chaffed under territorial government in which Mexican Americans were influential and twice, in 1903 and 1905, tried to annex themselves to Texas. Failing this, in 1906 Anglos in Eddy County resorted to more sophisticated, southern-inspired techniques for eliminating Hispanos from the electoral process: an all-white primary election and a poll tax. Each attempt met with violent objections from Mexican Americans and moderate Anglos and was defeated. On the other side of the territory, in the southwestern corner, a mining region, Anglos had become the majority group by the 1870s. There, too, they displayed aversion to political influence by Mexicans, many of whom labored in the mines. In the 1870s Grant County, in southwestern New Mexico, attempted to annex itself to Arizona in order, as one newspaper put it, to be better represented by an "American" legislature.[24]

By the 1890s, then, Hispanos no longer dominated all of New Mexico, but they did retain control of the north central portion, and continued to outnumber Anglos in the territory's total population. The railroad crossed New Mexico in the early 1880s. In contrast to the situation in southern California and southern Arizona, however, the coming of the railroad did not severely weaken Mexican American influence, for it failed to attract large numbers of permanent immigrants to the territory. The railroad had its greatest impact on the non-Hispanic mining and cattle-ranching areas of New Mexico.[25]

Having numerical superiority in the territory would have been of little consequence for Mexican Americans had they not proved adept at playing the Anglo political game. Contrary to the assertions of some sociologists that Mexican Americans are too individualistic to work effectively in organized politics, the Nuevo Mexicanos outregistered and outvoted Anglos, as well as outnumbering them. Hispano politicos dominated the key elective office of territorial delegate from 1850 to 1911 and controlled the territorial legislature at least through the 1880s, remaining well represented until New Mexico became a state in 1912.[26] At least as late as 1859, all sessions of the legislature were held in Spanish. Rather than resist Anglos from outside the system, Hispanos had learned to work within it. As staunch a leader of the resistance forces of 1846 as Diego Archuleta joined his former enemies and served for fourteen years in the territorial assembly.[27]

Mexican Americans' political astuteness won them the respect of many of their Anglo American colleagues. One of New Mexico's first Anglo governors, W. H. H. Davis, who had little appreciation for Mexican culture, described the Hispano politicos as "keen, cunning men in politics—quite a match for the Americans."[28] The politicos won more than respect; they defended their culture and institutions remarkably well, even to the extent of preserving the privileges of the upper class. The Hispano-dominated Territorial Assembly, for example, refused to abolish the institutions of Indian slavery or of peonage. Only an act of Congress in 1867 was able to outlaw those practices in the territory, and that act, one newspaper observed a year later, was "indifferently observed."[29] Hispanos also successfully opposed public education for the territory until 1891, in large part because they opposed the Americanizing effect of public schools and preferred parochial schools where lessons would be taught in Spanish and Roman Catholic principles would be transmitted to the next generation. Bills to establish public schools in the territory met with crushing defeats until 1891, when Hispanos supported a bill in order to prevent the federal government from forcing one on them and in order to improve their chances of obtaining statehood and home rule.[30]

Perhaps the most remarkable thing about Hispano resistance to

Americanization of New Mexico was that it was done while the territory was under a "colonial" rule.[31] The territorial system of government remained in force until 1912, with key officials (the governor, secretary, and federal judges) being appointed in faraway Washington. Under this system, a minority of Anglos was able to control the top offices in a territory where Hispanos were the majority.

Ironically, that New Mexico remained a territory for sixty-two years was due in part to the Hispanos' effectiveness at politics. Many Anglos opposed statehood, fearing that it would give the Hispanos the chance to take over completely. Hispanos' success at preserving their language and customs made New Mexico too "foreign" for the taste of many influential Easterners. As the *Chicago Tribune* put it in 1889, New Mexico's population was "not American, but 'Greaser,' persons ignorant of our laws, manners, customs, language, and institutions."[32] That viewpoint, which endured into the first decade of the twentieth century, was a major argument advanced by those opposed to New Mexico statehood.[33] Finally, many Hispanos themselves opposed statehood for New Mexico. In 1890 they voted overwhelmingly against statehood because a new constitution threatened the parochial school system. The Mexican American vote, encouraged by church leaders, went against the wishes of some of the most important Hispano oligarchs and was probably decisive in defeating the movement for statehood in 1890.[34]

If many Nuevo Mexicanos were not anxious for statehood, it was in part because they had learned to use the territorial system to their own advantage. The federal government, for example, paid many of the territorial government's expenses. Although it occurred somewhat accidentally, by 1897 the Hispanos had one of their own in the governor's chair—thirty-seven-year-old Miguel Antonio Otero. The first and only Mexican American to occupy the territory's highest office, Otero was the son of a prominent family, had been educated in Missouri and New York, and was described as "the representative of a new generation of Spanish-Americans who felt equally at home in both cultures."[35] Otero held onto the governorship for nine years (1897–1906), enjoying widespread popularity, especially among Mexican Americans.

By the turn of the century most of New Mexico's Hispanos favored statehood. Some argued that they should draw up a state constitution while they still held a majority in the territory. Thus, they could include protections for the future, when Anglos would inevitably be more numerous.[36] That, essentially, is what they did.

Of the 100 delegates to the 1910 constitutional convention, 35 were Hispanos who, under the leadership of Solomon Luna, formed an effective bloc. The 1910 constitution, which went into effect in 1912 when New Mexico became a state, declared that the rights granted by the Treaty of Guadalupe-Hidalgo would remain in force in the new state. It provided that the right of any citizen to vote, hold public office, or sit on juries could not be restricted because of "inability to speak, read or write the English or Spanish languages." The first state legislature put English and Spanish on an equal basis for all state business, thus making New Mexico officially a bilingual state. The Constitution of 1910 also provided for the training of bilingual teachers and prohibited separate schools for Anglo and Hispano children. Finally, these provisions were made difficult to amend.[37] Thus, although the constitution has been violated in practice, the Hispanos of New Mexico had effectively laid the legal groundwork for the protection of their civil rights and their culture.

III

Politics was not the only vehicle for Mexican Americans struggling to preserve their culture and to accommodate to Anglo American culture. The Spanish-speaking community also relied on the work of church groups, parochial schools, newspapers, and private clubs to give it unity and direction.

The most common private clubs were mutual benefit societies. Although information about these is scanty, they seem to have existed across the Southwest, becoming most popular toward the end of the century. Most of these groups were fraternal orders of workingmen, established as social clubs which would also provide insurance, medical benefits, and other services for their members and give the group some power politically. The *Club Recíproco*, for example, was founded in Corpus Christi, Texas, in 1873 with the stated purpose of "the protection of the poor and the mutual benefit of its members, calculated to assist society and elevate all who may wish to associate with the members of the club." By 1910, twelve such Mexican American societies existed in Corpus Christi alone, with names such as the *Sociedad Ignacio Allende* and *Sociedad Ignacio Zaragoza*. Most of these organizations seem to have been exclusively male. One exception, and doubtless there were others, was the *Sociedad Beneficencia*, founded in 1890 by women in Corpus Christi.[38]

The most successful of these organizations in the pre-1912 period was *La Alianza Hispano-Americana*, founded in Tucson in 1893. By 1906 the *Alianza* had twenty-two chapters which ranged throughout Arizona and spilled over into New Mexico mining towns such as Silver City and Santa Rita, and as far east as El Paso, Texas.[39] By 1929 the society had 15,000 members, with chapters ranging from San Diego, California, to Brownsville, Texas, and as far north as Cheyenne and Chicago. According to one of its founders, Ignacio Calvillo, the *Alianza* was formed in 1893 to "protect and fight for the rights of Spanish-Americans in Tucson, for at that time there was a lot of strife and ill-feeling between us and the Anglo-Saxon element caused in great part by prejudice, misunderstanding and ignorance."[40] Interestingly, the membership of the first Tucson chapter cut across class lines, with oligarchs Carlos Velasco and Manuel Samaniego as its principal founders. Since the *Alianza* was to be nonpolitical, the Tucson chapter also formed the Mexican Democratic Club as a political action front.

It is significant that these activities took place in Tucson in the 1890s, at a time when the influx of Anglos, who entered southern Arizona on the railroad, forced Mexican Americans to seek a new way to protect their political position and their culture.[41] That a similar organization was formed in Corpus Christi in the 1870s probably indicates the earlier need for mutual aid in Texas. That no chapter of the *Alianza* existed in Santa Fe, New Mexico, until 1906, may indicate that the Hispanos there had less need to form an exclusive club until after the turn of the century. Of course, groups other than mutual benefit societies functioned to preserve Mexican culture and institutions in the Southwest. Most famous are the *Penitentes*, who have provided dynamic leadership in a struggle to preserve religious practices in rural New Mexico, resisting even the hierarchy of the Roman Catholic church. Occupational groups such as livestock associations, and associations formed for the maintenance of irrigation ditches in New Mexico continued in existence from the colonial period.[42]

One of the most pressing needs of the Mexican American community was the need to form labor unions. In the pre-1912 Southwest, as

Professor Juan Gómez-Quiñones has shown, a surprising number of labor organizations were formed and strikes were carried out.[43] These strikes, ranging from those against railroads in Texas and California to strikes against mines in Colorado and Arizona, tended to involve industrial labor more than agricultural workers. Leadership in these efforts sometimes came from experienced union organizers who had been forced out of Mexico by the repressive regime of Porfirio Díaz. Perhaps the most active of these Mexican organizers were representatives of Ricardo Flores Magón's *Partido Liberal Mexicano*. Although Mexican laborers scored occasional victories in their attempts to raise wages and reduce working hours, more often they endured frustrating failures, for the odds against their success were considerable.

Newly arrived laborers, fresh from Mexico, were willing to work for lower wages than were Anglos or Mexican Americans, and a double wage scale became common across the Southwest. In Arizona in the late 1850s, for example, Mexican miners earned $12.50 a month and $6.00 worth of flour for the same work for which Anglos received $30 a month. A similar inequity still existed in Arizona mines at the end of the teritorial period, and there is evidence that Mexicans who had become American citizens worked for "Mexican wages," too. Since even the lowest wages for laborers in Arizona were higher than wages in Mexico, the new immigrants tended not to complain. Nor did they dare. Brief work stoppages, or walking off the job completely, were generally the only recourse of disgruntled workers, because those who were dissatisfied could be replaced with Indian laborers or with strikebreakers imported from Mexico.[44] Thus, as Juan Gómez-Quiñones put it, Mexican laborers were in the paradoxical situation of being "involved both as strikers and strikebreakers." Moreover, because they had a reputation as strikebreakers, and because ethnocentric Anglo union leaders regarded them as difficult to organize, Mexican laborers fell into disfavor with established unions such as the American Federation of Labor and the Western Federation of Miners. As so often happened, then, Mexican Americans were caught in the middle of a situation not entirely of their making, and their wages remained low, their hours long, and their working conditions miserable. Nonetheless, despite the odds against them, Mexican laborers participated in a number of strikes, one of which was the biggest strike in the history of Arizona Territory and, possibly, the pre-1912 Southwest.[45]

The strike broke out in the Clifton-Morenci district of southeastern

Arizona, the territory's first major copper-producing area, developed in the 1870s with Mexico labor. In June 1903, some 3,500 men went out on strike at Clifton-Morenci. Eighty to ninety percent of these men were of Mexican descent. They were angered over their employer's failure to comply with a state law guaranteeing an eight-hour day. The strike was apparently carried out without an effective union. As one newspaper editor noted upon first hearing of the trouble: "The miners of the district have no organization." He predicted that a strike by the "unruly" Mexicans would fail. When the strike succeeded in paralyzing the mines, the same editor, searching for an explanation, reported that the Mexicans "belong to numerous societies and through these they can exert some sort of organization to stand together."[46] Those "societies" were clearly mutual benefit organizations such as the *Alianza*, which apparently served as a *sub rosa* labor union in Arizona and elsewhere.[47] The Clifton-Morenci strike of 1903 ended when heavy rains and flooding destroyed part of the communities involved, especially the homes of the poorer workers. The flooding stopped the strike prematurely and probably averted a clash between federal troops and the armed strikers. Another major strike occurred in the Clifton-Morenci district again in 1915. This time the results were favorable to workers and, as the *Los Angeles Labor Press* explained it: "Everyone knows that it was the Mexican miners that won the strike at Clifton and Morenci by standing like a stone wall until the bosses came to terms."[48]

The task of forming organizations and accommodating the Mexican American community to the dominant Anglo culture was facilitated considerably by Spanish-language newspapers, which often regarded themselves as defenders of Mexican American rights and culture. Wherever there was a substantial number of potential readers, Spanish-language newspapers appeared. In territorial Arizona, for example, newspapers for Mexican American readers existed not only in large population centers such as Tucson and Phoenix, and in the border town of Nogales, but in mining communities such as Clifton, Morenci, and Douglas, where Mexicans labored.[49] In communities with mixed Anglo-Hispano populations, the leading English-language paper frequently published a Spanish edition or a Spanish page, as did the *Los Angeles Star* and the *Santa Fe New Mexican*.[50] As was true of frontier newspapers in general, most enjoyed brief lives, but Spanish-language papers especially must have failed due to the smaller number of literate and affluent subscribers they could muster.

Mexican Americans across the Southwest recognized the need either to have their own schools or to have public schools in which Spanish would be taught. We have already discussed the importance of this issue in New Mexico politics, and there the Hispanos were most successful in retaining parochial schools and bilingualism. Retention of parochial schools was an important issue in southern Arizona, too. There, however, Mexican Americans lost ground[51] because schools which treated Mexican American children fairly, and which encouraged them to take pride in their culture, could only be achieved where the Spanish-speaking were powerful politically. In Texas, for example, where Mexican Americans probably had the least political clout, there was open talk of not establishing public schools at all because Mexican children might attend them and become "ruined"—that is, no longer willing to work at a menial task for a pittance.[52] In the case of San Francisco, Mariano G. Vallejo described the important role played by political power in keeping Spanish in the school curriculum: "French and German," Vallejo said, "were taught in the San Francisco schools because those two groups could produce 30,000 votes; as the Hispanic-Americans could only muster 4,000, Spanish was not part of the curriculum."[53]

In the end, then, as Vallejo's comment illustrates, it was largely numbers that determined whether or not Mexican Americans would retain their cultural identity and institutions. Mexican Americans used all of the resources at their disposal to wage a struggle against overwhelming odds. Indeed, given the rapid rate at which they were being outnumbered, historian Rodman Paul's respectful question is quite appropriate: "How did they manage to preserve their identity at all?"[54] It appears that by the 1880s the struggle was being lost. Assimilation was taking place more rapidly than accommodation, as the railroads brought more and more Anglo Americans westward. Except in rural enclaves, traditional Mexican American culture was rapidly being supplanted by Eastern dress, food, architecture,[55] and even religion. As one Presbyterian minister put it, "Divine Grace is able to make even a Mexican honest."[56] In rural areas, too, Mexican Americans who were being pushed off their lands, or those who found their land no longer adequate to support growing families, began taking jobs on railroads, in mines, and in the incipient agribusiness. Mexican culture in the rural Southwest could not remain insulated from Anglo American economic penetration, either.

IV

In the last decade of the nineteenth century, as Anglo Americans threatened to overwhelm completely the Mexican American minority in the Southwest, a large-scale counter-immigration of Mexicans got under way. This immigration, which labor historian Ernesto Galarza has termed "one of the major mass movements of people in the western hemisphere,"[57] had a profound impact on the Mexican American community and on the attitudes of Anglo Americans toward Mexican Americans.

Massive immigration from Mexico is usually thought to have begun in the 1910s, when the burgeoning economy of the Southwest and World War I created enormous demands for labor in the United States, and the social dislocation of the Mexican Revolution began to push Mexicans across the border in search of jobs and stability. Nearly a quarter of a million Mexicans immigrated to the United States during the 1910s, according to official count, and nearly a half million in the 1920s.[58] By 1910, however, the year that the Mexican Revolution began and Congress passed legislation enabling New Mexico and Arizona to become states, a substantial number of Mexican immigrants had already entered the United States, and clear trends had developed which would be accelerated in the 1910s and 1920s.

The number of immigrants from Mexico who settled in the United States by 1910 can only be roughly approximated. Neither the United States nor Mexico kept careful records.[59] For some years (1886–93), the United States Immigration Service kept no records at all. What records were kept are highly inaccurate, reflecting apparently only those Mexicans who bothered to stop and report to a government official when they crossed into the United States. The Immigration Service, for example, reported that 5,162 Mexicans immigrated to the United States in the decade of the 1870s. Yet within that same decade, the Bureau of Census reported that the number of Mexican-born persons living in the United States had increased by some 26,000. Even had the Immigration Service wanted to keep records or to control the number of Mexicans who entered the United States each year, it did not have the manpower to patrol the border effectively.

Minor legal restrictions on Mexican migrant labor, then, such as the head tax of 1882 or the Contract Labor Law of 1885, were not strong deterrents to Mexican immigrants.[60]

According to federal census figures, which may be unrealistically low, the Mexican-born population of the United States increased steadily from 1870 on, more than doubling by 1900 when some 103,000 Mexican-born persons were recorded as living in the United States. That figure, of course, does not include American-born persons of Mexican descent. In the first decade of the twentieth century, the census reported that the Mexican-born population of the United States had further increased by nearly 63,000. The number of immigrants accelerated sharply during that decade. One government report of 1908 noted that some 50,000 Mexicans were arriving in the United States annually; it estimated conservatively that about 20,000 of them would remain permanently in the United States.[62]

The sharp increase in Mexican immigration toward the turn of the century was due in part to conditions in Mexico under Porfirio Díaz. By 1910 the Díaz government had come to deplore the emigration, for it created severe social disruption in communities throughout Mexico. Border towns especially were showing signs of strain. Yet, Díaz's policies in themselves contributed to the loss of population that he lamented. Opponents of the Díaz regime correctly charged that the oppression of a tyrannical government forced Mexicans out of the country, and labor leaders and politicians were among the emigrants. The chief impetus for immigration, however, was economic.[63] Enormous population growth in the last two decades of the Díaz government had been accompanied by declining food production, declining wages for workingmen, and declining opportunity to obtain land, as Díaz permitted members of the elite to increase the size of their already mammoth estates. Lower-class Mexicans had little choice but to seek opportunites elsewhere if they were to survive. Mexican railroad construction, which accelerated greatly under the Díaz regime, provided former peons with the opportunity and means to leave for the United States. Much of the railroad-building took place in northern Mexico, where lines pushed north toward border towns such as Nogales, El Paso, and Piedras Negras. Mexican farm workers, who took jobs on the railroads, or in mines in the north, found themselves cut off from their village and family ties and, often for the first time, introduced to the money economy. Then, learning that wages in the United States were double those in Mexico, many continued north to find similar employment on the other side of the border.

Concurrently, railroad lines had been moving across the Southwest, creating demands for labor and providing low-cost transportation, which promoted the economic development of the region. As the need for labor increased across the Southwest, Orientals, who had been the mainstay of the cheap labor force, became less available due to the Chinese Exclusion Act of 1882 and the Gentleman's Agreement with Japan of 1907. Thus, the work of building and maintaining Southwestern railroads, of mining and smelting, of picking sugar beets and cotton, and the menial tasks on ranches and farms, fell to Mexican laborers, whose backs and arms built the modern Southwest. This pattern was already set by 1910.[64]

The new immigrants were finding work as far east as Louisiana and as far north as Illinois and Wyoming, by 1910, but most remained close to the border in the four Southwestern states and in Colorado. Los Angeles had already become the largest urban center of Mexican population in the Southwest. Most Mexican immigrants, however, worked in rural areas, in jobs that frequently required migratory labor, and at lower wages than Anglos received for comparable work. These conditions, combined with the normal tendency of people of similar culture to seek out one another, contributed to keeping Mexican immigrants living together in *colonias* or barrios which were effectively segregated from the Anglo community. In these towns or neighborhoods, low wages meant mean living conditions. Separatism meant that Mexican culture would be reinforced and acculturation would proceed at a snail's pace.

Anglo American views of Mexican inferiority easily translated into social pressures which also contributed to ostracizing and segregating Mexicans and Mexican Americans into their own communities, or to the proverbial "other side of the tracks." To ensure the ethnic and racial purity of their neighborhoods, Anglos in many Southwestern communities invoked property restrictions against Mexicans, and encouraged segregated schools, stores, restaurants, barbershops, and theaters. In a remarkable study, Professor Paul S. Taylor found these conditions in the 1920s in communities ranging from the Imperial Valley in southeastern California, to northeastern Colorado and South Texas.[65] The trend, however, was already clear by 1910.

Anglo Americans made little effort to understand the historical and sociological circumstances that determined the life-style of Mexican immigrants. If Mexicans lived in poverty, a report of the United States Immigration Commission declared in 1911, it was because they were "without amibition and thrift." Mexicans, according to the same report, tend to require public charity, are of low intelligence, do not value education, are criminally inclined, and do not assimilate as do other ethnic groups. Thus, the report concluded, the Mexican "is less desirable as a citizen than as a laborer."[66] On the scale of values of some Anglos in the first decade of the twentieth century, Mexicans remained slightly above Negroes and below Indians.[67] These attitudes reflect, of course, the longstanding stereotypes which we examined in chapter two.

Mexican Americans of the first, second, and third generations could only view the new immigrants, and the hostility that they engendered from Anglos, with a mixture of sympathy and alarm. Those Mexican Americans who retained strong cultural ties with Mexico seem to have reacted with compassion and understanding for the plight of their brothers from the south. At the same time, however, Mexican immigrants competed with Mexican Americans for jobs and helped to lower the wage scale across the Southwest. Moreover, the negative impression that Anglos had of the newcomers carried over to anyone of Mexican extraction, unless perhaps the Anglo happened to know him personally. The result, as one observer put it in 1908, was that the Mexican American "considers himself above the immigrant, and does not want to be confounded with him in public opinion."[68]

The new wave of Mexican immigration, then, resulted in a schism in the Spanish-speaking community in the Southwest which was evident by 1910 and remains to the present day. By the 1920s, if not earlier, older residents of New Mexico began to refer to themselves as *Spanish Americans,* or *Spanish Colonials,* in order to disassociate themselves from the opprobrious term *Mexican.*[69] The same process occurred in California and Arizona, and in Texas, where older residents came to prefer the term *Latin American.*[70] Frequently accompanying this change in name was the self-delusion that the older Mexican residents of the Southwest were of "pure" Spanish blood and racially superior to Mexicans. This attitude of superiority antagonized Mexican immigrants, of course, occasionally leading to friction between the two groups.[71]

The tendency of older Mexican American families to hispanize their heritage coincided with a growing Anglo American appreciation for the Southwest's "Spanish" heritage. Beginning in the 1880s, the region's exotic "foreign" atmosphere appealed increasingly to Anglo American scholars, writers, artists, and to communities interested in tourism. Crumbling missions began to be restored as the most dramatic symbols of the period when the Southwest was part of the Spanish Empire. Yet, the boosters of the Southwest's Spanish heritage were careful to sanitize their product so that no one would confuse the romance of the "Spanish Pioneers" with the reality of thousands of struggling Mexican workers, some of whom were descended from those very pioneers.[72] Thus, as noted in chapter 1, a curious dichotomy between things Spanish and things Mexican left Mexicans in the Southwest without a history, unless they chose to identify themselves as Spanish. Few of the migrants from Mexico could or would do that.

With new immigrants from Mexico traveling over the same trails that explorers and homeseekers from Mexico had covered some four centuries before, the circle was complete. Mexican culture was further impressed upon the Southwest, and the flames of ancient Yankee prejudices were rekindled, ready to flare up at the first sign of economic competition. Massive immigration from Mexico created a new generation of completely unassimilated Mexican Americans nearly every decade. Those new arrivals from Mexico, however, were in a sense not immigrants at all, and certainly they were unlike immigrants from Europe. According to one well-known model, European immigrants went through a process of assimilation in which the second generation completely rejected the culture of its parents and the third generation sought to rediscover it.[73] Mexicans who settled in the Southwest usually did not have that opportunity, for they entered a society which had already determined the role that dark-skinned Mexicans who spoke little English would play. Thus, instead of rejecting the culture of the previous generation, "every generation of Mexican Americans has, in ignorance, been reliving its history," as Rodolfo Alvarez has aptly explained.[74] Individuals might break out of the pattern, but by 1910 Mexican Americans as a group seemed fated to remain foreigners in a land that had been native to their ancestors.

1. "Revenge took possession of me"

Tiburcio Vásquez, 1874*
Joaquín Murrieta, 1854**

Although Tiburcio Vásquez is remembered as a romantic Robin Hood figure, there is no hard evidence that he robbed from the rich to give to the poor. Yet he seems to fit the pattern of the social bandit, for members of the Mexican community in California sheltered him from the law, and he enjoyed a popular following at the end of his career.

Beginning with a killing in 1851, Vásquez took to robbing stage coaches and stealing cattle. In 1857 he was captured and sent to San Quentin, remaining there until 1863 (except for a brief escape in 1859). Vásquez returned to cattle rustling and then to the penitentiary again from 1867 to 1870. Up to this point, he remained an obscure criminal. A robbery and murders at Tres Pinos in 1873 brought him notoriety for the first time. With a reward of $3,000 on his head, Vásquez was captured in 1874, given a trial, and hung the following year. During his last days, he was a popular figure, entertaining many visitors in his cell. Among them was a newspaper reporter to whom Vásquez gave the following explanation of what had driven him to a life of crime.[1]

Vásquez's explanation, whether fact or rationalization, may very well be true. It makes even more interesting reading when compared with John Ridge's fictional account, included here, of why Joaquín Murrieta embarked on his bloody career. Both of these accounts should also be compared with Antonio F. Coronel's actual experiences in the mines (document number 3 in chapter 4).

Although not all bandidos fall into the category of social bandits, it seems clear that conditions existed in California to produce an ample number of them.

---

*Los Angeles Star, May 16, 1874. This account also appears in Robert G. Cleland, Cattle on a Thousand Hills: Southern California, 1850–1880 (San Marino: 1951), pp. 274–75.

**From The Life and Adventures of Joaquín Murieta: The Celebrated California Bandit, by Yellow Bird (John Rollin Ridge). New edition copyright 1955 by the University of Oklahoma Press. Reprinted by permission of the publisher. Although Ridge spelled Murrieta with one r, I prefer the double r spelling.

1. Ernest R. May, "Tiburcio Vásquez," Historical Society of Southern California Quarterly, 29, nos. 3–4 (September–December 1947): 123–34. See also Jackson, Bad Company, pp. 297–395, and Ralph Rambo's popular Trailing the California Bandit Tiburcio Vásquez (San Jose, Calif.: 1968).

TIBURCIO VASQUEZ
AN INTERVIEW WITH THE NOTED BANDIT

We interviewed Tiburcio Vasquez yesterday. He seemed but little the worse for his wounds. Sheriff Rowland has provided him with a comfortable spring mattress, and the dinner which was brought to him during our stay in his cell was good enough for anybody. He laughed and talked as gaily and as unconstrainedly as if he were in his parlor instead of the clutches of the violated law. In reply to our questions he gave the following account of himself, substantially:

"I was born in Monterey county, California at the town of Monterey, August 11, 1835. My parents are both dead. I have three brothers and two sisters. Two of my brothers reside in Monterey County—one unmarried and one married. The other resides in Los Angeles county; he is married. My sisters are both married. One of them lives at San Juan Baptista, Monterey county; the other at the New Idria quick-silver mines.

"I was never married, but I have one child in this county a year old. I can read and write, having attended school in Monterey. My parents were people in ordinarily good circumstances; owned a small tract of land and always had enough for their wants.

"My career grew out of the circumstances by which I was surrounded as I grew to manhood. I was in the habit of attending balls and parties given by the native Californians, into which the Americans, then beginning to become numerous, would force themselves and shove the native-born men aside, monopolizing the dances and the women. This was about 1852.

"A spirit of hatred and revenge took possession of me. I had numerous fights in defense of what I believed to be my rights and those of my countrymen. The officers were continually in pursuit of me. I believed that we were unjustly and wrongfully deprived of the social rights which belonged to us. So perpetually was I involved in these difficulties that I at length determined to leave the thickly-settled portion of the country, and did so.

"I gathered together a small band of cattle and went into Mendocino county, back of Ukiah and beyond Fallis Valley. Even here I was not permitted to remain in peace. The officers of the law sought me out in that remote region, and strove to drag me before the courts. I always resisted arrest.

"I went to my mother and told her I intended to commence a

different life. I asked for and obtained her blessing, and at once commenced the career of a robber. My first exploit consisted in robbing some peddlers of money and clothes in Monterey county. My next was the capture and robbery of a stagecoach in the same county. I had confederates with me from the first, and was always recognized as leader. Robbery after robbery followed each other as rapidly as circumstances allowed, until in 1857 or '58 I was arrested in Los Angeles for horse-stealing, convicted of grand larceny, sent to the penitentiary and was taken to San Quentin and remained there until my term of imprisonment expired in 1863.

"Up to the time of my conviction and imprisonment I had robbed stage coaches, houses, wagons, etc., indiscrimanately, carrying on my operations for the most part in daylight, sometimes, however, visiting houses after dark.

"After my discharge from San Quentin I returned to the house of my parents and endeavored to lead a peaceful and honest life. I was, however, soon accused of being a confederate of Procopio and one Sato, both noted bandits, the latter of whom was afterward killed by Sheriff Harry Morse of Alameda county. I was again forced to become a fugitive from the law-officers, and, driven to desperation, I left home and family and commenced robbing whenever opportunity offered. I made but little money by my exploits, I always managed to avoid arrest. I believe I owe my frequent escapes solely to my courage. I was always ready to fight whenever opportunity offered, but always tried to avoid bloodshed.

JOAQUIN MURRIETA

I sit down to write somewhat concerning the life and character of *Joaquin Murieta*, a man as remarkable in the annals of crime as any of the renowned robbers of the Old or New World, who have preceded him; and I do this, not for the purpose of ministering to any depraved taste for the dark and horrible in human action, but rather to contribute my mite to those materials out of which the early history of California shall one day be composed. The character of this truly wonderful man was nothing more than a natural production of the social and moral condition of the country in which he lived, acting upon certain peculiar circumstances favorable to such a result, and, consequently, his individual history is a part of the most valuable history of the State.

....

Joaquín Murieta was a Mexican, born in the province of Sonora of respectable parents and educated in the schools of Mexico. While growing up, he was remarkable for a very mild and peaceable disposition, and gave no sign of that indomitable and daring spirit which afterwards characterized him. Those who knew him in his school-boy days speak affectionately of his generous and noble nature at that period of his life and can scarcely credit the fact that the renowned and bloody bandit of California was one and the same being. At an early age of his manhood—indeed, while he was yet scarcely more than a boy—he became tired of the uncertain state of affairs in his own country, the usurpations and revolutions which were of such common occurrence, and resolved to try his fortunes among the American people, of whom he had formed the most favorable opinion from an acquaintance with the few whom he had met in his own native land. The war with Mexico had been fought, and California belonged to the United States. Disgusted with the conduct of his degenerate countrymen and fired with enthusiastic admiration of the American character, the youthful Joaquín left his home with a buoyant heart and full of the exhilarating spirit of adventure. The first that we hear of him in the Golden State is that, in the spring of 1850, he is engaged in the honest occupation of a miner in the Stanislaus placers, then reckoned among the richest portions of the mines. He was then eighteen years of age, . . . and the frank and cordial bearing which distinguished him made him beloved by all with whom he came in contact. He had the confidence and respect of the whole community around him, and was fast amassing a fortune from his rich mining claim. He had built him a comfortable mining residence in which he had domiciled his heart's treasure—a beautiful Sonorian girl, who had followed the young adventurer in all his wanderings with that devotedness of passion which belongs to the dark-eyed damsels of Mexico. It was at this moment of peace and felicity that a blight came over the young man's prospects. The country was then full of lawless and desperate men, who bore the name of Americans but failed to support the honor and dignity of that title. A feeling was prevalent among this class of contempt for any and all Mexicans, whom they looked upon as no better than conquered subjects of the United States, having no rights which could stand before a haughtier and superior race. They made no exceptions. If the proud blood of the Castilians mounted to the cheek of a partial descendant of the Mexiques, showing that he had inherited the old chivalrous spirit of his Spanish ancestry, they looked upon it as a saucy presumption in one so inferior to them. The prejudice of color, the antipathy of races, which are always stronger and bitterer with the ignorant and unlettered, they could not overcome, of if they could, would not, because it afforded them a convenient excuse for their unmanly cruelty and oppression. A band of these lawless men, having the brute power to do as they pleased, visited Joaquín's house and peremptorily bade him leave his claim, as they would allow no Mexicans to work in that region. Upon his remonstrating against such outrageous conduct, they struck him violently over the face, and, being physically superior, compelled him to swallow his wrath. Not content with this, they tied him hand and foot and ravished his mistress before his eyes. They left him, but the soul of the young man was from that moment darkened. It was the first injury he had ever received at the hands of the Americans, whom he had always hitherto respected, and it wrung him to the soul as a deeper and deadlier wrong from that very circumstance. He departed with his weeping and almost heart-broken mistress for a more northern portion of the mines; and the next we hear of him, he is cultivating a little farm on the banks of a beautiful stream that watered a fertile valley, far out in the seclusion of the mountains. Here he might hope for peace—here he might forget the past, and again be happy. But his dream was not destined to last. A company of unprincipled Americans—shame that there should be such bearing the name!—saw his retreat, coveted his little home surrounded by its fertile tract of land, and drove him from it, with no other excuse than that he was "an infernal Mexican intruder!" Joaquín's blood boiled in his veins, but his spirit was still unbroken, nor had the iron so far entered his soul as to scar up the innate sensitiveness to honor and right which reigned in his bosom. Twice broken up in his honest pursuit of fortune, he resolved still to labor on with unfliching brow and with that true *moral* bravery, which throws its redeeming light forward upon his subsequently dark and criminal career. How deep must have been the anguish of that young heart and how strongly rooted the native honesty of his soul, none can know or imagine but they who have been tried in a like manner. He bundled up his little movable property, still accompanied by his faithful bosom-friend, and again started forth to strike once more, like a brave and honest man, for fortune and for happiness. He arrived at "Murphy's Diggings" in Calaveras County, in the month of April, and went again to mining, . . .

He had gone a short distance from Murphy's Diggings to see a half-brother, who had been located in that vicinity for several months, and returned to Murphy's upon a horse which his brother had lent him. The animal proved to have been stolen, and being recognized by a number of individuals in town, an excitement was raised on the subject. Joaquín suddenly found himself surrounded by a furious mob and charged with the crime of theft. He told them how it happened that he was riding the horse and in what manner his half-brother had come in possession of it. They listened to no explanation, but bound him to a tree, and publicly disgraced him with the lash. They then proceeded to the house of his half-brother and hung him without judge or jury. It was then that the character of Joaquín changed, suddenly and irrevocably. Wanton cruelty and the tyranny of prejudice had reached their climax. His soul swelled beyond its former boundaries, and the barriers of honor, rocked into atoms by the strong passion which shook his heart like an earthquake, crumbled around him. Then it was that he declared to a friend that he would live henceforth for revenge and that his path should be marked with blood. Fearfully did he keep his promise, as the following pages will show.

2. "To defend ourselves" Juan Nepomuceno Cortina, 1859*

A slender man with reddish-blond hair and grey eyes, Juan N. Cortina was thirty-four years old when he began his famous "war" in 1859. His family had lived along the Rio Grande for three generations, his great-grandfather having arrived with the first colonists in the area under José de Escandón. Born on the south side of the river at Camargo, in 1824, Cortina moved to his

---

*U.S., Congress, House, *Difficulties on the Southwestern Frontier*, 36th Cong., 1st sess., 1860, H. Exec. Doc. 52, pp. 70–82. Cortina's name in these documents appears as "Cortinas," leading to considerable confusion about the spelling of his name. Most knowledgeable writers have settled on "Cortina" as the correct spelling.

mother's ranch near Brownsville on the north side of the Rio Grande in the 1840s and seems to have considered himself a United States citizen after the Mexican War.

Like other Mexicans in the area, Cortina's family had experienced difficulties with Anglos over land grants, and Cortina himself had been personally abused by Anglos. Cortina's war started on July 13, 1859, when he shot the sheriff of Brownsville, who was beating a Mexican. Escaping across the border, Cortina raised a small force and boldly attacked Brownsville on September 28. He did not plunder the city, but freed twelve Mexicans from jail, killed three Anglos whom he regarded as corrupt, and then retired to his mother's ranch. From there he issued two proclamations which explained his grievances. Portions of his first proclamation follow.

Although Cortina lost his war, he went on to become governor of Tamaulipas and mayor of Matamoros; he fought for Benito Juárez against the French invaders of Mexico and aided Union forces in Texas during the Civil War. Until 1876, when he was arrested and imprisoned in Mexico City, Cortina was rumored to be the head of a ring that stole cattle in Texas. A remarkable man, and a hero to his people, Cortina earned his nickname: The Robin Hood of the Rio Grande.

Proclamation

Juan Nepomuceno Cortinas to the Inhabitants of the State of Texas, and especially to those of the city of Brownsville.

. . . There is no need of fear. Orderly people and honest citizens are inviolable to us in their persons and interests. Our object, as you have seen, has been to chastise the villainy of our enemies, which heretofore has gone unpunished. These have connived with each other, and form, so to speak, a perfidious inquisitorial lodge to persecute and rob us, without any cause, and for no other crime on our part than that of being of Mexican origin, considering us, doubtless, destitute of those gifts which they themselves do not possess.

To defend ourselves, and making use of the sacred right of self-preservation, we have assembled in a popular meeting with a view of discussing a means by which to put an end to our misfortunes.

The assembly organized, and headed by your humble servant, (thanks to the confidence which he inspired as one of the most aggrieved,) we have careered over the streets of the city in search of our adversaries, inasmuch as justice being .administered by their own hands, the supremacy of the law has failed to accomplish its object.

Some of them, rashly remiss in complying with our demand, have perished for having sought to carry their animosity beyond the limits allowed by their precarious position. Three of them have died—all criminal, wicked men, notorious among the people for their misdeeds. The others, still more unworthy and wretched, dragged themselves through the mire to escape our anger, . . .

These, as we have said, form, with a multiple of lawyers, a secret conclave, with all its ramifications, for the sole purpose of despoiling the Mexicans of their lands and usurp[ing] them afterwards. This is clearly proven by the conduct of one Adolph Glavecke, who, invested with the character of deputy sheriff, and in collusion with the said lawyers, has spread terror among the unwary, making them believe that he will hang the Mexicans and burn their ranches, &c., that by this means he might compel them to abandon the country, and thus accomplish their object. This is not a supposition—it is a reality; and notwithstanding the want of better proof, if this threat were not publicly known, all would feel persuaded that of this, and even more, are capable such criminal men as the one last mentioned, the marshal, the jailer, Morris, Neal, &c.

All truce between them and us is at an end, from the fact alone of our holding upon this soil our interests and property.

Innocent persons shall not suffer—no. But, if necessary, we will lead a wandering life, awaiting our opportunity to purge society of men so base that they degrade it with their opprobrium. Our families have returned as strangers to their old country to beg for an asylum. Our lands, if they are to be sacrificed to the avaricious covetousness of our enemies, will be rather so on account of our vicissitudes. As to land, Nature will always grant us sufficient to support our frames and we accept the consequences that may arise. Further, *our personal*

*enemies shall not possess our lands until they have fattened [them]
with their own gore.*

We cherish the hope, however, that the government, for the sake of
its own dignity, and in obsequiousness to justice, will accede to our
demand, by prosecuting those men and bringing them to trial, or
leave them to become subject to the consequences of our immutable
resolve.

Juan Nepomuceno Cortinas
Rancho Del Carmen
County of Cameron, September 30, 1859

3. Las Gorras Blancas
Nuestra Plataforma, 1890*
Felix Martínez, 1890*

Although Las Gorras Blancas, or the White Caps, were
dismissed as criminals by most territorial officials (including
Governor Miguel Antonio Otero who termed them "rough
necks"),[1] they had a clear program and seem to have had the
support of a majority of the Hispanos in San Miguel County,
where they were strongest. To an impartial outsider, such as the
newly arrived Justice of the Territorial Court, James O'Brien, the
"outrages" of the White Caps were "protests of a simple,
pastoral people against the establishment of large landed
Estates, or baronial feudalism."[2]

For those who remained uncertain as to what White Cap
violence meant, a number of the group made a visit to Las Vegas
and nailed copies of their program on various buildings on the
night of March 11, 1890. The "platform," published the next day
in a Las Vegas newspaper, the *Daily Optic,* is reprinted here.

Las Vegas Daily Optic, March 12, 1890.

Las Vegas Daily Optic, August 18, 1890.

1. Miguel Antonio Otero, *My Life on the Frontier, 1882–1897,* 2 vols. (Albuquerque: 1939),
2:251.

2. O'Brien to Governor L. Bradford Prince, July 30, 1890. Prince Papers, White Caps Folder,
State Records Center, Santa Fe, New Mexico.

3. *La Voz del Pueblo,* editorial of March 21, 1891; and information supplied by Robert
Rosenbaum, Department of History, University of Texas.

Unable to bring the White Caps under control, San Miguel County officials staged a meeting in Las Vegas on August 16. With the governor himself in attendance, the meeting was supposed to find ways to stop the White Caps. Judging from the following account of the meeting, much of the citizenry had little intention of stopping the White Caps, but instead sympathized with them. Felix Martínez, who made a popular speech at this meeting, was publisher of *La Voz del Pueblo*, the Spanish-language paper in Las Vegas, which took the same position that Martínez expressed in the public meeting.[3]

NUESTRA PLATAFORMA--

Our purpose is to protect the rights and interests of the people in general and especially those of the helpless classes.

We want the Las Vegas Grant settled to the benefit of all concerned, and this we hold is the entire community within the Grant.

We want no 'land grabbers' or obstructionists of any sort to interfere. We will watch them.

We are not down on lawyers as a class, but the usual knavery and unfair treatment of the people must be stopped.

Our judiciary hereafter must understand that we will sustain it only when 'Justice' is its watchword.

We are down on race issues, and will watch race agitators.

We favor irrigation enterprises, but will fight any scheme that tends to monopolize the supply of water sources to the detriment of residents living on lands watered by the same streams.

The people are suffering from the effects of partisan 'bossism' and these bosses had better quietly hold their peace. The people have been persecuted and hauled about in every which way to satisfy their caprices.

We must have a free ballot and fair court and the will of the Majority shall be respected.

We have no grudge against any person in particular, but we are the enemies of bulldozers and tyrants.

If the old system should continue, death would be a relief to our suffering. And for our rights our lives are the least we can pledge.

If the fact that we are law-abiding citizens is questioned, come out to
our houses and see the hunger and desolation we are suffering;
and 'this' is the result of the deceitful and corrupt methods of
'bossism.'

The White Caps 1,500 Strong and Gaining Daily

FELIX MARTÍNEZ AT A CITIZENS' MEETING--

Responding to a call from Chairman Booth, on behalf of the county
commissioners, a large crowd assembled Saturday night in the main
court room of the court house, about eight o'clock. The inclemency of
the weather did in no wise effect [sic] the attendance, and the county,
including most of the outlying precincts, was very well represented.
Chariman Booth called the meeting to order, and said that he did not
know as it was necessary for him to state the object of the assemblage,
but after the election of Margarito Romero as clerk of the session, he
had the court interpreter read aloud the notices in both Spanish and
English. Mr. Booth said in a prefatory way that the idea in calling this
meeting was to get the expression of opinion as to the outrages being
committed, and the idea of all the people in the county as to the best
means of bringing them to an end. He wished those who might speak,
to do so freely, but with brevity and strictly to the point, . . . After a
silence of a few moments, Mr. Raynolds arose and said:
"Mr. Chairman, and Gentlemen, I move that a committee of five be
appointed to draft resolutions, which shall definitely express the sense
and purpose of this gathering. I also move that a second committee of
equal number be appointed to devise ways and means of safety. There
is no doubt now that there exists among us a very dangerous element
which has damaged every interest in this Territory, as well as in San
Miguel county and Las Vegas. It behooves every good citizen to have
this fence-cutting and these commissions of other depredations
stopped immediately. Every one thought that when this fence-cutting
commenced it was for the purpose of preventing the grants from
being fenced up, but it has expanded now all over the county. It is
time to call a halt. With that said in view I should like the chair to
appoint a committee of safety and another committee to draft
resolutions which shall express the sense of this meeting."
The motion was seconded on all sides, but Don N. Segura arose to
have the motion amended. He wished to know, first why the meeting

had been called. Thought it very strange that such committees of ways and means, etc., should be appointed when those present did not know why they were present. He lived in the north of the county where in at least eight or ten precincts no such notices as those read had been posted. He had come to town on business and not to attend the meeting, consequently he wanted to know why he was there. If for a purpose, in the name of the northern part of the county, he demanded to know for what purpose. For the purpose of resisting invasions? To appoint five men to prevent all illegal fence-cutting or just fence-cutting? (Much applause). Before proceeding, he wanted to know why those present had assembled. . . . After some silence, some discussion in undertones, etc., Felix Martinez was called for. He came forward amid ringing cheers from the audience. Here Nestor Montoya acted as interpreter, relieving Antonio Lucero, who was quite tired, and the two thereafter alternated, both serving efficiently. Mr. Martinez addressed the chairman and those present in English, saying in substance:

"Mr. chairman and gentlemen, I coincide with both speakers who have preceded me. This meeting has a two-fold object, to devise means to stop the wrongdoing, and do the right. The people are to rise in their might and squelch the land grabber as well as the fence-cutter, the fence-cutting which was begun with the plea of giving the people their rights, has, in the heat of passion, been permitted to go too far. The fence-cutters in their lawlessness must be suppressed, but the land-thief in his evil-doing must also be put down, and put down to stay. Many of you present are down on both alike. If the tax-payer and prosperous citizen of this county were to join hands and cooperate with the poor people, a conclusion would soon be reached. Politics can not be allowed to enter this question at all and it can not be traced out as the source of this trouble. It is to be traced to the landgrabber at the beginning. On the one hand you have the power of money, the rich landgrabbers, on the other hand, the physical might of the people. True, the innocent with good titles are made wrongfully to suffer on account of the land thieves. The good decision of a just judge was that the Vegas grant belonged to the town, meetings held, to what result? The man Millhiser is more than the community, because he is guarded by dogs. The people must be suppressed, but Millhiser, under the protection of his bloodhounds, holds the community at bay. He, and other landgrabbers are not greater than the mighty will of the people and should be ordered by the courts to vacate. Then there would be no fence-cutting, but peace." Mr. Martinez stopped here amid vociferous applause. Rev. Brush, Colonel Blake and Juan Jose Herrera then gave their views.

4. "In Sympathy"   N. A. Jennings, c. 1875*

Although Mexican Americans might be a majority in some communities, pressures exerted by Anglo American officials made majority rule difficult or impossible. There were subtle ways, however, of fighting back against the Anglo minority which held power. Young N. A. Jennings, a Philadelphia-born Anglo American who lived in Laredo from 1847 to 1875, described such an incident.

As he later remembered, Laredo "had about three thousand Mexicans and about forty Americans for its population. Of course, it was 'run' by the Mexicans." While Jennings was in Laredo, Hamilton G. Peterson, a United States commissioner, wielded considerable influence in politics. Although Peterson was able to force Laredo's Mexican American mayor to appoint Jennings chief of police, Peterson could not keep Jennings in office against the wishes of the Mexican American community. Jennings, in a candid, self-deprecating manner, tells why.

"How would you like to be on the police force?" he asked. "We ought to have at least one American on the police here, and, if you want to try it, I will get the appointment from the mayor for you."

I said I would try it, and he sent me with a note to the mayor. Peterson's influence with the authorities since his threat to put a stop to the smuggling would have made a Tammany leader in New York turn pale with envy.

The mayor read the note and at once appointed me chief of police!

To do this he had to depose a Mexican, but he would have turned out his own brother if he had thought he could please Peterson by so doing. I assumed my new duties at once. I hadn't a very clear idea of what they were, but I knew I had them to perform and that there was

---

*N. A. Jennings, *A Texas Ranger*. Foreword by J. Frank Dobie (Dallas: 1930), pp. 25–28.

money to be made in doing it. I received $2.50 from the town for every arrest that I made, and $1 a day was allowed me for every prisoner in the "calaboose," as the jail was called. As it cost me but forty cents a day to board each prisoner, there was a clear profit of sixty cents a day. This system was certainly open to criticism, as it encouraged the policemen in making as many arrests as possible.

I had ten Mexicans under me on the police force. They detested me from the beginning, partly because I had been the cause of the ousting of their former chief, but mainly because I was a "Gringo." The Mexicans on the border called all Americans "Gringos." The Americans retaliated by calling the Mexicans "Greasers. . . ."

....

I had not been at the head of the Laredo police force two days before stories of vague threats having been made by some of the policemen under me began to reach my ears. I was young and did not pay much attention to the threats. I reasoned that if the men should become openly hostile I could easily dismiss them from the force. There was no civil-service-reform nonsense about the city government of Laredo.

The third day after my appointment I made my first arrest. The mayor had given me a silver badge, which I put on my coat. I had a .45 calibre six-shooter in a holster, slung to a cartridge-belt about my waist, and I was impressed with the sense of my own dignity and appearance. On this day of my first arrest, I was walking quietly down the street when I saw a Mexican standing on the corner. He was giving a series of wild yells, and as I approached I saw that he was very, very drunk. I went up to him and grasped his arm to lead him to the "calaboose." He looked at me in blank amazement for a moment and then jerked his arm away. Before I could get hold of him again, he reached down to his boot-leg and, drawing a big knife, made a savage pass at me with it, and I retreated a couple of steps. I drew my revolver, cocked it, pointed it at his head and told him to drop the knife and hold up his hands. To my utter astonishment he did nothing of the kind. He backed slowly away.

I did not want to shoot him, nor did I care to get so close to him that he could use his knife on me. I was in a quandary. He backed up to a grocery store and then turned suddenly and ran inside. I ran in after him. There were half a dozen persons in the store, and when they saw me rush in with a revolver in my hand they dodged down behind the counter and boxes and barrels. The man I was after darted out through a rear door.

Before I could follow him, two women ran up to me and threw their arms about my neck. They held tightly to me in this embrace, screaming as loud as they could. I attempted to explain the circumstances to them, but my knowledge of the language was slight, and not at all equal to exciting occasions like this. When I finally did get into their heads the fact that I was a police officer and only wanted to arrest the man for drunkenness, he had disappeared.

I was mad clear through then. I went at once to the policemen on my force, and ordered them to hunt up the drunken man. They did not seem very anxious to obey, but I spoke imperatively and they started out on the search. I took one of them with me, and we began a hunt in that part of the town where I lost the man. We found him late in the afternoon, asleep in a little adobe house belonging to one of his friends. We went in and arrested him and took him to the "calaboose," but he fought like a tiger all the way. The next morning he had to pay a fine of $10.

This incident, although small in itself, led to more important results. The man whom I arrested was a great favorite with his native townsmen, and I did not make a bid for popularity in taking him to jail. One night a week later I was shot at in the street. I heard the bullet whistle by my head and hit the door behind me with a thud. I ran toward the place whence the report of the pistol had come, but could find no one there. The streets were very dark.

Half an hour later I was shot at again. Once more I failed to find the man, who had fled, although I hunted diligently. It was getting very uncomfortable. That night I was shot at five times. I told my policemen about it, and they apparently made great efforts to find the man or men.

There was something in the way they went about it, however, that aroused my suspicions, and I at last came to the conclusion that they were in sympathy with my unknown assailant. Indeed, I was not sure it was not one of my own men who had been firing at me. Be that as it may, I decided I had had enough of chieftainship, and the next day went to the mayor and resigned.

He accepted my resignation without hesitancy. He did not ask me why I resigned, nor did he ask me to remain on the force.

5. "Volunteers, both Mexicans and Americans"

Juan I. Téllez, 1926*

Anglo Americans who took up ranching in such sparsely settled areas as southern Arizona before the coming of the railroad cooperated with Mexican American rancheros for survival and fellowship, and depended on Mexican American labor to operate their ranches. The Anglo newcomers also frequently married women of Mexican descent, thus lessening the social distance between ethnic groups. The well-known television series "High Chaparral" portrays to some extent this period of harmony between Mexicans and Americans in southern Arizona. John Cannon, the program's main character, had a true-to-life predecessor in Pete Kitchen, who came to Arizona in 1853, married Rosa Verdugo, and operated the ranch of El Potrero some five miles north of the Mexican border at Nogales. Many of Kitchen's ranch hands were Mexicanized Ópata Indians who worked under the supervision of Kitchen's brother-in-law, Francisco Verdugo, and ranch foreman Manuel Ronquillo.[1]

Harmonious relations between Mexicans and Americans in southern Arizona came about partly because of the Apaches, who were hostile to both groups and prompted them to band together for common defense. Contrary to popular stereotypes about Mexican docility and cowardice, Mexican Americans such as Merejildo Grijalva[2] served with distinction as Indian fighters, as Anglo and Hispano fought together against the common enemy. In the selection that follows, Juan I. Téllez, who fought Indians until the 1880s in southern Arizona, recalls those days.

My great grandfather came from El Paso to Arizona in very early days while it was still part of Mexico. My father was born in Tucson and so were all of his children including myself. We children, four boys and four girls, were all born on Main Street right where Elias' corral now stands (west side, between Messila and Broadway).

*Reminiscences of Juan I. Téllez (as told to Mrs. George F. Kitt [1926])," *Arizona Historical Review* 7, no. 1 (January 1936): 85–89. Reprinted by permission of the Arizona Historical Society.

1. Gil Procter, *The Trails of Pete Kitchen* (Tucson: 1964), a popular account.

2. " 'El Chivero' Merejildo Grijalva," *Arizoniana* 1, no. 3 (Fall 1960): 8–9, is a brief biography.

My grandfather owned 160 acres of land where the Indian school now stands. The Indians sometimes raided the place and drove off all the cows and left only the calves. He had a big reservoir there made of dirt. The water ran back half a mile and was enough to irrigate all the land. My father sold the place to Pedro Aguirre, he sold it to a relation of Royal A. Johnson, and he to the Presbyterian Mission.

....

As a boy I went to Tucson private schools and then for ten months I went to Industrial College in Lawrence, Kansas. My father sent me there because he was a great friend of Sam Hughes and he recommended it. Mr. Hughes took me there but I could not stand the climate; got malaria and had to come home. When I returned I went to school under John Spring.

I can remember much Indian trouble, some that my father and grandfather told me and some that I had myself.

I was a small boy at the time of the Camp Grant massacre but I can remember some things about it and some things my father told me. He was one of the party. They met near Cabadilla ranch and went through the pass. There were many Indians and not quite so many Mexicans and Americans, pretty nearly as many Americans as Mexicans. Among the Americans were Jimmy Lee, Sam Hughes, Chas. Shibell, Jim Douglas (Mrs. Tilly Sutherland's father), Bill Oury, and lots of others.

On their way back they met an Arivaipa Apache driving off a fine buckskin race horse which belonged to a man in Tucson. The horse was being ridden by a big squaw and a little girl. They shot the squaw and one of the men was leading the girl off by the hand, for he was going to keep her, when Placido Soza up with his gun and shot her. They also had a yoke of oxen and this proved that it was the Arivaipa Indians who were doing the stealing and killing.

Indians were often seen around my grandfather's ranch—the one on this side of the river just east of Cat Mountain where the Indian school now stands. There were several ranches right there together; Mrs. Guadalupe Pacheco's, Mrs. Wm. Oury's, Ramón Castro's and José Herera's [sic], and they built their houses all within hailing distance of each other. My father's was on the northeast corner of his land. The houses were built with a four-foot wall extending above the flat dirt roof to be used as breastworks. There were holes in the wall and a ladder of poles with smaller branches tied on with cowhide for rounds was always placed against the wall. The corrals were close to the house and made of brush piled between upright posts. Around the corral on the outside was a ditch deep enough that the cattle would not jump it should the fence be torn down. All of this was to make it as hard as possible for the Indians to get the cattle which were locked in these corrals at night and herded in the daytime. The calves were generally kept in the corrals all the time.

One time, a long time after the Camp Grand massacre in 1871, the citizens of Tucson got word that some Indians who had been raiding in Mexico were bringing a large band of horses and cattle up through Sasabe and would come through Puerto del Amol (Amole Pass) in the Tucson Mountains, cross to the north point of the Santa Catalinas, and make their way to the reservation by way of Canyon del Oro. I do not know whether they were Arivaipa or San Carlos Apaches. A large party of Mexicans, I do not know how many, but my father was one of them, went out to the Puerto del Amol and waited for the Indians. When they appeared both sides began to shoot. The Mexicans got most of the horses and cattle, but whether they got any Indians or not they never knew.

I never was in but one Indian fight and I guess I would not have been in that if I had had any idea that we would ever catch up with the Indians. It was in the spring of 1886. The Indians were very bad all over the country and had been raiding in Mexico. Word was brought in early one morning that Indians had raided my father's ranch fifteen miles east of Tucson, in the Pantano Wash, and carried off the seven-year-old son of Juan Castelo, the man in charge, and stoned the mother but did not kill her. M. G. Samaniego and R. N. Leatherwood got together fifteen or twenty men including myself and we rushed to the ranch. We rode fast and reached there about noon. We started out on the trail immediately and after going some distance found a beef that the Indians had killed, with the blood still warm. Halfway between the Téllez ranch and Martínez, ten miles from the ranch, at about 4 o'clock we ran across the Indians and surprised them eating supper. Most of them were down in a low place but some were up on higher ground with two bunches of horses each with a bell mare. Four of us, Jesus Padres, Pedro Aguirre, a soldier, and myself started after the Indians with the horses. We saw the boy on a big buckskin horse up on a knoll to our right and called to him. He was all alone and without any shirt on. The Indians had taken it. He did not seem to be at all frightened but came over to us. We fired several shots at the Indians and they left the horses and dropped down behind the rocks as if killed. We wanted to go up and get the horses but Mr. Samaniego said no, that the Indians might be fooling us. Meanwhile the other men had driven the rest of the Indians out of the low place onto the hills and they had disappeared among the rocks. We do not know whether we killed any or not as they scattered and hid in the brush.

By that time it was quite late so we went on to the Martínez ranch and camped. In the night a lot of other men joined us. Next morning we got up very early, a long time before daylight, and went on toward Cedidello Pass as we knew that was where the Indians would go through to the San Pedro. We surprised them again at Morosco's ranch. They had left their horses on a hill to the south and were just crawling down on foot to raid the ranch. When we began to fire at them they ran back to their horses. Some stayed in the rocks on the top of the hill and shot at us while the others got away. We must have kept up the shooting for half an hour and then the Indians ran. They seemed very careful of their ammunition. I do not think they had much. Some of the men followed them into the San Pedro and as far as Tres Alamos so as to warn and help protect the ranchers but most of us went back to Tucson.

We found out later that they were a band of Apaches who had been raiding in Mexico and were run out by Lieut. Lawton. The soldiers had tracked them as far as the Rincons.

After that Mr. Samaniego and Mr. Leatherwood formed a company of volunteers, both Mexicans and Americans, whom the government provisioned and sent out to fight. . . .

6. "Now or Never"

La Voz del Pueblo, 1906*
Constitution of New Mexico, 1912**

In New Mexico, as in southern Arizona, the first decade following the Mexican War saw Mexican Americans and Anglo Americans cooperate. The New Mexicans, however, remained numerically dominant throughout the territorial period and so were better able to protect their institutions and culture than were Mexican Americans in Arizona. Nevertheless, Spanish-speaking New Mexicans sensed that they would not always constitute a majority and that as long as they remained a territory, Congress could enact unfavorable legislation without their consent. The following newspaper article, from *La Voz del Pueblo*, outlines the danger and suggests a solution.

That solution was a new state constitution which was written in 1910 and went into effect in 1912. Hispano delegates to the constitutional convention saw to it that Spanish-speaking citizens in New Mexico would be entitled to the rights of citizens whether or not they knew English, and that New Mexico would legally become a bilingual state. Relevant portions of the constitution follow.

PROBABILITIES AND POSSIBILITIES

. . . If New Mexico commits the mistake of voting against [the statehood bill], then only God knows what will be done with us upon seeing our insincerity and deceit demonstrated. Surely during the last half century we have been bothering Congress, and taking its time. Upon seeing that we reject that which we have so insistently asked for, it [Congress] will consider us unworthy of the name of American citizens and could treat us, perhaps, as uncivilized tribes.

Having kept our attention fixed on the mood of Congress toward New Mexico for a good number of years, and most especially during

---

*This article seems to be an editorial from the Las Vegas, New Mexico, paper *La Voz del Pueblo*, published in Las Vegas, New Mexico, and reprinted and endorsed in *El Labrador* (Las Cruces), August 10, 1906. Trans. David J. Weber.

**Constitutions of the United States: National and State* (Dobbs Ferry, N.Y.: 1962), 2:7, 25–26, 37.

the discussion of the Statehood Bill before the Committee on Territories of the House and before the congressional bodies themselves, we have clearly seen that a hostile sentiment has unfolded regarding the necessity of having interpreters in our courts and in our conventions, etc. This sentiment has hardened a true antagonism against the Spanish-speaking element. It was so pronounced among the majority [of Congress] that, if it had not been for the fact of the establishment of the Hamilton Law, through which if we accept [statehood] we will have our own government, legislation would have passed to prevent persons who are not able to speak and understand English well from serving on juries. In fact, Senator Spooner from Washington made such a proposition. . . .

The other question of restricting suffrage from those who do not know English, was also much discussed, and this discussion took place in Washington and in the other states, as well as inside our own territory. And do not believe that it will stop at this point. In order to better prove the tendency of the American government toward the establishment of the English language in this country, we will cite the citizenship law that was decreed by the congress which just adjourned. This prescribed that hereafter no person will be admitted as an American citizen until he knows the English language.

Reflect, fellow citizens, on what this means if we remain longer under the tutelege of Congress. This is not a theory, it is a real and positive fact. For that reason we say that if we decline to accept the liberty of statehood, it is *more than probable* that the next congress will decree legislation to define the qualifications for suffrage, as well as for the exercise of the duties of jurors and of public employees, based on knowledge of the English language. Cut out this paragraph and keep it well guarded in order that later you can see that the sincere and disinterested friend of the people warned you in proper time, *La Voz del Pueblo.*

There is another probability, and this we wish the Neo-Mexicanos as well as the Arizonenses of Hispanic-American origin would make note of. If we form our own constitutional convention today, we are in numerical condition to see that the fundamental law will be one that does not deny us any of our rights. After being written, the constitution will be submitted to the vote of the people for their ratification or rejection. If it contains something that might be detrimental to our people, we will be able to reject that clause or article while we are yet in numerical condition to do it, and we are able to do it. But if we reject statehood now, and we are admitted in ten or fifteen years, by that time the outside immigration will have drowned us numerically and then will be very late to defend our rights. The constitution is the cement of a government; now is the time to construct that cement. If we do not do it now, perhaps tomorrow will come antagonistic peoples, and then will be very late and we will see ourselves compelled to accept that which is given us, irrespective of our will.

....

To conclude this editorial we will say to our fellow citizens, as did Lerdo de Tejada when Juárez seemed to vacillate about whether or not to have Maximilian executed and end forever monarchic pretentions in Mexico, "NOW OR NEVER."

Our salvation depends on our action today. Tomorrow will be too late. NOW OR NEVER, FELLOW CITIZENS.

CONSTITUTION OF NEW MEXICO 1912

Article II.

Sec. 5. *Rights under treaty of Guadalupe Hidalgo preserved.* The rights, privileges and immunities, civil, political and religious, guaranteed to the people of New Mexico by the treaty of Guadalupe Hidalgo shall be preserved inviolate.

Article VII.

Sec. 3. *Religious and racial equality protected; restrictions on amendments.* The right of any citizen of the state to vote, hold office, or sit upon juries, shall never be restricted, abridged or impaired on account of religion, race, language or color, or inability to speak, read or write the English or Spanish languages except as may be otherwise provided in this Constitution; and the provisions of this section and of section one of this article shall never be amended except upon a vote of the people of this state in an election at which at least three-fourths of the electors voting in the whole state, and at least two-thirds of those voting in each county of the state, shall vote for such amendment.

Article XII.

Sec. 8. *Teachers to learn English and Spanish.* The legislature shall provide for the training of teachers in the normal schools or otherwise so that they may become proficient in both the English and Spanish languages, to qualify them to teach Spanish-speaking pupils and students in the public schools and educational institutions of the State, and shall provide proper means and methods to facilitate the teaching of the English language and other branches of learning to such pupils and students.

Sec. 10. *Educational rights of children of Spanish descent.* Children of Spanish descent in the State of New Mexico shall never be denied the right and privilege of admission and attendance in the public schools or other public educational institutions of the State, and they shall never be classed in separate schools, but shall forever enjoy perfect equality with other children in all public schools and educational institutions of the State, and the legislature shall provide penalties for the violation of this section. This section shall never be amended except upon a vote of the people of this State, in an election at which at least three-fourths of the electors voting in the whole State and at least two-thirds of those voting in each county in the State shall vote for such amendment.

7. "Por la raza y para la raza"

Congreso Mexicanista, 1911*

The popularity of mutual benefit societies in the Southwest toward the end of the nineteenth century indicated a growing awareness that group action was more effective than individual efforts in protecting the Mexican American community from oppression and in fighting for justice. This philosophy of group action was carried to its logical conclusion in Texas in 1911, when members of various societies came together in a state-wide convention, the *Congreso Mexicanista.*

This extraordinary meeting, which brought together delegates from twenty-four Texas communities at the border town of Laredo, had been prompted by extraordinarily bad times for

---

*Primer Congreso Mexicanista, Verificado en Laredo, Texas, EE. UU. de A., 14 al 22 de Septiembre de 1911. *Discursos y Conferencias por la raza y para la raza* (Laredo, Tex.: 1912), pp. 35–37. Trans. David J. Weber.

Mexicans in Texas: the beating to death of a Mexican boy, Antonio Gómez, in Thorndale, Texas, and the burning at the stake of Antonio Rodríguez by an angry mob in Rock Springs, Texas. This latter incident gained considerable publicity and resulted in a wave of anti-American riots in Mexico City.

These events gave an urgency to the stated purpose of the Congress: "to unite and protect all the Texas Mexicans." Unity became the key word at the Congress, and its slogan, *"por la raza y para la raza,"* is similar to the well-known saying in English: "All for one and one for all." To achieve unity, the Congress formed a central organization called the *Gran Liga Mexicanista de Beneficencia y Protección.* The following excerpts from a speech by the Reverend Pedro Grado touches on the three issues of most concern to the delegates: justice, mutual protection, and education.

Farewell Address
The Reverend Pedro Grado

Mr. President:

Respectable Audience:

My turn has arrived in the progression of the program of the *Congreso Mexicanista* to step in the place from which have come forth words full of erudition; ideas that, although heterogeneous, demonstrated with few exceptions beloved unity in the objective that occupies our attention. . . . In this conversation, and it is nothing more, I will touch on some of the points or topics which are most interesting to review, and which may be most useful to us in placing the first bricks of the great social edifice that this Congreso Mexicanista proposes.

There are two black points that, with a prophetic threat, sprout forth and grow in the pure heaven of our liberty and which day by day, worry all good Mexicans, all true patriots, and all persons who shelter altruism and philanthropy in their souls.

The first of these points concerns the oppression and the abuses that the sons of Uncle Sam commit daily to our countrymen, especially in the State of Texas.

The second is the imprudent conduct of men and women, our fellow citizens, in the State of Texas.

The first point has the following classification: I. Bad application of the law when it deals with Mexicans. II. Unpunished molesting of

Mexicans by particular Americans. III. The exclusion of Mexican children from the American schools.

Order demands that the bad application of the law in treating Mexicans be discussed. The disease has its remedy, and it is here that the utility of the Congreso Mexicanista is illustrated, inasmuch as experience teaches us that isolation causes weakness and that weakness produces failure. Reason tells us to make ourselves strong. . . .

The Congreso Mexicanista can and should enhance the Mexican press of Texas. The newspaper is the scourge of the unjust and the denouncer of the abusers of office. It is a powerful medium to carry complaints to the desks of officials and demonstrate by turns that we are not indolent, that we are concerned about the poverty of our countrymen, and that we are able to do all that is within the law for them.

The Congreso Mexicanista can and should embrace wealthy, influential men because of their morality, their knowledge, and their contacts. These are the ones who, in case of difficulty, will have access to elevated representatives of the law.

The Congreso will broaden itself admirably, and admirable will be the results, if it tries to attract to it all the secret societies of the Masonic type, or whose members might be our countrymen, or the lodges that might be of this kind. It should do the same with the mutual societies and those that simply have altruism as their ideal. How surprising will be the effect of a petition, or a request, or of a communication backed by thousands of individuals! What greater satisfaction for a needy person than the loving hand of thousands of his fellow citizens, ready to put to flight the terrible anxiety which poverty causes. Considering that this Congreso will come to be that which I suppose, with the elements now established, the oppressions of the authorities will stop. . . .

The unpunished vexations of particular Americans may continue. This problem is more difficult to solve. . . . The Mexican braceros who work in a mill, on a hacienda, or in a plantation would do well to establish *Ligas Mexicanistas*, and see that their neighbors form them. Thus, once united, with the help of the press, and with the valuable group of philanthropists of wealth or influence in some department, they will be able to strike back at the hatred of some bad sons of Uncle Sam who believe themselves better than the Mexicans because of the magic that surrounds the word *white*.

It remains for us to say something of the exclusion of Mexican children from the Anglo-Saxon schools in the majority of the counties of the State of Texas. We can say this is a difficult but not unsolvable problem.

What happens in Laredo, Texas, in San Diego of the same state, and in other river communities where the Mexican children have free access to the American schools and high schools? The purpose of this question is to go to the reasons, because if these reasons are transmissible, the problem is not far from resolving itself. . . . In the aforementioned towns, the Mexican element dominates and is intimately bound to the Anglo-Saxon by ties of commerce and other kinds. In these same towns there are respectable Mexicans with prominent positions in the court houses, so that we find in this one of the causes, or the reason, for the Mexican children's access to American schools. Would we be able to make these means transmissible, and make the influence of those men extend to many miles round about? Yes, it is possible when all in mass distinguish themselves as *mexicanistas* and take interest in their countrymen. Whatever may be the reasons they exclude Mexicans from the schools, I do not find another solution than the influence and heterogeneous powers of *mexicanismo.* . . .

8. A Sample from the Press   El Labrador, 1904*

One of the most important tools for organizing the Mexican American community in the nineteenth century, as today, was the Spanish-language press. While these papers often served special interest groups, many of them had the broader interests of Mexican Americans in mind.

The following sampling from *El Labrador,* published in Las Cruces, New Mexico, demonstrates the desire of the editor to have Mexican Americans work within the American system, yet

---

*The three articles which follow come, respectively, from the March 20, July 15, and December 30, 1904 issues of *El Labrador.* The last article first appeared, apparently, in *El Independiente* of Las Vegas, New Mexico, then was reprinted in *El Labrador.* All three items translated by David J. Weber.

preserve a sense of ethnic pride. Hence, *El Labrador* urged its readers to join organizations such as *La Alianza Hispano-Americana;* to become citizens and vote; to have pride in their own language, as well as to learn English. Unfortunately, too few copies of these Spanish-language papers have survived to the present day.

LA SOCIEDAD ALIANZA HISPANO-AMERICANA DE TUCSON, ARIZONA

During the last week a project was carried out rather successfully, for the purpose of organizing a lodge of the *Sociedad Alianza Hispano-Americana,* whose headquarters, or Supreme Lodge, is located in the city of Tucson, Arizona Territory.

There is no place in Arizona, no matter how small it might be, that has not established mutual societies. In New Mexico, unfortunately, among the Hispanic American people, it is entirely the opposite. It must be confessed that in Arizona our brothers [*nuestros hermanos de raza*] are ahead, inasmuch as they have arrived at the grand conclusion that in union there is strength, and from the societies proceeds the well-being and progress of the people.

The *Sociedad Alianza Hispano-Americana* has branches or lodges in Phoenix, Jerome, Congress, Tempe, Nogales, Yuma, Kofa, Clifton, Morenci, Metcalf, and other places that we do not recall in the territory of Arizona. In New Mexico they have finally been established in Silver City and Hillsboro, and there are hopes that many more might be established in different places.

This institution was established in Tucson, Arizona, in the year 1898 [1894]. The benefits which it offers are enormous, protecting the wife and children with $1,000 in case of the death of the member, and in the case of the death of the wife, $200 for a decent funeral. Besides these benefits, there is weekly help of a doctor, medicine, and cash money.

It is a demonstrated fact that by means of societies our people progress, and the society which concerns us [*La Alianza*] is solidly based with the funds it holds in reserve, and has always met its contractual obligations punctually.

Every two years it has its conventions where all of the delegates of each lodge gather together to elect supreme officials, and to make whatever reforms might be necessary in the bylaws. The next convention will take place in Phoenix, capital of the territory of Arizona, and it is hoped that a large number of delegates will attend since the Lodge there is making great preparations to worthily receive all the delegates.

Young people have never had a better opportunity than now to join a good society such as this. It costs them an extremely low monthly fee and we hope that all will make a good effort to join, in order that thus our people may be represented in a society that in every sense protects the interests of the Hispano Americanos.

EDITORIAL MESSAGE

Morenci, Arizona. July 1, 1904. . . . Here, as in Metcalf, two miles to the north, the mines are fabulously rich in copper. The number of miners and other workers is estimated at three thousand men.

The societies prosper in Morenci and Metcalf. *La Alianza Hispa-no-Americana*, *La Saragoza*, and *Obreros*, have very good lodges. Men of high standing make up these organizations. But despite this good fellowship, the public administration is very weak, and abuses in the area of justice are shameless. It is charged that the Justice of the Peace in Metcalf has seized a family and has detained them until they pay certain bills they owe. In other words, he uses the tool of a criminal case to solve a civil case. In Morenci it is assured that the justice of the peace is a little more than a businessman. In various cases the prosecuting witnesses have been fined for the simple reason that the accused did not have the money to pay his Honor. . . .

The political condition is demoralized in the extreme, and there is only one remedy that can save the situation. That is that many of the Mexicans who live in these mining camps become American citizens in order that, with their vote, they give their due to the multitude of greedy Pilates who today live off the toiling miners. . . .

. . . The fact that there is almost not a man among those who know how to read who is not a subscriber to some newspaper demonstrates that there generally exists good communication, and all that is lacking is that the great majority make themselves citizens in order to use the sword of suffrage in the defeat of corruption.

THE SPANISH LANGUAGE AND ITS IMPORTANCE
FOR THE NATIVES OF NEW MEXICO

It has become fashionable here in New Mexico to treat with a kind of reproach and contempt not only those who speak Spanish, but the language itself. It is as if they are guilty of some crime in speaking the language which came down from their forefathers, and as if it is not one of the most respected and best perfected modern languages that is spoken in Europe and America. They try to demand that all the native people of New Mexico know the national language, which is English, though knowing this has been impossible because we have not had the means or the facilities to learn it. Even knowing this, there has been no lack of those who want Spanish to be a prohibited language, and that those who speak it be despoiled of their franchises and rights of citizenship. It is as if the natives of this Territory are the only ones inside the boundaries of the United States who speak a foreign language. They forget that there are millions of foreigners in this country who have emigrated from European nations and do not know another language than that which they originally learned in their respective countries, and that they are not now of an age to learn the national language, despite having all of the facilities for learning it. The New Mexicans have a better excuse for ignorance of English because they have not had a way of learning it.

Nevertheless, although it is to the native people's advantage to learn the national language when there is an opportunity for it, this is not a reason for them to belittle and despise their own tongue. Moreover, Spanish is the language that nearly eighty million souls speak in all Spain and its colonies, Central and South America, Cuba and Mexico, and some of the islands of the West Indies, which occupy a territorial extent nearly four million square miles. It can be firmly maintained that among the modern languages only English is more extended and diffused. German, Italian, and French are very far behind in all respects. This demonstrates that Spanish is a language which has great importance in the world and is one of those that has the greatest probability of lasting and developing in the future, because it is the native language of independent peoples who occupy extensive territories in different parts of the globe.

So it is that the native people of New Mexico do not have reason for being ashamed of their language. Honor and self-respect should impel them to conserve it and to perfect themselves in it by all possible means, even when this continues being the occasion for those who throw the darts of contempt and proscription with which they have tried to treat us up to now. This will not be an impediment for those sons and descendants who may learn the English language when they have sufficiently ample opportunities to learn it. But until that time comes, it is necessary that they do not allow it to be trampled under foot or cut down by those who, with an axe of a different language, would like to relegate Spanish-speaking people to a state of isolation and political slavery. . . . The rights of our citizens in that which appertains to their language and customs are protected by the laws and the treaties and none has the right of abolishing them or limiting them. . . . This is a question of honor and of the conservation of political rights, and merits the most serious attention and consideration. Any reduction and disqualification which the language receives at the hands of legislators or public officials, fully catches up with those who speak and practice it, and may place them in a position of inferiority that is extremely prejudicial to their interests and well-being.—*El Independiente.*

9. Workers from Mexico: Three Views

Mexican: Diario del Hogar, 1910*
Anglo American: Samuel Bryan, 1912**
Mexican American: El Labrador, 1904***

By 1910, increased immigration from Mexico had made persons of Mexican descent the most important laboring group in the Southwest, whose toil kept mines, farms, ranches, and transportation facilities operating. In retrospect, it appears that the attitudes which many Anglo Americans, Mexican Americans, and Mexicans hold toward these Mexican laborers in the United States today had been clearly articulated by the end of the first decade of the twentieth century.

Newspapers in Mexico, such as *Diario del Hogar,* generally viewed Mexican emigration as undesirable, suggesting that

---

Diario del Hogar (Mexico City), August 2 & 8, 1910. Trans. David J. Weber.

**Samuel Bryan, "Mexican Immigrants in the United States," *The Survey* 28 no. 23 (September 1912): 726, 730.

***El Labrador* (Las Cruces, New Mexico), August 19, 1904. Trans. David J. Weber.

Mexicans would be badly treated in the United States, and expressing concern over the loss of laborers in Mexico.

Anglo Americans like Samuel Bryan also viewed Mexican immigration as undesirable, yet regarded it as a necessary evil. Underlying Bryan's thinking was the assumption that Mexicans were not a disadvantaged ethnic group because of historical and environmental circumstances, but that they were in fact an inferior people who enjoyed illiteracy and poverty. This stereotype of Mexicans, which we examined in chapter 2 of this study, remained alive in 1910. Yet as long as cheap labor was in demand in the United States, few would concern themselves with the "evils to the community" that Bryan thought he foresaw.

Mexican Americans, in the meantime, were caught in the middle again. They viewed the new immigrants with sympathy, for they understood the conditions in Mexico which drove lower-class Mexicans to the United States. At the same time, Mexican Americans regarded Mexican immigrants as a threat because they lowered the working man's wage scale. The Spanish-language newspaper *El Labrador,* of Las Cruces, New Mexico, expressed these sentiments in 1904. An article from *El Labrador* constitutes the final reading in this section and concludes this study on an appropriately ambivalent note.

MEXICAN IMMIGRATION
THE STATE OF GUANAJUATO PROVIDES THE GREATEST PROPORTION

According to the news provided by the Office of Emigration, annexed to the *Jefatura Política* of the Bravos District [apparently at El Paso], between the first and the fifteenth of the month [of July], 3,142 persons who crossed the boundary line registered at that office. They came from the following States of the Republic: 1,322 from Guanajuato; 931 from Michoacán; 600 from Jalisco; 207 from Zacatecas; the rest from Durango, San Luis Potosí, Aguascalientes, Coahuila, Sinaloa, and Tamaulipas.

As can be seen from the foregoing alarming figures, the greater part of those unfortunates emigrate from our state, in search of work which undoubtedly is not found on our soil. . . .

. . . Perhaps there are other reasons that oblige our workingmen, so attached to the land, to abandon the country, even at the risk of the

Yankee contempt with which they are treated on the other side of the Bravo [Río Grande].

One newspaper says we must make known the innumerable prejudices, hardships, and oppression that they receive far from the fatherland, to all those persons who are deluded by the offers of the so-called "recruiters" [enganchadores] and go abroad in search of work which they believe to be better recompensed. The greater part of the time they will be unsettled and abandoned among people whose language they do not know and may not be able to use, not even to beg for help.

What our government should do, we say, is lower the high taxes which weigh heavily upon the people, and put a stop to bossism, in order that our workingmen will not abandon their birthplace, despairing of the misfortune which grinds them down.

There are persons who have gone abroad, fleeing from the persecutions of the government, and others who go in search of work. But whatever the reason, we do not approve of their absence. We have the idea that rather than leave we should struggle with more faith in the establishment of a government that guarantees our rights and that complies strictly with the law, whose precise application supports harmony of the governors and the governed, . . .

In regard to the workers, reality has taught them that in practice, illusions bring sad results. They ought to do whatever is possible to return to their native soil and struggle for the progress of the nation.

Diario del Hogar, 1910

MEXICAN IMMIGRANTS IN THE UNITED STATES

Comparatively few people in the United States have any conception of the extent to which Mexicans are entering this country each year, of their geographical distribution, or of their relative importance in the various industries in which they are employed after their arrival. Nor are the social problems resulting from the influx of Mexicans fully appreciated by many persons who are not acquainted with the situation at first hand. This is primarily because the attention of students of the race problem has been focused upon the more important development of European and eastern Asiatic immigration to the eastern states, and upon Chinese, Japanese, and East Indian immigration to the Pacific coast. Other factors in diverting attention from Mexican immigration have been the relatively noncompetitive character of their employment in certain parts of the country, and the lack of adequate data with regard to their numbers.

Socially and politically the presence of large numbers of Mexicans in this country gives rise to serious problems. The reports of the Immigration Commission show that they lack ambition, are to a very large extent illiterate in their native language, are slow to learn English, and in most cases show no political interest. In some instances, however, they have been organized to serve the purposes of political bosses as for example in Phoenix, Arizona. Although more of them are married and have their families with them than is the case among the south European immigrants, they are unsettled as a class, move readily from place to place, and do not acquire or lease land to any extent. But their most unfavorable characteristic is their inclination to form colonies and live in a clannish manner. Wherever a considerable group of Mexicans are employed, they live together, if possible, and associate very little with members of other races. In the mining towns and other small industrial communities they live ordinarily in rude adobe huts outside of the town limits. As section hands they of course live as the members of the other races have done, in freight cars fitted with windows and bunks, or in rough shacks along the line of the railroad. In the cities their colonization has become a menace. The unwholesome conditions of the Mexican quarter in El Paso, Tex., have been described with photographic illustration in previous articles in *The Survey*. In Los Angeles the housing problem centers largely in the cleaning up or demolition of the Mexican "house courts," which have become the breeding ground of disease and crime, and which have now attracted a considerable population of immigrants of other races. It is estimated that approximately 2,000 Mexicans are living in these "house courts." Some 15,000 persons of this race are residents of Los Angeles and vicinity. Conditions of life among the immigrants of the city, which are moulded to a certain extent by Mexican standards, have been materially improved by the work of the Los Angeles Housing Commission, upon which Johanna Von Wagner has served as an expert social worker. However, the

Mexican quarter continues to offer a serious social problem to the community.

As is to be expected under the circumstances, the proportion of criminals and paupers among the Mexicans is noticeably greater than among the other foreign-born or among the natives. In Los Angeles county, California, the Mexicans comprised 11.4 per cent of the total number of persons bound over for felonies in 1907. In 1908 and 1909 the percentages were 12.6 and 13.4 respectively. During the year ending July 1, 1908, the chief of police of Los Angeles estimates that approximately 20,000 police cases were handled, in 2,357 or 11.8 per cent of which Mexicans were the defendants. In Arizona, where the proportion of Mexicans to the total population is greater than in Los Angeles, a correspondingly large proportion of the inmates of the various penal institutions are of this race. In 1908, 24.2 per cent of the prisoners in the jail at Tucson, Ariz., were Mexicans, while in the Pima county jail they comprised 62 per cent of the inmates. The territorial prison reported in the same year that 61 per cent of those incarcerated were Mexicans. In both Arizona and California the offenses for which they were committed were in the large majority of cases traceable to gambling or excessive drinking. Most of the serious trouble with Mexicans, however, arises from quarrels among themselves which interfere very little with the white population.

In the matter of poor relief, Mexican families were concerned in 11.7 percent of the cases dealt with by the Associated Charities of Los Angeles in 1908. The proportion has increased since that time, and in 1910 it was estimated that Mexicans comprised fully one-third of those given relief from this source. The county authorities had charge of approximately 3,000 individuals in 1908, of whom about one-third were Mexicans. The proportion of Mexicans among those dependent upon the County Board of Charities has continued about the same, for the month of November, 1910, which was said to be typical of that year, 30.1 per cent of the applications for aid were made by members of that race.

In conclusion it should be recognized that although the Mexicans have proved to be efficient laborers in certain industries, and have afforded a cheap and elastic labor supply for the southwestern United States, the evils to the community at large which their presence in large numbers almost invariably brings may more than overbalance their desirable qualities. Their low standards of living and of morals, their illiteracy, their utter lack of proper political interest, the retarding effect of their employment upon the wage scale of the more progressive races, and finally their tendency to colonize in urban centers, with evil results, combine to stamp them as a rather undesirable class of residents.

Samuel Bryan
Stanford University

MEXICANS IN THE UNITED STATES

The great number of Mexican workers who pass daily from Mexico to the United States ought finally to make both governments open their eyes. There is not a day in which passenger trains do not leave from the border, full of Mexican men who are going in gangs to work on railroad lines in the United States. The Mexican government loses the labor which could make its fertile lands very productive, its mines more developed, its herds larger, and the country more prosperous and united.

This [Mexican government] should be able to develop love of the native land, and not as a Platonism [or ideal] born only of spiritual reasons or patriotic affection, but for practical reasons. It should make life easier in the country, establishing colonies where the worker is able to become a landowner—well-organized colonies that are able to make life more independent and the spread of education completely unrestricted.

Once the foundation of these colonies has been laid, preparing young people to develop themselves, they should be fit for the struggle of life. They will no longer have to leave their country to go in search of life in a foreign country, where they are always viewed as inferiors. No longer will Mexico have to experience the delay [of progress] that comes from the scarcity of workers.

For its part, the American government ought to put an end to this disagreeable immigration. The American journeyman is more at the level of modern methods of work. Once invaded by the competition of the Mexican worker who, for lack of familiarity with American money and ignorance of the machinery of the country, works for what he is given, he [the American] will be demoralized, and with reason. He is made more insecure and his living more disagreeable.

El Labrador, 1904

Afterword to the Original Edition

To many observers, the ferment among Mexican Americans which began in the mid-1960s seemed to represent the first stirrings of the nation's second largest minority. Journalists wrote of the "end of the long siesta" and of the awakening of the "sleeping giant." Mexican Americans, of course, had never slept. Even a brief overview of the Mexican American past, as the foregoing pages provide, should make it clear that the roots of the present-day activism run deep into the nineteenth century.

Before massive immigration from Mexico got underway in the second decade of the twentieth century, Mexican Americans had been active in ways which have a surprisingly contemporary ring. They had displayed considerable resilience in participating where possible in state and local politics, in working in labor organizations, in forming groups for mutual protection and well-being, in fighting for ancestral lands, in seeking equal justice, and in nourishing the culture they had inherited from Mexico, while at the same time trying to accommodate to United States culture and institutions.

Of course, there was no uniformity of opinion or action in the Mexican American community of the nineteenth century. There were those who viewed accommodation with Anglo Americans as impossible or undesirable. Some Mexican Americans tried, and a few succeeded, to assimilate entirely into Anglo American society. Others resisted American culture entirely, either through violence or through quiet retreat. Diversity and complexity, then, characterized the Mexican American community of the nineteenth century, and these remain important characteristics today.

By ending *Foreigners in Their Native Land* with the year 1910, I do not mean to suggest that the processes that I have described also ended in that year and remained dormant until the mid-1960s. Yet 1910 does seem to mark a turning point in Mexican American history. Beginning about 1910 a flood of new Mexican immigrants, forced out of Mexico by the political and social upheaval of the revolution, poured into the Southwest more rapidly than ever. As a group, Mexican Americans could not simultaneously absorb countless new members and still enjoy upward social mobility in American society. Incessant waves of new immigration meant that Mexican Americans as a group seemed always to be first generation immigrants. Moreover, Anglo American intolerance and discrimination toward Mexicans, already intense because of official hostility between the United States and Mexico from about 1910 to 1940, increased as the number of Mexican immigrants grew. As Roger Daniels and Harry H. L. Kitano argued in their study *American Racism* (1970), a minority group's ability to assimilate diminishes as the group becomes larger, more feared, and a clearer target for discrimination.

The struggles that some nineteenth-century Mexican Americans led for political power, justice, education, job opportunities, and cultural pluralism were dealt a severe blow by the increase in immigration from Mexico after 1910. Nonetheless, these struggles continued throughout the twentieth century, frequently subdued by events and circumstances that were beyond the community's control. Then, in the 1960s, a new set of circumstances enabled the community to play a more conspicuous role.

The late 1960s saw Mexican Americans capture the attention of the nation as they struggled to ameliorate and dramatize the problems they faced. The struggle that won greatest notice was that of the California farm workers, led by César Chávez. Their *huelga* or strike against grape growers began at Delano in 1965. It did not end until 1970, by which time a remarkable national boycott against nonunion grapes had helped Chávez's workers achieve a startling victory. Having forced a substantial number of grape growers to sign union contracts, Chávez then turned the energies of his United Farm Workers' Organizing Committee toward unionizing the Salinas Valley lettuce growers.

While the strike against grape growers progressed in California, in New Mexico Reies López Tijerina won national publicity in his efforts to restore Hispano ownership of land grants that date from the Spanish and Mexican periods. Tijerina's organization, the Alianza Federal de Mercedes (The Federal Alliance of Land Grants), formed in 1963, has thus far failed to regain any acreage, but it has succeeded in focusing greater attention on New Mexico's rural poverty and on the circumstances that led to the loss of the Hispano's ancestral lands.

It has also heightened a sense of ethnic identity among some of the state's already proud Hispano population. At the same time, however, Tijerina's militant tactics won him a jail sentence and even alienated many Hispanos.

In Colorado, operating with broader goals than Tijerina, Rodolfo "Corky" Gonzales organized a civil rights group known as the Crusade for Justice in Denver in 1965. Gonzales's organization has sought to improve conditions for Mexican Americans in areas such as education, housing, medicine, employment, and the law.

Individuals such as Gonzales, Tijerina, and Chávez have not only captured the headlines, but their causes have won broad support in the Mexican American community, especially among young people. Across the Southwest, Mexican American youths have formed groups such as MAYO (Mexican American Youth Organization) and MECHA (Movimiento Estuadiantil Chicano de Aztlán) on the high school and college level. These groups have demanded that educational institutions become more tolerant of ethnic diversity and that they recognize the importance of Mexican American culture, history, and language. Frequently combining the politics of confrontation with carefully reasoned proposals, student groups have heightened the sensitivity of university and high school administrators and teachers in many areas. The students have won notable victories in revamping curriculum and in raising the numbers of Mexican American students in universities across the nation. In many cases young people have also prodded their parents into more militant stances.

The increased activism of the Mexican American community has caused politicians of both major parties to take greater notice of Mexican American needs and aspirations. Some Mexican Americans, dissatisfied with the major parties, have founded their own independent groups. The most successful of these independent parties has been La Raza Unida. Founded in South Texas in 1970 by José Angel Gutiérrez, La Raza Unida quickly won control of the school board in Crystal City and placed its members in control of city councils in two nearby communities. These victories at the ballot box in South Texas have served to inspire similar groups across the Southwest.

The events of recent years have been discussed in a legion of articles and books, to which most readers have access. It is not my purpose to analyze these current events, but only to suggest that men such as César Chávez, Reies López Tijerina, and "Corky" Gonzales had counterparts in the nineteenth century. The causes that the leaders of the 1960s represent and the solutions they have put forth are not especially novel. Rather, these leaders have modified old solutions to meet the conditions of modern America. Thus, the activists of recent years have behind them a long tradition. That tradition should engender both pride and caution. It may be a source of pride and joy to view in historical perspective the progress made in recent years by Mexican Americans. At the same time, a long view of current events suggests that problems which are rooted deeply in the past will not succumb to shallow or easy solutions, but will crop up again and again until profound solutions are conceived and carried out.

Afterword to the Thirtieth Anniversary Edition

In the spring of 1968, during my second semester as a history professor, I taught a course on the American Southwest at San Diego State University. I began the course with the early 1800s, when the first Anglo Americans pushed into what was then Spanish territory. From there I moved through Mexico's acquisition of the region in 1821, the Texas war for independence (1836), the U.S.-Mexico War (1846–1848), and on into the territorial period and statehood for New Mexico and Arizona (1912). I had much to say about Anglo-Mexican relations in the early part of the course. After the U.S. acquired the region, however, my script included only Anglos and Indians. Mexicans fell from view as I took students through the Turnerian kaleidoscope of the Gold Rush, the cattlemen's frontier, the Indian wars, the construction of new transportation networks linking East to West, the machinations of American politicians in territorial governments of Arizona and New Mexico, and the federal government's efforts to bring a steady supply of water to a thirsty region.

Mexicans in the post-1848 Southwest had not been part of the story that I had learned in graduate school, and their absence seemed striking in the presence of students with names like Chávez, Martínez, and Rodríguez. My course, in fact, seemed irrelevant on a college campus where Mexican-American students had begun to demand that teachers pay more attention to their history and culture, and conspicuously disconnected to events beyond the campus. I had begun teaching about the "American" Southwest in the midst of a decade of Chicano militancy—a period of ferment that began, as I can now see in retrospect, with the United Farm Workers strike at Delano, California in 1965 and ran out of steam by the mid-1970s.

In the autumn of 1968, Juan Gómez-Quiñones joined our history department to teach Chicano history. We commiserated about the scarcity of books and articles on Mexican Americans and lamented the fact that there was so little to assign to students or to inform our lectures. We outlined a project of our own that would feature primary sources and short essays to provide context. We envisioned two books for classroom use. I would do the era before 1910; Juan would do the rest of the twentieth century.

I began work on my half of the project in the spring of 1969 when I taught a new and improved version of the History of the Southwest. By then I had found Carey McWilliams' *North from Mexico*, first published in 1949. It became my starting point and principal source. I also found some pioneering scholarly articles and monographs, including George I. Sánchez's *Forgotten People: A Study of New Mexicans (1940)*, C. L. Sonnichsen's *El Paso Salt War* (1961), Cecil Robinson's *With the Ears of Strangers: The Mexican in American Literature* (1963), Leonard Pitt's *The Decline of the Californios: A Social History of the Spanish-Speaking Californians, 1846–1890* (1966), and Américo Paredes's remarkable retelling of the story of Gregorio Cortez, *"With His Pistol in His Hand." A Border Ballad and its Hero* (1958). Paredes's book soon became required reading for my course on southwestern history and remains on the syllabus to this day. These early works, while few in number, shaped the trajectory of Chicano historiography and many remain worth reading.

My progress on the book slowed during 1970 when I spent the year as a Fulbright Lecturer at the Universidad de Costa Rica, but resumed speed when I returned in 1971. Meanwhile, the historical literature had also expanded, with the appearance of new books like Nancie L. González's *Spanish Americans of New Mexico: A Heritage of Pride* (1969); *The Mexican-Americans: An Awakening Minority*, edited by Manuel P. Servín (1970); and *A Documentary History of the Mexican Americans*, edited by Wayne Moquin (1971), a potential competitor that, happily for me, slighted the nineteenth century. Two new journals had begun publication in 1970, *Aztlán: Chicano Journal of the Social Sciences and the Arts* and *The Journal of Mexican American History*. These joined *El Grito: A Journal of Contemporary Mexican-American Thought*, which dated to 1967. At the same time, scholarly articles on Mexican-American history had begun to appear in regional historical journals. Together with unpublished theses and dissertations, these published works guided me toward the primary sources that I hoped to anthologize and gave me a context for understanding them. So, too, did studies such as Howard Roberts Lamar's *Far Southwest, 1846–1912. A Territorial History* (1966), whose focus was not on Mexican Americans, but who had much to say about them nevertheless.

By the late spring of 1972 I had roughed out the introduction and the first three chapters of the book and mailed them to the University of

New Mexico Press, whose encouraging managing editor, Jack Ritten-house, sent them out to readers. That summer my wife and I moved our little family from San Diego to Albuquerque so I could avail myself of the fine library at the University of New Mexico and make a side trip to Austin to look for sources in Texas. Librarians at the University of New Mexico understood what I was up to, but at the University of Texas in Austin one prominent librarian-historian told me I would waste my time searching there for sources on Mexican Americans. Anglos and Mexican Americans got along so well in Texas, she said, that I would find nothing of interest! She was wrong, of course, but the story of Texas Mexicans was so forgotten that I had difficulty finding a complete copy of the memoirs of one of the most prominent Tejanos of the era of the Texas war for independence, Juan Nepomuceno Seguín. Since then, Seguín's memoirs have been reprinted. First in facsimile a book that I edited, *Northern Mexico on the Eve of the United States Invasion. Rare Imprints Concerning California, Arizona, New Mexico, and Texas, 1821–1846* (1976), and more recently in a richly analyzed and annotated edition by Texas historian Jesús F. de la Teja, *Revolution Remembered: The Memoirs and Selected Correspondence of Juan N. Seguín* (1991). Seguín has also become the subject of a motion picture and a comic book and an equestrian statue now stands in the Texas town that bears his family name.

As I completed work on the manuscript in 1972, two fresh overviews of Mexican-American history appeared: *The Chicanos: A History of Mexican Americans,* by Matt S. Meier and Feliciano Rivera, and *Occupied America: The Chicanos' Struggle toward Liberation,* by Rodolfo Acuña. Neither of these books, the first general histories since the publication of Carey McWilliams's *North from Mexico* in 1949, examined the nineteenth century in depth. Each, however, treated the twentieth century, which I did not. By then Juan Gómez Quiñones had put the twentieth-century half of our project on the back burner and had given me leave to publish my book on my own. That was a worry. Would there be a market for a book on Mexican Americans that stopped in 1910, before massive immigration from Mexico? It seemed like a foolish gamble, but my wife encouraged me to re-imagine the book as a stand-alone volume that treated "Historical Roots of the Mexican Americans."

It also began to dawn on me that my intervention in this field might be unwelcome. Chicano scholars had begun to write their own history, and Chicano militancy had increased in the academy. Would an Anglo American writing about Chicano history have credibility? I had tentatively titled the book "*Las raíces históricas de la raza,*" but a Chicano specialist advised UNM Press against it, arguing that "it seems a bit presumptuous . . . because the author is an Anglo." In the spring of 1973, as *Foreigners in Their Native Land* moved through production, the new managing editor at UNM Press, Carl Mora, called to my attention an attack on John Womack, Jr. in the *New York Review of Books*. Womack, the author of a celebrated book, *Zapata and the Mexican Revolution* (1969), had written a lengthy essay reviewing fifteen new books on Chicanos. Rudolph O. de la Garza, then a professor of Political Science at the University of Texas, El Paso, expressed his disappointment that the *New York Review of Books* had not assigned the essay to a "Chicano scholar." Chicano scholars, he argued, could "empathize with the Mexican American people rather than attempt to write from a purely 'objective' perspective." He expressed dismay that scholars like Womack and publishers like the *NYRB* would "continue to exploit the public's interest in ethnic studies." De la Garza, editor Mora told me, represented a point of view among "some Chicano academics . . . that only a Chicano can write about Chicanos," and he warned me that my book would receive criticism "on the same untenable grounds."

Would my book be dismissed because I was not a Chicano? I had begun to give public lectures on Mexican-American history even before completing the book, and audiences' responses suggested that the answer was "yes" and "no." Some younger and angrier listeners made clear their belief that a *gringo* could not understand *their* past. Mexican Americans who had moved beyond their student years, however, often commented that it was good to hear an Anglo American describe the racist environment in which they had grown up. Coming from an Anglo, they said, descriptions of the formidable social and structural obstacles to Mexican-American advancement in the United States did not sound like special pleading.

Happily, Chicano historians accepted me as a collaborator in their larger project. Colleagues like Rodolfo Acuña, Pedro Castillo, Carlos Cortés, Juan Gómez-Quiñones, José Roberto Juárez, and Ramón Eduardo Ruiz (who wrote a foreword for the first edition), generously gave me their time and advice. Over the years since its publication, still other Chicano historians have used *Foreigners in Their Native Land* in their classes or cited it in their work and have had kind words to say about it—John Chávez, Mario T. García, Manuel G. Gonzales, David Gutiérrez, Oscar J. Martínez, David Montejano, Ricardo Romo, and Vicki L. Ruiz come readily to mind.

Ethnocentrism, then, has not afflicted this field, but I did come to understand that an Anglo writing Chicano history would have poor prospects for employment in academic departments that understandably wanted to hire Chicanos to teach Chicano history. My training had been as a Borderlands historian, and so I continued to write about the Southwest, but moved back to a politically safe era when the region belonged to Spain and Mexico, before Mexicans became United States citizens. My course on the "American Southwest," however, has never been the same.

As Arnoldo De León makes clear in his generous Foreword to this edition, historical writing on Chicanos has mushroomed over the last thirty years. As it has grown in size, it has followed general trends in the historical profession, moving into urban history, social history, women's history, and comparative history. It has felt the influence of neo-Marxist materialism and dependency theory, and more recently deconstructionist, postmodernist, and postcolonial "turns" in historical studies. Historians and literary scholars writing *about* Mexican Americans have also uncovered more writing *by* Mexicans in nineteenth-century America. If I had to do it over again, *Foreigners in Their Native Land* would be informed by this richer historiography and its analysis would be deeper and more satisfying.

The new scholarship would also have spared me from some embarrassing errors. I had assumed, for example, that Guadalupe Vallejo was a nephew of Mariano Guadalupe Vallejo, who shared his uncle's name (chapter 1, source no. 10). Instead, Guadalupe Vallejo was his niece (an error I have corrected in this edition). I had also assumed the fidelity of the published translation of the memoirs of Angustias de la Guerra Ord (chapter 3, source no. 9). The English translation of her memoirs has her say that "the conquest of California did not bother the Californians, least of all the women." The original Spanish version, however, says: "*La toma del país no nos gustó nada a los californios, y menos a las mujeres.*" That is, the seizure of California by the United States "gave absolutely no pleasure to the Californians, least of all the women." The shocking mistranslation, which turns her meaning upside down, is a dramatic example of why historians should not rely on translations (for more, see my correction in the text).

Although it is not without errors of commission and omission, *Foreigners in Their Native Land* continues to find a home in classrooms because the primary sources that it reproduces and the questions that they address remain timeless. Then, too, Mexican-American history has become the subject of discussion in a growing number of classrooms all over the country. Responding to the burgeoning numbers of Mexican Americans and informed by a multicultural sensibility, instructors now teach Mexican-American history as a discrete subject and incorporate it into general courses on national and regional history.

I remain proud of my early contribution to explaining the Mexican-American past. Just a decade before completing *Foreigners,* I had graduated from college in western New York, my home state. I had visited the Southwest on just one occasion before moving to New Mexico to pursue graduate work. A complete outsider to the region, I could not bring Chicano "empathy" to my subject, but I could bring an interest in explaining to my students and to myself how Mexicans came to feel like foreigners in a land that had once been theirs.

David J. Weber
Dedman Professor of History and
Director, Clements Center for Southwest Studies
Southern Methodist University
Dallas, Texas
Spring 2003

Notes

INTRODUCTION

1. Census figures released at the time of this writing place the number of persons of Latin heritage in the four Southwestern states at 5,901,895. Since most persons of Latin heritage in the Southwest are of Mexican ancestry, an estimate of at least 5 million Mexican Americans seems conservative. Forthcoming tabulations are expected to provide more specific information on country of origin in the 1970 census. *Los Angeles Times*, March 8, 1972.

2. Helen Rowan, "A Minority Nobody Knows," *The Atlantic* June 1967, pp. 47–52.

3. Leo Grebler, Joan W. Moore, Ralph C. Guzman, *et al.*, *The Mexican-American People: The Nation's Second Largest Minority* (New York: 1970), p. 10. Those who consult this volume should also read: "The Mexican-American People: A Review Symposium," *Social Science Quarterly* 52, no. 1 (June 1971): 8–38, especially the comments of Rodolfo Alvarez, who argues that the book is seriously weakened by its failure to include an adequate discussion of the nineteenth century.

4. A pioneering and highly influential essay was Octavio Ignacio Romano-V., "The Anthropology and Sociology of Mexican-Americans: The Distortion of Mexican-American History," *El Grito* 2, no. 1 (Fall 1968):13–26. In a more systematic fashion Nick C. Vaca has explored the same theme in "The Mexican-American in the Social Sciences, 1912–1970," *El Grito* 3, no. 3 (Spring 1970): 3–24; and 4, no. 1 (Fall 1970): 17–51. Vaca finds that cultural determinism has prevailed over structural-environmental determinism as an explanation for Mexicans' status in the United States. In forthcoming parts of his study he promises a critique of past theories and "The Development of a New Theory of Mexican-American Culture." Some of the questions that Mexican American sociologists will be attempting to answer are asked by Fernando Peñalosa in his perceptive "Toward an Operational Definition of the Mexican American," *Aztlán* 1, no. 1 (Spring 1970):1–12.

5. Celia S. Heller, *Mexican American Youth: Forgotten Youth at a Crossroads* (New York: 1966), p. 15.

6. Mario T. García, reviewing Manuel Servín's *Mexican-Americans*, in *El Grito* 3, no. 4 (Summer 1970): 34.

7. In 1972 two surveys appeared, both written by historians: *The Chicanos: A History of Mexican Americans*, by Matt S. Meier and Feliciano Rivera (New York: 1972), and *Occupied America: The Chicano's Struggle Toward Liberation* (San Francisco: 1972).

8. Carey McWilliams, *The Mexicans in America: a Student's Guide to Localized History* (New York: 1968), p. 4.

9. A brief and well-documented discussion of the Southwest's "Hispanic Legacy" is in Richard L. Nostrand, "The Hispanic-American Borderlands: Delimitation of an American Cultural Region," *Annals of the American Association of Geographers* 60, no. 4 (December 1970): 652–55.

10. As did the *Journal of Mexican-American History* in its opening issue (Fall 1970).

271

11. See, for example, Julian Nava, *Mexican Americans: Past, Present, and Future* (New York: 1969).

12. *La Verdad* (San Diego, Calif.), October 1969.

13. Michael D. Coe, *Mexico* (New York: 1962), p. 153 suggests that Aztlán may have been in the state of Nayarit. Scholars are in general agreement that Aztlán was somewhere in northwest Mexico. One study, which has won no acceptance among scholars, places Aztlán in the area of California's Salton Sea: Ralph L. Cain, *Historic Azlán and the Laguna de Ora* [sic] (Los Angeles: 1962). Ronald Hilton has recently cautioned Chicanos against romanticizing and exaggerating their "Aztec" heritage in "Is Intellectual History Irrelevant? The Case of the Aztecs," *Journal of the History of Ideas* 33, no. 2 (April–June 1972): 337–44. In a similar vein, John Womack recently dismissed the idea of "the return of the Indian Mexico to the land of his origins," as "the daffiest current Chicano propaganda." *The New York Review of Books* (August 31, 1972), p. 17.

14. Abraham Hoffman, reviewing Wayne Moquin and Charles Van Doren's *A Documentary History of the Mexican Americans* (New York: 1971), in *The Journal of Mexican American History* 2, no. 1 (Fall 1971): 46. On this question see Nancie L. González, *The Spanish-Americans of New Mexico: A Heritage of Pride* (Albuquerque: 1969), p. 184.

15. An excellent analysis of Indian-Spanish relations is in Edward Spicer's *Cycles of Conquest: The Impact of Spain, Mexico, and the United States on the Indians of the Southwest, 1533–1960* (Tucson: 1962).

16. John L. Kessell, *Mission of Sorrows: Jesuit Guevavi and the Pimas, 1691–1767* (Tucson: 1970), p. 93.

17. Quoted in Magnus Mörner, *Race Mixture in the History of Latin America* (Boston: 1967), p. 86. See also Samuel Ramos, *Profile of Man and Culture in Mexico*, trans. Peter G. Earle (New York: 1962), p. 169.

18. Mario T. García, "José Vasconcelos and La Raza," *El Grito* 2, no. 4 (Summer 1969): 50.

19. Rodolfo Alvarez, "The Unique Psycho-Historical Experience of the Mexican-American People," *Social Science Quarterly* 52, no. 1 (June 1971): 20–21.

20. Juan Gómez-Quiñones, "Toward a Perspective on Chicano History," unpublished manuscript, p. 21 (to be published in a forthcoming issue of *Aztlán*).

21. Jesús Chavarría, "A Précis and a Tentative Bibliography on Chicano History," *Aztlán* 1, no. 1 (Spring 1970): 133.

22. Charles Gibson, *Spain in America* (New York: 1966), p. 189. Gibson's chapter on the Borderlands is an excellent short synthesis.

23. Pierre Goubert, "Local History," in *Historical Studies Today*, ed. Felix Gilbert and Stephen R. Graubard (New York: 1972), p. 304.

24. So Octavio Romano has argued in "The Historical and Intellectual Presence of Mexican-Americans," *El Grito* 2, no. 2 (Winter 1969): 44–45.

25. *Los Angeles Times*, February 6, 1970.

I. New Spain's Far Northern Frontier

1. Dario Fernández-Flóres, *The Spanish Heritage in the United States* (Madrid: 1965), p. 179.

2. In a remarkable article, "Pohé-Yemo's Representative," *New Mexico Historical Review* 42 no. 2 (April 1967): 85–126, Fray Angélico Chávez suggests that Domingo Naranjo, son of a mulatto father and a Tlascaltec mother, impersonated the god Pohé-Yemo.

3. Lansing B. Bloom, "New Mexico Under Mexican Administration, 1821–1846," *Old Santa Fe* 1, no. 1 (July 1913): 27–30, discusses the complex question of how populous New Mexico was.

4. Odie B. Faulk, *The Last Years of Spanish Texas, 1778–1821* (The Hague, Netherlands: 1964), p. 102.

5. In the Spanish period, well before the secularization of the California missions, California settlers were charged with exploiting Indian labor and themselves abhorring manual labor. See C. Alan Hutchinson, *Frontier Settlement in Mexican California: the Híjar-Padrés Colony and Its Origins, 1769-1835* (New Haven: 1969), p. 81.

6. Gibson, *Spain in America*, p. 190.

7. Gonzalo Aguirre Beltrán, *La población negra de Mexico, 1519–1810* (Mexico: 1946), p. 200. Aguirre Beltrán adds that "black and white together never represented more than one to two percent of the total population of the country."

8. Joel Roberts Poinsett, *Notes on Mexico, Made in the Autumn of 1822* . . . (London: 1825), p. 185.

9. Jack D. Forbes, "Black Pioneers: The Spanish-speaking Afroamericans of the Southwest," in *Minorities in California History*, ed. George E. Frakes and Curtis B. Solbert (New York: 1971), pp.20–33.

10. A provocative article on this theme will appear in a forthcoming issue of *The Journal of San Diego History:* "California's Hispanic Heritage: A View into the Spanish Myth," by Manuel P. Servín. See Forbes, "Black Pioneers," pp. 24–25, for census figures which reveal graphically how the "Whitening" process worked in California.

11. France V. Scholes, "Civil Government and Society in New Mexico in the Seventeenth Century," *New Mexico Historical Review* 10, no. 2 (April 1935): 98. By the eighteenth century, when Texas, southern Arizona, and California were being settled, racial distinctions were becoming hopelessly blurred throughout Mexico. So it was not, of course, the frontier alone that heightened social mobility in these places.

12. See, for example, Frank W. Blackmar, *Spanish Institutions of the Southwest* (Baltimore: 1891), pp. 187–88; Odie B. Faulk, *Land of Many Frontiers: A History of the American Southwest* (New York: 1968), p. 79, argues that Mexicans on the frontiers of New Mexico and Texas were too lazy even to feed themselves.

13. See, for example, David J. Weber, "Spanish Fur Trade From New Mexico, 1540–1821," *The Americas* 24, no. 2 (October 1967): 122–36, which explains why New Mexicans did not fully exploit local fur resources.

14. See, for example, readings 6 and 7 in this chapter.

15. Ygnacio Sepúlveda, "The Spanish-Californians: An Historical Memoir (1874)," *Touring Topics* 21, no. 11 (November 1929): 31.

16. There are a number of studies of aspects of Mexican folk culture in the Southwest. One of the most popular works of synthesis has been Roland F. Dickey's *New Mexico Village Arts* (Albuquerque: 1940).

17. Ronald L. Ives, "The Lost Discovery of Corporal Antonio Luis: A Desert Cure for Scurvy," *Journal of Arizona History* 11, no. 2 (Summer 1970): 101–14.

18. Donald J. Lehmer, "The Second Frontier: The Spanish," in *The American West: An Appraisal*, ed. Robert G. Ferris (Santa Fe: 1963), p. 144.

19. Sherburne F. Cook, *The Conflict Between the California Indian and White Civilization: The American Invasion, 1848–1870.* Ibero-Americana Series, vol. 23 (Berkeley, 1943), p. 5.

20. Silvio Zavala, "The Frontiers of Hispanic America," in *The Frontier in Perspective*, ed. Walker D. Wyman and Clifton B. Kroeber (Madison: 1965), p. 45.

21. See, for example, John Francis Bannon, *The Spanish Borderlands Frontier, 1513–1821* (New York: 1970), p. 138, and Hutchinson's discussion of the undemocratic nature of the frontier in *Frontier Settlement in Mexican California*, pp. 397–99.

22. McWilliams, *North from Mexico*, p. 44. Italics are mine.

II. Yankee Infiltration and the Hardening of Stereotypes

1. This is suggested by Richard S. Gronet, "United States and the Invasion of Texas, 1810–1814," *The Americas* 25, no. 3 (January 1969): 281–306.
2. Quoted in Samuel H. Lowrie, *Culture Conflict in Texas* (New York: 1932), p. 95.
3. See Weber, *The Taos Trappers: The Fur Trade in the Far Southwest, 1540–1846* (Norman, Okla: 1971,) which focuses on this period.
4. Quoted in Weber, "Mexico and the Mountain Men, 1821–1828," *Journal of the West* 8, no. 3 (July 1969): 373.
5. See Max L. Moorhead, *New Mexico's Royal Road: Trade and Travel on the Chihuahua Trail* (Norman, Okla.: 1958), pp. 193–97 for a discussion of Mexican merchants and the impact of American merchants on New Mexico.
6. Ward Alan Minge, "Frontier Problems in New Mexico Preceding the Mexican War, 1840–1846" (Ph.D dissertation, University of New Mexico, 1965), pp. 303–5.
7. Quoted in John A. Hawgood, "The Pattern of Yankee Infiltration in Mexican Alta California, 1821–1846," *Pacific Historical Review* 27, no. 1 (February 1958): 27, whose insights I have relied upon in this paragraph.
8. Quoted in Eugene C. Barker, "Native Latin American Contributions to the Colonization and Independence of Texas," *Southwestern Historical Quarterly* 46, no. 3 (January 1943):318.
9. Ibid., p. 325.
10. See Lowrie, *Culture Conflict in Texas*, for the fullest exposition of this thesis. Cecil Robinson, "Flag of Illusion: The Texas Revolution Viewed as a Conflict of Cultures," *The American West* 5, no. 3 (May 1968): 10–17.
11. Harry Bernstein, *Making an Inter-American Mind* (Gainesville, Fl.: 1961), pp. 6–10. See also Stanley T. Williams, *The Spanish Background of American Literature*, 2 vols. (New Haven: 1955), 1: 9, 18.
12. Philip Wayne Powell, *Tree of Hate: Propaganda and Prejudices Affecting United States Relations with the Hispanic World* (New York: 1971), p. 118. Mr. Powell's work is the best history of the Black Legend in English. *The Black Legend: Anti-Spanish Attitudes in the Old World and the New*, ed. Charles Gibson (New York: 1971), contains well-chosen selections of anti-Spanish writing.
13. *The Personal Narrative of James O. Pattie*, introduction by William H. Goetzmann (Philadelphia: 1962), p. 38.
14. Cecil Robinson makes this point in *With the Ears of Strangers: The Mexican in American Literature* (Tucson: 1963), p. 29. Robinson, however, shows little awareness of the Black Legend origins of American attitudes toward Mexicans and probably overstates his case. There were Americans who admired the Mexican frontier, too (see, for example, Pike, document no. 6, chapter 1), and Americans who thought that even the most cultured and urbane Mexicans were inferior.
15. For a general discussion of American attitudes towards Mexicans during this period see ibid, pp. 31–66.
16. James H. Lacy, "New Mexico Women in Early American Writings," *New Mexico Historical Review* 34, no. 1 (January 1959): 41.
17. Gene M. Brack, "Mexican Opinion, American Racism, and the War of 1846," *The Western Historical Quarterly* 1, no. 2 (April 1970): 161–74.
18. Sessions of August 20, 1832, and February 5, 1833, Santa Fe Ayuntamiento Journal, 1829-36, MS, Coronado Room, Zimmerman Library, University of New Mexico, Albuquerque, N.M.
19. From a story in Albert Pike, *Prose Sketches and Poems Written in the Western Country (with Additional Stories)*, ed. Weber (Albuquerque: 1967), p. 106.
20. I am here following Gene Brack's interpretation, "Mexican Opinion, American Racism, and the War of 1846," pp. 173-74. For a discussion of Mexican attitudes toward Anglo

Americans in a broader context, see José de Onís, *The United States as Seen by Spanish American Writers, 1776–1890* (New York: 1952).

III. CULTURES COLLIDE

1. Quoted in Gronet, "United States and the Invasion of Texas, 1810–1814," p. 306.

2. Lowrie, *Culture Conflict in Texas,* pp. 31–37.

3. I am here following a thesis best developed by Lowrie, ibid., but originated by such Texas historians as Eugene C. Barker (see his *Mexico and Texas, 1821–1835* [Dallas: 1928], p. 146). This thesis continues to enjoy wide acceptance. See, for example, Ray Allen Billington, *The Far Western Frontier, 1830–1860* (New York: 1956), chapter 6. The thesis has also come under attack. For a good, concise statement see Connor, *Texas: A History,* pp. 118–22.

4. Lowrie, *Culture Conflict,* pp. 118, 116, 105. Eugene C. Barker also took the position that Texas Mexicans worked with Anglos in Texas toward similar goals, but using different methods. See Barker's "Native Latin American Contributions to the Colonization and Independence of Texas," pp. 317–35.

5. Quoted in Allaine Howren, "Causes and Origin of the Decree of April 16, 1830," *Southwestern Historical Quarterly* 16, no. 4 (April 1913): 397.

6. José María Tornel y Mendívil, "Relations Between Texas and the Mexican Republic" (Mexico: 1837), trans. and ed. Carlos E. Castañeda, *The Mexican Side of the Texan Revolution* (Dallas: 1928), p. 351.

7. Walter Lord, *A Time To Stand* (New York: 1961), pp. 87–88. This highly readable account of the Alamo supersedes Amelia Williams' pioneering "A Critical Study of the Siege of the Alamo and of the Personnel of Its Defenders," published serially in the *Southwestern Historical Quarterly,* vols. 36–37 (1933–34).

8. Some Mexican views of the Alamo are translated in Casteñeda's *Mexican Side of the Texan Revolution.* A current Mexican view of the Alamo, although brief and carelessly assembled, is General Miguel A. Sánchez Lamego, *The Seige and Taking of the Alamo,* trans. Consuelo Velasco (Santa Fe: 1968), first published in Mexico City in 1966. Although American and Mexican literatures exist, neither has addressed itself to the question of Texas Mexicans.

9. Whereas Amelia Williams counted 9 Mexicans dead in the Alamo, the latest count is 7, assuming that Carlos Espalier of San Antonio was Mexican. See Lord, *A Time to Stand,* pp. 212–19, and Thomas Lloyd Miller, "The Roll of the Alamo," *Texana* 2, no. 1 (Spring 1964): 54–64, who puts the total number of dead defenders of the Alamo at 175, 5 less than the traditional estimate.

10. In a doctoral thesis which unfortunately came to my attention after I had finished this chapter, Fane Downs confirms my judgment on this matter: "The History of Mexicans in Texas, 1820–1845" (Texas Tech University, 1970), p. 35.

11. Dr. Amos Pollard at San Antonio, January 16, 1836. Not all Yankees shared his opinion. Just two days earlier Col. James C. Neill reported from San Antonio to Sam Houston: "I can say to you with confidence that we can rely on great aid from the citizens of this town in case of an attack. . . ." Both quoted in Amelia Williams, "Siege of the Alamo," *Southwestern Historical Quarterly* 36, no. 4 (April 1933): 270, 268.

12. Quoted in Williams, "Siege of the Alamo," *Southwestern Historical Quarterly* 37, no. 1 (July 1933): 24.

13. Thomas Lloyd Miller, "Mexican-Texans at the Alamo," *Journal of Mexican-American History* 2, no. 1 (Fall 1971): 36–38, 41.

14. James Presley, "Santa Anna in Texas: A Mexican Viewpoint," *Southwestern Historical Quarterly* 62, no. 4 (April 1959): 489–512, concludes that even if Santa Anna had won at San Jacinto, logistical problems would have forced his withdrawal from Texas anyway.

15. Rubén Rendón Lozano, *Viva Tejas: The Story of the Mexican-born Patriots of the Republic of Texas* (San Antonio: 1936), p. 5. This scarce booklet, published on the 100th anniversary of the Texas Revolution, provides brief biographical sketches of some of the known Texas Mexicans who fought on the Texas side. Written in the same spirit is *Bits of Texas History in the Melting Pot of America*, ed. José Tomás Canales (San Antonio: 1950), which treats acts of kindness on the parts of Mexicans toward Anglo prisoners during the revolution.

16. Joseph Milton Nance, *After San Jacinto: The Texas-Mexican Frontier, 1836–41* (Austin: 1963), p. 62. In this study, and in *Attack and Counterattack: The Texas-Mexican Frontier, 1842* (Austin: 1964), Professor Nance chronicles border troubles between Mexico and Texas in extraordinary detail.

17. The importance of California in bringing on war with Mexico is the theme of Norman A. Graebner, *Empire on the Pacific: A Study in American Continental Expansion* (New York: 1955).

18. Gene M. Brack, "Mexican Opinion, American Racism, and the War of 1846," p. 163.

19. Allan Nevins, ed., *Polk: The Diary of a President, 1845–1849* (New York: 1929), pp. 81–83.

20. Examples are: Charles G. Sellers, *James K. Polk, Continentalist: 1843–1864* (Princeton: 1966); Frederick Merk, *The Monroe Doctrine and American Expansion, 1843–49* (New York: 1966); Glenn W. Price, *Origins of the War with Mexico: The Polk-Stockton Intrigue* (Austin: 1967). Price criticized United States historians for following the well-researched but chauvinistic interpretation of Justin H. Smith, *The War with Mexico*, 2 vols. (New York: 1919). Smith's nationalistic point of view remains influential, however, as evidenced by the appearance in 1971 of Seymour V. Connor and Odie B. Faulk, *North America Divided: The Mexican War, 1846–1848* (New York: 1971), which contains an excellent annotated bibliography. Seymour Connor analyzed that bibliography in "Attitudes and Opinions about the Mexican War, 1846–1970," *Journal of the West* 11, no. 2 (April 1972): 361–66. Interestingly, some of the most influential studies of the war have assumed American expansionism to be the central explanation, then proceeded to ask why. See Ramón Eduardo Ruiz, ed., *The Mexican War: Was it Manifest Destiny?* (New York: 1963), and Peter T. Harstad and Richard W. Resh, "The Causes of the Mexican War: A Note on Changing Interpretations," *Arizona and the West* 6, no. 4 (Winter 1964): pp. 289–302. A concise, measured examination of United States and Mexican historiography on the causes of the war by a Mexican historian has appeared since this chapter was completed: Josefina Vázquez de Knauth, *Mexicanos y Norteamericanos ante la Guerra del 47* (Mexico: 1972). This study contains primary and secondary readings.

21. Manuel de Gorostiza, quoted in Gene Brack, "Mexican Opinion and the Texas Revolution," *Southwestern Historical Quarterly* 72, no. 2 (October 1968): 182.

22. This is the thesis of Brack's "Mexican Opinion, American Racism, and the War of 1846," p. 61–74.

23. Daniel Tyler, "Governor Armijo's Moment of Truth," *Journal of the West* 11, no. 2 (April 1972): 307–16, contains some new information about Armijo's painful decision and suggests a similar interpretation.

24. *Ruxton of the Rockies*, ed. LeRoy R. Hafen (Norman, Okla.: 1950), p. 188.

25. Christian Kribben, Santa Fe, October 20, 1846, quoted in John Porter Bloom, "New Mexico Viewed by Anglo-Americans, 1846–1849," *New Mexico Historical Review* 34, no. 3 (July 1959): 198.

26. Lawrence R. Murphy, "The United States Army in Taos, 1847–1852," *New Mexico Historical Review* 47, no. 1 (January 1972): 38–41.

27. See, for example, the comments of Brevet Colonel John Munro, described by Colonel George Archibald McCall in *New Mexico in 1850: A Military View*, ed. Robert W. Frazer (Norman, Okla.: 1968), p. 70, n. 40. Even Carey McWilliams underestimates the strength of New Mexicans' allegiance to Mexico. See his *North From Mexico*, p. 118. The question needs further study.

28. Quoted in Dwight L. Clarke, *Stephen Watts Kearny: Soldier of the West* (Norman, Okla.: 1961), pp. 205–6. Theodore Grivas, *Military Government in California, 1846–1850* (Glendale,

Calif.: 1963), pp. 187–88, takes the position that Californios were reconciled to the military government and rumors to the contrary were the work of alarmists.

29. Andrew F. Rolle, *California: A History* (New York: 1963), p. 202. The most detailed account of the Battle of San Pascual, which includes a list of nearly forty Californios who fought under Andrés Pico, is Arthur Woodward's *Lances at San Pascual* (San Francisco, 1948), published originally in vols. 25 and 26 of the *California Historical Society Quarterly*.

30. Quoted in Clarke, *Kearny*, p. 298.

31. Hubert Howe Bancroft, *History of California* (San Francisco: 1886), 5:586. Walter Colton, *Three Years in California* . . . (New York: 1850), pp. 144–47, 152–53, 155.

32. Louis Robidoux to Manuel Alvarez, Jurupa, California, June 17, 1848, in "Louis Robidoux: Two Letters from California, 1848," trans. and ed. David J. Weber, *Southern California Quarterly* 54, no. 2 (June 1972): 111.

33. From a speech given in New York, c. February 1848, in Amelia W. Williams and Eugene C. Barker, eds., *The Writings of Sam Houston, 1813–1863*, 6 vols. (Austin: 1938–41), 5:33–34.

34. Quoted in Norman F. Graebner, "The Treaty of Guadalupe Hidalgo: Its Background and Formation" (Ph.D dissertation, University of Chicago, 1950), p. 430.

IV. ALL THE RIGHTS OF CITIZENS

1. McWilliams (*North from Mexico*, p. 52), first made this widely agreed-upon reckoning. Geographer Richard L. Nostrand recently suggested a higher figure of 82,250 ("The Hispanic American Borderland," pp. 646–47), but the question needs further study.

2. Luis G. Zorrilla, *Historia de las relaciones entre México y Los Estados Unidos de America, 1800–1958*, 2 vols. (Mexico: 1965), 1:218.

3. Quoted in Bancroft, *History of California*, 5:591.

4. "Exposición de motivos presentada por los Comisionados de México," March 1, 1848, in Antonio Peña y Reyes, ed., *Algunos documentos sobre el Tratado de Guadalupe y la situación de México durante la invasión Americana* (Mexico: 1930), p. 158.

5. Thomas Ewing Cotner, *The Military and Political Career of José Joaquín de Herrera, 1792–1854* (Austin: 1949), pp. 268–69.

6. "McCall's Report on Conditions in New Mexico," in *New Mexico in 1850*, p. 80. McCall thought that Mexico was especially trying to lure its wealthy citizens home. For documents regarding Father Ortiz's difficulties in New Mexico see H. Bailey Carroll and J. Villasana Haggard, eds. and trans., *Three New Mexico Chronicles* (Albuquerque:1942), pp. 144–52.

7. Leonard Pitt, *The Decline of the Californios: A Social History of the Spanish-speaking Californians, 1846–1890* (Berkeley: 1966), pp. 210–13. *Arizona Sentinel*, June 1, 1878, quoted in Joseph F. Park, "The History of Mexican Labor in Arizona during the Territorial Period" (M.A. thesis, University of Arizona, 1961), p. 103.

8. Charles C. Cumberland, "The United States-Mexican Border: A Selective Guide to the Region," *Rural Sociology* 25, no. 2 (June 1970): 135.

9. John Russell Bartlett, *Personal Narrative of Explorations and Incidents in Texas, New Mexico, California, Sonora, and Chihuahua*, 2 vols. (New York: 1854), 1:213–14. D. W. Meinig, *Southwest: Three Peoples in Geographical Change, 1600–1970* (New York: 1971), p. 32.

10. *The San Francisco Weekly Chronicle*, May 10 and August 16, 1856, quoted in Park, "Mexican Labor in Arizona," p. 4. Charles D. Poston, *Building a State in Apache Land* (Tempe, Ariz.: 1963), p. 72. Hilario Gallego, "Reminiscences of an Arizona Pioneer," *Arizona Historical Review* 6, no. 1 (January 1935): 78.

11. Jack E. Holmes, *Politics in New Mexico* (Albuquerque: 1967), p. 10.

12. Park, "The History of Mexican Labor in Arizona," p. 118. I have relied heavily on this excellent thesis in interpreting the role of Mexican Americans in Arizona.

13. Quoted ibid., p. 237.

14. Ibid., p. 243.

15. In twelve of twenty-five territorial assemblies, no one of Spanish surname was elected. See the lists of public officials in Jay J. Wagoner, *Arizona Territory, 1863–1912: A Political History* (Tucson: 1970), pp. 495–529.

16. B. Sacks, "The Creation of Arizona Territory," *Arizona and the West* 5, no. 1 (Spring 1963): 48–49.

17. Congressman Moon [not of Arizona], in U.S. Congress, House, Committee on the Territories, *Statehood for Arizona and New Mexico,* 59th Cong., 1906, p. 22.

18. Constitution of the Republic of Texas, General Provisions, sec. 8, in H. P. N. Gammel, *The Laws of Texas,* 10 vols. (Austin: 1898), 1:1079.

19. Downs, "Mexicans in Texas," pp. 249–53.

20. Frederick L. Paxson, "The Constitution of Texas, 1845," *Southwestern Historical Quarterly* 18, no. 4 (April 1915): 387.

21. William F. Weeks, *Debates of the Texas Convention, 1845* (Houston: 1846), pp. 235–36, 157.

22. Ibid., p. 159. Since the constitution specifically forbade those of African and Indian descent from voting, Navarro argued that the word white was superfluous and might be applied to Mexicans. He did not object, however, to denying people of color the vote. Navarro was an exceptionally "safe" Mexican delegate. He had participated in the Texan-Santa Fe expedition of 1841 and had been captured and imprisoned in Mexico City. There one newspaper urged that he be hung as "a traitor to his native land." Joseph Martin Dawson, *José Antonio Navarro: Co-creator of Texas* (Waco, Tex.: 1969), p. 79. Navarro's own *Apuntes históricos interesantes de San Antonio de Béxar* (San Antonio: 1869), is a disappointing source for Mexican American history.

23. Ralph A. Wooster, "Membership in Early Texas Legislatures, 1850–1860," *Southwestern Historical Quarterly* 69, no. 2 (October 1965): 167. Terry G. Jordan, "Population Origins in Texas, 1850," *Geographical Review* 59, no. 1 (January 1969): 96.

24. Downs, "Mexicans in Texas," pp. 255–57. Carlos E. Castañeda, *Our Catholic Heritage in Texas, 1519–1936,* vol. 7: *The Church in Texas Since Independence, 1836–1950* (Austin: 1958), p. 85.

25. Frederick Law Olmsted, *A Journey Through Texas: or, a Saddletrip on the Southwestern Frontier* (New York: 1857), p. 163. Jordan ("Population origins in Texas, 1850" p. 96), finds that Texas Mexicans were not disenfranchised at this time: "Average voter turnouts for the presidential elections of 1848 and 1852 indicate that the proportion of the free population voting in Spanish-surname counties was identical with other counties." Intimidation, however, need not go to the extreme of disenfranchisement in order to be effective.

26. Alwyn Barr, *Reconstruction to Reform: Texas Politics, 1876–1906* (Austin: 1971), p. 17. See also Paul S. Taylor, *An American-Mexican Frontier: Nueces County, Texas* (Chapel Hill, N.C.: 1934), chap. 27, and Ozzie G. Simmons, "Anglo-Americans and Mexican-Americans in South Texas: A Study in Dominant-Subordinate Group Relations" (Ph.D. dissertation, Harvard University, 1952), p. 272.

27. E. L. Dickens, "The Political Role of Mexican-Americans in San Antonio, Texas" (Ph.D. dissertation, Texas Tech University, 1969), pp. 35–36, and Douglas O. Weeks, "The Texas-Mexicans and the Politics of South Texas," *American Political Science Review* 24, no. 3 (August 1930): 606–14. See also the commentary of Alonso S. Perales, who agrees with Weeks's analysis and offers some solutions: *El Mexicano Americano y la Politica del Sur de Texas* (San Antonio: 1931).

28. Sister Paul of the Cross McGrath, *Political Nativism in Texas, 1825–1860* (Washington: 1930), pp. 67–68, 103–4.

29. Barr, *Reconstruction to Reform,* pp. 16, 203. A grand jury reported in 1910 that in Bexar County, Mexican nationals often voted. Some were even permitted to pay the poll tax without proof that they were United States citizens. *San Antonio Light,* September 2, 1910.

30. Paul S. Taylor, *Mexican Labor in the United States,* University of California Publications

in Economics, vol. 6 (Berkeley, 1928–30), pp. 398–410. Barr, *Reconstruction to Reform*, pp. 205–8.

31. Barr, *Reconstruction to Reform*, p. 233. More research needs to be done on the reaction of Texanos to Anglo political control in the last half of the nineteenth century, as evidenced by Félix D. Almaráz, Jr., "The Historical Heritage of the Mexican American in 19th Century Texas, An Interpretation," in *The Role of the Mexican American in the Southwest* (Edinburg, Tex.: 1969): 12–23, which, despite its title, focuses almost entirely on well-known events before the Texas Revolution. Published reminiscences of Texano oligarchs, as already noted in the case of José Antonio Navarro, are disappointing. See, too, José María Rodríguez, *Memoirs of Early Texas*, 2d ed. (San Antonio: 1961), and Antonio Menchaca, *Memoirs*, vol. 2 of Yanaguana Society Publications (San Antonio: 1937), neither of which evince interest in the post-1836 period. Rodríguez, however, is critical of Anglos who want to "run out" the Mexicans in Laredo (pp. 75–76).

32. Pitt, *Decline of the Californios*, pp. 37–42.

33. Donald E. Hargis, "Native Californians in the Constitutional Convention of 1849," *Historical Society of Southern California Quarterly* 26, no. 1 (March 1954): 3–13.

34. Pitt, *Decline of the Californios*, p. 46.

35. Rolle, *California*, pp. 211, 309.

36. Richard Morefield, "The Mexican Adaptation in American California, 1846–1875" (M.A. thesis, University of California, Berkeley, 1955), p. 50.

37. Pitt, *Decline of the Californios*, pp. 140–41, 148.

38. Morefield, "The Mexican Adaptation in American California," Appendix B.

39. Ibid., pp. 51–52, and Pitt, *Decline of the Californios*, p. 270.

40. Morefield, "Mexican Adaptation," p. 31.

41. Pitt, *Decline of the Californios*, pp. 97–98.

42. Ibid., pp. 130–47. The research of Charles Hughes reveals San Diego to be an exception to Pitt's generalizations about Southern California. Anglos outnumbered Californios in San Diego County by 1850 and controlled political offices in the county throughout the 1850s. The results of Hughes's research will be available in a forthcoming M.A. thesis at Caifornia State University, San Diego.

43. Pitt, *Decline of the Californios*, p. 50.

44. Otis E. Young, Jr., "The Spanish Tradition in Gold and Silver Mining," *Arizona and the West* 7, no. 4 (Winter 1965): 299. For a fuller treatment of this subject see Young's *Western Mining: An Informal Account of Precious Metals Prospecting, Placering, Lode Mining, and Milling on the American Frontier from Spanish Times to 1893* (Norman, Okla.: 1970).

45. William Robert Kenny, "Mexican-American Conflict on the Mining Frontier, 1848–1852," *Journal of the West* 6, no. 4 (October 1967): 584–86.

46. Luis de la Rosa, Mexican minister to the United States, to John M. Clayton, secretary of state of the United States, Philadelphia, October 19, 1848, in William R. Manning, ed., *Diplomatic Correspondence of the United States. Inter-American Affairs, 1831–1860* (Washington, D.C.; 1937), 9:346–47.

47. Kenny, "Mexican-American Conflict," pp. 489–91. See also Richard H. Morefield, "Mexicans in the California Mines, 1848–53," *California Historical Society Quarterly* 35, no. 1 (March 1956): 37–46, and Leonard Pitt, "The Beginnings of Nativism in California," *Pacific Historical Review* 30, no. 1 (February 1961): 23–38, who identifies the "respectable middle class" as anti-foreign.

48. Roger Daniels and Harry H. L. Kitano, *American Racism: Exploration of the Nature of Prejudice* (Englewood Cliffs, N.J.: 1970), pp. 36–38. An outstanding analysis of American responses to European immigrants is John Higham, *Strangers in the Land: Patterns of American Nativism, 1860–1925*, 2d ed. (New York: 1963).

49. The finest discussion of nativism in the mines and its relationship to the Californios is Pitt, *Decline of the Californios*, chap. 3.

50. Ibid., pp. 73–74. William B. Secrest, *Juanita* (Fresno, Calif.: 1967), p. 26.

51. Pitt, *Decline of the Californios*, pp. 70, 202. See also ibid., chap. 9.

52. *El Clamor Público* (Los Angeles), March 7, 1857.

53. Reference to Santa Anna in a novel, *Piney Woods Tavern*, by Samuel Hammett (1858), quoted in Robinson, *With the Ears of Strangers*, p. 71. See also Frank Triplett, *Conquering the Wilderness* (New York: 1883), p. 313, wherein a Kentucky boatman says to a Mexican: "Here's at you—you greaser, you nigger!"

54. *Columbian Planter* (Columbia, Tex.), September 9, 1856, in "Letters and Documents," *Texana* 3, no. 2 (Summer 1965): 181. For similar incidents see Olmsted, *A Journey Through Texas*, pp. 163–64, 245. McGrath, *Political Nativism in Texas*, pp. 66–67, cites two such incidents which occurred in 1854.

55. John J. Linn, *Reminiscences of Fifty Years in Texas* (Austin: 1935), pp. 352–54. See also McGrath, *Political Nativism in Texas*, pp. 166–69.

56. Taylor, *American-Mexican Frontier*, p. 54. J. Frank Dobie, *A Vaquero of the Brush Country* [1st ed., 1929] (London: 1949), p. 119.

57. See Américo Paredes, *"With His Pistol in His Hand": A Border Ballad and Its Hero* (Austin: 1958), pp. 23–32, for an unusual glimpse at the Rangers from a Texas Mexican point of view.

58. Dobie, *Vaquero of the Brush country*, p. 54. Ben H. Procter, "The Modern Texas Rangers: A Law-Enforcement Dilemma in the Rio Grande Valley," in *Reflections of Western Historians*, ed. John A. Carroll (Tucson: 1969), pp. 215–31, discusses Ranger activities during the Rio Grande City strike of 1967.

59. U.S. Commission on Civil Rights, *Mexican Americans and the Administration of Justice in the Southwest* (Washington, D.C.: 1970).

60. Downs, "Mexicans in Texas," pp. 254–55, 248. Miller, "Mexican-Texans at the Alamo," pp. 36–38.

61. Downs, "Mexicans in Texas," pp. 36–37, 247, 63–64. See also Taylor, *American-Mexican Frontier*, pp. 17–21.

62. T. R. Fehrenbach, *Lone Star: A History of Texas and the Texans* (New York: 1968), p. 283. Olmsted, *A Journey Through Texas*, p. 163. A well-known example is the case of Martín de León, founder of Victoria, and his son Fernando. See J. W. Petty, Jr., ed., *Victor Rose's History of Victoria* (Victoria, Tex.: 1961), pp. 154–56, and a sympathetic but unscholarly biography by A. B. J. Hammett, *The Empresario Don Martin de Leon, The Richest Man in Texas* (Victoria, Tex.: 1971).

63. Fehrenbach, *Lone Star*, pp. 510, 290.

64. Thomas Lloyd Miller, *The Public Lands of Texas, 1519–1970* (Norman, Okla.: 1972), p. 9.

65. Taylor, *American-Mexican Frontier*, pp. 179–80. See also George M. Blackburn and Sherman L. Richards, "A Demographic History of the West: Nueces County, Texas, 1850," *Prologue* 4, no. 1 (Spring 1972): 20, which finds that "in a remarkably short time, the Americans in Nueces County had emerged as the dominant economic force. . . ."

66. Florence Johnson Scott, *Historical Heritage of the Lower Rio Grande Valley*, rev. ed. (Waco, Tex.: 1966), p. 165. Scott's study describes the work of the Bourland-Miller Commission of 1850 in investigating claims in the lower Rio Grande Valley. J. J. Bowden, *Spanish and Mexican Land Grants in the Chihuahua Acquisition* (El Paso, 1971), chronicles some cases in southwest Texas. No work, however, adequately examines the disposition of Spanish and Mexican period grants in Texas as a whole.

67. W. W. Robinson, *Land in California: The Story of Mission Lands, Ranchos, Squatters, Mining Claims, Railroad Grants, Land Scripp, Homesteads* (Berkeley, 1948), p. 106.

68. Ray H. Mattison, "Early Spanish and Mexican Settlements in Arizona," *New Mexico Historical Review* 21, no. 4 (October 1946): 290. All land grants in Arizona were located in the Gadsden Purchase area. The Gadsden Treaty made it more difficult to confirm titles by stipulating that they would be valid only if confirming evidence was found in Mexican archives.

69. Olen E. Leonard, *The Role of the Land Grant in the Social Organization and Social Processes of a Spanish-American Village in New Mexico* (Albuquerque: 1970), pp. 102–3. See ibid., pp. 90–117 for a discussion of New Mexico's communal properties. An excellent comparison of New Mexico and California is in White, Koch, Kelley, and McCarthy, Attorneys at Law, and the New Mexico State Planning Office, *Land Title Study* (Santa Fe: 1971), pp. 40–41.

70. Howard R. Lamar, "Land Policy in the Spanish Southwest, 1846–1891: A Study in Contrast," *Journal of Economic History* 22, no. 4 (December 1962): 504, 507–8; Pitt, *Decline of the Californios*, pp. 97–98.

71. Paul W. Gates, "California's Embattled Settlers," *California Historical Society Quarterly* 41, no. 2 (June 1962): 99–130, argues that the major shortcoming of the Land Act of 1851 was its failure to make public land available to those who made improvements on the land—Anglo and Californio alike.

72. Pitt, *Decline of the Californios*, chap. 5.

73. See Victor Westphall, *The Public Domain in New Mexico, 1854–1891* (Albuquerque: 1965), and William A. Keleher, *The Fabulous Frontier: Twelve New Mexico Items* (Albuquerque: 1962), pp. 107–9.

74. See Paul W. Gates, "Adjudication of Spanish-Mexican Land Claims in California," *The Huntington Library Quarterly* 21, no. 3 (May 1958): 213–36, and Gates, "The California Land Act of 1851," *California Historical Quarterly* 50, no. 4 (December 1971): 395–430.

75. This often repeated charge needs further investigation. At the moment, one can only wonder at what kind of evidence exists to suggest that the upper-class Californios were more extravagant and wasteful than their Anglo counterparts. For a balanced contemporary statement see Horace Bell, *On the Old West Coast, Being Further Reminiscences of a Ranger*, ed. Lanier Bartlett (New York: 1930), p. 5.

76. See, for example, in the case of California, Robert Glass Cleland, *Cattle on a Thousand Hills* (San Marino, Calif.: 1951); Robinson, *Land in California;* and Pitt, *Decline of the Californios*.

77. Keleher, *Fabulous Frontier*, p. 107. Also, Keleher, "Law of the New Mexico Land Grant," *New Mexico Historical Review* 4, no. 4 (October 1929): 350–71. Most writers on New Mexico land grants agree with Keleher. See, for example, Herbert O. Brayer, *William Blackmore: The Spanish-Mexican Land Grants of New Mexico and Colorado, 1863–1878*, 2 vols. (Denver: 1949), 1:16, and Ralph E. Twitchell, *The Leading Facts of New Mexico History*, 2 vols. (Cedar Rapids, Iowa: 1912), 2: 467. Attorney-historian Gilberto Espinosa, on the other hand, takes the view that "the United States, fully and well, complied with its obligations toward its new citizens." ("About New Mexico Land Grants," *Albuquerque Bar Journal* 7, no. 2 [September 1967]: 5–15.)

V. Accomodation, Assimilation, and Resistance

1. Eric J. Hobsbawm, *Bandits* (New York: 1969), p. 15, and *Primitive Rebels* (New York: 1959), pp. 23–24. This theme is analyzed in two soon-to-be-published essays by Chicano historians: Carlos E. Cortés, "The Chicano Social Bandit as Romantic Hero" (to be published in *The Romantic Mind*, Robert Gleckner and Hugo Rodríguez Alcalá, eds.), and Pedro Castillo, "Social Banditry and Revolution in the American Southwest" (to be published in *New Perspectives on Chicano History*, Castillo and Cortés, eds.).

2. Pitt, *Decline of the Californios*, p. 256.

3. Joseph Henry Jackson, *Bad Company. The Story of California's Legendary and Actual Stage-robbers, Bandits, Highwaymen and Outlaws from the Fifties to the Eighties* (New York, 1949), pp. xii–xiii.

4. See Joseph Henry Jackson's introduction to *The Life and Adventures of Joaquin Murieta* by John Rollin Ridge (Norman, Okla.: 1955), and William B. Secrest, *Joaquin: Bloody Bandit of the Mother Lode. The Story of Joaquin Murrieta* (Fresno, Calif.: 1971). Although Murrieta is usually spelled with one *r*, as Ridge has spelled it, the double *r*, as used by Secrest, is the more likely spelling.

5. Pitt, *Decline of the Californios*, p. 262.

6. "Letter from Major Heintzelman," in U.S. Congress, House, *Difficulties on the Southwestern Frontier*, 36th Cong., 1st sess., H. Exec. Doc., no. 52, ser. 1050, p. 109.

7. José T. Canales, *Juan N. Cortina: Bandit or Patriot?* (San Antonio, 1951), pp. 4–5.

8. *New York Times*, January 13, 1860, reference courtesy of Bonnie Royer. The best biography of Cortina to date is Charles W. Goldfinch, *Juan N. Cortina, 1824–1892: A Re-appraisal* (Brownsville, Tex.: 1950), but Cortina clearly deserves a major biography. Professor Michael Webster, of Trinity College, San Antonio, has such a study under way. For a more typically unfavorable view of Cortina see Tom Lea, *The King Ranch*, 2 vols. (Boston: 1957), 1: 158–69, 262–92.

9. Olmsted, *A Journey Through Texas*, p. 164.

10. The best published accout of this affair is by C. L. Sonnichsen, in *Ten Texas Feuds* [1st ed., 1957] (Albuquerque, 1971), pp. 108-56, also published separately as *The El Paso Salt War, 1877* (El Paso, 1961). Testimony by many participants and witnesses, including Mexican Americans, is in U.S. Congress, House, *El Paso Troubles in Texas*, 45th Cong., 2nd sess., H. Exec. Doc. no. 93, ser. 1809.

11. Andrew B. Schlesinger, "Las Gorras Blancas, 1889–1891," *Journal of Mexican American History* 1, no. 2 (Spring 1971): 87–143.

12. A fine essay on this subject is William F. Cheek, *Black Resistance Before the Civil War* (Beverly Hills, Calif.: 1970).

13. See, for example, Howard Roberts Lamar, *The Far Southwest, 1846–1912: A Territorial History* (New Haven, 1966), pp. 86–87, 101–2, 135, 166, and Porter A. Stratton, *The Territorial Press of New Mexico, 1834–1912* (Albuquerque: 1969), p. 90. For a case study of Mexican American disunity see Seb. S. Wilcox, "The Laredo City Election and Riot of April, 1886," *Southwestern Historical Quarterly* 45, no. 1 (July 1941): 1–23.

14. The foregoing is drawn from Pitt, *Decline of the Californios*, especially pp. 130–47, 204–5, 244–49.

15. James E. Officer, "Historical Factors in Interethnic Relations in the Community of Tucson," *Arizoniana* 1, no. 3 (Fall 1960): 14. I have relied heavily on Officer's interpretation in discussing Tucson. He elaborates his thesis and adds documentation in his unpublished doctoral dissertation "Sodalities and Systemic Linkage: The Joining Habits of Urban Mexican-Americans" (University of Arizona, 1964), pp. 43–69.

16. Park, "Mexican Labor in Arizona," pp. 186–87.

17. Officer, "Sodalities and Systemic Linkage," pp. 57–58, 61.

18. David Erland Vassberg, "The Use of Mexicans and Mexican Americans as an Agricultural Work Force in the Lower Rio Grande Valley of Texas" (M.A. thesis, University of Texas at Austin, 1966), pp. 14–20. D. W. Meinig, *Imperial Texas: An Interpretive Essay in Cultural Geography* (Austin: 1969), pp. 83–84, 99–101.

19. Stratton, *The Territorial Press*, p. 126.

20. Nancy L. González, *The Spanish-Americans of New Mexico: A Heritage of Pride* (Albuquerque: 1969), p. 80.

21. A warm, personal reminiscence of life among sheepmen and cattlemen on the eastern plains of New Mexico is Fabiola Cabeza de Baca, *We Fed Them Cactus* (Albuquerque: 1954), especially pp. 50, 57, 63, 72–74, 144–50, 174–76. See also the reminiscences of José Ynocencio Romero, "Spanish Sheepmen on the Canadian at Old Tascosa," *Panhandle-Plains Historical Review* 19, (1946): 45–72.

22. *Santa Fe New Mexican*, January 27, 1874, quoted in Oliver Lafarge, ed., *Santa Fe: The Autobiography of a Southwestern Town* (Norman, Okla: 1959), p. 88. See also Philip J. Rasch, "The Horrell War," *New Mexico Historical Review* 31, no. 3 (July 1956): 223–31; Meinig, *Southwest*, pp. 32–35; and Keleher, *Fabulous Frontier*, p. 109.

23. *Hagerman Messenger*, 1906, quoted in Stratton, *Territorial Press*, p. 132.

24. *Grant County Herald* (Silver City), 1876, quoted in Stratton, *Territorial Press*, p. 127. Conrad K. Naegle, "The Rebellion of Grant County, New Mexico," *Arizona and the West* 10, no. 3 (Autumn 1968): 225–40, puts these events in a broader context.

25. Lamar, *Far Southwest*, pp. 170, 175; Meinig, *Southwest*, pp. 41–44, 53.

26. *The New Mexico Blue Book, 1882* (Santa Fe: 1882), pp. 98–117; *The New Mexico Blue Book, 1913* (Santa Fe: 1913), pp. 99–100. In 1914, the only year that voters were classified according to ethnic origin, 26,563 Hispanos were registered compared to 20,150 Anglos. (*The New Mexico Blue Book, 1915* [Santa Fe, 1915], p. 142. Benjamin M. Read, *Illustrated History of New Mexico* [Santa Fe: 1912], pp. 610–12.)

27. Lamar, *Far Southwest*, pp. 91; 106. My view of the political role of the Hispanos contrasts sharply with that of George Sánchez, who argued that because of "cultural inadequacy," the Hispanos were unable to cope with Anglo American society and so "they became cannon fodder for political guns." *Forgotten People: A Study of New Mexicans* (Albuquerque: 1940), pp. 13, 18. But neither Sánchez nor I have space to explore this complex question to the extent it deserves.

28. Quoted in Lamar, *Far Southwest*, p. 90.

29. Lamar, *Far Southwest*, p. 90; LaFarge, *Santa Fe*, p. 56.

30. Lamar, *Far Southwest*, pp. 89, 167, 187; Stratton, *Territorial Press*, p. 143. Of course, not all Hispanos had opposed public education in New Mexico. See Sánchez, *Forgotten People*, pp. 17–25.

31. The best overall discussion of how this colonial system worked is in Earl S. Pomeroy, *The Territories and the United States, 1861–1890: Studies in Colonial Administration*, 2d ed. (Seattle: 1969).

32. Quoted in Robert W. Larson, *New Mexico's Quest for Statehood, 1846–1912* (Albuquerque: 1968), p. 148.

33. See, for example, John Braeman, "Albert J. Beveridge and Statehood for the Southwest, 1902–1912," *Arizona and the West* 10, no. 4 (Winter, 1968): 318, 339.

34. Larson, *New Mexico's Quest for Statehood*, pp. 159–68. Stratton, *Territorial Press*, pp. 106, 142, 239 n. 132. Lamar, *Far Southwest*, p. 189, points out that the constitution also threatened the right of non-English speakers to sit on juries.

35. Lamar, *Far Southwest*, 198–99.

36. Ibid., p. 200. Stratton, *Territorial Press*, p. 98.

37. Reuben W. Heflin, "The New Mexico Constitutional Convention," *New Mexico Historical Review* 21, no. 1 (January 1946): 60–68. Constitution of New Mexico, Article II, sec. 5, Article VII, Sec. 3, and Article XII, sec 8 & 10, in *Constitutions of the United States: National and State* (New York: 1962), pp. 7, 25–26, 37.

38. Taylor, *American-Mexican Frontier*, pp. 173–74; Pitt, *Decline of the Californios*, p. 266.

39. *El Labrador* (Las Cruces, N.M.), May 11, 1902.

40. Quoted in Kaye Briegel, "La Alianza Hispano Americana: A Preliminary Interpretation" (Paper presented to the 13th Annual Arizona Historical Convention, May 6, 1972, Nogales, Arizona). Briegel also generously shared ideas about the *Alianza* with me.

41. Officer, "Sodalities and Systemic Linkage," pp. 53–57.

42. González, *The Spanish-Americans of New Mexico*, pp. 86–89. For the *Penitentes* as a political force see Holmes, *Politics in New Mexico*, pp. 33–49.

43. Professor Gómez-Quiñones kindly provided me with the manuscript of his important, pioneering article, to be published in *Aztlán*: "The First Steps: Chicano Labor Conflict and Organizing, 1900–1920," which has influenced my interpretation heavily.

44. For examples see Pitt, *Decline of the Californios*, p. 114, and Vassberg, "Mexicans and Mexican Americans as an Agricultural Work Force," p. 28.

45. Park, "Mexican Labor in Arizona," pp. 62–63, 243–60, describes this strike well.

46. *Bisbee Daily News*, quoted in the *Arizona Daily Star* (Tucson), June 5 and 7, 1903.

47. Societies, for example, also played a significant role in the Imperial Valley strike of 1928 (Taylor, *Mexican Labor in the United States*, p. 45).

48. Quoted in Gómez-Quiñones, "The First Steps," p. 25. This strike is described in James R. Kluger, *The Clifton-Morenci Strike: Labor Difficulty in Arizona, 1915–1916* (Tucson: 1970). Kluger does not adequately explore the role of Mexican labor in the strike (see his pp. 23–24).

49. Estelle Lutrell, "Newspapers and Periodicals of Arizona, 1859–1911," *University of Arizona Bulletin* 20, no. 3 (July 1949). Herminio Ríos and Lupe Castillo have drawn together a list of Spanish-language newspapers which, although by no means complete, illustrates their proliferation throughout the Southwest: "Toward a True Chicano Bibliography: Mexican-American Newspapers, 1848–1942," *El Grito* 3, no. 4 (Summer 1970): 17–24.

50. See William B. Rice, *The Los Angeles Star, 1851–1864: The Beginnings of Journalism in Southern California*, ed. John Walton Caughey (Berkeley, 1947), pp. 14–15. Lafarge, *Santa Fe*, pp. 75, 111.

51. Richard J. Hinton, *The Handbook to Arizona: Its Resources, History, Mines, Ruins and Scenery* (1878; reprint ed., Tucson, 1954), p. 378.

52. E. L. Dickens, "The Political Role of Mexican-Americans in San Antonio, Texas" (Ph.D. dissertation, Texas Tech University, 1969), p. 31.

53. Mariano G. Vallejo, "Historia de California," ms., Bancroft Library, Berkeley, quoted in Morefield, "The Mexican Adaptation in American California," p. 51.

54. Rodman W. Paul, "The Spanish-Americans in the Southwest, 1848–1900," in *The Frontier Challenge: Responses to the Trans-Mississippi West*, ed. John G. Clark (Lawrence, Kan.: 1971), p. 41. Paul's conclusion, however, is quite different from my own. Farther on in his essay he says: "It is hard to see that in any of the Southwestern states Spanish-speaking cultures proved resilient or resourceful in meeting the challenge of the aggressive, acquisitive Anglo American intruding groups" (p. 52).

55. Burl Noggle, "Anglo Observers of the Southwest Borderlands, 1825–1890: The Rise of a Concept," *Arizona and the West* 1, no. 2 (Summer 1959): 124–31. Pitt, *Decline of the Californios*, chap. 15.

56. Carolyn M. Remy, "Protestant Churches and Mexican Americans in South Texas" (Ph.D. dissertation, University of Texas, 1970), p. 114. Little study of the response of Mexican Americans to Protestantism has been done. A recent article, however, leaves no doubt that many Protestant missionaries viewed Mexicans as inferior, and that Presbyterians set a higher standard for Mexican converts than for Anglos (R. Douglas Brackenridge, Francisco O. García-Treto, and John Stover, "Presbyterian Missions to Mexican Americans in Texas in the Nineteenth Century," *Journal of Presbyterian History* 49, no. 2 [Summer 1971]: 103–32). The reminiscences of José Policarpio Rodríguez describe some of the difficulties of a Texano convert to Protestantism: *José Policarpio Rodríguez, "The Old Guide." Surveyor, Scout, Hunter, Indian Fighter, Ranchman, Preacher* (Nashville, Tenn., 1897).

57. Ernesto Galarza, *Merchants of Labor: The Mexican Bracero Story* (Santa Barbara, Calif.: 1964), p. 17.

58. Leo Grebler, *Mexican Immigration to the United States: The Record and Its Implications. Mexican-American Study Project, Advance Report 2* (Los Angeles: 1965), pp. 19–22. Grebler, et al., *The Mexican American People* (New York: 1970), pp. 63–64.

59. Mexican historian Moisés González Navarro has found some figures from Mexican states, but for an overall view he relied on United States census records: "Los braceros en el Profiriato," *Estudios Sociológicas*. Quinto Congreso Nacional de Sociología. 2 vols. (Mexico: 1964), 2:262–63.

60. Julian Samora (with Jorge A. Bustamante F. and Gilbert Cardenas), *Los Mojados: The Wetback Story* (Notre Dame: 1971), pp. 34–35. Some Mexican laborers were denied entrance to

the United States, but probably not a significant number. See González Navarro, "Los braceros," pp. 263–64.

61.   Census and Immigration statistics for the nineteenth century are available in such studies as Lyle Saunders, *The Spanish-Speaking Population of Texas* (Austin: 1949), p. 16, and *Mexicans in California: Report of Governor C. C. Young's Mexican Fact-Finding Committee* (San Francisco: 1930), pp. 19, 29.

62.   Victor S. Clark, *Mexican Labor in the United States,* Dept. of Commerce and Labor, *Bulletin of the Bureau of Labor,* no. 78 (Washington, D.C.: 1908), pp. 520-21.

63.   González Navarro, "Los braceros," pp. 274–77. Gómez-Quiñones, "The First Steps," has a fine discussion of conditions in Mexico which encouraged emigration.

64.   Clark, *Mexican Labor,* pp. 469–71, 477–501. John Ramón Martínez, "Mexican Emigration to the United States, 1910–1930" (Ph.D. dissertation, University of California, Berkeley, 1957), pp. 2–5. Galarza, *Merchants of Labor,* p. 27.

65.   Taylor, *Mexican Labor in the United States,* pp. 75–94, 192–211, 388–431.

66.   U.S. Congress, Senate, Dillingham Commission, *Abstracts of Reports of the Immigration Commission,* 61st Cong., 3d sess., 1911, S. Doc. 747, vol. 1, pp. 683, 689–91.

67.   Clark, *Mexican Labor,* p. 512.

68.   Victor, *Mexican Labor,* pp. 113, 521–22.

69.   González, *The Spanish-Americans of New Mexico,* p. 203, citing reminiscences of Mary Austin and Erna Fergusson. See also Lafarge, *Santa Fe,* pp. 178–79, who says that in speaking Spanish, "Hispanos" continued to refer to themselves as *Mexicanos.*

70.   Connor, *Texas,* p. 351, says that this preference began in the 1930s in Texas.

71.   For some interesting conversations on this subject see Taylor, *Mexican Labor in the United States,* pp. 212–16, 410–14.

72.   See McWilliams, *North from Mexico,* pp. 35–47. Noggle, "Anglo Observers of the Southwest Borderlands," pp. 128–31. Earl Pomeroy, *In Search of the Golden West: The Tourist in Western America* (New York: 1957), pp. 35–37, 41–44.

73.   Elucidated in such works as Marcus L. Hansen, *The Problem of the Third Generation Immigrant* (Rock Island, Ill.: 1938).

74.   Rodolfo Alvarez, "The Unique Psycho-Historical Experience of the Mexican-American People," p. 29.

Index